SILICON VALLEY

"Silicon Valley's Enterprises" by
John Kevin Waters

Produced in cooperation with
the County of Santa Clara
Board of Supervisors and
the County of Santa Clara
Historical Heritage Commission

Windsor Publications, Inc.
Chatsworth, California

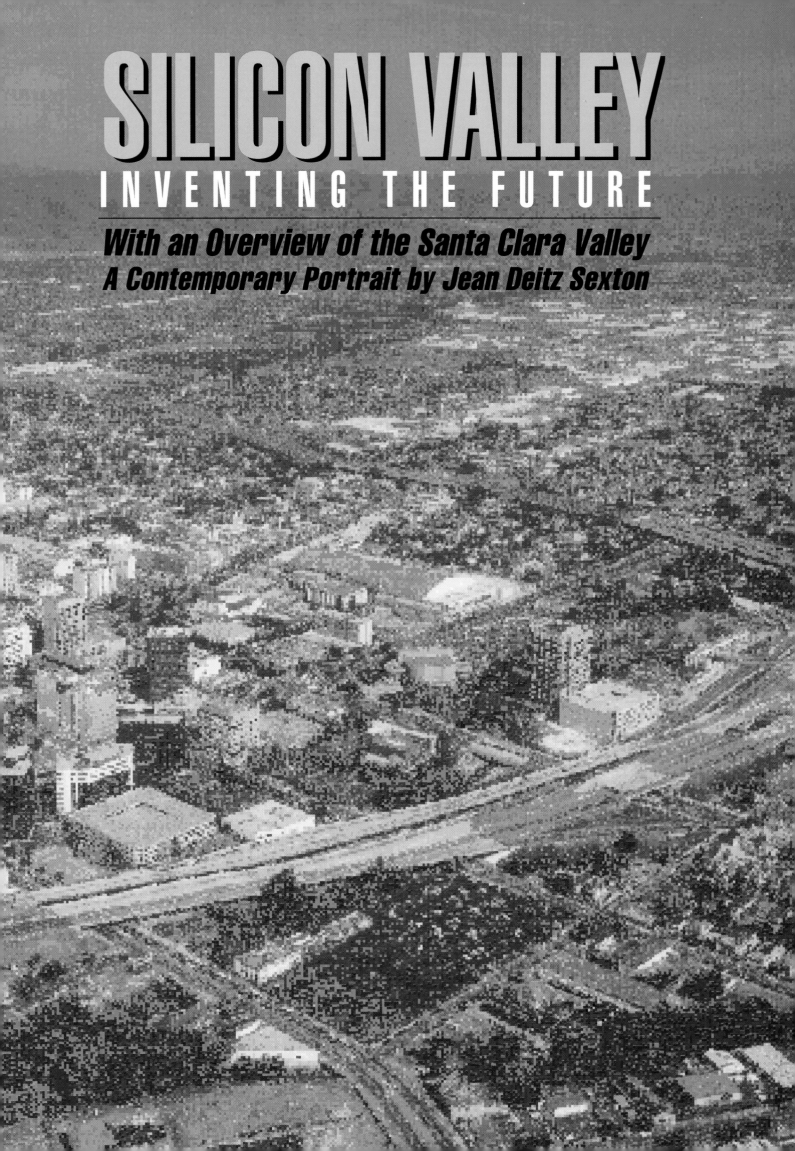

SILICON VALLEY
INVENTING THE FUTURE

With an Overview of the Santa Clara Valley
A Contemporary Portrait by Jean Deitz Sexton

Windsor Publications, Inc.—Book Division
Managing Editor: Karen Story
Design Director: Ellen Ifrah
Executive Editor: Pamela Schroeder

Staff for *Silicon Valley: Inventing the Future*
Manuscript Editor: Michael Nalick
Photo Director: Susan L. Wells
Senior Editor, Corporate Profiles: Jeffrey Reeves
Photo Research Assistants: Elizabeth Anderson, Darlene Huckabey
Proofreader: Annette Nibblett Arrieta
Customer Service Manager: Phyllis Feldman-Schroeder
Editorial Assistants: Alex Arredondo,
Kate Coombs, Lori Erbaugh, Wilma Huckabey, Michael Nugwynne
Publisher's Representatives, Corporate Profiles: Harriet Holmes,
Gina Waters
Layout Artists, Corporate Profiles: Kristi Johnson, Trish Meyer
Designer: Christina L. Rosepapa

Windsor Publications, Inc.
Elliot Martin, Chairman of the Board
James L. Fish III, Chief Operating Officer
Mac Buhler, Vice President/Acquisitions

County of Santa Clara Board of Supervisors:
Chairperson, Dianne McKenna
Rod Diridon; Ron Gonzalez; Mike Honda; Zoe Lofgren

County of Santa Clara Historical Heritage Commission:
Chairperson, Ed Teresi
Paul Bernal; Elisa Boyden; Jack Douglas; Sue Harper
Joanna Herz; Nancy Mason; Art De Mattei; David McKinney
Ed Sakauye; Beth Wyman
Dr. Arthur Ogilvie, Volunteer Advisor
Frank Fenton, Parks Department Staff

Library of Congress Cataloging-in-Publication Data
Sexton, Jean Deitz, 1948-
Silicon Valley : inventing the future : a contemporary portrait /
by Jean Deitz Sexton. — 1st ed.
p. 464 cm. 23X31
Includes bibliographical references.
ISBN: 0-89781-389-8
1. Santa Clara County (Calif.)—Description and travel. 2.
Santa Clara County (Calif.)—Description and
travel—Views. 3. Santa Clara County (Calif.)—Economic conditions. 4.
Santa Clara County (Calif.)—Industries.
I. Title
F868.S25S49 1991
979.4'73—dc20   91-20998
CIP

FRONTISPIECE: Photo by Gerald L. French/The Photo File

RIGHT: Photo by Andrew Van Dis

For my mother and father, Jean and Robert Francis Deitz

 *Contents*

11

High Technology and Manufacturing 301

Silicon Valley is a mecca for a flourishing high-tech manufacturing and research and development industry.

12

Marketplace 375

Silicon Valley's retail establishments, service industries, and products are enjoyed by residents and visitors alike.

13

Building Silicon Valley 387

As the gatekeepers of Silicon Valley's skyline, developers, contractors, and real estate professionals all help to shape and enrich this growing metropolis.

14

Business 421

Business firms and government offices combine to demonstrate Silicon Valley's innovative leadership.

15

Quality of Life 433

Medical and educational institutions contribute to the quality of life for Silicon Valley residents.

Foreword

The Santa Clara Valley, always evolving, has seen its way through several major revolutions. From the original hunting and gathering Ohlone Indians to the cattle-ranching Spanish Rancheros, from the fields of grain covering the valley to the orchards upon orchards of fruit trees, our face has changed many times. With the arrival of World War II came the conversion of the agricultural and food-packaging industry to defense production. During that era enormous companies like FMC began producing weapons instead of food machines, and Lockheed Missiles and Space Company, the valley's largest employer, was established. While San Jose State University, Santa Clara University, and Stanford University researched the latest in high technology, innovative individuals like Bill Hewlett and David Packard produced that technology in their garage. That kind of synergy earned Santa Clara County the name Silicon Valley and a reputation as the world's capital of high technology.

Becoming more irrefutable every day, however, is the fact that leading the world in technological innovation and providing thousands of people with remarkable employment opportunities has a downside: fouled air, traffic congestion, and skyrocketing living costs.

The challenge for the future is to write a new chapter in the Silicon Valley saga, protecting the best of our past and leaving behind the worst. No longer can we search for a scapegoat to blame. Rather industry, government, and—most important—private citizens must coalesce to create new alliances to combat our common crises.

Again we find ourselves at a turning point. Not too unlike the Indians who held their ears to the ground to detect horses rumbling in the distance, current valley leaders feel the pulse of change at their fingertips. Many hypothesize that the next transition will involve a shift in Silicon Valley's high-tech research and production capacity from defense to environmental protection, putting our valley once again at the forefront of an emerging industry.

Heightened environmental awareness, growing impatience with traffic congestion, and a perennial water shortage have unleashed a demand for new technologies. In response local innovators have offered air pollution control equipment; water reclamation and purification devices; magnetic levitation for high-speed transit; "telecommuting" devices that allow people to work at home; and solar, wind, and other forms of renewable energy.

Though the transition to a more environmentally conscious community is complicated, involves millions of people, and could cost billions of dollars, it shouldn't be feared or avoided, but rather embraced. After all, one key to this valley's success has been our ability to take advantage of changing times.

This adaptation will require increased utilization of mass transportation to reduce traffic congestion, air pollution, and the overuse of petroleum fuel. Although the impetus of stringent federal and state legislation mandating cleaner air has led to dramatic improvements, we have a long way to go. Reduced reliance on fossil fuel, especially as used in motor vehicles, will bring continued air-quality improvement.

Instead of the single-family suburban dwelling typically preferred in today's American culture, more and more valley residents will live in less expensive condominiums clustered in downtown cities and on top of and around rail stations. New water-purification procedures like large-scale reverse osmosis will allow us to reuse sewage water, freeing us from the water importation requirements that degrade the bay delta. The water surplus created by new treatment practices will return our streams and rivers to their natural state, moving swiftly—full with salmon and steelhead—and keeping the air cool and the hills green.

The most important ingredient for continued success in the valley is the remarkably dynamic mix of risk-taking and creative individuals who have been and will continue to be attracted to the valley. Although darker episodes in our history have included prejudice and discrimination, residents now celebrate our ethnic diversity, realizing that the mix existing in this valley is an unparalleled asset.

That critical mass of creative genius and management expertise, coupled with the burgeoning supply of risk capital generated by our prior successes, will be catalyzed by our challenge to return to environmental excellence and will make Santa Clara Valley the next century's Paris of the West.

Supervisor Rod Diridon
Santa Clara County Board of Supervisors

Acknowledgments

Writing a book about the Santa Clara Valley is like trying to get your arms around an elephant as it's jogging down the road.

The valley is physically immense, ethnically diverse, and in constant flux, driven ever forward by the force of technology.

Nothing stays the same. In many ways the valley is the archetypal modern culture. At any point in time it remains contemporary because, whether it wants to be or not, it is in the maelstrom of change.

Santa Clara Valley invents the future almost by the minute—multicultural population surges; the rebirth of a major city; RISC chips; 3-D modeling; multiple organ transplants.

There's a particular challenge to describing the Santa Clara Valley. Satisfaction comes with wrapping up a region into a neat package of description, of feeling. But it's virtually impossible to do so in this instance. Is the valley a former agricultural heaven turned to asphalt and industry? Is it a home for tomorrow's technocrats? Is it a valley rich in history, trying to redefine itself? Is its identity the Santa Clara Valley or Silicon Valley?

Literary pigeonholing doesn't work here. The Santa Clara Valley is really a work in progress. Its deadline has no boundaries for it is the future.

From December 1989 to February 1991, I interviewed more than 100 people for *Silicon Valley: Inventing the Future*. People make a project work or fail. I am indebted to each and every person who graciously spent time being interviewed.

The wealth of talent and intellect in Silicon Valley cannot be overstated. It was wonderfully stimulating to talk with scientists, venture capitalists, and other movers and shakers who continue to propel the valley into a hopefully rosy future.

I am thankful for

• Computer visionary Alan Kay who thinks about how to think, who teaches that extrapolation is a futile process when trying to predict the future;
• J. Lindsey Wolf, who recommended me as the author;
• Santa Clara County Supervisor Rod Diridon for his interest and encouragement;
• Linda Noble, the marvelous researcher at the Alum Rock Library;
• Mike Nalick, my compassionate book editor;
• Phil Kohlenberg, analyst for the state Employment Development Department, a patient source and all-around nice guy;
• Richard Carlson, president of Spectrum Economics, a good analyst and a delightful interview;
• Paul Ely, Burt McMurtry, and other Silicon Valley luminaries who enthusiastically gave their time;
• Dr. Ed Feigenbaum of Stanford;
• Marilyn Lewis of the San Jose Mercury News who was kind enough to point me in the direction of a few sources;
• Brenna Bolger, who opened doors to the business elite of Silicon Valley.

Family and friends are the anchors of sanity when one's mental health is threatened by the work at hand. For their moral support I thank Diane Deitz, Janeen Muse, William Jones, Gloria Chacon, John Waters, Cecelia Dirstine, Mimi Baca, Stuart McFaul, Jan Bright, Lori Cooke, Kathy Linton, Janet and Bob Dietz, and Frances and Stanley Bielen.

And last but not least, I thank my husband Jim for his fabulous sense of humor and his patience.

Jean Deitz Sexton

1

Inventing the Future

Traveling Through Santa Clara County

■ *Future Past*

For many people in the modern world, Santa Clara County became interesting when the late Robert Noyce filed a patent for the integrated circuit in 1959.

Santa Clara County has always been fertile breeding ground, for new ideas and for the gifts of nature. Long before technological innovations imprinted the phrase "Silicon Valley" on the global consciousness, the area bustled with another major industry: agriculture.

Although urbanization has consumed most of its cropland, the county still retains some of the breathtaking beauty that inspired its title as "The Valley of Heart's Delight." It is evidenced in rolling foothills that turn dusky purple at day's end, bright orange California poppies that dot the valley in springtime, and the gentle gray mist of a winter's rain.

Encompassing 1,315 square miles, Santa Clara County consists of the Santa Clara Valley, which is nestled between the Diablo mountain range to the east and the Santa Cruz mountain range to the west, and the foothills of both mountain ranges. Santa Clara County's 1.5 million residents are blessed with a mild Mediterranean climate, which prompts a year-round love affair with the outdoors.

This lovely carousel comes alive with color and music at Great America. Photo by Mark E. Gibson

The valley's lush soil still produces crops for commercial distribution. But, along with garlic, mushrooms, onions, and cherries, Santa Clara County now produces microprocessors, workstations, personal computers (PCs), and disk drives.

"The Valley of Heart's Delight." "Silicon Valley."

Santa Clara County has a dual identity. As it approaches the twenty-first century, the fertile breeding ground continues to thrive.

■ Early Days

Tucked away in San Jose's Kelley Park is a delightful reconstruction of the city's Victorian era. In the Pacific Hotel run by the San Jose Historical Museum, visitors can stop in the old-fashioned soda shop for an ice-cream treat and pretend they live in the days of the Old West.

On the second floor of the Pacific Hotel are the museum archives where history lovers spend countless hours, captivated by original volumes dating back to the 1800s.

In its book and photo collections, the museum sketches a vibrant picture of Santa Clara Valley's colorful past, covering the valley's transformation from a land of scattered mission settlements to a bustling center of commerce.

An 1896 publication titled *Sunshine, Fruit and Flowers* reveals street after street of splendid commercial buildings and elegant Victorian homes, many of them designed by noted architect Theodore Lenzen. Unfortunately many of those buildings were either razed or lost in the 1906 earthquake. But a few from that era remain: the renovated St. Joseph's Cathedral and the old downtown courthouse overlooking St. James Park are two prominent examples. The courthouse was damaged in the Loma Prieta earthquake of October 17, 1989, and its fate is now uncertain. Some of the Victorian homes have been preserved, particularly in the downtown area.

Santa Clara Street was the heart of San Jose's downtown a century ago. The city's late twentieth-century downtown pretty much mirrors the same geography: the new Fairmont Hotel and Fairmont Plaza are just a few minutes' walk from St. Joseph's Cathedral.

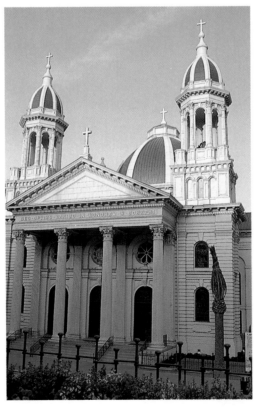

In the late 1800s San Jose was a major distribution center for produce from the valley, shipping an impressive 87.1 million pounds in one year. Gilroy alone produced 1.3 million pounds of cheese annually. Elsewhere the mountain ranges supplied redwood timber, providing work for the early residents of Los Gatos and Saratoga, and the San Francisco Bay and its ports provided accessible shipping points.

The city of Santa Clara enjoyed early prosperity because it was near San Jose's business center. An electric streetcar line connected the two cities and was used from early morning to late evening.

ABOVE: Strawberries are plentiful in south Santa Clara County. Photo by Mark E. Gibson

LEFT: The San Jose Civic Center is the headquarters of city governmental offices and services. A light rail system connects the civic center and adjacent county offices to the downtown commercial district. Photo by Gerald L. French/The Photo File

FACING PAGE BOTTOM: The movement to refurbish and rebuild downtown San Jose extends to its religious institutions. European craftsmen were brought to California specifically to put finishing touches on the inside of the recently reopened St. Joseph's Cathedral. Photo by Gerald L. French/The Photo File

By the early 1900s the Santa Clara Valley was a robust blend of emerging cities. Manufacturing and other commercial endeavors added to the valley's agricultural economy.

Later the post-World War II economy and the birth of the technology industry generated new prosperity, bringing record numbers of people to the region.

With so much of the land having been developed for new industry and housing, the end of the twentieth century became a time for many of the valley's cities to review growth policies and to protect open space.

The latter half of the century was also a time for cities to preserve their character and heritage amidst a rapidly changing environment. Saratoga and Los Gatos have defined themselves as genteel residential communities. In contrast Gilroy and Morgan Hill, surrounded by acres of vacant land, have struggled to maintain their rural nature.

Other cities have undergone radical change as high-technology industries create new demands for industrial space and residential housing. Santa Clara, its early roots in manufacturing and seed farms, became a headquarters town for many significant companies. Sunnyvale burgeoned quickly when Lockheed moved in, thrusting the city into the middle of the technology boom.

Without question the city which marked the most change was San Jose. During the 1980s San Jose regained its prominence as an urban center and declared itself the Capital of Silicon Valley.

■ San Jose: Reaching For The Sky

San Jose is California's oldest city, established November 29, 1777, as San Jose de Guadalupe and incorporated March 27, 1850. It served as the first state capital and the site of the inaugural session of the California legislature, held in the

While much of San Jose's downtown image is centered on the new and modern, this old French clock serves as a reminder of the rich traditions of the region. Photo by Gerald L. French/The Photo File

city on December 15, 1849.

At the end of the twentieth century, the city is again making history. Rapid population growth in the 1980s catapulted San Jose to its new status as the 11th most populous United States city, with 791,600 residents. San Jose now has more residents than San Francisco.

But the city still has a low-key style reminiscent of a simpler time. It remains, for the most part, an amalgam of quiet, unpretentious neighborhoods. Modern San Jose is a city of young families. About a quarter of the city's population is school-age. One especially appealing element for families is San Jose's distinction of being the safest of the top 40 American cities.

The 1980s were also a boom time for San Jose commerce. A downtown building renaissance which virtually reshaped the San Jose skyline began during the decade and continues into the 1990s. The majestic business palaces of the city's past have been replaced by luxurious new office towers.

With its downtown modernization well under way, the city is refining its business image. San Jose is emerging as the Northern California trade center for the Pacific Rim and is establishing links with other international markets.

Flags along the streets of San Jose are changed regularly to remind passersby of upcoming community events. Photo by Gerald L. French/The Photo File

■ Hometown

San Jose has retained its warm, homey style, a tribute to its agricultural roots and the many immigrant families who have settled in the city over the last two centuries.

"We still have a small-town ambience even though we are now a major urban area," says Tom McEnery, who in 1990 ended his eight-year tenure as San Jose's mayor.

Few leaders of modern American cities have made as positive an impact as McEnery. With a lineage dating back to early San Jose, McEnery followed the tradition of his family and devoted himself to public service. His father, John P.

McEnery, was a political power and served as Democratic party state chairman in 1948. McEnery's maternal grandfather, Ben Sellers, served as city councilman in San Jose's third ward from 1914 to 1918, and his paternal grandfather, Patrick McEnery, was an editor for the old *San Jose Mercury Herald* during the early 1900s.

The McEnerys were early San Jose landowners. The Farmers Union Corporation, a farmers cooperative that supplied materials and arranged credit, was established in 1874 and operated out of McEnery-

Visitors to San Jose can identify key historical sites throughout the downtown area via prominent markers, such as this. Photo by Gerald L. French/The Photo File

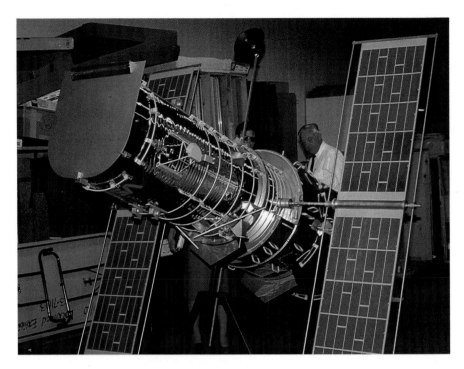

The Technology Center of Silicon Valley features new and exciting high-tech innovations that will rocket the nation into the twenty-first century. Courtesy, Technology Center of Silicon Valley

owned buildings at San Pedro and Santa Clara streets. The corporation is now run by the McEnery family as a private property-management firm, whose signature project has been the revitalization of San Pedro Square.

History has also become an avocation for the former mayor. He authored a fictional account of Captain Thomas Fallon, who in 1846 raised the American flag of independence in front of San Jose's town hall. McEnery also led the effort to restore the Peralta Adobe.

The shape and tone of San Jose as it moves into the twenty-first century is largely the work of McEnery who made an indelible stamp on the city's evolution during his two terms as mayor. A strong political leader who commanded a voting majority on the city council, McEnery determined what the modern look of San Jose would be. He led the redevelopment movement that transformed the sleepy downtown into a glittering skyline with a bustling cultural district. During McEnery's administration, San Jose gained two new museums—Children's Discovery Museum and the Technology Center of Silicon Valley—the Fairmont Hotel and Plaza, an expanded San Jose Museum of Art, a new convention center, plus numerous new commercial buildings, restaurants, and entertainment spots.

At the beginning of his tenure McEnery had a distinct vision of how San Jose should evolve. Abhorring urban sprawl he drew a ring around the city and declared the city would not stretch beyond those boundaries so space could be saved for a greenbelt. New development in San Jose would have to occur within existing boundaries, via higher-density projects.

To fuel the city's economy land was set aside for industrial use. McEnery ensured a balance of usage by establishing planning policies that situated new housing and parks near industrial developments.

Respectful of the environment, McEnery supported the opening of San Jose's Office of Environmental Management, one of the first such departments in the nation. San Jose now has the nation's largest curbside recycling program.

As San Jose heads into the next century, McEnery feels the city will retain its "delicate balance" between economic success and quality of life. "San Jose will remain very much what it is now with a few new embellishments," McEnery says, referring to the new museums, a major new sports arena under construction, and the planned Guadalupe River Park, which McEnery says will rival Central Park in breadth.

San Jose's toughest critics, its own residents, approve of the work of McEnery and his city staff. "I'm most pleased with how the people who live here think of us. Of our residents, 80 percent believe San Jose is a good place to raise a family," McEnery says.

The Capital Of Silicon Valley

By the mid-twenty-first century San Jose will be one of the nation's leading centers of international trade. The high-technology global community likes San Jose's manageable downtown and its nearness to San Jose's North 1st Street industrial sector and other Silicon Valley business centers.

Notably, the Pacific Rim is choosing San Jose as a primary trade location. In 1990 San Jose International Airport announced that nonstop flights would begin to Tokyo to serve the increasing traffic between Silicon Valley and Asia.

San Jose made a formal commitment to world trade in 1990 when it opened the Center for International Trade and Development. Its intent is to attract foreign investment in San Jose and the surrounding metropolitan area.

The city's trade office is located downtown where a varied mix of service businesses are grouped, the result of recruitment efforts by the Redevelopment Agency and the Office of Economic Development. These firms—high-tech sales and marketing, banking, legal, and accounting—serve both Silicon Valley-based businesses and the increasing number of international firms who want a San Jose presence.

Redevelopment Agency executive director Frank Taylor, who with McEnery captained the transformation of downtown, enjoys the eclectic feeling the downtown now has: "It's a diversified work force, not just your traditional white-collar style. I love having lunch at Eulipia and seeing someone dressed in L.L. Bean next to a table of Brooks Brother suits."

With high-technology industry now a primary tenant of San Jose, it is common for software developers in sneakers to find themselves next to financial executives in pinstripes. To Taylor it is a "unique sharing of environment."

This aerial photo features the North 1st Street industrial sector in San Jose. Photo by Gerald L. French/The Photo File

RIGHT: San Jose International Airport connects commuters and travelers quickly with other regional and international destinations. Photo by Gerald L. French/The Photo File

BELOW: The Fairmont Hotel is a luxurious landmark in downtown San Jose. Other amenities located downtown include a light rail system, shopping mall, and a new convention center. Photo by Gerald L. French/The Photo File

"What we've done is create a place for networking and brainpower to come together. The clustering of talent in San Jose and its metropolitan area is unbeatable. It's an incredible collection of brilliant people," Taylor declares.

While San Jose's downtown is now a vibrant place to work, Taylor sees his job as only half completed. The 1980s were a time for the city to underwrite public amenities—museums, parks, a new transit mall, a new convention center—and to work in concert with private enterprise. For Taylor the 1990s will focus on private development, especially new housing downtown. San Jose will also complete major public projects such as the Guadalupe River Park.

Taylor believes San Jose's downtown success is in part due to its "partnership of quality" with major developers such as the Swig family, which owns the San Jose and San Francisco Fairmont hotels.

The Swigs spent several million dollars alone on exquisite art and furnishings for the San Jose Fairmont. San Jose matched the Fairmont's opulence with equally fine materials in its public facilities, Taylor notes. Granite paving of the transit mall and the new convention center's hand-painted tile facade and terrazzo floors are examples of the city's attention to a "particular level of elegance."

Setting a level of luxuriance has also enabled San Jose to attract "Class A" office structures, Taylor says. The Fairmont Plaza and the River Park Towers, with their marble, brass, and copper adornments, reflect San Jose's new business style.

To further solidify its position as an international trade center, San Jose is adding other amenities. The city's convention center, which opened in 1989 and added $28 million to the San Jose economy during its first full year of operation, is one of the 20 largest such facilities in the United States. Occupying a space about the size of 10 football fields, the center handles major conventions and trade shows. Since its opening the center has booked a variety of clients,

LEFT: The Fairmont Hotel's elegant Les Saisons restaurant is a classic way to begin or end an evening. Photo by Gerald L. French/The Photo File

BELOW: The abstract mural by Danish artist Lin Utzon graces the San Jose McEnery Convention Center. The downtown facility is the size of 10 football fields and is a major center for business conferences and conventions. Photo by Gerald L. French/The Photo File

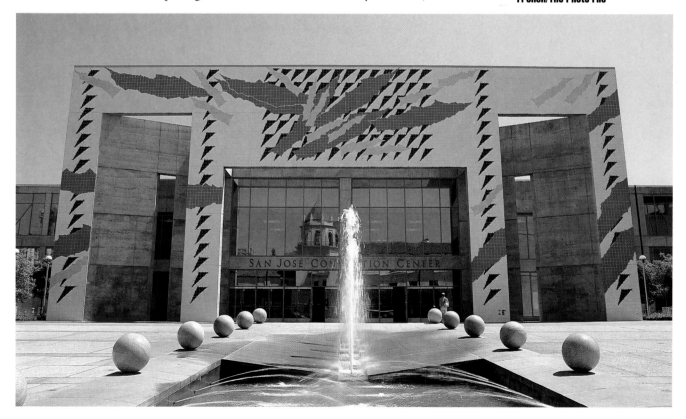

from prestigious technology shows such as the Seybold Computer Publishing Conference to the Harvest Festival and other local interest shows. It is now the home of Silicon Valley's major charity event: the Silicon Valley Charity Ball.

To accommodate convention guests and business travelers, San Jose is soliciting additional new hotels for downtown. Currently planned are two hotels that will flank the convention center; a San Jose Hilton will be built by developer Lew Wolff on the western side.

The historic DeAnza Hotel, built in 1931, is reopening for business after a two-year restoration, providing 100 new downtown hotel rooms.

Temporary guests are one focus of San Jose's redevelopment efforts; full-time residents are another. The Redevelopment Agency is currently stepping up efforts to provide downtown housing for its permanent residents. "We want to reinforce the concept of downtown living," says Taylor, whose aim is the establishment of an additional 5,000 housing units.

Indicative of the type of housing San Jose planners want downtown is the Paseo Plaza, a 210-unit condominium complex to be accompanied by its own retail services. The high-density development at Third and San Fernando streets, to be completed in 1992, will serve nearby office workers. With more people living downtown and staying there after office hours, San Jose will become what it desires to be—a round-the-clock city.

■ *Attracting Industry*

Redevelopment in San Jose's downtown paralleled the sweeping expansion of its North 1st Street industrial sector, now one of the leading centers of high-tech industry in Silicon Valley.

San Jose, with 40 percent of the county's remaining developable land, has become a favorite of corporations that need additional space and can't grow at their original sites. Asian-based corporations are also choosing San Jose. Major North San Jose tenants include Amdahl Corporation and the Korean-based Goldstar.

San Jose's other industrial redevelopment priority is the Edenvale corridor, whose major tenants include IBM, United Technologies, and Litton Applied Technology.

Industrial redevelopment has created 70,000 new jobs for San Jose, according to the Redevelopment Agency. An economic benefit is the additional $5.4-billion tax base which has helped pay for many of the public facilities constructed by the city.

Since land is increasingly scarce in Silicon Valley, San Jose is always under pressure to develop industrial space. The Coyote Valley—one of the prime parcels of undeveloped land in the city—has been held in reserve by city leaders. A balance of jobs and housing must be assured in Coyote Valley before any development could be considered, according to city policy. San Jose's philosophy, crafted during the administration of Mayor Tom McEnery, is that housing and jobs need to be linked to prevent sprawl and further congestion.

The golden hills of the Santa Clara Valley envelop the rapidly growing city of San Jose; its freeway system provides quick access to communities both north and south. In 1990 voters approved measures to bring a variety of road and transit improvements to Santa Clara County. Photo by Mark E. Gibson

■ *Sunnyvale: A Company Town*

Martin Murphy, Jr., knew a good thing when he saw it. In 1850 Murphy purchased 4,800 acres of Rancho Pastoria de los Borregas from Mariano Castro. The prime piece of land, stretching from the San Francisco Bay to El Camino Real and from Mountain View's Castro Street to the Lawrence Expressway, became the heart of the city of Sunnyvale.

Murphy, a legendary Santa Clara Valley pioneer, built one of California's first framed homes. The residence became a favorite for the valley's social and political gatherings. One of the largest individual landowners and cattlemen in the state, Murphy enjoyed a good party. When he and his wife Mary celebrated their 50th wedding anniversary in 1881, the revelry lasted three days. Newspapers reported as many as 10,000 people attended.

After Murphy died in 1884 and his wife in 1892, the Murphy estate was divided equally among their heirs. Modern-day Sunnyvale really began in 1898 when a Murphy heir sold 200 acres to developer W.E. Crossman.

After subdividing his property Crossman began promoting his concept of a new town: "Sunnyvale, The City of Destiny." Sunnyvale soon became a city of orchardists and industrial concerns such as the Joshua Hendy Iron Works, Sunnyvale's first manufacturer.

Just months before the thriving town of Sunnyvale incorporated on December 24, 1912, an ad in *Colliers Magazine* described it as "the manufacturing suburb of San Francisco." But the mainstay of Sunnyvale's economy continued to be agriculture until World War II demanded industrial mobilization.

NASA Ames Research Center and nearby Lockheed Missiles and Space Company in Sunnyvale help keep Santa Clara County in the forefront of the nation's most important scientific and aeronautical developments. Lockheed is one of the largest employers in Silicon Valley. Photo by Roger Lee/The Photo File

After the war Sunnyvale permanently shifted to an industrial focus. With the arrival of Lockheed in 1956, the city entered the technological era. Lockheed's impact on Sunnyvale was dramatic. As Silicon Valley's largest employer—in 1989 it had 22,000 personnel—it created a tremendous and immediate demand for new housing. Sunnyvale's orchards gave way to subdivisions to house its many new workers.

Since 1956 Sunnyvale's resident population has grown to 117,000, making it the second most populous city in Santa Clara County. Lockheed has been joined by more than 600 technology firms, including Amdahl, Advanced Micro Devices, and ESL.

In the 1980s the Sunnyvale City Council set growth limits on industrial development when it saw that land for housing was becoming alarmingly scarce. Sunnyvale is continuing that policy into the 1990s by rezoning land from industrial to residential usage.

With a climate that encourages outdoor adventure year-round, Santa
Clara County allows residents ample
opportunity to participate in the
recreational activity of their choice.
Photo by Tim Davis

"We've become very biased towards housing," declares Larry Stone, a councilman who has served two terms as mayor. With housing costs high in Sunnyvale, the council sees new higher-density construction as a more affordable alternative for the future. High density is a departure from the typical Sunnyvale single-family neighborhood, Stone notes, and some of Sunnyvale's long-term residents will likely resist such a change.

One thing is for certain. People love to live in Sunnyvale. Its low crime rate, manicured neighborhoods, award-winning parks and recreation services, and healthy fiscal state make it a highly desirable city. The city has a full complement of schools to serve its families. There are 12 elementary schools, 3 intermediate schools, and 2 high schools as well as Catholic parochial schools, the South Peninsula Hebrew Day School, and the Sunshine Christian School.

Sunnyvale's public safety department—in which personnel are trained as both police and fire fighters—was considered an offbeat concept when introduced in 1949. But Stone says it saves the city millions of dollars each year, and many other cities have embraced the concept.

The city's practice of planning its budget for a 10-year time frame instead of the usual two-year cycle, helps to make it a financially strong community, Stone says. With a solid financial base Sunnyvale can plan for new public facilities.

During the 1990s the city plans to redevelop the area occupied by the Town and Country Village Shopping Center, north of Washington Avenue between Mathilda and the Murphy Avenue Heritage District. Murphy Avenue, a popular street full of restaurants and shops, was restored during the 1980s. According to the city's plan the shopping center would change to a mixed-use development. One of the focal points would be a new performing arts theater with a maximum 800 seats to house the California Theatre Center, a popular producer of children's shows.

Sunnyvale's long-term future, Stone believes, will be basically the status quo. Most likely there will be new high-density housing developments. But the essential nature of Sunnyvale, that of a pleasant, well-run, suburban community, will remain intact.

Throughout the Santa Clara Valley, considerable effort is often made to restore older buildings to their original splendor. Photo by Gerald L. French/The Photo File

Santa Clara: The Mission City

On January 12, 1777, Father Junipero Serra founded the Mission Santa Clara de Asis, the eighth of 21 missions established by Spain to colonize California.

To the Franciscan padres the fertile lands of the Santa Clara Valley seemed a good place to build the next mission. Santa Clara's mission settlement thrived until 1836, when civil commissioners gained power. After a period of deterioration the mission was eventually transferred to the Jesuits for use as a new school of higher learning.

Remnants of the settlement still exist on the campus of Santa Clara University (originally known as Santa Clara College), which has occupied the site since 1851. The mission church that the Jesuits inherited was later destroyed by fire; in 1928 an enlarged replica of the mission was dedicated. Surrounded by beautiful grounds, the graceful, historically significant building is a very popular choice for the weddings of university graduates.

About the time that Santa Clara University was founded, the land surrounding the mission began to assume the shape of a small town. William Campbell surveyed the hamlet and parceled the land into lots of 100 square yards. Each citizen received a lot with the caveat that a house would be built on the land within three months or the property would be revoked.

Santa Clara incorporated as a town in 1852 and can be considered one of the state's first exporters: the Eberhard Tannery, which began as the Wampach Tannery, exported fine leather goods to the East Coast and Europe until closing its doors in 1953.

The city's good soil supported acres of flower and vegetable seed farms. J.M. Kimberlin and Company, the largest seed grower on the West Coast, was established in Santa Clara in 1875. It was followed by C.C. Morse and Company which grew to be the world's largest producer of seed.

Orchards flourished in Santa Clara, producing an abundance of crops for the world. Pratt-Low Preserving Company, one of Santa Clara's numerous produce companies, shipped canned apricots, pears, peaches, cherries, and plums to other parts of the United States, England, and Asia.

By the early 1900s Santa Clara had become a magnet for people seeking manufacturing or produce jobs and desiring to live in its mild climate.

About 5,000 people lived in Santa Clara in 1906, and the city's geographical shape remained relatively unchanged until after World War II, when it expanded beyond its nineteenth-century boundaries. Homes and businesses soon overtook the orchards.

Santa Clara, its historical roots in manufacturing, played an important role in the beginning of Silicon Valley. By the early 1960s Intel and National Semiconductor were established in Santa Clara. Both firms have their corporate headquarters in Santa Clara and continue to be among the city's biggest employers. In 1990 Intel was planning to consolidate some of its operations, using Santa Clara as a base and bringing the number of Intel people employed in the city to 4,500.

National Semiconductor and other first-generation Silicon Valley companies permanently changed Santa Clara's landscape. Many high-technology start-ups moved in, replacing the remaining orchard land with stark modernistic buildings. Santa Clara became one of the leading industrial cities of the new Silicon Valley.

ABOVE: The Triton Museum of Art in Santa Clara, the oldest public art center in the valley, shows traveling exhibitions and displays of its permanent collection of nineteenth- and twentieth-century American art. The adjoining sculpture garden contains works of contemporary regional sculptors. Photo by Joseph Sohm/Chromosohm

High technology remains a part of everyday life in Santa Clara. By 1990 there were close to 500 manufacturing plants in the city, producing everything from integrated circuits to mini-computers. Santa Clara's ratio of residents to daytime workers is 93,000 to 130,000, making the city one of the region's largest importers of workers.

The town began as a collection of hard-working families, and it has retained that character. Santa Clara is very much a middle-class community, says city manager Jennifer Sparacino. Half of its housing units are rentals occupied by families, the elderly, and Santa Clara University students. In 1990 construction began on Fairway Glen, which will provide 2,100 new housing units and have its own park and library. The city's families are served by 14 elementary schools, 2 junior high schools, 3 high schools, and 4 parochial schools.

Residents and businesses have enjoyed the benefit of several innovative energy-source services initiated by city management. Santa Clara and Palo Alto are the only two cities in Santa Clara County that have their own electric utilities. As a result residents in Santa Clara pay 35 percent less on an average utility bill, and businesses 15 percent less. The city also runs a solar energy utility that heats swimming pools, residential hot water, and industrial process water.

For years Santa Clara also had the distinction of being the first city in the nation to own and operate its own theme park. In 1989 the city sold the Great

Major hotel chains, such as the Doubletree in Santa Clara, serve the substantial business and convention demands of Silicon Valley. Photo by Joseph Sohm/Chromosohm

LEFT: Thousands of people come each season to the Great America Theme Park in the city of Santa Clara. Traditional rides and a giant antique carousel attract children and adults. Photo by Mark E. Gibson

The carousel at the Great America Theme Park in Santa Clara is a signature attraction. Photo by Tom Tracy/The Photo File

America Theme Park to Kings Entertainment, retaining the park's land and leasing it back to the company under a 50-year agreement. It will realize $5.3 million yearly in lease payments plus a percentage of the gross income. The money will be used to pay off the $42-million parkland debt, after which the revenue will be applied to other city services.

A diversified economy, combining high technology and tourism, has given the city fiscal strength, Sparacino says. To further encourage tourism and entertainment trade, Santa Clara during the 1980s developed a new trade and convention complex near Great America. The convention center, which opened in 1986, divides its shows evenly between corporate events and public interest shows for antique collectors, home remodelers, and the like. During their leisure time conventioneers who want to enjoy art can visit the Triton Museum, which opened a new $3-million facility in 1987 and is located near Santa Clara's city government center. Other elements in the convention center complex include a Doubletree Hotel and Techmart, a high-technology sales and marketing center.

For sports enthusiasts Santa Clara has developed the municipal Golf and Tennis Club adjacent to the convention center. It features an 18-hole tournament-level course and seven lighted tennis courts. Santa Clara is also home base for top swimmers who use the Olympic-level International Swim Center.

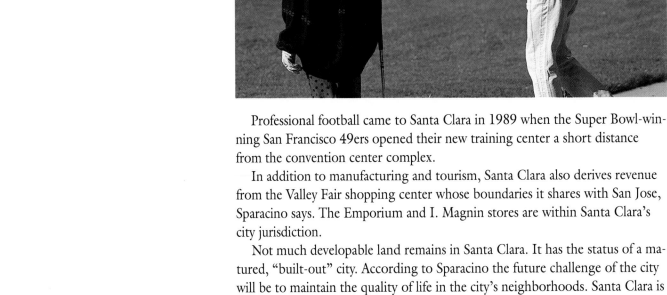

Professional football came to Santa Clara in 1989 when the Super Bowl-winning San Francisco 49ers opened their new training center a short distance from the convention center complex.

In addition to manufacturing and tourism, Santa Clara also derives revenue from the Valley Fair shopping center whose boundaries it shares with San Jose, Sparacino says. The Emporium and I. Magnin stores are within Santa Clara's city jurisdiction.

Not much developable land remains in Santa Clara. It has the status of a matured, "built-out" city. According to Sparacino the future challenge of the city will be to maintain the quality of life in the city's neighborhoods. Santa Clara is basically divided into two segments: the north has industrial while the south has residential. "The council wants to retain that demarcation," Sparacino says.

■ *Mountain View: By The Bay*

Mountain View, described as "the interesting town between the mountains and the bay" in *Sunshine, Fruit and Flowers,* has come full cycle. Early in Mountain View's history freight cars loaded with wine and produce embarked from the city. At one time there were 22 wineries operating in the vicinity of the city.

In the 1990s Mountain View is once again a wining and dining mecca, having completed an ambitious overhaul of its downtown, the centerpiece being a new Castro Street performing arts and government center.

There are no less than two dozen restaurants dotted along Castro and nearby streets. Silicon Valley workers make Mountain View a favorite stop to indulge tastes ranging from sausages at the Tied House Brewery to French cuisine at Jacqueline's.

Castro Street officially became Mountain View's downtown in 1990 when the city celebrated its $60-million revitalization project with a street festival.

In Mountain View, contemporary eateries blend with the architectural styles of the past. Sausages are a specialty of the Tied House Brewery. Photo by Joseph Sohm/Chromosohm

Economic development manager Ken Alsman describes the area as "the traditional concept of a downtown." There is an emphasis on foot traffic and sidewalk interest, encouraged by the innovative use of flexible sidewalks which double as additional walkways or extra parking spaces.

Redevelopment of Castro Street was the linchpin for Mountain View's landmark downtown projects: a Castro Street plaza containing a new city hall and performing arts theater, which opened in 1991; a 400-unit housing complex with office and retail space built by Prometheus Development; and a new Bryant Street garage offering 300 spaces of free parking for downtown visitors.

Mountain View's new prominence as a local entertainment center also reflects its history. It has always been a crossroads city, serving people from many of its surrounding communities. The city, which incorporated in 1902, began as a town servicing the stage line between San Francisco and San Jose. Its northern Santa Clara Valley location and its land fronting on San Francisco

ABOVE: The Silicon Valley community of Mountain View is situated between San Jose and Palo Alto and is home to many high-tech companies. Photo by Joseph Sohm/Chromosohm

RIGHT: Palo Alto Central bustles with activity on a bright sunny afternoon. Photo by Joseph Sohm/Chromosohm

Bay made it a practical shipping location for orchardists and vintners.

In 1890 Mountain View was shipping up to 4 million pounds of freight per month. Early Mountain View settlers such as Henry Rengstorff built wharves and warehouses to accommodate shipping from the baylands. Vintners, wishing to find an alternative to expensive rail shipping, used the wharves to transport their wine on schooners.

Now Mountain View docks are no longer used to ship freight; rather, the city has opted to maintain its baylands in the form of Shoreline, a 644-acre open space preserve. Shoreline is a favorite place for bird-watchers since it is the home of many birds indigenous to Northern California and the migratory path for many others. The schooners of Mountain View's past have been replaced by recreational sailboats. Shoreline also features nature trails, picnic areas, and a championship-level golf course.

Adjacent to Shoreline is the late Bill Graham's Shoreline Amphitheatre, an outdoor entertainment complex that contributes one million dollars annually in city revenues.

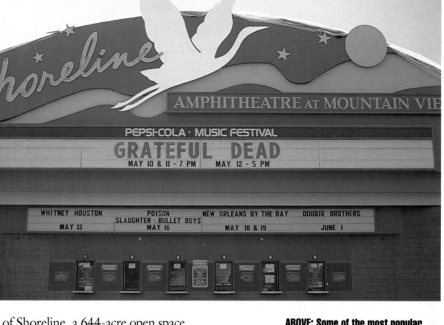

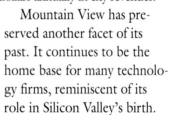

Mountain View has preserved another facet of its past. It continues to be the home base for many technology firms, reminiscent of its role in Silicon Valley's birth.

In 1955 Mountain View was the home of William Shockley's lab located near El Camino Real. The late Shockley, who won the Nobel Prize in 1956 for developing the electronic transistor, hired men who later founded some of Silicon Valley's most important companies. Eugene Kleiner, Gordon Moore, and Robert Noyce were three of his original hires. A difficult personality, Shockley in just a few years watched his brilliant recruits leave to form Fairchild

ABOVE: Some of the most popular musical groups in the entertainment industry perform at Mountain View's Shoreline Amphitheatre. The Grateful Dead is a particular favorite throughout the Bay Area, drawing fans who travel great distances to attend each performance. Photo by Joseph Sohm/Chromosohm

LEFT: A leader in the computer industry is Sun Microsystems, headquartered in Mountain View. The company has developed the UNIX computer operating system, one of the industry standards. Photo by Joseph Sohm/Chromosohm

Semiconductor, housed in a building on Charleston Road in Mountain View. Noyce then went on to invent the integrated circuit, and Silicon Valley was born.

Noyce's legacy of invention has been inherited by new generations of companies. Sun Microsystems, one of the city's biggest employers with 2,600 workers, exploded the workstation market during the late eighties and early nineties. Another Mountain View resident, Silicon Graphics, is a leader in workstation graphics.

Mountain View also has GTE, Hewlett-Packard, Raytheon, Acuson, Abbot Critical Care, and Spectra-Physics as major employers. Almost half of Mountain View's 71,000 jobs are in manufacturing and wholesaling.

The city is also a neighbor of Moffett Field, a 1,500-acre military site that houses the NASA Ames Research Center and the U.S. Naval Air Station. Adjacent to Moffett is the Onizuka Air Force Base. In April 1991 Moffett Field made the list of bases that could be closed in a federal budget-cutting move. If the base were to close, the NASA Ames facility would most likely remain, with NASA possibly taking over some of the flight facilities. NASA currently owns about 400 of the 1,500 acres.

Similar to other Silicon Valley cities, Mountain View wants to decrease traffic congestion by making it possible for people to both live and work in town. Its housing density is already high compared to neighboring cities. Two-thirds of the city's 65,000 residents live in apartments and condominiums. Projects such as the new Prometheus Development on Castro Street are indicative of Mountain View's commitment to high-density housing, according to Ken Alsman.

For the future Mountain View is looking at converting older industrial and commercial areas into housing space. Evelyn Avenue and the Ellis/Middlefield

Santa Clara County was once largely farmland, but residential and industrial uses now prevail, as here in Morgan Hill. Photo by Gerald L. French/The Photo File

industrial area, where Fairchild was located, are two possibilities, Alsman says.

Families in Mountain View have nine elementary schools, two intermediate schools, and one high school to serve their children. "On the drawing board," says Alsman, is the NASA (National Aeronautics and Space Administration) Air & Space Center, a new museum and educational resource. It will feature a "space camp" which teaches kids how to become astronauts.

"Mountain View is a community willing to step out and try things. The excitement and innovation of Silicon Valley rubs off here," Alsman declares.

El Palo Alto

When early Santa Clara Valley explorers spotted a majestic double-trunked redwood in 1769, they called it *El Palo Alto* (the tall tree). The tree served as a landmark for some of the first travelers to the valley. Eventually the surrounding community took the name Palo Alto.

The history of Palo Alto, founded in 1894, is entwined with that of Stanford University, which has set the tone for the town. Railroad magnate Senator Leland Stanford and his wife Jane founded the university in memory of their son, who had died of typhoid fever.

"If there's a single factor which makes Palo Alto different from the rest of the Peninsula," says city manager William Zaner, "it's the influence of Stanford University on the city."

Stanford University spawned Silicon Valley's first industrial park, whose famous tenants still include Hewlett-Packard and Varian Associates. In 1939 William Hewlett and David Packard, who both studied engineering at Stanford, founded Hewlett-Packard in a garage on Addison Street in Palo Alto. In 1954 the Varian brothers, who invented the klystron tube in Stanford's physics lab, became the first tenant in the Stanford Industrial Park.

"Stanford also affects this community in other ways," says Zaner. "You can see it in the school system. This is the school district everybody wants to get into because Palo Altans care about education and support it."

Although it has an enrollment of only 9,000 students, the Palo Alto Unified School District has a budget of more than $32 million. Special education needs are served by three schools and a medical therapy unit. Private schools include

Palo Alto's University Avenue is one of the area's livelier shopping districts. The historical film programs at the restored Varsity Theater and many bookstores attract Stanford students and residents of neighboring communities. Photo by Gerald L. French/The Photo File

Castilleja, a prestigious girls school, and nine others teaching grades K-12.

Although Palo Alto continues to be a birthing place for Silicon Valley ideas, the physical landscape of the town remains far from industrial. In fact only one-tenth of Palo Alto's land is used for commercial or industrial purposes. The community has a firm commitment to preservation of the local environment and open space. Palo Alto maintains 30 parks covering some 3,300 acres, and the original redwood, *El Palo Alto,* still stands by the railroad trestle at the intersection of El Camino Real and Alma Street.

If there is one word to describe Palo Alto living, it is *gracious.* Modern Palo Alto's 60,000 residents live in a community known for its beautiful, mature trees and impeccable landscaping. Stately Victorian homes and Spanish-influenced architecture give the town an old-world elegance.

"Palo Altans have a community in which they enjoy an enormous variety and depth of services," says Zaner. "This is a community with a strong set of values. People here care about the environment and open-space issues. In the future I believe Palo Altans will continue to maintain a very high level of services and will support their values with their dollars."

A popular mode of transportation in Santa Clara County is bicycling, especially on the sprawling Stanford University campus. Photo by John Elk III

ABOVE: This Palo Alto rose garden is proof of the rich growing conditions found throughout the Santa Clara region. Photo by Gerald L. French/The Photo File

LEFT: Committed teachers prepare students for higher education, whether they will be attending private universities such as Stanford and Santa Clara, or public universities in the California State University system. Photo by Liane Enkelis

The Apple Corporate Center in Cupertino is headquarters and the nerve center for this corporation that is frequently gossiped about and watched as an indicator of the general health of the computer industry. Photo by Joseph Sohm/Chromosohm

■ *Cupertino: A City Of Rainbows*

A person driving down DeAnza Boulevard in Cupertino any workday will have a unique visual experience. There are all these rainbow-colored signs—on trucks, buildings, and passing cars. For Cupertino is Apple Computer territory; in fact, it's the company's hometown.

A believer in karma, Apple Computer has been wooed by other cities but has never broken its emotional ties with the city in which it began. Its rainbow-colored apple logo remains a common Cupertino symbol.

Apple Computer now dominates the DeAnza and Stevens Creek Boulevard junction of Cupertino, having expanded its campus of buildings as it has grown exponentially over the years.

Besides Apple many other leading Silicon Valley companies call Cupertino home. Tandem Computers and Measurex are among the city's long-term tenants.

Like many other Silicon Valley cities, Cupertino is a blend of high-tech corporate campuses and housing for high-tech workers. An ethnically diverse community of 40,000, Cupertino appeals to Silicon Valley families who want their children to benefit from its excellent school system.

Cupertino, a largely affluent community, has always attracted families who want to live close to Santa Clara Valley jobs. The city began during the mid-

The local police force maintains a diligent presence. Photo by Joseph Sohm/Chromosohm

1800s as a small village called West Side. Cupertino's western-central position makes it a convenient location from which to commute.

The city's geographic origin, at the crossroads of DeAnza Boulevard and Stevens Creek Boulevard, was for years the site of the Cali granary and feed plant. During the 1980s the landmark of Cupertino's agricultural past was razed. Apple Computer now occupies the high-rise buildings that replaced the granary.

Shortly before the turn of the century, West Side changed its name to Cupertino, the name originally given to Stevens Creek by Spanish explorers. Through a series of annexations the city grew from its original size of 4 square miles to 13 square miles.

Cupertino has grown in stature along with Silicon Valley. It now has some of the most expensive housing in the valley, with homes priced at a million dollars and more being built on the hillsides.

City residents and others have DeAnza College as a cultural and educational resource. DeAnza, a noted community college, operates Flint Center which enjoys an international reputation for its acoustics. Flint Center has hosted performers from Itzhak Perlman to Johnny Mathis, from the Peking Acrobats to the Irish Rovers.

With Cupertino's high regard for education, it's not surprising that the Cupertino Library is the most extensive in the Santa Clara County Library system. It has a collection of more than 200,000 books, records, compact discs, audio and video cassettes, periodicals, and pamphlets.

"Over the years Cupertino has established a good blend of residential, commercial, and industrial developments," says former mayor Barbara Rogers. "In the future we will strive to maintain that balance, continuing to expand our services and focusing on the quality of life for our residents."

■ Milpitas: Boomtown

Next to the glossy suburbs of Silicon Valley, Milpitas was long regarded as an unloved stepchild. Located on the eastern fringe of the Santa Clara Valley, Milpitas seemed to be nothing more than a way station for people traveling to Alameda County.

Yet, just as Cinderella made the magical transformation from floor scrubber to a prince's love, Milpitas has been transformed into a highly desirable address for Silicon Valley businesses and residents.

While other Silicon Valley cities enjoyed public attention during the valley's boom years, Milpitas was quietly gaining an economic vitality of its own. Its population doubled to a recorded 50,000 between 1970 and 1990.

"The American dream, the little house in suburbia—that was Milpitas," recalls Steven Burkey, associate planner for the city. Milpitas became a city of young families attracted by housing prices that were more affordable than the valley median, and it remains largely a city of single-family homes.

Milpitas forever shed its stepchild status during the 1980s when Shapell Homes, the single largest residential builder in the city, began building luxurious homes in the $400,000 price range.

Shapell changed how Milpitas was perceived. It became a coveted address for those wishing to escape the congestion of other Silicon Valley communities.

The legendary Apple Computer considers the city of Cupertino its lucky home base. Photo by Joseph Sohm/Chromosohm

The change in perception paved the way for Milpitas' 1990s phenomenon—hillside homes in the million-dollar (and higher) price range.

With available land for housing shrinking along with the rest of the valley, the city government decided to allow custom home development in the nearby hills. But the development has met with mixed reactions. Since July 1989 a Hillside Review Committee (HRC) has been meeting to construct a hillside plan. By 1992 the plan is expected to have been completed and presented to the Milpitas City Council, with council action taken.

Milpitas' pristine hillside, which is appreciated from the valley floor, is the city's most-prized natural treasure. In the future developers will most likely be confined to building on the eastern face of the hills, which can not be seen from the valley floor.

During the 1980s Milpitas also changed from a bedroom community to a city with its own industrial base. The same dynamics which created its housing boom were at work. High-technology companies in search of significant acreage at a reasonable price began to seriously consider Milpitas.

"In 1978 we opened Oak Creek Industrial Park. It was our first high-tech industrial development, and it was fabulously successful," Burkey relates.

Modern Milpitas is now part of the Fremont industrial corridor, which also developed during the 1980s. Sun Microsystems—looking to expand beyond its home base of Mountain View—LSI Logic, and Quantum are among Milpitas' high-technology residents. There are now 24 industrial parks in Milpitas.

Success is not without its costs. With more people living and working in Milpitas, its roads are now clogged. As a thoroughfare to both Alameda County and other parts of Silicon Valley, Milpitas is wrestling with the worst traffic congestion it has ever experienced.

For Pete McHugh, who was elected mayor of Milpitas in November 1990, traffic alleviation is a top priority. The upgrading of Highway 237 to freeway status will help, McHugh says. On workdays traffic backs up on Calaveras Boulevard, which feeds into freeways 237, 880, and 680. According to McHugh, Santa Clara County plans to extend its Tasman Corridor light rail line and to constuct an overpass and interchange at Tasman across 880, which will help alleviate commuter traffic.

McHugh is working on improving the internal flow of traffic on the well-traveled Milpitas Boulevard. Extension of surrounding feeder streets would help to divert some of that traffic, McHugh says.

The problems that Milpitas faces today consist of traffic congestion and other typically urban dilemmas. In contrast its past was a bucolic one, as the Spanish name *Milpitas* (little cornfields) suggests. Originally settled by the Costanoan Indians, Milpitas existed as a collection of ranchos until the gold rush of the 1800s. One of its largest ranchos, measuring 4,458 acres, was granted to Jose Maria Alviso and called Rancho Milpitas.

American settlers eventually moved into Milpitas. After World War II many returning veterans chose to make Milpitas home. There were 840 residents when Milpitas incorporated as a city in 1954.

The city was largely a blue-collar community until Silicon Valley transformed the region. "Our community has changed and come of age. Now we're a full-fledged member of Silicon Valley," says Mayor McHugh.

Campbell: The Prune Capital

In the early 1900s the city of Campbell was known as the home of the world's largest fruit-drying facility, a distinction that earned the rural community the title "Prune Capital of the World."

Campbell was founded in 1846 by its namesake, Benjamin Campbell, but the city did not incorporate until 1952. Since then Campbell has grown to be a busy San Jose suburb with a population nearing 35,000. Covering approximately six miles Campbell is bordered by San Jose, Saratoga, and Los Gatos.

"We've seen an awful lot of changes in our short history, but we've managed to maintain our small-town feeling," says city councilwoman Jeanette Watson, a former mayor and author of *Campbell, the Orchard City.*

Campbell has a mixed commercial and industrial tax base. Its most notable commercial development is the Pruneyard, which includes 250,000 square feet of retail space, a 110-room hotel, and the Pruneyard Towers, with more than 200,000 square feet of office space.

Land for expansion within Campbell is virtually nonexistent, but the city continues to maintain a pro-growth stance, focusing on infill projects and redevelopment.

Because vacant land is so scarce, the city is concentrating on providing higher-density housing in its downtown redevelopment plan. By adding more housing the city council also hopes to attract after-work patrons to downtown businesses.

Changes may occur, but Campbell residents remain dedicated to preserving their community's identity and history. For example residents

LEFT: Maintaining lush, beautiful landscaping is a worthwhile chore and source of pride for many Campbell residents. Photo by Mark E. Gibson

BELOW: The Pruneyard Shopping Center on the edge of San Jose in Campbell has an easy-going ambience. Photo by Gerald L. French/The Photo File

raised more than one million dollars to relocate and save Campbell's historic Ainsley House.

"[Saving the Ainsley House] is just one example of our community spirit," says Watson. "We have a fierce pride in our past, and we want our citizens now and in the future to remember it."

Shimmering Suburbs

Los Angeles has Beverly Hills, Brentwood, and Bel Air. Silicon Valley has a medley of suburban villages along its western rim where the Mercedes and Jaguars are as plentiful as stock shares.

When Silicon Valley's executive elite travel home at the end of a workday, more than likely they will head towards Saratoga, Los Gatos, Monte Sereno, Los Altos Hills, or Los Altos.

Saratoga: McCartysville

The quintessential Silicon Valley village is Saratoga. With its fairy-tale downtown and exquisite homes, Saratoga represents a genteel way of life. But it didn't start out that way.

Saratoga began as a toll station for a lumber mill that needed to ship its wood out of the Santa Cruz Mountains. An Irishman named William McCarty built a toll road from the mill down to a little settlement at the base of the mountains. The village which developed was first called Toll Gate and later McCartysville. In the 1860s citizens changed the name to Saratoga, based on the

Senator James Phelan left his mark on Santa Clara County with his magnificent Villa Montalvo in Saratoga. Photo by Audrey Gibson

fact that the mineral water from a nearby spring was similar to the water found in the Saratoga Springs spa in New York.

By the early 1900s Saratoga had changed from a lumber town to a pleasant village whose business centered on the orchard industry. Saratoga became a country haven for wealthy San Franciscans. Villa Montalvo, the palatial Mediterranean-style estate built by Senator James Phelan, has been preserved and is used as an arts center.

As the Santa Clara Valley economy thrived, Saratoga retained its status as an elegant suburb. It incorporated in 1956 and formally became a bedroom community; there is no land zoned for manufacturing in the city limits.

Only 12 miles southwest of San Jose is the picturesque town of Los Gatos, which takes its name from "the cats" (mountain lions) that were once prominent in the area. Photo by Gerald L. French/The Photo File

Saratoga's zoning requirements for houses have created a community with large lot sizes and therefore limited population growth. The city has 30,000 residents and doesn't expect to grow much in the future, according to city manager Harry Peacock.

The city is not only a bedroom community but also one of Silicon Valley's favorite playgrounds. In addition to the downtown village and Villa Montalvo, Saratoga has the Mountain Winery (formerly Paul Masson) and its summer music series, the Congress Springs winery, and the posh Inn At Saratoga.

While Saratoga's housing prices are steep, Peacock is pleased the city does not have the "ostentatious" air of a Beverly Hills. "In town we do have limits on house sizes," says Peacock. However, in the Saratoga hills, houses have been allowed to be oversized. In 1984 one resident built a 10,000-square-foot recreation of Windsor Castle. Peacock says city officials are considering an ordinance to limit all houses, regardless of location, to 7,000 square feet.

Housing development will likely remain limited in Saratoga's future since the villagers are largely content with the character of the town as a quiet bedroom community.

Los Gatos: Town Of The Cats

In the late 1800s mountain lions and wildcats roamed the hills in the Santa Cruz Mountain range. One of the Spanish land grants, Rancho Rinconada de los Gatos (corner of the cats), was named after the wild animals.

Los Gatos was founded about 1868 as a portion of the land grant and incorporated in 1877. Through the early 1900s Los Gatos remained a small, rural community supported mostly by orchards.

Modern-day Los Gatos has retained a small-town feeling in its downtown shops and surrounding neighborhoods. Its picturesque streets and charming older homes make it a popular place for a stroll or a bike ride. During the 1989 Loma Prieta earthquake, Los Gatos suffered major damage to some of its historic homes and to the downtown commercial area. Expensive restoration has taken place and the town has largely recovered from the damage.

Los Gatos is a place, says former mayor Tom Ferrito, "where people can walk down Main Street with their families, see familiar faces, and know the merchants with whom they do business."

With a population nearing 30,000, Los Gatos is a mix of residential and commercial zones, with some light industry. The town expands out approximately 10 square miles from its downtown core and is geographically divided by Highway 880.

To meet the educational needs of its young citizens, Los Gatos has six elementary schools, one junior high school, one middle school, and two high schools.

Similar to Saratoga, Los Gatos has remained a stable community for decades, and Ferrito doesn't expect it to change: "For a hundred years Los Gatos has managed to retain its small-town character. I think we can manage to do it for a hundred more."

Monte Sereno

Tucked in between Los Gatos and Saratoga is the tiny hamlet of Monte Sereno—population 3,600. The smallest city in Santa Clara County, Monte Sereno is a little over one square mile. It has no chamber of commerce and industry; Monte Sereno, however, does have wealthy residents. The median price of a home is more than $500,000, but there are plenty well above that price range.

Monte Sereno incorporated in 1956 to prevent annexation by the city of Los Gatos, relates Rosemary Pierce, chief administrative officer.

Along with its neighbors, Saratoga and Los Gatos, the hamlet's future will be more of the same since 93 percent of its lots have already been developed, according to Pierce.

Los Altos Hills: The Pinnacle

Rising to an elevation of more than 1,300 feet, Los Altos Hills has some of the most sought after real estate in the Santa Clara Valley. For those who have reached the pinnacle of success in Silicon Valley, what better place to perch than a community of sweeping vistas?

Los Altos Hills was discovered in 1776 by the Spanish explorer Juan Bautista de Anza on his way to the Bay of San Francisco. The area became part of the Spanish land grant Rancho la Purisima Concepcion. It was later divided and sold.

Although modern-day Los Altos Hills is geographically larger than the city of Los Altos, which serves as its downtown, its population of about 9,000 is one-third that of Los Altos due to its requirement that lots be a minimum of one acre in size. Los Altos Hills, which incorporated in 1956, also excludes any commercial enterprises or multifamily housing projects.

"We have attempted to maintain a large-lot, open-space life-style and have done so very effectively, though the pressures of growth have been tremendous," declares city councilwoman Barbara Tryon.

Los Altos Hills' lack of commercial or industrial developments leaves the community with a minimal budget for local services. "We depend largely on volunteer efforts," says Tryon. "And we have a high level of involvement. Residents participate in everything from our volunteer emergency preparedness network to putting together the town newsletter."

The town is committed to protection of its open space. "It's going to be an ongoing struggle to maintain the rural atmosphere and quality of life we have established here," says Tryon. "But we are trying to maintain something very special—something few communities have been able to manage—and I think we will succeed."

Los Altos: The Hills' Downtown

At the base of the Los Altos Hills is Los Altos, with a population of nearly 28,000. "You can tell you're in Los Altos," says city manager Diane Gershuny, "when you look around and there are no sidewalks."

Los Altos, bordered in part by the busy cities of Sunnyvale and Palo Alto, has sheltered itself from Silicon Valley and managed to sustain a country town atmosphere. During the post-World War II building boom, Los Altos decided it wanted to determine its own fate and incorporated in 1952. It then established its current minimum lot size of at least one-quarter acre, allowing it to preserve much of its open space and wooded areas.

Today Los Altos remains a semirural community of primarily single-family residences. "This is something of a bedroom community," says Gershuny, "but we also have some very healthy and active commercial areas. Unlike some bedroom communities we maintain the services to support the area." The city operates its own police and fire departments.

Los Altos was originally part of a Spanish land grant called Rancho San Antonio. The approximately seven square miles comprising the city were developed largely through the efforts of Paul Shoup, a Southern Pacific rail executive who envisioned the area as a commuter town, a rail stop linking the cities of Palo Alto and Los Gatos.

Instead of a commuter town Los Altos has become a town where commuters come home to rest and play. Los Altos' downtown village, at Main and State streets, has boutique shops and restaurants. And for outdoors lovers, the city maintains 10 parks.

Los Altos echoes the goals of its neighboring Los Altos Hills: both wish to preserve their semirural nature in the face of outside pressures.

■ South County

About 20 minutes outside of San Jose's metropolitan area, the landscape along Highway 101 dramatically shifts from subdivisions and sound walls to a breathtaking pastoral scene that winds for miles and miles. It is South County, a land of rolling hills and grazing cattle. The viewer is gently reminded that all of the Santa Clara Valley was once like this, a verdant blanket of orchards and ranches.

The cities of Morgan Hill and Gilroy and the unincorporated area of San

Morgan Hill's Machado School, one of the first educational sites in south Santa Clara County, is still in use today. The land for this site was donated by cowboy Barney Machado, who married into one of the ancestral families of Morgan Hill. Photo by Gerald L. French/The Photo File

Built on land that was once part of a Spanish land grant, the community of Morgan Hill, 15 miles south of San Jose, has grown from a strictly agricultural area to an expanding suburban community. The sense of the past is visible in the architecture of some of the well-maintained homes. Photo by Gerald L. French/The Photo File

Martin make up South County. In geographic distance and culture South County seems far removed from the hustle and bustle of urban Silicon Valley. South County still feels rural, unhurried, and friendly. And that is precisely its appeal.

With developable land at a premium in the cities to the north, South County is viewed as the next target for new housing or industrial space. Both Morgan Hill and Gilroy, respectful of their history, are trying to balance the need to preserve open space with the need to maintain economic vitality in their cities.

Morgan Hill

The story of Morgan Hill might be titled *Love's Labour's Won,* for the early history of the town has a decidedly romantic flavor.

In 1851 Daniel Murphy, the youngest son of landowner and pioneer Martin Murphy, Sr., married Maria Fisher. It was a marriage of land dynasties. Murphy Sr. had in 1845 purchased 9,000 acres known as the Rancho Ojo de Agua de la Coche, part of a vast Spanish land grant which dated back to the original settlements of California by the Spanish crown.

Maria Fisher had her own dynasty. She was heiress to the neighboring 19,000-acre Rancho Laguna Seca. Daniel and Maria had one daughter, a precocious lady, Diana, who in 1882 secretly married a dashing San Franciscan named Hiram Morgan Hill.

When Daniel Murphy died, Diana inherited 4,500 acres of Rancho Ojo de Agua de la Coche and promptly built an estate known as Villa Mira Monte on the property. Train operators began referring to Villa Mira Monte as Morgan Hill's Ranch, and eventually the name was shortened to Morgan Hill.

By 1896 Morgan Hill was a growing community of 250 with a post office, rail depot, two hotels, and a restaurant. Morgan Hill incorporated as a city in 1906.

Villa Mira Monte, Hiram Morgan Hill's home, is virtually unchanged, having been preserved by the Morgan Hill Historical Society.

During the twentieth century Morgan Hill has grown at a leisurely pace, gradually adding manufacturing and commercial ventures to its original agricultural economy. The wine industry and companies that grow mushrooms and flowers now comprise most of the city's agricultural business. High technology has come to the city. Wiltron, Innowave, and Cermoss are among the city's largest manufacturers.

In 1990 the city recorded 25,300 residents, 60 percent of whom commute to Silicon Valley and other regions for jobs. "When Silicon Valley grew, people started looking to the south for a bedroom community," says city councilwoman Lorraine Barke. During the late seventies and early eighties, Morgan Hill added thousands of residents.

Santa Clara County residents often find more affordable homes if they are willing to commute from outlying areas to the work site. These new Morgan Hill homes are 15 miles south of San Jose. Photo by Gerald L. French/The Photo File

Families in Morgan Hill are served by the wide-ranging Morgan Hill Unified School District, which covers 296 square miles including a portion of San Jose and the unincorporated area. The district is one of Morgan Hill's largest employers. It maintains eight elementary schools, two middle schools, and two high schools.

With Morgan Hill's increasing Silicon Valley influence, "our downtown changed from department stores selling bib overalls to stores catering to the boutique crowd," Barke recalls.

Morgan Hill's Redevelopment Agency has been instrumental in providing the town with a tonier image. It spent $3 million revamping downtown, which lies along Monterey Road between Dunne and Main avenues. Monterey Road now has chic restaurants and stores.

Along with Morgan Hill's tonier image have come new custom homes catering to Silicon Valley's affluent executives. "Our goal is to have livable neighborhoods with some individuality. We also want to maintain a rural feeling," says city manager Jan Perkins.

While expensive custom homes have been added to the city's housing inventory, Councilwoman Barke says affordable housing remains a council priority.

What Morgan Hill wants, according to Perkins, is a balanced community. "We have below market rate housing which doesn't price out the people who were born here and which young families starting out can afford."

As Morgan Hill gains in prestige, government is working to ensure the city avoids "the L.A. sprawl syndrome," according to Perkins. "We want to retain a greenbelt around the community, to preserve the rural element."

Gilroy: The Garlic Capital

Gilroy, which bills itself as the Garlic Capital of the World, owes its name to a famous defector.

The city should rightfully be named Cameron, since John Cameron was the real name of the man who jumped ship from Queen Victoria's fleet in Monterey Bay. After jumping ship Cameron assumed his mother's surname and made his way to the Santa Clara Valley. He met and married Clara Ortega, daughter of a Spanish land-grant family which owned Rancho San Ysidro at the southern end of the Santa Clara Valley. At the time the area later to be called Gilroy was known as Pleasant Valley.

John Gilroy settled in his namesake area in 1813 and was followed nine years later by another Monterey Bay sailor, Philip Doke, who married Lugarda Castro, heiress to the Las Animas land grant. By 1850 Gilroy was a local center of commerce, with five stores, a hotel, and a stable. The town incorporated in 1870, having elected its first Board of Town Trustees just two years prior. One of the city government's first acts was to purchase a $200 bell for the volunteer fire company.

Tobacco was one of Gilroy's early industries, with J.D. Culp running the local cigar factory. At the Panama Pacific Exposition in 1915, Gilroy won a silver medal for its tobacco exhibit.

Gilroy has some of the most fertile agricultural land in the world. Agriculture remains Gilroy's largest industry, but the amount of land available for cultivation has decreased, notes Roberta Hughan, mayor of Gilroy.

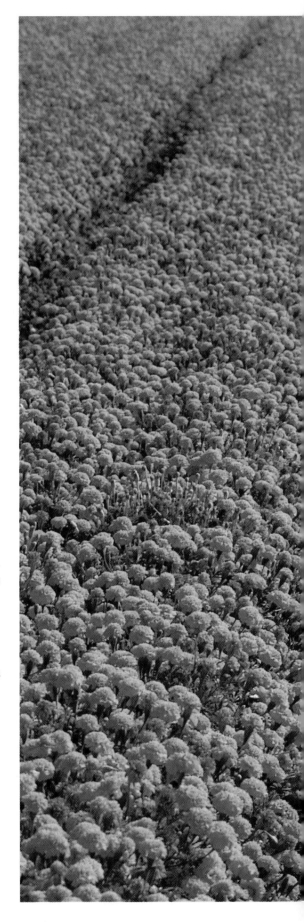

Flowers such as these marigolds, as well as a rich variety of agricultural produce, are grown in the farmland in south Santa Clara County around Gilroy. Photo by Mark E. Gibson

ABOVE: The farmland around Gilroy not only produces garlic, but also yields a variety of flowers such as these zinnias produced for commercial sale. Photo by Mark E. Gibson

RIGHT: The annual Gilroy Garlic Festival is the event that put the city on the map. Almost anything that can be done with or made from garlic is found here, from garlic jelly and garlic spaghetti to garlic corsages. Photo by Mark E. Gibson

Production of garlic powder and other food-processing staples is now the primary activity while growing and canning have shifted more to the Central Valley, Hughan explains.

Garlic and onions are two of Gilroy's best-known products. A&D Christopher Ranch is a major garlic-grower while Gilroy Foods is the city's largest food-processor. Gilroy Canning and Garden Valley Foods provide seasonal canning jobs. Gilroy is also the corporate home of the Nob Hill Foods supermarket chain.

For 12 years Gilroy has staged its Garlic Festival, earning it international fame as the Garlic Capital of the World. The annual three-day festival relies on 4,000 volunteers. "One of the most outstanding things about Gilroy is our spirit of volunteerism," Hughan declares.

Besides agriculture, Gilroy has a mix of small manufacturers and service establishments. About half of Gilroy's 30,000 residents leave the city to work.

For more than a decade Gilroy has enforced a managed-growth policy, limiting the number of new building permits each year.

Mayor Hughan, a strong managed-growth advocate, believes Gilroy's biggest challenge ahead will be to strike a balance between jobs and housing. Hughan emphasizes that, before any major housing development occurs, there should be new jobs to accompany that growth.

As of yet Gilroy's industrial base has "no real high-tech presence," Hughan says. The city's housing stock caters largely to middle-income workers rather than high-paid executives. The exception is some scattered new homes, particularly in the hills, where prices are as expensive as Silicon Valley's.

Almost one-third of Gilroy's residents are students. They are served by nine elementary schools, seven private schools, one junior high school, and two high schools.

For Gilroy's future, preservation of its identity as a rural small-town community is of paramount importance to Hughan. One way this can be accomplished is to establish a greenbelt around the city, Hughan says.

South County's two cities—Morgan Hill and Gilroy—appear to be in consensus on the need to prevent urban sprawl and protect open space.

■ Variations On The Theme

Santa Clara Valley's cities are three variations on a theme of urban evolution. Maturing full-service cities such as San Jose and Sunnyvale are trying to balance the need for more housing with industrial strength. High-density housing is becoming the commonly accepted solution since developable land is scarce in many cities.

In contrast the valley's affluent bedroom communities, such as Saratoga and Los Altos Hills, are carefully guarding against new development, desirous of preserving their semirural landscape.

Morgan Hill and Gilroy—quiet, rural South County communities for decades—are finding themselves in a vortex of opposing pressures of development and protection of their agricultural heritage. These two communities represent the last vestiges of Santa Clara Valley's past. How they manage their growth will determine the quality of life in South County for the next century.

2

Coming Together

■ A Prism Of Cultures

I n 1783, six years after the Spanish government founded "el Pueblo de San Jose de Guadalupe," California's first civil settlement, the San Jose *padrón* (census) recorded nine original landholders: three Spaniards, one Coyote (half Indian/ half white), one Indian, two mulattoes, one mestizo, and one "unknown," according to Clyde Arbuckles' 1985 *History of San Jose*.

From the early days the roots of San Jose and the Santa Clara Valley—first reached by Spanish explorers in 1769 near the present city of Palo Alto—have reflected cultural diversity. Indians lived in the valley for thousands of years before the Spanish arrived. Black history dates from the valley's period of Spanish exploration. Christian blacks and mulattoes who spoke Spanish were pressed into service by the Spanish crown during its colonization of Alta California. When San Jose became the first civic pueblo in 1777, one-quarter of the population was mulatto.

Indians, Spanish, and blacks were followed by English, Americans, Chinese, Japanese, Filipinos, Mexicans, Portuguese, Italians, and other European immigrants to make up the cultural mix of Santa Clara Valley that dominated until the second half of the twentieth century.

Santa Clara County has a rich ethnic mix of cultural diversity. African-Americans, Spanish Americans, and Asians from Japan, China, Vietnam, Korea, the Philippines, and other Pacific Rim nations bring an international tone to Santa Clara County. Photo by David Lissy/The Photo File

San Jose, the focal point of new settlers, changed to American rule in 1846 when Captain Thomas Fallon raised the American flag in front of the *juzgado* (town hall). The war with Mexico was the culmination of the growing political sentiment of Manifest Destiny. American expansionists believed that Heaven had preordained the Pacific Ocean as the United States' rightful Western border. As more Americans moved into California, a political war was inevitable.

After the end of the Mexican-American War, the

Santa Clara Valley was relatively stable until John Marshall discovered "el dorado" and the Gold Rush began in 1848. Prospectors combed the Santa Cruz mountains for gold and silver, but adjacent Santa Clara Valley had found its own cache: valuable cinnabar (red ore) and quicksilver. The New Almaden quicksilver mines flourished since the primary use of quicksilver was the separation of gold and silver from impure ores.

Between 1847 and 1864 the New Almaden mines in San Jose produced a total of $15 million in quicksilver. After gold fever subsided, production at the mine gradually declined. During World War I the mine again became important since the mercury was used in the manufacture of bombs.

By 1852 the Gold Rush and California's agricultural strength had swelled the Santa Clara Valley population to almost 7,000. The valley's growth necessitated a regular means of travel to San Francisco, which was first accomplished by a nine-hour stage service between San Jose and its northern neighbor. Later, rail service opened between the two cities with completion of a new rail line in 1864.

Part of the California railroad boom, the new line brought Chinese workers to Santa Clara Valley. After the railroad was completed, they were recruited to work in the orchards. The Chinese worked hard and were paid below standard wages. Due to the Chinese Exclusion Act of the 1880s, the Chinese work force in the valley diminished. Japanese, who first came to the valley around 1890, began working in the orchards. They were also paid substandard wages.

Eventually many Japanese became agricultural entrepreneurs, establishing their own farms and becoming major suppliers of vegetable and berry crops.

As the nineteenth century drew to a close, blacks found employment in the valley as laborers, gardeners, barbers, and cooks. Soon Portuguese and Italian immigrants joined the valley's agricultural work force. Local canneries provided jobs, but low pay was again the norm. During the 1920s and 1930s Mexican and Filipino immigrants came to work in the valley's fields, harvesting many crops. When the Depression came, whites worked in the orchards, accepting the reality of low wages.

Shopping centers designed to serve the many cultures found in the county bring familiar products to customers and help them maintain ties to their homeland. This mall in East San Jose provides a range of ethnic products. Photo by Richard L. Kaylin

The well-known Fung Lum Chinese restaurant provides a friendly atmosphere on South Bascom Avenue in Campbell near the Pruneyard Shopping Center. Photo by Gerald L. French/The Photo File

During World War II Japanese-Americans in Santa Clara Valley had to leave their farms when they were disenfranchised and forced to live in internment camps. Decades later Congressman Norman Y. Mineta of San Jose successfully led the movement to seek redress for Japanese-Americans. Former President Ronald Reagan signed the redress bill, drafted by Mineta, in August 1988. The U.S. government made an official apology to the Japanese-Americans who were mistreated. The law also called for a $20,000 cash payment to each person affected and for an educational fund to be established. As a result of the law, the government is considering the reinstatement of Japanese-Americans who were dishonorably discharged from the U.S. Armed Services during the war. "They would all be given an honorable discharge," Mineta says.

"We want this to be a lesson so that in the future it will never happen again," says Mineta.

Throughout the latter half of the twentieth century, as the Santa Clara Valley evolved from an economy largely based on agriculture to what is now known as Silicon Valley, the area continued to be the choice of immigrants from all over the world. The fast-growing, fast-paced economy meant jobs and some measure of financial security for immigrants, many of whom came from troubled, unstable countries.

Now, on the eve of the twenty-first century, Santa Clara County people represent a rich blend of cultures. Their European predecessors who passed

People from all over the world come to Santa Clara to ply their trades. Besides growing flowers outdoors in south Santa Clara County fields, many horticulturists grow flowers indoors in hothouses. Photo by Michael O'Callahan

through Ellis Island and their Spanish ancestors who first settled Alta California have been joined by new waves of immigrants from the Pacific Rim countries and India.

The faces may change, but the timeless search for a better way of living continues.

■ *To The Land Of Freedom*

The record numbers of Asian and Hispanic immigrants who came to America from 1970 to 1990 contributed to Santa Clara Valley's changing demographics. They came for different reasons: to escape war, to live and work in a better economic climate, to join their families, and to invest in the United States.

Asian immigration patterns changed after 1965 when amendments to the U.S. Immigration and Nationality Act abolished the national origin of the population as a basis for quotas. This action gave Asian countries a chance to send large numbers of people to America. Simultaneously limits on immigration from the West were established, contributing to a steady decline in the number of European-born immigrants. During this same period Latin Americans, especially Mexicans, continued to immigrate at a consistently high rate.

In the 1990s the face of Santa Clara County is a pluralistic one, reflecting the statewide demographic changes that took place during the 1980s. California, long the golden dream of immigrants, reached a record population of 30.3 million in 1990, according to the California Department of Finance. Unprecedented numbers of Hispanic and Asian immigrants and their offspring contributed to the 26-percent increase in the state's population between 1980 and 1990.

Santa Clara County's 1.5 million residents represent the new pluralism. According to 1990 census data 42 percent of the county's population is non-Anglo. The old labels of "majority" and "minority" no longer apply since the county now has a highly diverse mix of ethnic groups living and working in its borders.

Hispanics comprise 21 percent of the county's population while Asians make up 17.5 percent. During the 1980s Santa Clara County's Asian population grew 162 percent, with Vietnamese and Asian Indians recording the highest growth rates, followed by Chinese, Koreans, Filipinos, and Japanese. In total numbers there are approximately 65,000 Chinese; 62,000 Filipinos; 54,000 Vietnamese; 27,000 Japanese; 21,000 Asian Indians; and 16,000 Koreans.

According to the 1990 census figures, there are 56,211 blacks and 1,032,190 whites in Santa Clara County.

As educators and politicians sift through the census data, it is clear the Golden State will be making some changes to respond to the ethnic pluralism. Schools, political campaigns, retailing and entertainment trends—all facets of California and Santa Clara County life—will be affected by the new faces that have arrived in the state.

■ *Cosmopolitan People*

Food and the arts provide satisfying and stimulating ways to learn about different cultures, and San Jose's East Side, home to an eclectic mix—Italian, Portuguese, Mexican, black, and Vietnamese, to name a few—affords a graduate-level course in ethnicity.

Daytime San Jose continues the education as office workers spend their lunch hours sampling exotic foods—from the banana leaves with stuffing at the 13th Street Chez Sovan to the pad thai noodle dish and chicken satay at Market Street's Bangkok Station.

Santa Clara Valley's Mexican roots are celebrated in the many *panaderias* (bakeries) and *taquerias* (taco stands) throughout San Jose. The Guadalajara Market on Empire Street is a favorite of locals who want a tasty, cafe-style lunch.

The lunchtime crowd is noisy and happy, munching on homemade Italian sausage sandwiches at Antipasto's Italian Deli on McKee Road in San Jose's East Side. Proprietor Nick DeRose dishes up the succulent food as fast as he can. Earlier in the day his son Gino made another batch of the popular sausage. Antipasto's is a reminder of the days when families had a local butcher and he knew every customer by first name.

Not far away from Antipasto's, Jesse's Ribs serves some of the best barbecue

The DeRose family stands surrounded by wares at Antipasto's, their popular East San Jose restaurant and deli. Photo by Richard L. Kaylin

in town, while Tamar's Portuguese Restaurant prepares popular seafood dishes.

"The ways in which we share food say a lot about our cultures," says Jim McEntee, Santa Clara County director of the Office of Human Relations. McEntee, who often mediates neighborhood disputes as new cultures learn to get along with one another, makes it a habit to attend as many ethnic gatherings as possible.

"Each culture wants to retain its independence, its unique image. We respect that and help people to become more sensitive to recognition of these different cultures," says McEntee.

Santa Clara Valley's many ethnic festivals also help to retain the unique identity of each culture. In San Jose's Japantown the annual Obon festival is celebrated with food, games of chance, and graceful formal dancing by local residents. Mexicans stage a yearly Cinco de Mayo parade, and Vietnamese celebrate the annual Tet Festival.

ABOVE: Hispanic organizations and dance groups parade in traditional costumes during the annual festival in San Jose commemorating Cinco de Mayo. Photo by Gerald L. French/The Photo File

RIGHT: U.S. Marines carry the colors during the annual Cinco de Mayo parade in San Jose. Photo by Gerald L. French/The Photo File

FAR RIGHT: Traditional music and dances of Mexico are performed each year during Cinco de Mayo. Photo by Gerald L. French/The Photo File

ABOVE: San Jose residents line the streets near the downtown Plaza Park fountain in preparation for the Cinco de Mayo festival. Photo by Gerald L. French/The Photo File

RIGHT: Hispanic dances of all kinds are performed during ceremonies celebrating San Jose's annual Cinco de Mayo festival. Photo by Gerald L. French/The Photo File

Ethnic artists are receiving increased recognition as the valley becomes more aware of the different forms of inspiration each culture has to offer. The Asian Heritage Council, a regional organization formed to promote Asians in visual and performing arts, encourages emerging new artists. With the Triton Museum of Art in Santa Clara, the council cosponsored a traveling show of Chinese contemporary artists.

"Asian-Americans are now emerging as recognized artists in the 'mainstream' art world," declares Flo Wong, Chinese artist and multicultural art advocate.

"Asians are now organized when it comes to art. We never were before," says Wong, who also serves as an officer of the Asian Heritage Council.

Emerging artists, new cuisines, new friends—Santa Clara Valley's future lies in cultural diversity. The valley is becoming a truly cosmopolitan place, one in which all people of the world can flourish.

■ The New Merchants

San Jose's East Side and downtown are microcosms of modern Santa Clara Valley, and they provide good examples of how immigrants assimilate and contribute to the area's economic health.

Each wave of immigrants that has settled in Santa Clara Valley has brought new foods, customs, and festivals. Families have pooled their resources to open retail stores, restaurants, and other businesses.

For example Santa Clara Street, an extension of Alum Rock Avenue near San Jose's downtown, now has many Vietnamese-owned and -operated establishments. One highly successful Vietnamese-style drugstore, Medex, exemplifies the entrepreneurial spirit that the Vietnamese have demonstrated. The store is really a combination drugstore and variety store, selling bolts of fabric in addition to medicines. Many Vietnamese buy medicines at the store and then ship them back to Vietnam, where their families lack access to modern medicine.

Medex and other small businesses get assistance from the San Jose Development Corporation, a nonprofit community-assistance program administered by Richard Rios, a former U.S. deputy secretary of Health, Education, and Welfare who ran the U.S. Community Services Administration during President Jimmy Carter's term in office. The corporation serves mainly Southeast Asian and Hispanic clients, putting together loan packages for small businesses and

Local politicians recognize the importance of participating in the affairs that reflect their constituencies. Eagerly taking part in the Cinco de Mayo festival is Mayor Susan Hammer of San Jose. Photo by Gerald L. French/The Photo File

Santa Clara County's blend of cultures can be seen in the wide range of dining options throughout its many communities. A combined menu from two Asian countries gives diners a variety of possibilities at Thanh Thanh Chinese-Vietnamese restaurant. Photo by Richard L. Kaylin

ABOVE: The tradition of mural painting has been taken up by the young. This image may be found on Miller Elementary School in East San Jose. Photo by Richard L. Kaylin

RIGHT: Hispanic murals with traditional themes may be found throughout the Santa Clara Valley. This one graces a supermarket in San Jose. Photo by Richard L. Kaylin

working with the Hispanic and Vietnamese chambers of commerce to encourage economic development.

"We look at their needs from a cultural viewpoint. Many of the Vietnamese have not had banking relationships. They carry over paranoia from the old country. So we help them start relationships and overcome these fears. We have a track record now, and word has gotten around that doing business here is safe. In fact, many are doing quite well," Rios declares.

For those Vietnamese who have been fortunate enough to amass significant sums of money, Santa Clara Valley's lucrative land development and real estate markets offer target investments. One Vietnamese entrepreneur developed million-dollar homes along the Calaveras Ridge in the city of Milpitas. The Lyon shopping plaza, a unique, modern center devoted to serving Asian clients, was developed by Asian businessmen.

By being industrious and ambitious, Vietnamese immigrants have taken their place in history alongside the land barons and merchants of yesteryear.

■ Work Force Of The Future

The children of today's immigrants are tomorrow's Silicon Valley work force. By the year 2000 it is estimated that more than 83 percent of people entering the work force for the first time will be women and ethnics.

From the multicultural population that comprises Silicon Valley, the educational system needs to produce a technically skilled labor pool in order to be able to fill the many high-tech jobs of the future. It's a big order, given the language and cultural barriers that must first be overcome. Women traditionally have not chosen careers that depend on math and science skills. Hispanic students drop out at an alarming rate in San Jose high schools. Technology companies, recognizing the need to have qualified workers for the future, are now financially supporting programs to help "at-risk" student populations. For example Hewlett-Packard, Tandem, and Apple have contributed more than one million dollars to the pre-college engineering programs (PEP), administered by MESA (Mathematics, Engineering, Science Achievement) headquartered at the University of California's Berkeley campus. Through counseling, mentoring, and providing special workshops, PEP encourages students to complete the high school math and science curricula required for acceptance to four-year colleges. The track record for PEP has been outstanding: 80 percent of the students get accepted to a four-year college. Of those, 83 percent choose math-based majors.

Part of the Santa Clara Valley's continuing commitment to superior education is carried out by Morgan Hill's Lewis Britton Middle School. Photo by Michael O'Callahan

Elementary schools such as Hester Elementary near downtown San Jose prepare students to ultimately attend the region's outstanding universities. Photo by Richard L. Kaylin

There is a positive payoff for technology firms that can hire from a local pool of skilled workers. These workers may be more committed to staying in Silicon Valley, greatly reducing the need for firms to recruit from outside the region. In the early 1990s Silicon Valley was the subject of news stories about the "reverse brain drain" from Taiwan, in which skilled Taiwanese engineers and other professionals would come to Silicon Valley, work for awhile, and then head back to their homeland, equipped with more technical knowledge. The only means of preventing these "brain drains" of the future is to have a domestically produced, skilled work force.

In developing a pool of workers for the future, resistance from some cultures is one of the challenges schools face, but language barriers present by far the toughest hurdle for educators.

"Half of our kids have a language other than English as their primary language," declares Jan Carey, public information officer for the Santa Clara County Office of Education. The office oversees 33 school districts and 4 community college districts serving close to a quarter of a million students.

"Bilingual education used to be the buzzword. Now we're a multilingual society . . . In the seventies the hot subject was computer training. In the eighties and nineties it's dealing with the multicultural school population at the same time there is increased pressure from government to improve school academic performance," Carey says.

A school population in which 10 primary languages and dozens of dialects can be spoken on one campus has had "a profound impact on the way teachers teach," Carey declares. "The techniques of 20 years ago don't work."

Educators now look at a variety of options in language instruction, Carey explains. Sheltered instruction, a new concept that uses a limited English vocabulary and nonlanguage teaching tools, is being tried. Other options include intensive language classes in a lab setting or the classic bilingual approach, which only works when the teacher is fluent in both languages. With a myriad of languages and dialects now heard in the schools, the bilingual approach isn't practical.

Curricula other than language have also been affected by Santa Clara County's diverse student population. "We need to look at a more global curriculum

Teachers work hard to help their students learn about the world outside their own region. Because students in some minority groups drop out of school in large numbers, local companies are beginning to support and promote math and science programs, hoping to ensure a stable work force for the future. Photo by Liane Enkelis

than we did decades ago. There is more focus now on Pacific Rim history, on Hispanic and Eastern European history," Carey says.

Santa Clara County's teachers have had to become more knowledgeable about many cultures to meet the demands of the new students. The Santa Clara County Office of Education offers teachers daily, year-round in-service training in multicultural subjects.

"We want the students to feel good about their different cultures. In order to do that, the teachers must first understand our multicultural society," Carey asserts.

Castro Elementary School

When Castro Elementary School principal Lonnie Hartman greets his class at the beginning of the school year, he knows that half of them won't be there the following June.

"It's a real revolving door here, and we just have to be flexible," says Hartman.

Situated in a low-income neighborhood in Mountain View, Castro Elementary School represents the challenges educators face in teaching a multiethnic, immigrant population.

"We get families who will take a kid out of school for three months to return to Mexico. The problem is that when the kid is in Mexico they don't go to school. Many of these families are from undeveloped areas that don't have schools," explains Hartman. When the student returns, he is behind the rest of the class, and it's quite difficult to catch up, Hartman says. To help the students

Castro Elementary School runs a migrant education program that provides additional tutoring. Half of the school's 600 students are in the program.

Families from Mexico, El Salvador, Guatemala, and Nicaragua first settle in apartments near the Castro Elementary School and send their kids down the block to the school. "When [the parents] get jobs and find new housing, they move," says Hartman. They are then replaced by the next wave of immigrant families. This constant flux results in a 50-percent turnover of the school's population during one school year.

Adding to Hartman's challenge is the fact that there are 42 languages and dialects spoken on the Castro campus. Teachers routinely send home information written in English, Spanish, and Vietnamese. Castro incorporates aggressive programs, including experimental nongraded classes, to help new immigrants learn English. In the evening the school offers English classes for more than 100 parents from the neighborhood.

Despite the fluctuating school population and the language barriers, the kids do learn—and learn well—at Castro, Hartman proudly reports. Castro Elementary School tests well above California state averages in student achievement tests. During 1990 the school installed a $35,000 IBM computer lab, which each child visits at least once a week.

Hartman attributes the school's success to an excellent staff and the support of the kids' families. "[The parents] can't make PTA meetings because many of them hold two jobs, but they really support our school and help us with fundraising," says Hartman. "Often they'll go to more affluent communities to raise the money."

Castro Elementary School demonstrates how parents and schools can work together to produce the most important result: a quality education for their children.

■ City Campus

San Jose's Independence High School on the East Side has won acclaim for its responsiveness to multiethnic students. Opened in 1976 Independence High School was created as an innovative "educational park" during the administration of Frank Fiscalini, former superintendent of the East Side Union High School District. From the beginning the school's mission was to accept and nurture cultural diversity in its students. Its sprawling campus, at Jackson Avenue and McKee Road on San Jose's East Side, is located in the middle of a high-density, multicultural community.

Proof of the region's high commitment to education is the large percentage of graduating high school seniors who pursue higher education at the California system of community colleges and public and private universities. Photo by Liane Enkelis

The school serves 4,000 students who speak more than 40 different languages and dialects. Independence is organized into four villas or minischools, three of which have their own principals. The fourth villa is organized to handle attendance and discipline. By organizing into villas, each school has an even mix of students and ethnic groups. The approach has proven both manageable and successful.

"Independence looks like the United Nations," says Mike Gibeau, who was a villa principal at Independence for 13 years. "Multicultural is the future. *Minority* is a passé word," he notes. After leaving Independence, Gibeau was appointed youth coordinator for the City of San Jose by former mayor Tom McEnery. He has coordinated the city's annual Youth Conference and worked with educators to design other youth programs.

In his office at San Jose's city hall, Gibeau keeps a collection of red, white, and blue, braided "friendship bracelets." To him they symbolize Independence's purpose. Students give the bracelets to each other to reinforce the school's philosophy "that people are different and that's okay," Gibeau explains.

Programs that cut across cultural lines and celebrate multiculturalism are Independence's trademark. "Independence has programs which focus on goals, on nonethnic issues, on the rites of passage from high school to being a young adult. The school wants to elevate a student's self-esteem, to celebrate the uniqueness of a person," Gibeau explains.

At the same time Independence recognizes the needs of students to identify with their ancestral cultures. Each year Independence holds a week-long multicultural rally. For students it's one of the most fun times of the year. "Other schools use our rally as a model," says Tom Marin, president of the Associated Student Body at Independence and member of the 1990 graduating class. "We have 20 different cultures represented at the rally." Each ethnic club serves its native foods. Parades, dancing, and entertainment cap the celebration.

Tom Marin, an 18-year-old senior and Mexican-American, and Van Duong, an 18-year-old senior who was born in Vietnam, represent those students at Independence who have been able to use the school as a means of achieving their personal goals. Duong serves with Marin on the students' executive council.

"Sure you have your everyday fights here, but in general everyone gets along," Marin says. As a teacher's aide in the school's self-esteem classes, he volunteers to teach freshmen who received poor grades in middle school how to improve their study habits. One of four children from a broken family, Marin considers himself a role model for the freshmen. "I show them that I was able to get through the family problems and yet maintain my grades and stay in sports."

Already politically astute, Marin says he wants "to be a power, a business entrepreneur" after he completes college. "I'm hungry," he says, "I want to make a difference."

For Van Duong, Independence and San Jose are a marked contrast from her earlier childhood in Eureka, California, where she immigrated as a three-year-old when her father, who was working with Americans, was forced to leave Vietnam as a result of the war.

"When I lived in Eureka, we were one of the few Asian families, but there was very little tension. In San Jose it's a lot easier to find Asian stores, to learn more about the Asian cultures, but there is more tension," Duong says. She is pleased that Independence promotes ethnic diversity and recognizes the large Asian population in the area. Asians hold the majority in elected student government offices at Independence.

Duong, a B+ student, is interested in law and politics. She is looking forward to attending UC Davis, which has the small-town atmosphere she prefers.

Marin and Duong, two students from highly different cultures, exemplify the spirit of Independence High School: each individual has uniqueness and value and can make a difference in this world.

▪ Politics: The Next Wave

Santa Clara County's multiethnic students eventually grow up and become voters. By the early twenty-first century, county politics will undoubtedly change further to reflect this new pluralism.

The 1980s and early 1990s saw the beginning of political change. Iola Williams, a black community leader, was elected to the San Jose City Council. She was joined by Blanca Alvarado, a Mexican-American representing the East Side. Ron Gonzales became the first Hispanic to be elected to the Santa Clara County Board of Supervisors, followed by the election of Mike Honda as the first Japanese-American to be elected to the county seat.

Three decades before, a union advocate set the stage for the ethnic politics. In the early 1960s Ben Gross was a hard-working union man, putting in his time with the Ford automotive plant in Milpitas. Having a natural inclination for politics, Gross, bolstered by his union's support, handily won a seat on the Milpitas City Council. It might seem like a typical marriage of union strength and local politics, but many considered the election of Ben Gross to be a radical departure from "politics as usual" for one reason: he was black.

Gross, who campaigned with the slogan, "A Better Milpitas," became the first person of any minority to be elected to a city council in Northern California, and one of a rare handful of minority elected officials in the state at that time. He was first elected in 1962, at the dawn of the national civil rights revolution. Gross became mayor of Milpitas in 1967 and served on the council until 1971, when the United Auto Workers hired him for a new position in Detroit.

Twenty-two years after Gross' watershed victory, Pat Amoroso became the first Filipino-American to be elected to a city council seat in the San Francisco Bay Area. Again the city was Milpitas.

Amoroso's success has inspired other Filipino-Americans, such as Maryles Casto, owner and founder of a multimillion-dollar travel agency serving Silicon Valley, to consider running for local office. But Amoroso believes it will be some time before many other Filipinos, Vietnamese, or other immigrant groups, realize political strength.

"When people come here, they first need to survive economically. Politics comes later," Amoroso declares.

Ben Menor, president of the Filipino-American Council, says, "There are phases of survival for every immigrant. Taking care of the family, through work and finding a home, [comes] first.

"The first generation is just happy to get out of the barrio. We're the second generation. We've been in America long enough to want to achieve more," says Menor.

Amoroso predicts that as each generation of Filipinos assimilates, individuals will become more active in community politics. "We've just started," he says.

To be successful in politics immigrants need to see the value of ethnic representation in elective office. Both Amoroso and Fernando Zazueta, a prominent Mexican-American lawyer and community leader, believe ethnics can achieve far more in politics than they have to date.

"Filipinos have to become more visible. We need to raise our level of expectations. Elective office will give us a stronger voice in economics. It is a stepping stone to greater success in all facets of life," Amoroso declares.

Hispanics and Filipinos suffer from the overall voter apathy in America, both men believe.

"The Hispanic community is just as apathetic as the general public. And they will be until they realize their vote really is their strength. We're not good at selling our own people on democracy," says Zazueta.

With time more Hispanics will become active in politics, Zazueta predicts. "People are coming up through the ranks. We have now a growing middle class of Hispanic professionals."

Zazueta, a San Jose High School alumnus and San Jose State University graduate, first became active in the community after listening to Cesar Chavez. "He asked those of us who were educated what we were doing for those who weren't able to go to college," Zazueta recalls.

Chavez's remarks became a personal challenge to Zazueta, who now is one of the most politically active Mexican-Americans in the community. During 1990 Zazueta served as treasurer in the successful mayoral election campaign of San Jose city councilwoman Susan Hammer, his neighbor. He is president of the Mexican Heritage Corporation, a nonprofit agency that will build a new Mexican cultural center in San Jose.

Also representative of the emerging Hispanic middle class is Rigo Chacon, an Emmy-award winning television reporter. The son of migrant workers, as is Zazueta, Chacon worked in the fields as a child. After graduating from San Jose High School and attending San Jose State University, Chacon began a television career that has made him one of the most popular and recognizable figures in the San Francisco Bay Area. He volunteers 90 percent of his leisure time to community service and is often encouraged to run for political office. "We have a strong reason to be proud of what the Hispanic community has achieved in the last 20 years in Santa Clara County in politics and in business," says Chacon.

Chacon and Zazueta demonstrate how working with the community can make a difference.

■ A County For All People

Santa Clara County's growing, diverse population has impacted all levels of services provided by the county government system, reports Sally Reed, who, as Santa Clara County executive, heads the administrative branch.

"We are becoming increasingly multilingual in all the services we provide," Reed declares.

The county now designs educational programs so that county managers in various departments can learn more about the new and varied cultures they serve, says Reed. "It's a top down effort. We want our leadership to understand cultural differences.

Vietnamese who have come to the Santa Clara Valley have begun to integrate themselves into the life and economy of the region. Photo by Renee Lynn

It's not just about assimilation. It's about enrichment," Reed says.

Santa Clara County government, one of the largest local employers, with a work force of 15,000, has also had to revise employee recruitment needs to respond to these multiethnic changes.

For example one-third of the employees in the county's GAIN (Greater Avenues for Independence) program are Indo-Chinese, according to Alette Lundeberg, education and employment program manager in the county Department of Social Services. Lundeberg oversees several county programs that serve refugees from Vietnam, Laos, Cambodia, and Ethiopia.

On the average, 100 refugee families per month arrive in the county seeking assistance, Lundeberg says. Initial help usually takes the form of welfare. Then the refugees begin the long process of education. About one-quarter of the 6,000 GAIN clients are refugees. GAIN offers comprehensive education, training, and employment services.

For newly arrived refugees English skills are the first priority. Then the clients can be placed in educational and job-training programs under the GAIN umbrella.

Lundeberg says the county has about 1,200 persons in English as a Second Language (ESL) programs. Another 1,500 are completing high school proficiency classes, and an additional 1,000 are in county-sponsored community college certificate programs.

The success that the Vietnamese, for example, have experienced in finding jobs, opening businesses, and buying property in the county proves that programs such as GAIN can aid in assimilation.

■ Superior Services

"Professionalism is a hallmark of government in this county," declares Reed, who believes quality service befits the pace and standards set by Silicon Valley industry.

In every county department highly educated and trained professionals bring a multitude of services to the county's residents. Exemplifying fine service is the Santa Clara Valley Medical Center, which is owned and operated by the county and located at 751 South Bascom Avenue in San Jose. The Santa Clara County Board of Supervisors serves as its governing board.

Santa Clara Valley Medical Center (VMC) serves as a teaching hospital for the Stanford University School of Medicine and is widely regarded as one of the leading public hospitals in the United States. For residents throughout the San Francisco Bay Area, VMC is known for its critical care and specialty services. Trauma patients are often flown to VMC via Lifeflight helicopter for treatment in its regional burn center or its rehabilitation center for patients with spinal cord or head injuries. VMC also provides an advanced neonatal intensive-care unit and a high-risk pregnancy program.

Stanford Medical College is one of the key medical training facilities in the area. Photo by Gerald L. French/The Photo File

Being a public hospital, VMC's "mission has been to provide quality care for those who cannot get access to treatment elsewhere, as well as to provide speciality services that are one-of-a-kind or highly unusual in the region," says Robert Sillen, the hospital's executive director.

The hospital, which was founded in 1876, celebrated a landmark year in 1989 with the opening of the new $45-million West Wing, a technologically advanced building housing VMC's critical-care units.

VMC and other health and public-safety agencies in Santa Clara County are linked to the county's communications system. The system provides emergency police, fire, and medical communications services. In October 1990 half of the county's communications operation was transferred to the City of San Jose when it opened its communications center.

In addition to social and medical services, Santa Clara County administers one of the busiest law and justice divisions in the San Francisco Bay Area. As the county has grown in population, there has been a parallel increase in the

ABOVE: A modern dispatching system allows San Jose police officers immediate communications to all parts of the city. Photo by Richard L. Kaylin

LEFT: Stanford Medical Center uses a helicopter as part of its Life Flight service to transport patients to emergency medical care without delay. Photo by Gerald L. French/The Photo File

The City of Morgan Hill has up-to-date fire-fighting equipment as part of the service citizens are provided. Photo by Michael O'Callahan

demand for court hearings, for crime prevention and intervention, and for jail space.

During the 1989-1990 fiscal year Santa Clara County expanded its court system by 25 percent, adding judges at both the superior court and municipal court level, for a total of 49 superior court and 32 municipal court judges. At a cost of $7.2 million, the court expansion generated a total of 285 new positions in the courts and in the probation, sheriff's, district attorney's, and public defender's offices.

At the same time the county saved almost $5 million by establishing its civilian-operated Department of Corrections, which manages the jails. In November 1988 the California Supreme Court upheld the board of supervisors' decision to create a new corrections department and transfer responsibility for the jails from the sheriff's office.

During the 1990 fiscal year the sheriff's office added a beat in South County, responding to the vigorous development taking place in the cities of Morgan Hill and Gilroy.

Working closely with the sheriff's office are the county district attorney's and public defender's offices. In addition to prosecuting all criminal offenses tried before the county courts, the district attorney's office administers a number of specialized programs. Its Family Support Unit aggressively enforces paternity and child-support financial obligations. The office also operates special prosecution units for "career criminals" and major drug offenders and a "gang violence suppression" unit.

Fire department personnel of Los Altos in the northwest county stand ready. Photo by Joseph Sohm/ Chromosohm

A paramedic from the Campbell Fire Department responds to a call. Photo by Eric Luse

For those individuals who are charged with a crime but can't afford a private attorney, the county public defender's office has the constitutional responsibility of defending them. As a result of the expanded court system, the public defender's office added 31 new positions during fiscal 1990.

Legal representation for Santa Clara County government is administered by the county counsel's office. The county counsel defends or prosecutes all civil actions in which the county, its officers, or employees are involved. It also advises all boards, commissions, and departments and drafts ordinances, resolutions, and other legal documents.

A Global Home

Both Santa Clara County government and private nonprofit agencies are responding to the new waves of immigrants with targeted help programs. These programs recognize the need of different cultures to assimilate socially and economically while retaining the unique identity of their ancestry.

As a new century draws near, Santa Clara County already reflects the future. It is one in which all the people of the world can live together in constructive pursuit of a healthy economy and their personal visions of "the American dream."

3

Moving In and Getting Around

■ **Scenario: The Year 2050**

T he sun is starting to peek through the summer early morning fog as Van Minh Niem and her husband Nguyen Van Niem prepare themselves for another Bay Area workday.

In their co-op apartment overlooking St. James Park in downtown San Jose, Van and Nguyen finish dressing their two young children. Everyone hurries out of the 20th-floor apartment and into the elevator, which quickly takes them to the ground-level day-care facility. They drop off their children and give them goodbye hugs. Since there are 600 families living in the twin 30-story St. James Towers, the day-care center is an essential service.

From the St. James Towers the two walk a few blocks to the light rail stop at North First and East St. James streets, passing a continuous stream of high-rise apartment towers much like their own. About 1.5 million people now live in San Jose, the most densely populated city in the Bay Area.

As they stroll they reflect on their good fortune. They were able to purchase a cooperative share in their apartment tower after being on a waiting list for several years. Both feel fortunate they do not have to endure the housing crunch and tedious work commutes their parents and grandparents experienced. Nguyen and Van were able to find housing that matched their means and was within a reasonable commuting distance from their respective employers.

While the San Jose light rail system has a fleet of new cars, restored antique cars also travel the system and add a sense of history. Photo by Kerrick James

At the light rail stop they board the line for a brief shuttle over to the Cahill Transfer Station. Van, an engineer with a fiber-optics company in Palo Alto, boards a northbound, high-speed "maglev" train. The magnetically levitated train, traveling at speeds of 315 mph over the old Southern

Pacific right-of-way, takes her to the Palo Alto Industrial Park stop. Total commute time: 10 minutes. Van then boards a solar-powered jitney that transports her and fellow workers down a specially designated lane to the front door of their employer.

Meanwhile Van's husband Nguyen boards a northeast-bound BART (Bay Area Rapid Transit) train to the Hostetter Transfer Station in the middle of the Milpitas/Fremont industrial corridor. From Hostetter Nguyen walks the few blocks to his job as a software developer at a Milpitas educational games company.

Having both been born in the year 2020, Van and Nguyen are the new generation of Bay Area residents who have never owned cars. Their daily commutes are made on mass transit. For leisure activities, they walk a few blocks to San Jose's cultural district, with its repertoire of entertainment and multiethnic restaurants. For weekend pleasure trips "maglevs" crisscrossing the state of California provide sufficient transportation. The Niems use a mix of mass transit and airplanes for long-distance travel.

In the year 2050 Van and Nguyen's Bay Area megalopolis is a crowded one, but the air is actually cleaner than it was in the previous century, when automobile usage reached a historical peak.

At the end of their workday, back in their co-op, the entire family enjoys the view from the 20th-floor flat. They look to the western horizon as the sun casts a red glow over the Santa Cruz Mountains. With their two young children, Van and Nguyen feel content with their home and life in San Jose.

■ Parts Of The Puzzle

The world of Van Minh Niem and her family is a harmonious one in which Bay Area communities cooperate with one another. This cooperation has produced

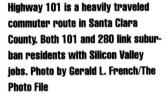

Highway 101 is a heavily traveled commuter route in Santa Clara County. Both 101 and 280 link suburban residents with Silicon Valley jobs. Photo by Gerald L. French/The Photo File

a linkage of transit connections along with affordable high-density dwellings built to serve mass-transit users.

By the year 2050 the Bay Area is a model of regionalism. Government and the private sector long ago realized that to maintain the Bay Area's high standards for quality of life, regionalism had to move from a theoretical concept to action.

Two significant quality of life issues—where people live and how they travel to and from work—spurred the seeds of regionalism in the 1980s and early 1990s. In Santa Clara County, civic leaders saw the impact one city's land-use policy had on another's traffic congestion, and vice versa. With Santa Clara County growing so rapidly in jobs and population, local governments had to start to view the area as interrelated. Addressing the "jobs-housing imbalance" meant adopting a regional approach. As the county developed in the boom, high-technology years of the 1970s and into the early 1980s, it became clear most people lived in one town and worked in another. A more logical approach to planning needed to be taken so that jobs and housing would achieve a better balance in each of the cities.

During the 1980s regionalism began to take shape with the Golden Triangle Task Force, which referred to the industrial sector bordered by highways 101, 237, and 880. Its mission was to create a uniform policy on transportation and land use. The task force was supported by the Santa Clara County Manufacturing Group (SCCMG) and its president Peter Giles, who now heads the Technology Center of Silicon Valley.

SCCMG, a Silicon Valley employers' association that takes an active role in local public policy, saw its member companies having to contend with two horns of a dilemma: because employees were having to live farther and farther from their jobs, traffic congestion and commute times were increasing.

By 1990, in addition to the Santa Clara County government, five cities remained active in the task force: Mountain View, Sunnyvale, San Jose, Palo Alto, and Milpitas. There was heightened concern about traffic and land-use issues. The significant population growth in the Bay Area pointedly demonstrated that the "jobs-housing imbalance" was still far from solved.

In 1991 the Golden Triangle Task Force merged with the new Santa Clara County Congestion Management Program (CMP) Agency, which is comprised of each of the county's municipalities and the county government. The agency resulted from state Proposition 111, which established CMPs in every county. Since its objectives are basically the same as the task force, CMP now becomes the lead local agency on such issues.

▓ *Finishing The Puzzle*

Regionalism in the San Francisco Bay Area took a dramatic step forward in 1988 with the formation of the Bay Vision 2020 Commission, a 32-person cross-section of private and public representatives from the nine Bay Area counties. Its mission is to construct a future scenario for the Bay Area, focusing on the issues of land use, transportation, and housing.

"Our major objective is to stop urban sprawl," says Santa Clara County supervisor Rod Diridon, one of the influential forces behind the group's formation.

Reconciling often conflicting needs—the need to maintain a strong regional economy and the need to protect the physical environment—is the core issue facing Bay Vision 2020. Among the group's concerns are the regional shortage of affordable housing, longer commutes between home and work, an increased demand on transportation, and dwindling open space due to urban sprawl.

Bay Vision 2020 is the combined product of two groups that were working independently but with the same goal: effective regional decision making. Supervisor Diridon, also former chair of the Metropolitan Transportation Commission (MTC), initiated one group that was comprised of governmental leaders from around the bay. The second group consisted of business and environmental leaders active in the Bay Area Council and the Greenbelt Alliance. When the groups realized they had essentially the same goals, they decided to combine resources and create Bay Vision 2020.

"One of our goals is to restructure regional government, to look at the possibility of merging some of the regional agencies," Diridon explains.

Bay Vision 2020 is a litmus test for whether or not regionalism will truly work in the San Francisco Bay Area. There is already consensus on the critical relationship between transportation and land-use policies and the Bay Area's quality of life. Such issues have been ebbing and flowing through the consciousness of Bay Area leaders for decades.

The extent to which the Bay Area can remain a desirable place to live and work depends largely upon state legislators, local governments, and the private sector taking the initiative and enacting the recommendations of Bay Vision 2020.

◼ *Impetus For Change*

While Bay Vision 2020 faces its ultimate test, several compelling factors are already forcing changes in transportation and related land-use policies. These include a combination of new state laws, one court case, and a sociopolitical climate that favors aggressive action to protect the environment.

Demographics have played a role. The number of people working in the Bay

Santa Clara County Supervisor Rod Diridon is one influential force behind Bay Vision 2020.

The manufacture and testing of computer components are a key part of the work done in the Silicon Valley. Photo by Liane Enkelis

Area increased significantly during the 1980s, intensifying demand for affordable housing and contributing to traffic congestion. In Santa Clara County, for example, the total number of jobs in manufacturing, service, retail, real estate, construction, and transportation rose from 675,400 in 1980 to 834,500 in June 1990, a jump of almost 160,000 new workers, according to the state Employment Development Department (EDD). By 1993 the EDD predicts another 50,000 jobs will be added to Santa Clara County, providing the economy remains relatively stable.

As more workers headed onto Bay Area roads, concerns about the pollution impact were reinforced by a rebirth of consciousness about environmental issues. People in the Bay Area and around the nation observed the 20th anniversary of Earth Day in April 1990. They gave themselves a relatively poor report card in treatment of the environment. The need to switch to cleaner forms of transportation was discussed in rallies, news shows, and literature.

Congruent with this newly reawakened environmental consciousness were public actions that mandated changes in transportation policy. Two actions created a pincer effect on local governments and agencies: the state's 1988 Clean Air Act and a successful 1989 environmental lawsuit put a tight grip on agencies responsible for air quality and traffic management.

Authored by Assemblyman Byron Sher of Palo Alto, the California Clean Air Act says that federal air pollution standards aren't strict enough. It mandates that ozone pollution levels cannot exceed .10 parts per million, compared to the federal standard of .12 parts per million.

Public-relations agencies such as this help companies maintain high-profile images and get a corporation's message out to potential clients. Many trained public-relations practitioners come from the degree-granting program at San Jose State University. Photo by Richard L. Kaylin

After the Clean Air Act a successful lawsuit was filed by the Sierra Club and Citizens for a Better Environment. Aimed at all causes of air pollution—including vehicle emissions and stationary sources such as bakeries—the lawsuit was designed to accelerate actions to clean up the Bay Area's air.

In the suit brought against the Metropolitan Transportation Commission, the Bay Area Air Quality Management District, and the California Air Resources Control Board, the plaintiffs argued that these agencies had long been in violation of the less stringent federal air standards and had failed to meet pollution reduction deadlines set under the federal law.

In September 1989 Thelton Henderson, a U.S. district court justice, ordered the agencies to create tougher pollution-control measures and adopt such a plan within nine months.

With two deadlines in effect—the judge's timetable for a new pollution-control plan and a 1997 date for compliance under the new state law—regional government went to work to create a strategy.

In 1990 the MTC released the first draft of a plan for 16 transportation control measures (TCMs) to meet the compliance standards of the new, more stringent state law (thereby also satisfying the less strict federal standards). By June 1991 the MTC and the Bay Area Air Quality Management District were expected to adopt a blueprint for regional compliance. This blueprint will be used by local jurisdictions to create their own implementation plans. Santa Clara County is scheduled to submit its plan by early 1992. The new Congestion Management Agency will play a key role in the plan design.

Aiming to cut vehicle pollution by 35 percent, the MTC plan focuses on methods of alleviating traffic congestion, intensifying use of mass transit by expanding transit systems and by making them more convenient, and imposing financial disincentives—such as higher Bay Area bridge tolls and fees for parking at the workplace—for those who do drive cars. The plan also referred to the need to locate new higher-density dwellings along transit corridors.

"It's really tricky. We need to beef up the transit system so it is a convenient, workable option," declares Arielle Leonard, former director of transportation and land use for the Santa Clara County Manufacturing Group, noting that the only way people will leave their cars at home is if there are attractive alternatives.

Market-based strategies such as charging employees to park "would be a radical change in corporate culture" in Santa Clara County, Leonard says. Such

financial disincentives are advocated by the Bay Area Economic Forum, a group of leaders from the public and private sectors who studied the air pollution issue and recommend market-based strategies as the solution.

While most air pollution reduction plans tend to focus on commute times, Leonard emphasizes that commute traffic represents less than 25 percent of total road trips. Shoppers and people driving to other daytime activities need to be considered in any incentive plan, Leonard believes.

Air pollution reduction became a primary topic among industry representatives such as Leonard during the years 1988 through 1990. The Clean Air Act of 1988 and the environmental lawsuit of 1989 created the momentum for change, and the June 1990 election ballot added a third compelling factor.

California voters approved propositions 108, 111, and 116, which created new sources of funding for road and transit improvements. Proposition 111 raised the state's gasoline tax by nine cents; revenue from the tax increase will fund a variety of highway and transit projects. Proposition 108 authorized the sale of one billion dollars in bonds for rail projects. Proposition 116 similarly created a $1.9-billion rail bond measure.

Of the new monies created by the three propositions, the Bay Area hopes to get almost $5 billion for new transit and road projects. Planned mass-transit improvements include extensions of BART and CalTrain, extension of the Santa Clara County light rail system, and a proposed intercity rail service between San Jose and Sacramento.

Proposition 111, the gas tax increase, will fund road improvements that alleviate traffic congestion. Plans include adding carpool lanes along Interstate 880 in Santa Clara and Alameda counties; along Highway 101 in San Mateo, Marin, and Sonoma counties; and on I-680 through Contra Costa County.

Ironically Santa Clara County, one of the most traffic-congested areas in the state, did not vote in favor of the gas tax increase. Political analysts conjecture that the negative vote resulted from a backlash associated with the passage of Measure A, a 1984 Santa Clara County law that raised the local sales tax to fund freeway expansion. Although they reside in one of the most affluent places in America, perhaps Santa Clara County voters didn't want to open their wallets again. However the county did vote for the two bond measures.

Perhaps the propositions will help to solidify regionalism as a way of doing business in the Bay Area. As the 1990s progress, local and regional governments ideally will work together to put the proposition money to best use. And always in the background will be the double specter of a new and tougher state clean air law and a federal judge who has deadlines for compliance.

■ *Everything Old Is New Again*

In its search for mass-transit alternatives to the car, government is finding out that history books can have the answers.

During the early 1900s the residents of Santa Clara County rode electric trolleys that linked the growing burgs of San Jose and Santa Clara to other parts of the county. At the peak of the era, nearly 130 miles of trackway were used—running from Los Gatos and Congress Springs near Saratoga on the western rim, to Alum Rock Park in the east foothills, south to the Almaden Mines, and north to Palo Alto and Stanford University.

The advent of automobile travel relegated trolleys to the history books until 1982 when the nonprofit San Jose Trolley Corporation, with Supervisor Diridon as president, began buying and restoring vintage streetcars.

During the 1990s visitors to San Jose will see a half-dozen colorfully restored trolleys running downtown. Happily Fred Bennett, a master car-builder, has been able to restore Car 124, one of the original trolleys from Santa Clara County's streetcar era. Other trolleys restored by the corporation have come from as far away as Milan, Italy, and Melbourne, Australia. Since restoration is costly and intricate, the San Jose Trolley Corporation is always seeking benefactors. The *San Jose Mercury News*, Heritage Cablevision, the Ray Collishaw Corporation, the Fairmont Hotel, the Hugh Stuart Center Charitable Trust, and the Metro A Trust Fund have contributed financing.

In addition to the downtown trolleys, Diridon says three more are planned for Kelley Park, where the San Jose Historical Museum is located. The trolleys would serve as the internal transit system for the 200-acre park.

Almost a century after elegant streetcars traversed the pathways of Santa Clara County, government is bringing them back with a modern twist. The trolleys now signify a desire for clean, nonpolluting travel. What was once quaint is now viewed as smart environmentalism.

The trolley's modern-day counterpart, Santa Clara County's light rail system, also has its roots in the region's travel history. Native Americans were the first settlers and travelers in the Santa Clara Valley. They pulled their travois down the river banks. The corridors they used now serve as the grid followed by the light rail lines and major roads. For example, Highway 101 and Almaden Expressway in the San Jose area run along the original Coyote River corridor.

Santa Clara County's first phase of the light rail system was named the Guadalupe Corridor Project, referring to the Guadalupe River, one of the Indians' main routes.

The 20-mile light rail system, which runs from south San Jose through the downtown Transit Mall and ends at a point along the Tasman Drive industrial sector in Santa Clara, is one of the longest to be built in the United States in five decades. Its first link was completed in 1988. The remainder of the first phase is due to be finished in 1991, when the line will extend to IBM and the Almaden Valley. Studies have already been launched to extend the system.

A clean alternative to the car, the light rail system is a "phenomenal success," Diridon observes. He notes that the system carries 10,000 riders daily, double the original expectations. Ridership figures are expected to increase dramatically when the IBM link is completed.

"Our positive experience with light rail shows there is a pent-up demand for mass transit we're just barely beginning to tap," Diridon says.

In Santa Clara County everything old is new again. The river corridors once traveled by the Native Americans are now bustling with trolleys and updated streetcars. A healthful side effect of this renaissance of rail usage is that each person taking a trolley or light rail car is staying off the road, lessening the amount of ozone leaked into the atmosphere.

■ *The Master Plan*

In order for the Bay Area to reach a 35-percent cut in vehicle emissions by 1997, it is clear a lot more people must start carpooling or taking mass transit.

As a densely populated center, Santa Clara County plays an important role in achieving the objective. The county's own Transportation 2000 master plan acknowledges that unless there is a greater use of mass transit and ridesharing, commute traffic could *increase* as much as 40 percent by the year 2000.

In line with Transportation 2000, Santa Clara County is undergoing major road improvements to mitigate traffic congestion. These improvements have been funded by Measure A, which added a half-cent to the county sales tax. The tax, which took effect April 1, 1985, has become a model for other California counties since it is a radical departure from the traditional means of obtaining road funding from the state or federal government. Voters in 13 other counties have since approved similar measures. Due to expire in April 1, 1995, the Santa Clara County tax could continue if voters approve a new measure that would partially fund the BART extension to Santa Clara County. The new measure is expected to be placed on the ballot in 1992.

Measure A funds the widening of Route 85, which runs along the northwestern rim of the county; the addition of 18 miles of Route 85, extending it south; the widening of Highway 101, to eight lanes from Bernal Road in South San Jose to the San Mateo County Line; and the upgrading of Highway

The freeway system around San Jose and throughout Santa Clara County provides access to the region's major industrial, educational, and recreational areas. State Highway 280 is shown here. Photo by Gerald L. French/The Photo File

237, which runs through the industrial sector from Milpitas to Mountain View, from an expressway with stoplights to a six-lane freeway. Route 85 and Highway 237 are due for completion in 1993; Highway 101 should be finished in 1992.

Road improvements funded by Measure A are part of the county's plan to encourage carpooling by constructing special high-occupancy vehicle (HOV) lanes. These commuter lanes can be used by two or more persons and are designed to ease the flow of traffic during peak commute hours. Upon completion there will be a 140-mile network of HOV lanes, to include Route 85; highways 101, 237, and 280; and San Tomas, Montague, and Lawrence expressways.

Even if another 5 percent of commuters carpool, "it will have a great impact" on ease of traffic, declares SCCMG's Peter Giles. "With a very slight improvement around the margin, we could basically have free-flowing traffic during commute time. That is the theory behind commute lanes," Giles explains.

Building the commuter lanes is only one part of the process, Giles believes. "We need to promote the advantages of carpooling, that people can save time."

Some companies such as Varian Associates in Palo Alto already have ridesharing programs in place. "Private industry wants to do a reasonable share," says Leonard, but she cautions that ridesharing will be the most successful when there are more mass-transit connections in the industrial sector. "People still want to get in their cars and leave the company at lunchtime," Leonard says. However, adequate transit availability could give employees the independence they desire.

The need for immediate information is met daily by media facilities of the Santa Clara Valley with electronic linkage to regions of the world. Photo by Tim Davis

■ *Linking Up*

Supervisor Diridon envisions a future in which residents travel on a full-fledged system of mass transit linked around the San Francisco Bay.

As former chair of the regional Metropolitan Transportation Commission, Diridon is coordinating a passel of studies focusing on where new rail links should be built. At the core of Diridon's work is the belief that people will leave their cars home if there are convenient and inexpensive mass-transit options, whether they be light rail, BART, or CalTrain. Rail expansion will also be networked to bus systems in the region.

History was made during the 1980s when Santa Clara County inaugurated its new light rail system. But civic leaders and consumers alike realized that the first links of the light rail line were just the beginning. Light rail must now extend outward like a spider web, connecting more housing centers with industrial sectors, fulfilling the goal of getting people off the road.

Silicon Valley industry will be served by the next light rail link. The Tasman Corridor, a 12-mile extension along Tasman Drive, will parallel heavily traveled Highway 237. It is scheduled for construction to begin in 1993 and to be in operation in 1996. The western end of the Tasman line will be situated near the Lockheed complex in Sunnyvale while the eastern end will serve Milpitas and northeast San Jose. Plans also call for a feeder line for Tasman—to the Mountain View CalTrain station.

Once Tasman is under way, the next priority is the seven-mile Vasona Corridor stretching from downtown San Jose through Campbell and into Los Gatos. Construction on Vasona is expected to begin in 1994.

In the concept stage are four other light rail studies. A DeAnza Corridor extension would run along Route 85 from the Oakridge Mall in San Jose, through Los Gatos, ending in either Sunnyvale or Mountain View. The Santa Teresa extension would link the IBM stop in South San Jose to the North Coyote Valley if that area is developed.

The eastern rim of the Santa Clara Valley would be served by two other proposed light rail links. An eight-mile Downtown/Evergreen Corridor would link the existing Guadalupe Corridor system with the Eastridge Mall via Senter Road and Capitol Expressway. Another option is the five-mile Capitol Corridor which would link the proposed new Tasman Corridor line to Eastridge Mall via Capitol Avenue.

In addition to expansion of the light rail line, Santa Clara County is negotiating the extension of BART to the valley. Currently BART ends in Fremont on the eastern side of the San Francisco Bay. One option would be for BART to run along the Southern Pacific right-of-way through Milpitas to downtown San Jose, then continue to Santa Clara University. A second option is to use the Union Pacific route parallel to Lundy Avenue and King Road, crossing the valley and also ending at the university. BART would be convenient to San Jose State University, the downtown Transit Mall, and the new San Jose downtown arena.

BART will be an expensive proposition for Santa Clara County. Diridon estimates the cost at $1.7 billion. Fifty percent would be funded by the federal Urban Mass Transportation Administration (UMTA), 25 percent by the state, and 25 percent by a new county measure.

Competition for federal dollars is tough, says Diridon, who is leading the BART negotiations. The first hurdle is to get UMTA to approve a full-fledged BART study. Diridon is working with San Jose congressmen Norm Mineta and Don Edwards to secure the UMTA funding. As chair of the House Subcommittee on Surface Transportation, Mineta has a good track record in securing transportation money for Santa Clara County. In the past he has obtained funding for the county's light rail system and for the Tasman Corridor extension.

Mineta will work with Edwards, who is dean of the California delegation, when the time comes to put the BART funding to a vote. As dean, Edwards wields a bloc of votes that is critical to the obtainment of funding. BART studies will be lengthy and complex. Diridon estimates the full range of studies will take until 1996 or 1997 to complete.

Santa Clara County is also joining with San Mateo and San Francisco counties in negotiating the purchase of the main Southern Pacific right-of-way between San Jose and San Francisco. The route is one used daily by CalTrain commuters. According to Diridon purchase of the right-of-way would save the commute line, which would continue with funding by Proposition 116.

Santa Clara County is also studying a 28-mile extension of the CalTrain commuter rail line from its endpoint in downtown San Jose to Gilroy. The link

Business travelers and residents alike appreciate the San Jose International Airport's proximity to central city firms and industrial parks. Photo by Gerald L. French/The Photo File

would allow south county's bedroom communities to travel by CalTrain to San Jose's transit mall, where they could board light rail or bus lines to take them to work.

The county's bus system will continue to be a part of the valley's transit future, serving primarily as a feeder and distribution link to rail lines, Diridon says. A fleet of more than 500 buses now serves the county.

For long-distance travel, residents, tourists, and people doing business in Silicon Valley are served by one major airport and three general-aviation airports.

San Jose International Airport serves 7 million passengers yearly and is expected to double its customer base by the year 2000. The airport, operated by the City of San Jose, is undergoing a $516-million expansion program. Three new terminals will be built, the first of which—Terminal A—has been completed and is now occupied by American Airlines. More than half of the airport's business is generated by American Airlines, which has made San Jose International one of its hubs.

In 1984 the airport adopted international status, with the addition of flights to Canada. It has since added service to Tokyo and Guadalajara. A federal customs inspection facility opened at the airport in 1990 to serve international travelers and businesses.

The San Jose airport complex is also home to corporate jets, which refuel at the San Jose Jet Center. Hewlett-Packard also maintains its corporate aviation headquarters at the airport.

Young travelers at the airport now have the benefit of KidPort, an aviation-themed play area with interactive exhibits. Kids can listen to communication in the air traffic control tower by using video-telephone hookups.

To serve general aviation customers Santa Clara County manages three airports: Reid-Hillview, in San Jose; Palo Alto Airport; and South County, in San Martin. More than 1,000 aircraft are based at the airports.

New light rail lines. Improved roads. An expanding airport. Santa Clara County is making an investment in its transportation future.

Reid Hillview Airport in East San Jose provides aeronautical services for South Bay pilots and companies. This is one of three general aviation airports managed by the county. Photo by Gerald L. French/The Photo File

■ *Stopping The Sprawl*

For much of the twentieth century the Santa Clara Valley was a classic suburban culture. People lived in single-family homes and drove to work. Subdivisions of

tract homes spread out around the valley, in no particular alignment to where jobs and industry were located.

Now, with the twenty-first century fast approaching, Santa Clara Valley is changing from a car-oriented suburban culture to a higher-density urban area in which mass transit will eventually supersede the automobile as the primary means of travel to work.

With this evolution comes a revamping of land-use policies focused on two main objectives: stopping the sprawl of housing to outlying areas, thereby preserving some open space, and encouraging the in-filling of new multifamily housing near transit corridors.

Santa Clara Valley is not alone in its concerns about urban sprawl and dwindling open space. Its neighboring counties face the same dilemma, the result of a Bay Area population surge that demands more housing.

"We're really at a critical point in land use. Without a change we will begin to duplicate the urban sprawl of Los Angeles," warns Bob Mang, president of the Greenbelt Alliance.

"Thankfully we are beginning to see a movement from all types of people who want to look at in-filling and increased density as a strategy. The philosophy is to use the land you have instead of leaving a mess behind and going on to the next area," says Mang.

Formed as People for Open Space to preserve the open space in the hills beyond Berkeley, the Greenbelt Alliance is now a 31-year-old organization with a regional perspective. "Open space and parks are a key component of what makes the Bay Area so attractive," Mang declares.

In 1990 the greenbelt concept received much attention from Santa Clara Valley governmental and business leaders. The November ballot asked voters to approve the creation of a new open-space authority, which would buy and preserve lands predominantly in the southern and eastern parts of the valley. Lands in the north are already owned and protected by the Midpeninsula Open Space District. The new authority would similarly make the lands available to the public for hiking, picnicking, and other low-key recreation.

One of the factors leading to the open-space measure was new, scattered

housing development in the Santa Clara Valley hillsides. It amplified the need for a public policy to check urban sprawl and protect one of the valley's environmental treasures: its spectacular hillsides.

The open-space measure enjoyed a unique consensus of support. All of the cities that would be affected and Santa Clara County government, whose unincorporated lands would be included in the new district, were in favor of the measure. Developers supported the measure even though it impacted their industry. People in both the private and public sectors agreed that if Santa Clara Valley were to avoid the sprawl of Los Angeles, its hillsides needed to be protected. To travel on the densely populated valley floor and look up at the hillsides and open space was a spirit-enhancing luxury few wanted to surrender.

Despite such support the measure failed. Since it would trigger a yearly property assessment—a maximum of $25 per developed parcel—to raise funds to buy the lands, the measure needed two-thirds vote in favor in order to become law. Traditionally such ballot measures have a difficult time passing. However, the measure did receive approximately 63 percent approval of votes cast.

■ Living In Town

Stopping the sprawl is one side of the land-use issue. The other is in-filling by building higher-density housing in already established urban corridors.

In-filling as a solution is complicated by the fact that cities have to make hard choices between land for new homes versus land for new jobs. The current disparity between the number of homes and the number of business locations is the result of many cities historically choosing jobs over housing. Industry brings a tax base to cities that housing does not, so cities looking to improve their revenue structure naturally choose to zone new land for jobs.

The imbalance between jobs and housing is starting to improve as cities take a regional approach, working towards interrelated goals. Some 15,000 housing units have been added since the Golden Triangle Task Force began looking at commute patterns in the valley.

Sunnyvale and San Jose have taken the lead in promoting new development that meets the in-filling goal. San Jose has always been a housing center for the valley. Sunnyvale, a city with a healthy tax structure and the home of industry giants such as Lockheed, began to question its land-use policies in the 1980s. "We found our industrial growth was proceeding three times as rapidly as what we had expected. Our ratio of jobs to housing was out of balance by 25,000 units," recalls veteran councilman Larry Stone.

An industrial moratorium was declared by the Sunnyvale City Council, which later rezoned 520 acres in the city from industrial to residential use.

Since then Sunnyvale has continued to legislate a balance of housing and jobs. Stone believes having adequate housing in the city is essential to keeping its industrial base. "One of the biggest problems for companies is finding housing for their employees. If we don't deal with this issue, eventually our industrial base will disappear," Stone asserts.

In 1990 Sunnyvale celebrated the ground-breaking of its flagship in-fill project—The Mark—an 822-unit residential development located near Highway 101 and the Lawrence Expressway. Its 21-story condominium tower will be the first of its type in the valley and a startling departure from the typically low-rise

local residential construction. It will also be the third-tallest, after the Fairmont Hotel in San Jose and the Pruneyard Towers commercial complex in Campbell. In addition the project will contain 622 apartments and 32 bi-level townhomes.

The $130-million joint venture of Japanese-owned Haseko and Trammell Crow Residential is situated in the middle of Silicon Valley and will eventually be marketed to affluent technology workers who want a respite from daily commuting. It will contain such amenities as a concierge, dry cleaners, health club, and restaurant. Due to the 1990-91 recession the 1993 opening date for The Mark has been postponed, and the construction schedule is being revised.

Selling high-rise condominiums at The Mark will be an experiment since there is no precedent in Santa Clara Valley for this type of ownership. "We'll soon find out whether people will buy them," says Councilman Stone.

To the south of Sunnyvale, San Jose has its own signature in-fill project: River Oaks, a major 2,100-unit complex, 1,400 of which are being developed by Shea Homes. It is located on River Oaks Parkway near San Jose's North 1st Street, in the Golden Triangle industrial sector. Shea's development will include close to 1,000 rental apartments. The remainder of the units are condominiums.

"It's a forerunner of housing trends, an attempt to bring housing closer to jobs," says Reid Gustafson, president of Shea Homes' Northern California division.

Interestingly enough, many older, affluent executives are buying condominium units for a pied-à-terre in town. They have primary residences in San Francisco, Saratoga, Santa Cruz, and other cities.

For the rental units Gustafson expects to market them to corporations that need temporary housing quarters and to professionally employed singles in the Golden Triangle. River Oaks is due to be completed in 1995.

In-town developments such as River Oaks are a harbinger of the future. It represents the new direction in land use in Santa Clara Valley, towards density and away from urban sprawl.

Land Economics

Higher-density residences make good sense not only in terms of the environment but also in basic economics, according to housing industry leaders in Santa Clara Valley.

By 1990 the cost of an average single-family home had well outdistanced the salaries of many Silicon Valley workers. Escalating home prices had provoked people to move as far away as Tracy, Modesto, Los Banos, and Salinas. They endured round-trip commutes of up to four hours in order to live in a city where they could afford to buy a home.

Silicon Valley's atmospheric housing prices can in part be traced to the high cost of land, which doubled during the 1980s. Attached housing became more prevalent as land costs necessitated a change in economics.

"In order to be profitable, builders had to go to higher density," explains Robert Livengood, former executive director of the Building Industry Association of Northern California and now a Milpitas city councilman.

The 1980s also brought an influx of new jobs without a complementary amount of new housing. "Demand went through the roof," Livengood remembers. And housing costs escalated drastically. By 1990, however, the housing market had flattened dramatically. There were 12,000 homes for sale in 1990.

"It's a perfectly reasonable correction," says John V. Pinto, former president of the San Jose Real Estate Board. "Both the 1970s and 1980s began with a slump, then there was tremendous demand, and then the cycle repeated itself."

A startling 85 percent of the houses available in 1990 were overpriced, Pinto believes. One reason is that half of the homes on the market were listed by discretionary sellers who wanted to take advantage of accrued equity by either buying a more expensive home or by cashing in and moving out of the area. Pinto says this dynamic means that people are holding on to houses they could sell for a little cheaper and denying themselves a better home they could get for a good price.

There is no quick panacea for those desiring to buy a traditional single-family home in Silicon Valley. "Middle-class families will have to redefine the American dream," says Pinto. Higher-density homes such as townhomes, row houses, and condominiums are what the middle class might be able to afford in Silicon Valley's future, according to Pinto.

For Silicon Valley workers at the low end of the income spectrum, the challenge is not to buy a home but to find any type of affordable housing.

"We're getting more working poor coming in to see us. They're low-paid clerical people or they might work at McDonald's," says John Burns, executive director of the Santa Clara County Housing Authority. The authority administrates federally subsidized housing and seeks financing packages to build more low-income housing.

Burns serves 9,000 families and has an equally long waiting list. Southeast Asians who have migrated to the county have also added to the demand, Burns says.

Since the federal government has stopped building low-income housing, the demand far exceeds supply. Burns predicts the future is going to "get a lot worse" for low-income families unless the Bush administration starts building new housing units.

Obtaining affordable housing for all levels of income—from middle-class professionals to low-paid service workers—is a complex, challenging task in the Santa Clara Valley of the 1990s.

South County: The Final Frontier

Land is now scarce and expensive in Santa Clara County. Developers look to both the Coyote Valley in South San Jose and the South County communities of Morgan Hill and Gilroy as the last frontier of open space that could be zoned for residential construction. But the political climate strongly favors preserving open space rather than freeing up additional land for development.

The City of San Jose has tied new housing construction in the Coyote Valley to completion of industrial development, in keeping with the goal of balancing housing with jobs.

"If we opened up Coyote Valley now, land costs would go up immediately," so housing wouldn't be any more affordable, declares Shirley Lewis, a San Jose city councilwoman and strong advocate of regional planning.

Lewis sees San Jose's future in higher-density housing with access to transit and in mixed-use development that combines housing with commercial and retail occupants.

The "last bastion" of developable land for single-family builders such as Reid Gustafson of Shea Homes is Morgan Hill, Gilroy, and the unincorporated area of San Martin. However the cities have taken what Gustafson calls an "antigrowth posture." And Santa Clara County government, which rules the unincorporated lands, discourages urban sprawl and supports in-filling as the answer.

For Mayor Roberta Hughan of Gilroy, managing growth and retaining the unique agricultural character of South County are primary goals. Both Gilroy and Morgan Hill want to prevent the urban sprawl they see elsewhere. "We want to define the city's boundaries so it isn't one big city from here to the rest of the county. We want open space through greenbelting," says Hughan.

The political message from South County in the 1990s is a clear one: new construction in the cities will be limited and managed carefully in order to prevent urban sprawl. City leaders and Santa Clara County government officials want South County to move cautiously into the future.

■ The Turning Point

Santa Clara County, and indeed the entire Bay Area, came to a critical phase by 1990. The relentless influx of new residents in the decades prior spurred a rethinking of public policy. No longer could one city take an egocentric approach to land-use planning. Each city—and on a larger scale, each county—was impacted by the other. Most people lived in one place and worked in another. The sheer increase in population exacerbated concerns about traffic congestion and the environment and helped to further skew housing availability and pricing against demand.

A regional approach to land use and transportation planning will help address such challenges. Forums such as the Golden Triangle Task Force and Bay Vision 2020 mark milestones in regional cooperation. Bay Vision's future scenario will demand intergovernmental collaboration on a new level. Only time will tell whether or not it succeeds.

One of the greatest opportunities for regional cooperation is the expansion of mass-transit systems around Santa Clara County, linking up with other established systems around the San Francisco Bay. With population projections showing the 1990s as another decade of influx and with highways already overused, mass transit is becoming a necessity. If cities cooperate, it will be easier to secure the tremendous sums of money needed to build these transit systems.

The willingness of people to reduce their dependency on the automobile and to live in higher-density neighborhoods will shape the environmental viability of Santa Clara County. By the middle of the twenty-first century, mass transit and high density will simply be a way of life for new generations of residents.

FOLLOWING PAGE: Known as the capital of Silicon Valley, San Jose is home to businesses that serve the technology industry. Photo by Ed Cooper/The Photo File

4

Pushing the Envelope

■ *Frontiers Of The Mind*

Pushing the envelope—it's a phrase that test pilots use to describe going beyond known limits. When pilot Chuck Yeager broke the sound barrier, he pushed the envelope. His courage inspired the first generation of astronauts.

America continues to produce pioneers who push the envelope. The Challenger astronauts gave their lives for space exploration. Since then new teams of astronauts have volunteered, undaunted by the high risk.

The daredevil days of Chuck Yeager live on, in a new fashion. Individual nerve is now linked to high technology. Yeager's successors use computer-graphics modeling and high-speed supercomputer-generated mathematics manipulation to see how far the envelope can be pushed.

Silicon Valley's advances in the use and speed of computers have made it possible for tomorrow's explorers to chart new frontiers. In fact, modern research has been permanently changed by the contributions of Silicon Valley and technology firms across America. Computers are now an integral part of virtually all science research, enabling scientists to calculate and manipulate data in untold ways.

As the twenty-first century draws near, it is likely that Silicon Valley, which remains one of the most fertile research and development (R & D) centers in the world, will continue to be a leader in technology innovation.

The use of the computer in design and graphics—and the resulting explosion in desktop publishing—has become one of the major new markets. Photo by Bill Morse/The Photo File

In truth the phenomenon of Silicon Valley might not exist if it were not for the value placed on research by one man—Leland Stanford—and the pushing-the-envelope activities of two others—William Shockley and Frederick E. Terman.

Upon founding Stanford University in 1885, Stanford, a former California governor and U.S. senator, adopted the German higher-education model, which stressed research along with teaching.

Stanford University's philosophical commitment to a strong research environment has enabled it, from its early days, to attract the world's best scientists.

One of Stanford's most-noted professors was William Shockley. A member of the research team that developed the first transistor at Bell Laboratories in New Jersey, Shockley won a Nobel Prize in 1956 for his work.

Shockley's research at Bell Laboratories was the genesis of modern electronics. In 1955 he left Bell Laboratories to return to his hometown of Palo Alto, after which he founded the Transistor Lab in Mountain View.

Originally funded by Beckman Instruments, Shockley's Transistor Lab is considered to be the beginning of Silicon Valley. It was staffed by such luminaries as Robert Noyce, inventor of the integrated circuit; Gordon Moore, who later cofounded Intel with Noyce and Andy Grove; and Gene Kleiner, whose venture-capital firm, Kleiner, Perkins, Caufield and Byers, has funded numerous technology stars. In 1957 Noyce, Moore, Kleiner, Julius Bank, Victor Grinich, Jean Hoerni, Jay Last, and Sheldon Roberts left Shockley to form Fairchild Semiconductor, becoming known as the "Fairchild Eight."

Fairchild Semiconductor became the progenitor of Silicon Valley chip companies. From the 1950s to 1980 more than 50 companies were documented as spin-offs.

As Shockley's lab diminished in size and impact, he was recruited by Frederick Terman, who developed Stanford's distinguished Department of Engineering, to participate in Stanford's fledgling solid-state program. Shockley began a long-term teaching relationship with Stanford. He was a professor emeritus at Stanford when he died in 1989. In his later years Shockley created controversy with his theories on eugenics and other studies. Known for his eccentricity, he reportedly taped all his telephone calls. Those who requested an interview with him first had to pass a Shockley-authored intelligence test.

Just several years before Shockley founded his lab, Terman presided over the opening of his own project—the Stanford Industrial Park. Terman believed that Stanford University needed to form a symbiotic relationship with industry and that Stanford could serve as the brain trust for new technology-based industries, thereby spawning a "community of technical scholars." The industrial park, on Stanford-owned property, would become a kind of collective petri dish for technical innovators.

ABOVE: Undeveloped land in Santa Clara County has been maintained by Stanford University to allow research projects to proceed without the intrusion of civilization. Photo by Renee Lynn

RIGHT: David Packard, one of Silicon Valley's legends, is co-founder of Hewlett-Packard with William Hewlett.

Stanford University leased the land in its industrial park to men who have become part of Silicon Valley legend: David Packard and William Hewlett, both former students of Terman, and Russell Varian, who coinvented the klystron tube—a device for producing high-power microwaves— with his brother, Sigurd, and Professor William Hansen of Stanford's Physics Department.

Now known simply as Research Park, Stanford's industrial park land still houses the corporate headquarters of Hewlett-Packard and Varian Associates. It is a testament to the longevity of Terman's vision and a validation of his concept of a university-industry marriage.

In the 1990s a first-time traveler to Silicon Valley will notice street after street of industrial parks. Terman's belief that research and development thrives in a campus-like setting has been embraced by scores of technology firms.

From the days of Terman and Shockley, Silicon Valley has evolved into a diffuse R & D environment. Every day there are a multitude of applied-research projects being conducted in the cubicles and laboratories of technology firms. With product development and marketing, or technology licensing, as the ultimate goal, these projects are closely guarded by firms and stamped "proprietary" until released.

Research and development, on a contract basis, is big business for Silicon Valley universities and private firms. The federal government has been Stanford University's biggest research customer and virtually the only source of funds for basic research, such as the atom-smashing research at the Stanford Linear Accelerator. However, in early 1991, Defense Department auditors revealed that the university had overcharged for research by as much as $180 million over a 10-year period. As a result, in May, the government dropped its overhead reimbursement rate

LEFT AND BELOW: The linear accelerator at Stanford is an important
research site for scientists and
their students. Left photo by Gerald
L. French/The Photo File; below by
John Elk III

ABOVE: NASA Ames Research Center scientists are involved in dynamic and important U.S. government projects, including the Galileo probe of Jupiter and the planned Space Station Freedom. Photo by John Elk III

FACING PAGE: Scientists at the NASA Ames Research Center need the most advanced equipment for their projects, such as this wind tunnel and evacuation sphere. Photo by John Elk III

from 78 to 55.5 percent. After the rate cut was announced, Stanford said it would cause a $76-million shortfall in the school's 1991-92 and 1992-93 budgets. Future relations between Stanford and the government will indeed require careful attention.

Fortune 500 firms and the United States and foreign governments are customers of SRI International, formerly Stanford Research Institute, an independent firm originally affiliated with the university.

Aerospace exploration has long been a mainstay of Silicon Valley research. NASA Ames Research Center and Lockheed Missiles and Space Company have made history with their technological developments in the aircraft and space industries.

Research and development—the lifeblood of Silicon Valley industry—is taken to the next steps of application, product development, testing, and eventually marketing by a support system of trained personnel. Santa Clara County's three universities and seven community colleges provide the education and training for these professionals. Local educational institutions work closely with Silicon Valley companies to ensure that graduates' skills match the specifications of industry. At the same time, industry is opening its doors to education in new ways, realizing that the bond between the classroom and the high-tech cubicle must be strengthened in order to keep pace with rapid technological change.

The community of technical scholars that Terman dreamed about decades ago has reached beyond the boundaries of the Stanford lands and encompasses all of Silicon Valley.

Some research projects look deceptively like everyday commercial aircraft. This helicopter at the NASA Ames Research Center is a research aircraft. Photo by John Elk III

DANGER
CONFINED SPACE

TEST ATMOSPHERE
BEFORE ENTRY

The arches and red tile roofs define the grounds of Stanford University in Palo Alto, one of the nation's leading private institutions of higher learning. Stanford is often called the "Harvard of the West." The school has eight Nobel Prize winners on its faculty. Photo by Tim Davis

■ *On The Farm*

A year after their son died of typhoid fever in 1884, Senator Stanford and his wife Jane founded the Leland Stanford Junior University in his memory. A leader in business as well as politics, Senator Stanford was one of the "Big Four" captains of industry who built the Western link of the first transcontinental railroad. He and his wife kept a rambling Palo Alto country estate, which also served as a horse farm. Stanford decided to situate the university on his country property, prompting its affectionate title— "The Farm."

Conceived as a West Coast alternative to what Senator Stanford believed to be inferior Eastern schools, Stanford University's mission was to teach practical courses for personal success and, at the same time, give the student a well-rounded education. Senator Stanford believed that a person would excel in business by being able to think creatively. A liberal arts education, combined with technical knowledge, prepared a person not only for business, but also for the world at large. "A man will never construct anything he cannot conceive," Stanford wrote.

Modern-day Stanford students have adhered to its founding principles. Personal success is a strong student ethic. The most popular undergraduate major is economics; the immediate goal, acceptance at Stanford's prestigious graduate school of business or one of the other elite graduate business schools in the nation.

Stanford's engineering school, one of the top ranked in America, is a draw for foreign students, 70 percent of whom are graduate students.

The university's preeminent position in research gives students in technology and science-related fields the luxury of being taught by, and working with, some of the world's top intellectuals. Stanford's faculty includes 8 Nobel Prize, 9 MacArthur Foundation, and 16 National Medal of Science award winners.

Representative of Stanford's stellar faculty is Dr. Stanley Cohen who created the biotechnology industry with his gene-splicing research. Cohen performed his work on campus, giving Stanford licensing rights to the technology. For Cohen's work and other inventions, Stanford earns close to $10 million annually in licensing revenue from companies.

At Stanford the Dr. Cohens of tomorrow are studying artificial intelligence, materials and earth sciences, and biology.

Stanford University remains true to the philosophy of its founder: it prepares

young men and women for personal success by giving them the best possible technical education, presented with a humanitarian perspective. Many life-saving and life-giving technologies have originated on "The Farm."

■ *Downtown University*

An unseen link threads through the many corridors of Silicon Valley firms. In a diverse, competitive business environment, technology workers often find they do have one thing in common: San Jose State University.

During its history the university has produced close to a quarter-million graduates, 80 percent of whom enter the San Jose-San Francisco job market. As a result San Jose State University is inextricably linked to the history of virtually every major Silicon Valley employer.

The oldest publicly funded institution of higher education in California, it was first known as the California State Normal School when it was founded in 1857 in San Francisco. In 1871 the campus moved to San Jose. It became San Jose State Teachers College in 1921. A half-century later it achieved university status, and in 1974 it was renamed San Jose State University (SJSU).

SJSU's original mission was teacher training. However, as the Santa Clara Valley changed from an agricultural society to a technology-based culture, the university changed along with it. Its curricula now reflects modern technological society. Majors offered in the schools of business, applied arts and sciences, engineering, and science total 57 percent of SJSU's enrollment.

As it looks ahead to the emerging Silicon Valley of the twenty-first century,

Graduation ceremonies at Stanford Stadium celebrate the achievements of some of the county's leading scholars. Seventy percent of Stanford students undertake graduate work. Photo by Gerald L. French/The Photo File

ABOVE AND FACING PAGE: San Jose State University is the oldest public institution of higher learning in California. Part of the California State University system, it has some 30,000 students. Eighty percent of SJSU graduates find employment in the Bay Area. Photos by Gerald L. French/The Photo File

SJSU is planning to meet the twin challenges of a rapidly changing technology world and the limitations of its physical campus. Located on the periphery of San Jose's downtown business and cultural districts, SJSU is at full capacity with a record-setting 30,000 students. University officials are discussing plans to build a new humanities and arts tower, a twin to the existing business tower. High-density construction offers one logical solution for the landlocked campus.

In 1988 SJSU opened the $47-million expanded School of Engineering facilities, adding a half-million square feet of space for classrooms, laboratories, and faculty offices. Silicon Valley companies and individuals contributed 40 percent of the funds for the engineering project. Mindful of the continuing need for qualified local personnel, high-tech firms basically invested in their own future by supporting SJSU.

According to Jay Pinson, dean of the School of Engineering, the expansion will allow undergraduate enrollment to increase by 50 percent and graduate enrollment to double. California schools are able to supply only half of the number of engineers needed for California industry, Pinson says, so expanding enrollment at SJSU and other engineering schools is an important objective.

Business' role in making the engineering expansion a success is encouraging, Pinson says, because "the survival of Silicon Valley is going to be related directly to the availability of a skilled work force, and the basic ingredient of that is education."

Pinson is an impassioned advocate of creating new partnerships between industry, education, and government. From Pinson's perspective the common goal these entities share is the desire to fight the erosion of America's standing in the global marketplace.

Pinson believes that deficiencies in the educational system have directly led to America's declining global market share in semiconductors. Japan, Korea, and Taiwan have a better educated work force in the areas of applied research, design, development, and manufacturing of semiconductors, he notes.

Pinson is determined to infuse Silicon Valley's semiconductor industry with new energy. His vitamin is the Applied Technology Institute for Microelectronics, which opened at SJSU May 1, 1990. With an initial five-year budget of $35 million, the institute serves as another example of partnerships at work. Private industry is expected to contribute half of the funds, with the remainder coming from the state and federal governments, the California State University system, SJSU, and community colleges.

The institute provides education, training, and technology transfer programs to support the semiconductor industry, the end result being improved microelectronic products and a skilled work force.

Silicon Valley's semiconductor industry must redirect its focus to applied research and to commercially viable products in order to survive, Pinson says. He

has a $35-million stake in seeing that the institute not only helps the semicon-
ductor industry develop new products but also that it supplies the talented pool
of workers necessary to bring the products to the marketplace.

With education the basic ingredient for the survival of Silicon Valley, it will
be educational leaders such as Dr. Pinson who supply the lifeline.

■ The Mission School

Today, students at Santa Clara University walk across campus lands that trace
the early history of California settlements. Santa Clara University's lineage dates
back to the eighteenth century, when 21 missions were established as the Spanish crown settled Alta California. Mission Santa Clara de Asis, the eighth
mission, was founded by Father Junípero Serra on January 12, 1777. For nearly
75 years Mission Santa Clara thrived as a religious and educational center for
Indians and settlers.

When California became a state in 1850 and the political force of the missions di-
minished, Mission Santa Clara came under the leadership of a Dominican bishop,
Joseph Alemany. In charge of the new diocese of California, Alemany was distressed
by the lack of educational institutions. His concern led him to discussions with two
Italian Jesuits—Michael Accolti and John Nobili—who had been exploring sites in
California for a Jesuit college. Alemany decided to offer Mission Santa Clara to the
Jesuits. On March 19, 1851, Santa Clara College opened as the first institution of
higher learning in California.

A fine Catholic private school from its beginning, Santa Clara College
attracted the sons of foreign consuls and many of California's pioneer families.
Founded on the nineteenth-century ideals of classical training, Santa Clara College offered scientific and commercial courses as well. In 1896 Santa Clara
hired a famous science faculty member—John J. Montgomery. Credited with
the first heavier-than-air flight in America (August 20, 1883), Montgomery
taught physics until 1911, when he was killed while testing one of his gliders.

For Santa Clara College 1912 marked a watershed year: it opened its schools
of engineering and law and became Santa Clara University. In the fall of 1961
the school reached another milestone when women were admitted, and it

became the first coeducational Catholic university in California.

Santa Clara University's rich history is still evident in its modern campus, which remains one of the most beautiful in the state. Its visual focal point is the Mission Santa Clara de Asis. Dedicated in 1928 the mission is an enlarged replica of the original building and includes some cover tiles dating back as early as 1790. Visitors to the campus will find many remnants of history, including the wooden cross in front of the mission, which is part of the original settlement.

Although steeped in history, Santa Clara University has been aggressive in modernizing its campus and expanding its facilities. During the 1980s the university's dynamic former president, William Rewak, S.J. (Society of Jesus), led a successful $56-million fund-raising campaign that financed the new Thomas Bannan Engineering Center and a $5-million addition to the Benson Student Center, among other projects.

Throughout its history Santa Clara University has adhered to its Jesuit ideals of preparing students to lead a humane life in the practical world after graduation. Santa Clara University asks that its students share a moral commitment to the world at large and to activate this commitment by serving others through various forms of leadership. It is no coincidence that the university has produced many business and political leaders in Santa Clara Valley. Thomas McEnery, who in 1990 finished the second of two terms as San Jose mayor, holds a master's degree in history from the university. Many community leaders, like McEnery, came to Santa Clara University from Bellarmine Preparatory School. Graduates from both schools are among those active in the business/political power structure in the county.

The Montgomery glider hangs from the ceiling of the San Jose International Airport as part of a historical presentation of aeronautical artifacts on display for airport visitors. Photo by Gerald L. French/The Photo File

In teaching moral values Santa Clara University has been fortunate to have among its professors such distinguished scholars as Theodore Mackin, a nationally recognized expert on the theology of marriage.

Balancing its adherence to Jesuit values with the need to offer students a practical education, Santa Clara University requires that all students receive a certain level of training in the humanities. For example in the School of Engineering, 25 percent of the curriculum covers the humanities and social studies.

In addition to following its historical principles, Santa Clara University realizes it has to serve the secular world of Silicon Valley. The university has instituted flexible graduate-level programs such as the "early bird" classes in the School of Engineering. Silicon Valley employees can take 7 a.m. classes and then go to work. It is a rousing success with companies, reports Dean Terry Shoup.

More than half of the School of Engineering's students do go on to graduate school, Shoup says. "They are recognizing that advanced degrees are necessary for success. With the increasing complexity of technology, there's more to learn."

In the School of Engineering the fastest-growing program is mechanical engineering, Shoup says, since "companies realize that mechanical engineering problems need to be solved in order to move technology forward." For example, Shoup notes, the race for higher-speed, higher-density chips creates a host of heat transfer problems.

Shoup, who was named dean in July 1989, plans on working closely with companies to continue the supportive working relationship between Santa Clara University and business. Technology firms are among those who contributed significantly to the engineering school renovation. The university also has its fair share of notable graduates, such as IBM president Jack Kuehler and Hewlett-Packard executive vice president Bill Terry, who support the school.

One of Shoup's long-term goals is to increase the research component of the school. As Silicon Valley looks for solutions to problems such as heat transfer, Shoup would like his faculty to be there with the answers.

■ Saplings Of Industry

Silicon Valley industry benefits from seven community colleges that offer both career-oriented training and leisure courses for workers who need some recreational respite.

DeAnza College in Cupertino and Mission College in Santa Clara are particularly focused on serving the technology industry. These colleges have the triple function of preparing students for four-year colleges, educating and training those already working in industry, and teaching contract courses to which many Silicon Valley firms subscribe.

Ranked as one of the top five community colleges in the nation, DeAnza College, a short distance from the corporate headquarters of Apple Computer and Tandem, serves as a blueprint for modern community colleges.

"Our students have bought into the idea of lifelong education," declares A. Robert DeHart, who has been president of the college since its founding in 1967.

One-quarter of DeAnza's 52,000 students served annually already have a degree, DeHart says. They come to DeAnza to add skills that will help in career advancement. An additional 5,000 students are taught every year on-site at

Using computers to design computer chips is one method of designing the future. Photo by Liane Enkelis

their place of employment as participants in DeAnza's contract instruction program. DeAnza earns one million dollars annually by instructing the employees of such companies as Hewlett-Packard and Intel.

To expand its technology curriculum DeAnza plans to build a $16-million, three-story building that will house programs in computers, engineering, science, math, and language arts.

DeAnza maintains its top ranking, DeHart believes, because the college practices its founding principles of "constant, purposeful innovation and improvement." There are no less than 45 task forces working on different aspects of the college. "We have no intention of standing still," DeHart says.

Serving the technology industry is just one aspect of DeAnza. As a full-service community college, it offers a long list of programs and courses outside the realm of business. "There's a lot of attention here to the job side of life, but there's a lot more to life than that," DeHart says. For pure pleasure DeAnza has the Flint Center performing arts complex, the California History Center, and the Minolta Planetarium.

On the other side of Silicon Valley, in the heart of the Santa Clara industrial sector, sits Mission College, the newest community college, founded in 1975. Technology firms intensively use the college as a resource. According to Betty M. Dean, former president of the college, 70 percent of its 12,000 enrolled students are currently employed in industry.

One of Mission's most important services is retraining workers for high-tech industry. "With such rapid changes in technology, employees find they need retraining to avoid being laid off," says Dean. "Since training isn't what industry does, they find it very cost-effective to use Mission College."

Mission College gets some interesting requests from industry. "We found a math teacher who was willing to teach the graveyard shift at a company. It wasn't easy finding someone to give a class at 2 a.m., but we did it," Dean recalls.

Although relatively new, Mission already operates beyond capacity. The single college building, which serves as an administration and classroom center, is one of seven phases in a master plan approved by the state community college chancellor. To complete the remaining six phases will cost $100 million, according to architect Theresa Yuen. Funding for a $3-million gymnasium has been identified. Next on the agenda will be completion of other athletic facilities. Due to Proposition 13, which cut property taxes, simultaneously cutting the revenues that flowed to schools, the master plan will have to be financed by a combination of governmental and private funding. Major projects in the plan include a new student center; library; math, engineering, and science building; auditorium and telecommunications center; and cultural and technical arts building.

Mission College and DeAnza College are joined by Foothill College, which also offers training on a contract basis and serves northern Santa Clara County; West Valley College in Saratoga; San Jose City College and Evergreen Valley College, which serve the densely populated San Jose metropolitan area; and Gavilan Community College in Gilroy, which serves southern Santa Clara County and neighboring San Benito County.

LEFT AND BELOW: Foothill College in Los Altos Hills is part of the vast California community college system that prepares students for four-year schools and provides continuing education to the work force of Santa Clara County. Photos by John Elk III

■ *Teaching With Technology*

It's a cruel irony that in the middle of Silicon Valley the average public school's use of computers as a learning tool remains so limited. Silicon Valley schools' inability to make full use of computers results from the same challenges facing schools across the nation: lack of funding to purchase both hardware and software, lack of easy access to computers for students, insufficient teacher training,

and lack of integration of the computer into all curricula.

For many schools the computer itself remains the teaching goal, although educational innovators agree that the computer should no longer be regarded as the end goal, but as a creative tool with which to learn virtually anything. Innovators also warn that unless students—the workers of tomorrow—become sophisticated computer users, they will not be able to economically survive in the knowledge-based industries of the twenty-first century. The ability to use computers to manipulate and process information, coupled with the ability to think independently and creatively, will be determining factors in whether or not the next generation of workers succeeds.

ABOVE: Large mainframe computers such as these are important for record keeping and data storage. Photo by Tom Tracy/The Photo File

FACING PAGE: The beautiful campus of Foothill College is tucked into the Los Altos Hills just off Highway 280, a major thoroughfare running north and south through the county. Photo by Gerald L. French/The Photo File

In Santa Clara County educational administrators realize that integration of technology in the classroom will not occur until teachers first possess a good degree of comfort with computers.

They recognize that the previous generation of teachers had already earned their educational credentials and were out practicing their profession when computers gained general acceptance. New teachers entering the profession now must have some level of computer literacy. But old and new teachers alike need training assistance in order to stay current with innovations such as laser disks and interactive video, which are used in multimedia presentations.

Silicon Valley teachers are able to get technology instruction through the Santa Clara County Office of Education's Educational Technology Consortium. Judy Powers, consortium director, decries the fact that district by district, schools in the county are very uneven in their use of technology. "The main thing holding us back is money and equipment," she says.

The consortium works to integrate technology in the instruction of language arts, math, science, history, and social science. Since computers are nonjudgmental and allow a student to repeat processes again and again, they give students the chance to learn at their own pace in a creative environment.

"If educators don't make the move to bring technology to the forefront of the curriculum, we're holding back the next generation of kids," Powers declares.

As an advocate Powers also participates in the California Technology Project funded by AB 1470. The five-county project, which includes Santa Clara and the central coast counties, supports legislation that funds technology in education; focuses on technology training for teachers; and promotes business and

industry tie-ins with technology-using educators.

The model for business-education partnerships is Apple Computer, whose corporate culture centers on educational innovation.

"Our desire to make a contribution to education is the single most passionate ethic in Apple," says David J. Barram, vice president of corporate affairs.

Apple Computer linked itself to education from its early days when it made history by donating an Apple to 10,000 California public and private schools. Apple's user-friendly interface and pleasing graphics made it a natural for students, who found they could intuitively learn how to use the computer. Teachers and students loved Apple from the very beginning. This early bonding has resulted in Apple's winning a 60-percent share of the educational market. There are now more than 2 million Apple II computers in elementary and secondary schools.

Apple's educational flavor is cultivated by the many former educators on its staff, says Sandra Bateman, K-12 education public relations manager. Bateman, who taught for 13 years, says, "Apple really works in partnership with education. We find ourselves in the middle of educational reform because our products enable people to do things they've never done before."

Since the educational system moves at a snail's pace compared to personal computer product development, Apple has by necessity taken the lead in advocating technology integration in the classroom and governmental funding of educational technology. "We make the case that technology is not a fad, that our kids will find very, very few jobs untouched by technology," says Bateman.

John Sculley, Apple's chairman and CEO, serves as chairman of the National Center for Education and the Economy (NCEE), a research center whose goal is to restructure the American classroom. The NCEE believes American students need a different education than the one they are currently receiving if they are to become globally competitive in industry as adults.

To encourage integration of technology in the classroom, Apple administers its Education Grants Program. The program, since its inception in 1979, has given millions of dollars to schools who use computers in innovative ways. Apple funds projects that take advantage of the computer's capabilities: interactive play, immediate feedback, graphics and information processing.

Apple also has put its staff educators to work in researching the role of computers in the classrooms of the twenty-first century. Its Apple Classroom of Tomorrow (ACOT) is a long-term research project that explores new learning environments for teachers and students, using interactive technologies.

ACOT classrooms have been created at public school sites across the nation. Apple equips the classrooms with a variety of computer-based technologies. Each of the classrooms is unique in its teaching style and educational focus. These "living laboratories" give Apple researchers the feedback they need and enable the researchers to translate their findings into suggested new curricula,

Youngsters are never too young to start experimenting with computers. Here kindergartners are introduced to some of the computer's limitless possibilities. Photo by Renee Lynn

learning tools, and environments. These innovations are then tested in ACOT classrooms; the cycle of study and innovation repeats itself.

In Apple's hometown of Cupertino the Stevens Creek Elementary School has an ACOT classroom. There, teachers work with second and third graders on learning keyboarding and word-processing skills. The school also uses software to prepare children for independent problem solving.

Following Apple's lead, other major computer companies are now creating educational alliances. IBM, for example, has donated $20 million of equipment to the California State University system. Given its scarcity of funding and the lag time in accepting technology, the American educational system needs all the help it can get from industry.

Young Explorers

As an alternative to the simulated world of computers, the Youth Science Institute (YSI) offers Silicon Valley kids a hands-on, analog exploration of nature.

Kids can stare at a snake, pet a rabbit, or view a live tarantula as part of YSI's animal loan program to schools.

Face-to-face interaction with nature occurs at YSI's three Discovery Centers—at Sanborn-Skyline County Park in Saratoga, Vasona County Park in Los Gatos, and Alum Rock in the east foothills of San Jose. YSI's "get wet" activities at Sanborn-Skyline and Vasona give kids a chance to identify the animals living in the valley's creeks and ponds. At Alum Rock kids can visit the live animal room, which houses more than 50 species of native birds, mammals, reptiles, and amphibians.

Founded in 1953 by the Junior League and the National Science Foundation for Youth, YSI is a nonprofit organization that has educated more than 50,000 Santa Clara Valley students during its history.

YSI hosted previous earth dwellers in 1990 when it brought a Tyrannosaurus rex, a baby Stegosaurus, and 15 other dinosaur models to San Jose in the Dinamation exhibit. The institute converted a 29,000-square-foot building to show the exhibit which featured robot-driven models. As the dinosaurs—some of which were full-size—moved and roared, Silicon Valley kids enjoyed an exciting glimpse of what life was like on earth eons ago.

The Knowledge Givers

Silicon Valley's brain trust, nourished by an above-average educational system and charged with the task of creating technologies for the future, requires access to trillions of bits of information each day. One important information source, for students and entrepreneurs alike, is the library.

The Santa Clara County library system, municipal libraries, and specialty libraries—such as the Silicon Valley Information Center (SVIC) and the Patent Information Clearinghouse in Sunnyvale—give the brain trust the luxury of easily accessible information on demand. Usually the information is free, one of the few exceptions being charges for special, complex data-base searches.

Technology is both the object of information searches and the facilitator for change in the valley's libraries. "We now have a CDROM (Compact Disk Read Only Memory) catalog listing the collections of all public libraries in the county with the exception of San Jose," Santa Clara County librarian Susan Fuller says proudly.

From her office in an industrial section of San Jose—the rent's inexpensive, she says—Fuller oversees the county's libraries, located in nine cities. The system also serves the unincorporated areas of the county. There is no "central" library in the system. "We see each library as an entry point from which you can get anything you want," explains Fuller. With the South Bay Cooperative Library System, which links county and municipal libraries by computer, a resident of Cupertino can walk into the Palo Alto City Library and find out whether or not a book is available at the Cupertino branch. If it isn't, the book can be transferred for loan on request. With a yearly circulation of 3 million in the county library system alone, streamlining operations by computer becomes vital to efficient service.

To answer the more than 300,000 reference questions each year, each of the nine county-run libraries has reference staff. For questions that can't be answered at the local level, the staff makes use of the cooperative system. Sometimes it takes an old-fashioned letter. "We've even written to Paris," says Fuller.

For business researchers the county library houses 900 periodicals. "Things are changing so fast that books are rarely up to date on technology," Fuller says. The county system also provides specialized reference materials such as the Overseas Business Reports and offers on-line search capability for a number of database services.

Libraries are an essential part of business development, Fuller believes. "They create a climate of inquiry and curiosity in a community. Business is, after all, the implementation of someone's ideas," she says.

"And for kids, I like to think of [libraries] as choice factories, where the next Steve Wozniak or Dave Packard can explore without limits," says Fuller.

Kids and adults curious about the origins of Apple, Hewlett-Packard, and other Silicon Valley corporate giants often visit the Silicon Valley

This sculpture stands—or sits—as a tribute to learning as it encourages reading in front of the Sunnyvale Library. Photo by Joseph Sohm/Chromosohm

Information Center (SVIC), housed in San Jose's Dr. Martin Luther King Jr. Main Library.

Opened to the public in 1986, the SVIC—exclusively a reference facility— was created because "there was an increasing number of requests about companies located here," recalls Wynne Dobyns, senior librarian. "We realized the information was in corporate libraries which the public didn't have access to."

History enthusiasts can scan the corporate archives, which contain documents donated by more than 600 technology firms and organizations. SVIC has a complete collection of Hewlett-Packard's *HP Journal,* dating back to 1949.

Realia aficionados will enjoy SVIC's historical collection of original technology company posters, T-shirts, coffee mugs, logos, decals, and just about anything else Silicon Valley marketers have dreamed up.

Job seekers and researchers make extensive use of SVIC's collection of company annual reports and of the staggering 23,000 clippings of newspaper articles the center has accumulated. These clips are referenced in an on-line bibliography that also catalogs SVIC's books and periodicials. Customers with the appropriate modem and communications software can dial up SVIC's on-line catalog.

About a quarter of SVIC's reference requests come from other parts of America and from around the world. "No one else is collecting the scope of information that we are on Silicon Valley," Dobyns asserts.

After a would-be entrepreneur learns the history of Silicon Valley companies at SVIC, the next stop might be the Patent Information Clearinghouse in Sunnyvale to find out if an idea for a product is truly unique.

"Most of our customers are individual inventors searching for product patents. We get a lot of start-ups," says Sandra Duncan, supervising librarian of the Clearinghouse. Large, established companies use their own corporate libraries and patent attorneys to do searches. The Clearinghouse also has an account list of more than 900 customers who pay for patent copies on demand.

A division of the City of Sunnyvale public library, the Clearinghouse is one of only four patent depository libraries in the state of California and the only one in the San Francisco Bay Area. In the unassuming quarters of a converted elementary school sits a fascinating collection of inventions that date back to 1790, when the first patent was issued (for potash). American ingenuity seems to be thriving since new patents from the U.S. commissioner of patents and trademarks come into the Clearinghouse at an average rate of 2,000 per week.

Before applying for a patent an entrepreneur has to perform due diligence and research prior patents. Many patent applications are rejected each year because they are duplicates. "Once something is patented it can never be patented again," explains Duncan.

Performing a patent search is an intricate task. Most thorough searches take several days, but Silicon Valley patent searches have been known to run as long as a thousand hours.

To facilitate searches the Clearinghouse introduced a "CASSIS" /CDROM catalog in 1989. CASSIS (Classification and Search Support Information System) contains patent abstracts for the years 1969 to the present. Patents from the years 1790-1969 are available on microfilm; the Clearinghouse also plans to add post-1970 years to microfilm. Eventually the Clearinghouse will be a paperless reference center. It is quickly running out of room to store the original paper patents.

Technology entrepreneurs comprise only one type of Clearinghouse customer. Horticulturists who aspire to invent a new rose scrutinize the color pictures of plant patents, and furniture designers research the many design patents in their category. Sarah Winchester—whose San Jose home, the Winchester Mystery House, still baffles tourists with its bizarre construction—holds several patents for her rather unique design approach.

Business researchers are also served by Sunnyvale's main public library, which houses a much-used small business reference section. Laura Nakamishi, business reference librarian, helps entrepreneurs find information on California law and directs them to the library's substantial collection of literature on importing and exporting. With trade increasing between Taiwan and the Unit-

The attractive climate of the Santa Clara Valley provides ample opportunity for students to make the most of the good weather as they pursue the challenges of their academic programs. Photo by Joseph Sohm/Chromosohm

ed States, Nakamishi finds that people in Taiwan will often write to a business associate in Silicon Valley and ask them to visit a library to conduct research for them.

Sunnyvale's extensive library resources are a natural response to the technology community in which the city has played a part for half a century. Since 1955, when Lockheed opened a new missiles and space division in the city, Sunnyvale has been firmly implanted in the technology world.

Tomorrow's explorers are welcome in Sunnyvale. "You can be anybody and walk into our library and get any information you need whether you're a new immigrant or the president of Lockheed . . . What we're about is taking opportunities and supporting innovation," says library director Beverley Simmons.

Sunnyvale, Santa Clara County, and specialty libraries provide the knowledge that Silicon Valley's creative intellect requires.

■ *Beyond The Envelope*

Two decades after man first walked on the moon, Americans continue to demonstrate their interest in space exploration, aware of its potential to help save the Earth's environment.

As record-level pollution ravages the world, the importance of space research increases. Space provides a seamless laboratory in which to monitor such phenomena as ozone depletion and to test the effects of various environmental conditions on plants and animals.

In 1989, to mark the twentieth anniversary of the Apollo moon landing, President George Bush committed America to a revitalized space program. Bush proposed a three-phase plan: a manned Space Station Freedom—to be launched during the mid-1990s as a preamble to the second phase, a permanent lunar settlement to be established during the twenty-first century, and last, a manned mission to Mars. During his speech Bush referred to space exploration's potential to help solve environmental problems such as global warming.

Silicon Valley has two institutions that are an integral part of America's invigorated space initiative: NASA Ames Research Center and Lockheed Missiles & Space Company. NASA Ames made space exploration history when Pioneer 11 carried out man's first trip to Saturn, in September 1979. Lockheed made history again in April 1990 when its Hubble Space Telescope, a NASA project, was placed in orbit by the space shuttle Discovery, giving astronomers their first observatory in space.

In 1995 NASA Ames' Galileo Probe is expected to make the first entry into the atmosphere of an outer planet—Jupiter. The Probe, launched in 1989, will fly down 400 miles into Jupiter's atmosphere. Its measurements of such mysteries as Jupiter's hurricane winds will produce new data that may give American scientists more information about the origin of the solar system and of the universe.

Before man can make a permanent home in a space station or on the moon, scientists must be able to construct a life-sustaining environment. NASA launched Spacelab Life Science-1 (SLS-1) in 1990 to conduct a nine-day battery of tests on how the human body reacts to space flight. SLS-1 is the first in a series of missions to prepare man for lengthy stays in space. NASA Ames acts as the lead research-agency on the nonhuman life-science experiments aboard SLS-1. The experiments include a study of the metamorphosis of jellyfish in space and a study on how rats, serving as surrogates for humans, react to potentially harmful physiological changes.

Since space suits will be a necessity for the microgravity climate aboard Space Station Freedom, NASA Ames is refining a version of its AX-5 model, a hard spacesuit that offers more protection than the soft suits used by space shuttle astronauts.

For Americans, whose tax dollars fund space programs, the payoff will come in new knowledge about the human body, the global environment, and materials. Aboard SLS-1, experiments may help scientists with new information on the causes of cardiovascular disorders or bone diseases. Space Station Freedom will study natural phenomena, such as solar radiation and tropical rainfall, that affect the earth's environment and climate. The space station's experiments in fabricating large, defect-free crystals, such as gallium arsenide, will directly impact Silicon Valley's high-tech industry.

While NASA readies Space Station Freedom, Lockheed's Hubble Space Telescope is providing scientists with unparalleled data, of use to them in their

This artist's conception accurately depicts Pioneer 10's view of the solar system and the center of the Milky Way. Courtesy, National Aeronautics and Space Administration

preparations. The Hubble, orbiting 593 kilometers above Earth, gives astronomers their first look at the universe without the distortion of the Earth's atmosphere. Its 2.4-meter primary mirror, developed by Hughes Danbury Optical Systems (formerly Perkin-Elmer), is the finest ever created. Lockheed designed and built the Support Systems Module that points and controls the 25,500-pound telescope in space.

The Hubble was launched by the Space Shuttle Discovery in April 1990 and sent back its first series of images on May 20, 1990. It carries five scientific instruments that are replaceable during its anticipated 15-year operating life.

Some of the most stunning visual images are coming from the Wide Field/Planetary Camera, which views galaxies and star fields. Another instrument, the European Space Agency's Faint Object Camera, has taken the clearest pictures ever of Pluto, the most distant object in our solar system.

Since the Hubble was launched there have been some technical problems, including a spherical aberration in the primary mirror. By using computer enhancement, scientists have been able to correct for the lessened focus as a result of the mirror flaw. However, Hubble's images continue to be better than the best images produced by ground-based telescopes on a clear night.

In 1993 a repair mission will take place. Scientists plan to correct for the spherical aberration by modifying the telescope's replacement instruments.

As man reaches beyond the envelope, Silicon Valley—with NASA Ames and Lockheed as two major contributors—will supply the technological tools to make it possible.

◼ *Research For The World*

In the late 1940s Stanford University's brain trust created Stanford Research Institute. No longer affiliated with the university, SRI International, as it is now known, operates as a private research and consulting firm that does business in excess of $330 million annually and employs 3,500 personnel at its Menlo Park headquarters and branches in the United States, Europe, the Middle East, and Africa.

SRI's client list consists of the U.S. and foreign governments and *Fortune* 500 firms. As the business world evolves into one global market, companies that want inside advice on how to trade overseas often retain SRI. The firm has a long-standing presence in Japan and frequently advises Western multinational organizations on the feasibility of doing business in the country.

From a better bar-code reader for the U.S. Post Office to a new 3-D image-processing technology that can be used in simulating head surgery, SRI researchers find useful applications for newfound technologies.

One of SRI's major accomplishments occurred in 1989 with the start of clinical trials for 10-EDAM, a promising new compound for treating inoperable tumors. SRI developed 10-EDAM with Memorial Sloan-Kettering Cancer Center in New York. Clinical trials are being conducted at Sloan-Kettering and at 20 other centers in the United States and Canada.

Research at SRI is generally organized into the physical and life sciences, engineering, manufacturing, and materials. On the consultant side of the business, SRI operates an international business division and a policy group, which, among other projects, surveys the changing educational system in America.

◼ *The Human Scale*

Medical history books of the twenty-first century will no doubt contain the name of Dr. J. William Langston, who in 1984 uncovered a new link between a toxin that kills brain cells and Parkinson's disease. Langston's discovery gave Parkinson's sufferers new hope for slowing down progression of the disease.

Langston, who at the time was chief of neurology at Santa Clara Valley Medical Center, now devotes himself full-time to Parkinson's research as president of the California Parkinson's Foundation, based in San Jose.

Research breakthroughs continue under the direction of Dr. Langston. In August 1989 he and his associate, Dr. James W. Tetrud, announced that a three-year clinical study of Parkinson's patients who had taken the drug deprenyl showed that deprenyl significantly slowed the disease's progression.

The first breakthrough in the treatment of Parkinson's occurred after Dr. Langston examined a young heroin addict who appeared to have all the symptoms of Parkinson's. Langston learned that the addict had used synthetic heroin, a "designer drug" that contained the compound MPTP. Langston and his colleagues then began a study of heroin addicts, which culminated in the 1984 announcement that a version of MPTP toxins apparently caused Parkinson's and that chemicals might be found to block the disease.

As for a cure Langston says his long-range goal "is to put [himself] out of business." The fact that deprenyl slowed progression of Parkinson's marks a major triumph in the fight against the disease. The treatment of other neurodegenerative diseases, such as Alzheimer's and Lou Gehrig's disease, may also benefit from Langston's research.

■ *Fertile Ground*

In Silicon Valley the dream that Frederick Terman had at Stanford University decades ago still flourishes. Educators and industry work and live in a symbiotic environment that supports innovation. Research and development breeds products that in turn breed success. Technology firms grow and spin off new ones. Silicon Valley has become a self-perpetuating phenomenon.

The laser's capabilities and promise in the field of medicine are becoming more evident as research is continued in hospitals and laboratories. Photo by Tom Tracy/The Photo File

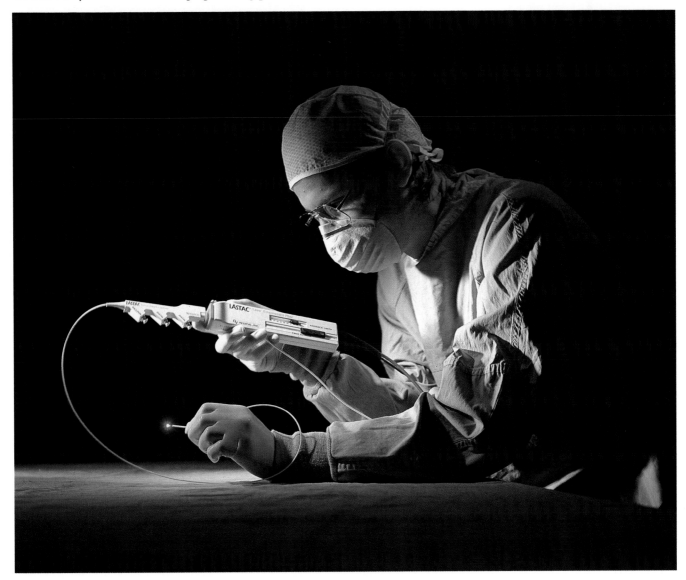

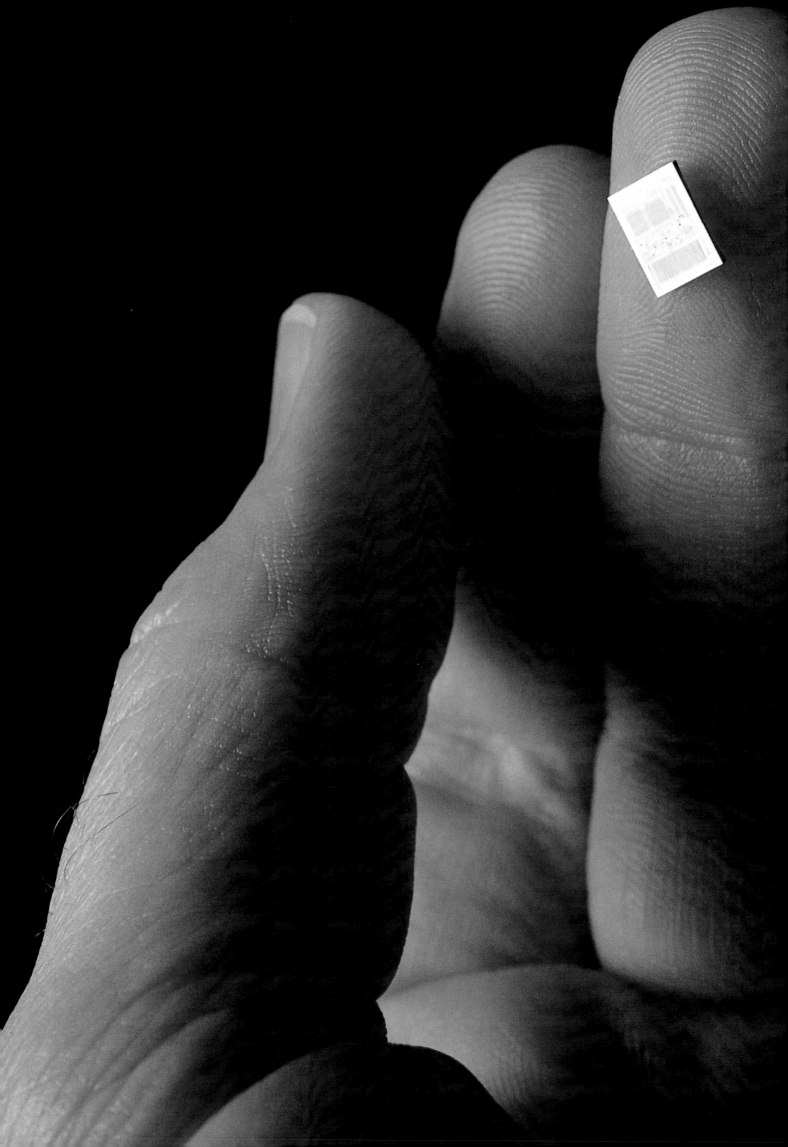

Taking Risks

■ Scenario: The Year 2020

I t is 8 a.m. on a Monday morning in Los Gatos, California. Jay Allen has just poured his second cup of coffee and sat down in front of his computer. Since Jay is a "telecommuter" —one of more than 30 million Americans who work at home or at nearby satellite offices—starting his workday means walking a few steps to his home office and switching on his computer.

A market analyst for a major workstation manufacturer, Jay contributes a high level of energy to his work since he escapes the dehumanizing grind of California freeway gridlock.

After logging on and reading his corporate electronic mail, Jay presses the screen icon for "news." The computer—using artificial intelligence—has already scanned all major network and cable broadcasts in the last 24 hours, as well as the morning editions of the *San Jose Mercury News,* the *Wall Street Journal* and *New York Times.* All items of particular interest to Allen have been sent to the "news" menu. He scans the list and selects a Cable News Network segment about a workstation competitor. Using a video disk and interactive software, he watches the segment on his computer screen, then asks the computer to display a transcript of the segment.

Allen sends the transcript into a "newsfile" directory he has created and then sends the transcript, via electronic mail, to one of his analyst colleagues in his corporation's Tokyo office.

One common goal of the computer industry is to make it small, as indicated by this tiny chip. Photo by Tom Tracy/The Photo File

Sitting in front of his computer screen for about a half hour, Allen has saved at least one hour of freeway driving time, seven to eight hours of television watching and newspaper reading, and about a half hour of computer-inputting time.

The computer has served as an *implement,* a basic tool of Allen's work; as *media* through which to receive and send information; and as a *knowledge* source, functioning as Allen's external brain.

With so much efficiency Allen should be able to take

off afternoons to play golf or to work in his organic garden. But the world of 2020 overflows with information, and every second freed by quicker computer processes is immediately consumed by the demands of more information generated and waiting to be massaged or manipulated in some fashion.

While Allen is scanning his newsfiles, his colleagues in Boston are preparing to electronically send him the latest Yankee Group analysts' report on the workstation market; his corporate headquarters in Menlo Park is completing its second-quarter sales report, which will be sent to him; and *Business Week*'s San Francisco bureau has just messaged him by public electronic mail, asking him for a comment on a workstation report by Japan's MITI (Ministry of International Trade and Industry).

The computers coming out of the valley no longer just store information. Today they design systems, facilitate intercontinental communications, and create art and music. Photo by Tom Tracy/The Photo File

Allen is the future, a knowledge processor whose main function is receiving and giving information. He represents an expanding stratum in the global economy of the twenty-first century. As robots assume many manufacturing functions, people—aided by computers—will do the one thing they do best: think.

The marriage of the internal human brain and the external brain of the computer will reach a new level of comfort. By the year 2020 two generations of Americans will have spent their entire lives before computers; computers will be an extension of people. A twenty-first-century person will spend time wondering what role the computer can next play in life. The focus will be on what new things the computer can do, on new applications.

Making one computer talk to another through a networking system is one of the key challenges developers face. The result is that workstations can communicate like the two shown here. Photo by Renee Lynn

For better or worse the computer has permeated most facets of a person's life. That penetration will deepen in the twenty-first century. Products will come and go; the computer is here to stay. It will serve as an implement, or tool, as another form of media, and as knowledge. In some ways the computer will seem almost transparent, but it has changed, and will continue to change, the nature of society, of how people work and live.

Silicon Valley: The Dream Lives On

Xanadu. Valhalla. Heaven. Man has many abstractions of beauty and wonderment. In the concrete business world man has created the abstraction known as Silicon Valley, the birthplace of the world's technology market.

Journalist Don C. Hoefler is credited with first using the phrase in print, to honor the substance from which semiconductors are made. In the two decades since Hoefler introduced the phrase, Silicon Valley has come to signify many things to many people. Discussions about what Silicon Valley means can be satisfying and endless. In reality everyone is probably a little bit right. For Silicon Valley is both a geographic collection of businesses with a common goal— growing the technology market—and an abstraction of the eternal American belief that hard work can breed untold riches and success.

And the dream lives on even though Silicon Valley has shed the headiness of youth and matured into a more conservative, cautious culture.

"There continues to be interesting opportunities for young entrepreneurs," says Burt McMurtry, general partner of Technology Venture Investors. One of the deans of Silicon Valley venture capitalism, McMurtry has been giving seed money to companies since 1969. ROLM, Microsoft, Triad Systems, KLA Instruments, Sun Microsystems, and Adaptec comprise just a handful of McMurtry's many investments.

ABOVE: One of the most innovative thinkers working in the computer industry is Bill Gates, head of Microsoft. Photo by Renee Lynn

RIGHT: Business conferences, consultant roundtables, and departmental coaching sessions are part of the everyday commercial tradition in this high-tech environment. The Santa Clara Valley work force has a strong commitment to training and education beyond the normal workday. Photo by Kim Frazier/The Photo File

In Silicon Valley's traditionally quirky style, Microsoft was funded after an unusual meeting between McMurtry's partner, Dave Marquardt, and Microsoft founder Bill Gates. "They couldn't get their calendars together so finally they decided to meet at a University of Washington football game. Neither watched any of the game, but they had a great meeting," McMurtry recalls.

Technology Venture Investors' initial 1981 investment of one million dollars in Microsoft, based in Redmond, Washington, has since earned the partners $250 million.

The potential for big successes such as Microsoft still exists. "It's a remarkable situation," observes McMurtry. "Computing has become so widespread that the markets being addressed now by electronic technology companies are huge markets."

"It used to be that a $50- to $100-million company was a major home run," McMurtry adds. "Now we have Sun Microsystems, which is a $2-billion company, or a one-billion-dollar Microsoft."

Innovation, the genetic essence of Silicon Valley, still thrives, according to Paul Ely, a general partner in Alpha Partners. "We get 20 qualified ideas each month. The difference now is not in the number of good ideas or good entrepreneurs but the fact there are far more venture capitalists scrambling to invest their money," Ely declares.

Ely personifies Silicon Valley's executive stratosphere. At 57 he says he has "the perspective of a relative newcomer" in the venture-capital business. But he already has a long industry track record as a former CEO of Convergent, bringing the company back from the brink of bankruptcy, and as a former director and executive vice president of Hewlett-Packard, where he increased its computer division revenues from $100 million to $3 billion. And Ely admits he actually has always dabbled in venture capitalism. During the more than 20 years he spent at Hewlett-Packard, Ely served on the board of Page Mill Partners, co-investing with Jack Melchor, whom Ely calls "the grand old dad of the investment industry," in companies such as Triad, ROLM, and Software Publishing.

Like several other venture-capital firms, Alpha Partners is located in the cluster of offices along Sand Hill Road in Menlo Park. But Ely chooses to maintain a small office suite above an antique shop in Menlo Park, communicating with the main office by fax machine.

"I think the future is rosy for Silicon Valley," Ely says, noting that the valley has a strong infrastructure of companies that support technology growth. "We have a wide-ranging group of professional entrepreneurs collected in one place. It's incredible the advantages it gives and the momentum it creates," he says. Software developers, plastics fabricators, engineering design consultants, VLSI (very large scale integration) chip manufacturers, and marketing firms are examples Ely gives of the valley's support network.

The dream of Silicon Valley lives on. McMurtry and Ely represent the venture capitalists' communal desire to fund innovation, thereby seeding the twenty-first-century generation of technology firms. Ely's Alpha Partners invests exclusively in Silicon Valley-based companies. "We find no shortage of opportunities here," notes Ely. "There are more good ideas than ever."

The Chess Game

On June 4, 1990, during his United States summit tour, President Mikhail Gorbachev of the now-defunct Soviet Union visited Stanford University. The center of Silicon Valley's brain trust, Stanford was the perfect spot for a visit. Gorbachev made a dramatic gesture that he understood the importance of technology in the world and, further, that he understood Silicon Valley's contribution. As Cold War relations between the Soviet Union and the United States continued to thaw, and as Eastern Europeans hungrily eyed American computer products, Silicon Valley once again took a bow.

Paul Ely is a Silicon Valley veteran. Formerly the director of a major division of Hewlett-Packard and chief executive officer of Convergent, he is now a venture capitalist. Photo by Liane Enkelis

During his Bay Area visit Gorbachev agreed to meet with South Korean president Roh Tae Woo. The invitation by Roh, whose ultimate objective is the re-unification of South and North Korea, was a significant diplomatic overture to end the Cold War in Asia. Roh cited economic cooperation with the Soviet Union as a key reason in South Korea's desire to meet with the Soviet president.

The Gorbachev visit is another indication that trade is no longer the byprod-uct of international relations, but the driving force. Eastern Europeans want the personal computers that Silicon Valley first marketed less than two decades ago. South Koreans are already thriving in the technology business and see the Sovi-et Union as a lucrative new market.

Since the early 1960s when Fairchild Semiconductor produced the world's first integrated circuits—invented by Robert Noyce, one of Fairchild's founders (and later Intel's)—the technology world has reached far beyond Silicon Valley to become an intrinsic part of many nations' economies.

Silicon Valley, once sole ruler of the computer world it invented, is now just one of many players on a global technology chessboard. The United States, with a head start advantage and an electronics industry that has grown to $200 billion annually, is now in imminent danger of dropping to second or third place in world market share, according to a 1990 report issued by the U.S. De-partment of Commerce. Japan is quickly closing in the race for first place, and South Korea is growing in importance, the report reveals.

The message is that business now functions in a truly global economy and this economy is the most complex in modern history. Doing business is now far more difficult, far more complicated, and far more competitive. Rather than just worrying about a few competitors down the block, an American company has to compete with firms all over the world and has to learn how to conduct business effectively in many nations.

"No one country will come out on top as the United States did in the post-World War II economy," predicts Tom Mandel, a futurist with SRI Internation-al. "The big question for Silicon Valley's future is," says Mandel, "How do you compete in a world in which many more people are playing the games we used to play exclusively?"

While Silicon Valley's "technical brilliance is still unmatched relative to world standards," the area has lagged far behind the Japanese in finance, marketing, design, and customer relations, asserts Richard Carlson, president of Spectrum Economics, a Mountain View economic-forecasting firm.

"The question is," says Carlson, "Can we move from purely technical leader-ship to these other areas? Right now, we're very one-dimensional."

Companies such as Hewlett-Packard are well positioned for the future, Carl-son believes. "HP is truly one of the greats. It is really good in technology, finance, and marketing," he says.

Alpha Partners' Ely believes America can still be a powerful player in the global marketplace. "I'm basically optimistic, but it's tenuous," says Ely, citing some improvement in product quality and cost performance as reasons for his optimism.

And on the global chessboard even the best of strategists can't always predict the king's move. "In 1980 the world economy was dismal. At HP we were told to pre-pare for inflation. Only three years later the whole outlook changed," Ely recalls.

If it's computer related, it's important to Santa Clara Valley. The design and development of disks and disk drives keep valley workers challenged as they attempt to store more information and retrieve it faster. Photo by John Lund/The Photo File

On The Edge

In the twenty-first century, global technology competition is certain to reach a historic pitch. Whether or not America can retain or gain market share will depend in part on public-policy actions taken during the 1990s. During the previous decade little was done in Washington to mitigate the competitve issues affecting the technology industry's ability to be a global player.

The most critical issue is the availability of capital. Compared to global competitors such as Japan, the U.S. is capital poor. Japan enjoys the benefits of an industrial policy that promotes cheap, available capital, and its government assists firms with funding. America's tax policies, however, are often adversarial to entrepreneurs.

Within Silicon Valley there is heated debate on whether or not the U.S. needs an industrial policy to aid technology industry. Those who favor a laissez-faire approach agree with President Bush, who has routinely opposed a formal industrial policy. Other Silicon Valley entrepreneurs and financiers argue in favor of some type of industrial policy.

"We don't need help. We need less 'help,' less meddling," declares Alpha

BELOW, RIGHT, AND FAR RIGHT: Three
of Santa Clara County's political lead-
ers are Representative Tom
Campbell of Stanford, below;
Congressman Don Edwards of San
Jose, right; and Congressman Norm
Mineta of San Jose, far right.

Partners' Ely, who is strongly against "protectionist measures for industries in trouble."

While an industrial policy "might be politically unattractive in the short-term, it will be beneficial in the long-term," asserts Peter Wallace, a principal in Hambrecht & Quist, one of the top investment-banking firms specializing in technology.

"No one wants to take the global responsibility of how to drive the economy," Wallace notes, observing that legislators, faced with ever-tightening federal budgets, find it politically difficult to divert money into such long-term, capital-intensive programs as research and development, and away from more immediate constituent needs.

Silicon Valley businesses that favor some form of an industrial policy look to Norm Mineta, San Jose's veteran Democratic congressman, and Tom Campbell, a Republican representative of Stanford. Both Mineta and Campbell are actively working to provide mechanisms that could free up capital for technology businesses and provide other support for key technologies.

In May 1991 the House Committee on Science, Space and Technology, of which Mineta is a senior member, approved Mineta's H.R. 1517, which would require the secretary of commerce to identify and study commercial industries critical to the U.S. economy. While the Bush administration has published a list of 22 key technologies, Mineta says the list is not supported by any commitment to study the economic impact of these technologies. Mineta's legislation would develop a 10-year plan to outline the public and private strategies needed to grow these critical industries. These strategies will include investment measures, work-force training, export policies, and tax and antitrust laws.

Mineta has also reintroduced his American Technology Preeminence Act, which failed to receive legislative support in 1990. The act was approved by the House Committee on Science, Space and Technology in May 1991 and will next be submitted to a House vote. One of the act's key provisions is a benefit for capital-poor technology firms. The provision will authorize the National Institute of Standards and Technology (NIST) to give long-term, low-cost loans to small- and medium-sized U.S. companies for the purpose of developing and commercializing advanced technologies.

Another important provision of the act is legislation cosponsored by Mineta and Don Edwards, a Democratic congressman of San Jose. Mineta and Edwards are proposing the removal of antitrust restrictions for companies that engage in joint manufacturing operations. This provision is an extension of Edwards and Mineta's successful removal of such restrictions for companies that share R & D expenses.

Another approach to a moderate form of industrial policy is being proposed by Campbell. He would have the National Academy of Engineering choose industries that would benefit from a special R & D tax imposed on consumers of their products. The monies raised would be earmarked for R & D and given to companies or institutions to be used for compatible research.

While Silicon Valley debates the merits of an industrial policy, there does appear to be consensus, however, on the need to make capital more available. The American Electronics Association, which represents 3,000 technology firms nationwide, is lobbying for public-policy reforms that will both increase the availability of capital and make it cheaper to get. The reforms would require a complex restructuring of policies to affect interest rates, increase the amount of American money dedicated to savings and investment, and establish tax incentives.

An important part of this tax reform, for many Silicon Valley entrepreneurs, is the revival of the capital gains tax reduction. Ed Zschau, a former Republican congressman who represented the northern portion of Silicon Valley, lobbied successfully for the reduction, which became law in 1978 and was rescinded during the Reagan administration. In 1990 an effort to revive the reduction became futile when President Bush, who had strongly favored it, let it become a political fatality during budget negotiations.

The failure of the capital gains tax cut to be reinstated was a disappointment for the valley's entrepreneurs. No doubt, the reduction will again be the focus of a political battle. In future fights of this nature, Silicon Valley is fortunate to have three astute representatives: long-term veterans Mineta and Edwards, and Campbell, a candidate for the U.S. Senate and a rising young political star.

In America, as the end of the twentieth century draws near, there are more manufacturing jobs in electronics than in all other major manufacturing industries combined. That means technology is no longer an esoteric occupation confined to Silicon Valley and a few other Silicon Gulches in the U.S. Technology now fuels America's manufacturing economy.

Public-policy changes will occur when Washington realizes technology workers *are* the new national constituency.

■ *Big Brother*

If "money is the mother's milk of politics," in the immortal words of the late California state treasurer Jesse Unruh, then federal defense spending is the baby food of Silicon Valley.

Much of the money that has poured into Silicon Valley R & D budgets has been defense motivated. Research institutions such as Stanford University have long relied on federal funds. Until the end of the Cold War, jobs directly related to defense accounted for about 10 percent of the valley's employment.

The end of the Cold War will impact R & D budgets, making it considerably tougher for Silicon Valley to obtain the money it needs for expensive, long-term science projects. As a result of the 1991 Persian Gulf War, some Silicon Valley defense contractors did gain additional business. However, the war did not appear to have an effect of the long-term prospects for R & D funding.

An omen for Silicon Valley is the changes in one of its earliest benefactors, the Defense Department's Advanced Research Projects Agency (DARPA). In October 1957, when the Soviets launched the Sputnik satellite, America was jolted out of its complacency and realized it could lose the space race. The federal government quickly mobilized, creating DARPA and expanding NASA from a small agency subdivision to a powerful new federal agency.

DARPA was the right agency at the right time in Silicon Valley. The technology industry was in its infancy. Hewlett-Packard and Varian were growing and the venture capitalists were starting to provide seed money for innovation. As all of this was happening, an anxious federal government poured research money into the valley.

The motivation for DARPA was the United States' desire to win the space race by developing superior defense-related technologies. But DARPA money has impacted far more than defense. Silicon Valley's basic computer research benefited greatly from the research funds that were made available. Historically many technologies originally developed for defense applications have made their way into civilian markets.

For years DARPA had a true commitment to innovation and was known for funding people, not projects. It put its faith in technology innovators. As the 1990s began, however, DARPA retained only a faint glimmer of its original self. The coup de grace may have been its decimating of the research budget for high-definition television (HDTV). HDTV and the flat-panel displays that will replace conventional television screens in the future constitute a potentially major new market with both consumer and military applications. The Japanese have gone into the HDTV and flat-panel display market with a vengeance. With the lack of support evidenced by the DARPA cutbacks, America will find it difficult to capture any share of the HDTV market.

The message is clear: without a real threat, such as the Russian Sputnik or a military situation that demands a new arms buildup, the federal government has cooled its commitment to research.

The opinion of many Silicon Valley businesses is that commercial research must become the responsibility of the private sector now to make up the deficit caused by defense retrenchment. But unless there are changes in federal monetary and tax policies, the private sector won't be able to afford committing large sums of capital to long-term research.

"One of the fallacies of the government is that it looks at big companies when deciding policy. It should target start-ups, the smaller companies where there's far more new technology and development. The smaller companies with a burning desire to succeed" are where the action is, says Peter Wallace of Hambrecht & Quist.

Federal cutbacks in R & D funding are "going to force businesses to think about R & D in innovative ways," predicts Tom Mandel of SRI International. "If they don't, we will fall even further behind" in global competition, he warns.

The winding down of the Cold War directly impacts jobs as Silicon Valley redirects a portion of its labor force from defense jobs to commercial endeavors.

Ed Feigenbaum, codirector of the Knowledge Systems Laboratory at Stanford University, has an optimistic view: "Thirty percent of our engineers have worked in defense. This hasn't helped us to grow competitive products. Now we will get back 30 percent of our talent."

■ *A Culture In Evolution*

Silicon Valley created the computer revolution in the twentieth century and for a time had virtually exclusive reign over its product manufacturing. As the twenty-first-century global technology economy takes shape, Silicon Valley's role in manufacturing will greatly diminish.

Several factors combined to spur a permanent exodus of electronics production from Silicon Valley, an exodus that reached a high pitch during the 1980s. Labor became prohibitively expensive, as did the commercial manufacturing space needed to house production facilities. Roseville, Folsom, and other more rural California sites became attractive places for major Silicon Valley firms to open new facilities. Labor and land were cheaper there. Offshore assembly, a factor in electronics production for decades, continued to be financially attractive.

From 1985 to 1990 semiconductor manufacturing—which gave Silicon Valley its very being—declined steadily as America's aggregate chip production continued to lose market share to other nations.

The fallout from the valley's diminished role in manufacturing could be significant. Is it enough that the valley remains a leader in technical innovation? There are few real leaders in American electronics outside of Silicon Valley. What place in

America will take up the slack left by the valley's economic change? Who will speak for the importance of manufacturing in our economy?

The twenty-first century will be a time when Silicon Valley further evolves from a manufacturing to a service-based technology economy. Of those jobs that are available in electronics manufacturing, a high degree of technical skill will be required. Basic production jobs will be located out of the area.

For the years 1987-1992, the California Employment Development Department (EDD) projects that 40 percent of new jobs will come from the service sector; 25 percent from electronics manufacturing; and the remaining 35 percent a mix of other manufacturing, wholesale and retail trade, government, finance, real estate, and construction.

In the twenty-first century, Silicon Valley industry will be dominated by knowledge processors: highly skilled and educated people who use the computer as a tool and knowledge source and who invent new ways of using technology. Compatible industries such as biotechnology, which in part relies on computer instrumentation, will forge new symbiotic relationships between the valley's computer brain trust and life scientists, creating new market opportunities.

Technology jobs with a rosy future, according to the EDD report, include electrical and electronic engineers, computer programmers, software developers, mechanical engineers, and biological scientists.

"In the valley there will be more brainy and wealthy people. The percentage of those types of people will be increasing," says Phil Kohlenberg, EDD labor market analyst.

The shift from production- to knowledge-based jobs is just one aspect of Silicon Valley's future. Its culture will also change with the shift in jobs, analysts believe.

While Silicon Valley is "obsessed with technology," the real story of its future will be written by people, says Tom Mandel, a futurist for SRI International who, since 1975, has earned a living predicting the future for corporations and governments.

"Technology is very easy to forecast. It's harder to say what people are going to do," Mandel says.

The future of the valley "is not a foregone conclusion," asserts Mandel. What choices people make on zoning, growth, and development policies and transportation will determine its fate. Add to this mixture the "global constraints" of environmental and energy policies and "wild cards" such as the October 1989 Loma Prieta earthquake, Mandel says, and the future of Silicon Valley becomes a rather complex question mark.

Just as Silicon Valley earned the title "LA North" for its traffic and smog, it is quickly on its way to earning the title "New York West" for its social stratification. In New York City the white-collar power elite and glitterati can afford to live in town. Lower-paid workers commute in from the boroughs of the Bronx, Brooklyn, and Queens. In Silicon Valley retail salespeople, waitresses, and janitors will commute in from Stockton, Tracy, Salinas, and San Benito, housing costs in Silicon Valley having long ago outdistanced their income. Only the technical elite and high-paid service professionals will be able to live in Silicon Valley, the culmination of a housing trend begun during the 1980s.

There is no guarantee, however, that lower-paid workers will meekly resign themselves to their fate and endure long daily commutes. "It may be tough to find people willing to take these jobs," says Kohlenberg.

High housing costs, traffic, smog, and other maladies have made Silicon Valley a less desirable address. Despite its problems, the valley will continue to be a magnet for technology innovators, believes Ed Feigenbaum of Stanford University.

"Urbanization has made living here much less attractive, but no one will move. Entrepreneurs will stay here because we have such an incredible support structure. We have people here who understand your problems," Feigenbaum says. "We've simply gone from a first-class heaven to a second-class heaven."

■ *The Computer As Implement*

From the beginning, practical computer design has been sparked by the original, conceptual thinking of such computer visionaries as Dr. J.C.R. Licklider and Alan Kay. Both Licklider and Kay made conceptual leaps, "flashes" as Kay likes to call them, which greatly expanded the horizon of computer technology.

In the beginning there was ENIAC (Electronic Numerical Integrator and Calculator), used by the U.S. War Department in 1945 to integrate ballistic equations, and later to compute problems involving atomic energy.

Howard Rheingold, in his fascinating book, *Tools for Thought,* describes ENIAC: ". . . 100 feet long, 10 feet high, 3 feet deep, weighing 30 tons—and

On the inside resembling a record player, a computer hard disk is a key component when users need to store large amounts of information or run programs requiring large amounts of memory. Photo by Tom Tracy/The Photo File

hot enough to keep the room temperature up towards 120 degrees [Fahrenheit] while it shunted multivariable differen-tial equations through its more than 17,000 tubes, 70,000 re-sistors, 10,000 capacitors, and 6,000 hand-set switches."

Ballroom-sized computers with thousands of tubes were the norm until the invention of the transistor, and later the integrated circuit, made it pos-sible to condense the calculat-ing power into smaller and smaller machines.

The original large-scale ma-chines were fed a calculating problem and then asked to solve it. Then in 1957 Licklid-er, an MIT researcher and pro-fessor, began a self-study that eventually led to the develop-ment of interactive computing. Dr. Licklider realized that many of his intellectual functions could in fact be performed by a machine. But the machine had

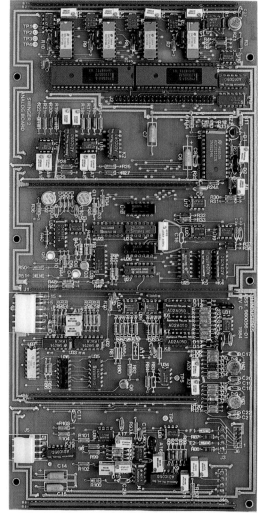

to be different; it had to interact with him, going beyond pure calculations into formulating models, using the data he supplied to arrive at hypothetical series of consequences. The computer had to work in close to real time, manipulating the data as the scientist fed it. It was no longer enough to feed the computer a problem and walk away. The computer could become a dynamic partner in in-tellectual thought.

During the early 1960s, when Dr. Licklider was a director at DARPA, he supported teams of scientists around the country who worked on the develop-ment of interactive computing. The notion that people should be able to inter-act freely with the computer signified a monumental step forward in computing technology. Combined with the natural evolution of the computer into a small-er size, the timing was right for computer visionary Alan Kay.

Personal computing, an enhancement of interactive computing, became tan-gible when Kay designed Dynabook, which he describes as "a PC for children of all ages." From 1967 to 1969, while a graduate student at the University of Utah, Kay designed FLEX, a desktop computer. Adults didn't respond well to FLEX, Kay recalls, "so I said, hell, make it for children." He then went to work on Dynabook which, Kay says, "had access and the ability to construct, in read-ing and writing. It was the forerunner of the Apple Macintosh, and other com-panies' workstations." Dynabook pioneered the use of windows on a display

RIGHT: Designs that once took hours to perfectly render can now be turned around in a fraction of the time due to the speed and flexibility of modern computers. Photo by Tom Tracy/The Photo File

FACING PAGE RIGHT: The drive toward increased miniaturization continually pushes for more portable computers such as this Poqet PC laptop. Photo by Renee Lynn

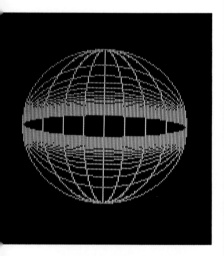

ABOVE: The calculating power of computers can make previously tedious designs, such as these ellipses, capable of quick and easy reproduction. Photo by Andrew Van Dis

screen and the use of icons as command symbols, basic elements of the Macintosh.

Kay worked on Dynabook during an 11-year association with Xerox's Palo Alto Research Center (PARC), from 1970 to 1981. He also wrote a new programming language, Smalltalk, which created a dynamic environment for the personal computer user. Smalltalk integrated text and graphics, another attribute found in the Macintosh. The goal of the language was to be understood by both children and adults.

Xerox's PARC attracted some of the brightest minds in computer science. At the time Kay worked there, other PARC scientists were also contributing to a new world of personal computing and to the eventual establishment of networked systems. Many of their designs were incorporated into Apple's computers. After PARC, Kay worked for a brief stint at Atari, leaving in 1984 to become a research fellow at Apple Computer.

"I was described as a technological bumblebee by Steve Jobs. I spend part of my time pollinating," declares Kay. As an Apple fellow, Kay chooses to be based in Los Angeles, having lived in the posh suburb of Brentwood since 1980. He directs Vivarium, an Apple research project that uses a Los Angeles school as an experimental site.

Kay appears more relaxed and amiable in his current position at Apple. Now well into his forties, his boyish haircut tinged with a little gray, Kay sips tea in one of Apple's numerous conference rooms and talks about the evolution of the computer and where it's headed.

The computer industry has moved incredibly fast, Kay believes. "We've had 400 years of history collapsed into 40." People's perception of what the computer is or does has spurred its evolution. From a remote calculating machine, the computer is now viewed by people as a tool capable of endless applications beyond pure calculation. "At PARC we shrunk the computer from above human scale to a tool," Kay says.

Technology will shrink the computer even further, according to Kay. "The next qualitative change is that the computer will become part of your clothing. The evolution has been from institutional to personal to intimate." Kay, who says he forecast the laptop computer in 1968, talks about "credit card-sized computer notebooks."

RIGHT: Electronic circuit board assembly is precision work. Photo by Liane Enkelis

RIGHT: Using computers such as this Silicon Graphics workstation for project design and simulated testing is one way computers and software designed and made in the Silicon Valley reduce the expense of a wide range of products. Photo by Tim Davis

BELOW: Andy Bechtolstein of Sun Microsystems, a Stanford graduate, is an innovative workstation designer. Courtesy, Sun Microsystems

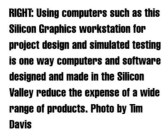

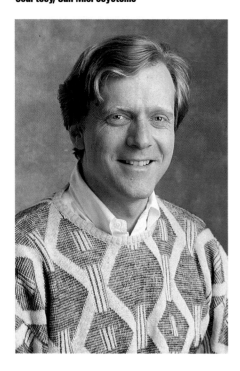

In the future these miniature computers will be used universally to do mundane tasks, Kay says. The role technology plays in people's lives will deepen.

Software publishing has lagged seriously behind hardware innovations, Kay says. In the twenty-first century software will have to catch up in order for the computer to truly realize its potential.

While the computer is shrinking to intimate size for mundane tasks, people are also demanding more power to perform complicated workplace tasks.

As an implement the workstation has taken its place in computer history as the next evolutionary phase in personal computing power. For people who use technology to create other technologies—PC boards, chips, computers, or software—the workstation is the system of choice. Described by one engineer as "a personal computer on steroids," the workstation is a high-powered computer that possesses considerably more memory than a PC. It usually runs on UNIX, an operating system more powerful than MS-DOS, a commonly used operating system for PCs.

A workstation's simulation ability has made it an invaluable tool for not only technical people but also anyone who wants to manipulate a theoretical environment in real time. Civil engineers can create a computer model of a bridge and test it under earthquake conditions. Student pilots can train in

simulated flight situations. Heat tests can be run on the space shuttle.

For "power users" who require extremely fast response to complicated inquiries and who need to make decisions in a real-time environment, workstations provide the speed. Engineers and financial analysts are two types of "power users" who now rely on workstations.

"A lot of the engineering design and development process is a repetitive, iterative thing. By using a workstation an engineer can perform these iterations at a much faster speed," explains Andy Bechtolsheim, the 35-year-old cofounder of Sun Microsystems, the country's premier workstation manufacturer.

LEFT: Sun Microsystems, one of Silicon Valley's many success stories, produces innovative workstations such as this. Photo by Tim Davis

"It used to take a day for one lab experiment. Now it takes 10 minutes on the workstation," Bechtolsheim notes.

While an average workstation costs $10,000, some of the software used can cost as much as $100,000. "It's a huge level of investment, but we are helping true entrepreneurs. By using a workstation you can create an entirely new business, so the investment in the software pays off," Bechtolsheim declares.

In the future all engineering will be simulation based, Bechtolsheim predicts. And by the year 2000 "every engineer will have the equivalent in power of the most expensive mainframe today," says Bechtolsheim.

Since the company's very beginning in 1982, Sun Microsystems has encouraged an open standard. As a graduate student at Stanford University, Bechtolsheim designed the first Sun (Stanford University Network) workstation. About the same time Sun cofounder Bill Joy was developing Sun's UNIX operating system at UC Berkeley. "Bill gave away software, and I gave away hardware," Bechtolsheim recalls. President Scott McNealy and Vinod Khosla were Sun's two other cofounders.

"Our business strategy was that we had to be different in order to be successful. We couldn't be another IBM," says Bechtolsheim, who believes the open standard educates the market. "In the fifteenth century clocks weren't standardized. Some went counterclockwise, and there were 15-hour days," he says.

Just as the clocks became standardized, Sun's way of designing workstations is becoming the standard, not by artificial market manipulation but by the power of education.

Sun's strategy has worked well. In 1990 the multibillion-dollar company achieved market dominance with a 30-percent share. Yet competition exists in Sun's own backyard, from Hewlett-Packard, which acquired Apollo, and from

BELOW: Mark W. Perry is executive vice president of Silicon Graphics, a workstation manufacturer specializing in 3-D simulation. Courtesy, Silicon Graphics

Silicon Graphics, a workstation manufacturer specializing in 3-D simulation.

Market competition, which serves to drive down the cost of the workstation, has made Silicon Graphics comparable in pricing to Sun. Mark W. Perry, executive vice president of Silicon Graphics, explains: "We've now been able to make this technology affordable, and so it's becoming a mainstream technology. In the past you'd have to spend $50,000 or more to get a workstation. Now it's available at an entry price of around $10,000."

Workstations have wide-ranging implications for the future of scientific research. The ability to fashion simulations is "fundamentally a new way of doing things," says Perry, who agrees with Bechtolsheim that in the future most prototypes will be computer generated. "It allows people to do things they've never done before." In medical research, for example, there are molecular models that allow scientists to simulate the AIDS (acquired immunodeficiency syndrome) virus and test it with computer-generated chemical formulas.

When a scientist cannot create a real-life event, such as an earthquake, the computer simulates the event, offering a more attractive alternative to the real thing.

Using a visual interface closely approximates the way the human brain works, Perry explains. "Over 50 percent of the neurons in the brain are linked into the visual interface, so the most productive way a human being can assimilate data is by sight," says Perry.

No doubt the workstation market will continue to reach beyond its original customer base of technical personnel. Workstations give advanced personal computer users everything they want: speed, power, real-time manipulation, and the ability to create and analyze with one machine.

From its beginnings with ENIAC the computer has evolved to a smaller, more powerful, more malleable implement for workers and thinkers. People now think of the computer as a basic tool of everyday life. They look to the future for ways in which the computer can help them work more efficiently and more creatively.

■ *The Computer As Media*

In the 1970s people found a new leisure activity: using "joysticks" to manipulate a bouncing ball on a video screen. Invented by Nolan Bushnell, Pong became the world's first commercially successful video game. It thrust Bushnell's new

Atari Corporation into the international spotlight, creating a billion-dollar video game industry.

Pong and later home video games showed consumers that electronics could interact in new ways. A home television monitor became the medium in which to play the game. Couples could sit on their living room floor, interacting with the screen by giving instructions.

From the days of Atari's Pong and Pac-Man, the computer itself has come to be viewed as just another medium. Enhanced interactivity with the computer and multimedia—the combining of the computer with other media such as video disks—has developed far beyond the video game level and found application in a variety of environments. The development of graphics software, with spectacular modeling capabilities and all the colors of a child's crayon box, has added a new dimension to the computer. Not only is it a medium but it is a visually exciting one as well. In the twenty-first century, interactivity will reach a new level when people use virtual imaging to place themselves in a computer simulation. They will be able to see the simulation from their own perspective, manipulating it as they wish, using three-dimensional enhancement and other technologies.

Advances in computer technology hold tremendous potential for education. Apple Computer funds experimental classrooms in which students use interactivity and multimedia to try new approaches to old-fashioned subjects. Traditional methods of teaching—lectures and notes—no longer suffice; students find it much more fun and interesting to listen to the sounds of a rain forest, to see the environment on a computer screen (projected there by video disk), and to access rain forest data, all at the same time.

"The idea of the computer as media is more cosmic," says Apple's Alan Kay, since it brings the computer down to the lowest common denominator. Both kids and adults can relate to the computer as just another form of media, similar to the telephone or television monitor.

Kay believes that by examining the intuitive thinking of kids it will be possible to design new ways of using the computer. The success of Apple's Macintosh is in some ways attributable to this theory. Macintosh users rely on an intuitive approach, finding the computer easy to use and manipulate.

Vivarium, the long-range Apple research project which Kay designed, involves 300 elementary school pupils at the Los Angeles Open Magnet School. The name, which means an enclosure for observing animals, signifies the students' work. They use a variety of media, including the Macintosh, to design animals and then simulate the environments in which they live. Students experiment with Apple's HyperCard, software which gives them the ability to create original multimedia displays that can incorporate voice, sound, video, and text.

A central purpose of Vivarium is to encourage kids to think creatively. By observing the kids Apple hopes to gain valuable knowledge about the nature of thinking and to use this knowledge to design new software or other products.

While kids are becoming the unofficial researchers of tomorrow's multimedia environments, the industrial world is focusing on how to integrate new forms of media into the everyday workplace. Improved presentations through the use of desktop publishing tools are one form of multimedia enhancement.

But researchers at Xerox's PARC believe the key to new media lies in the very essence of work communication: the document.

Dr. John Seely Brown, PARC vice president of advanced research, explains the importance of the document: "The fact is, the document really is the interchange medium for people to work together. Organizations function today because of the document. It is the substratum that allows them to work. So really, the document is our subject matter for focusing on people. Whereas computers tend to be just a technological notion, the document sits between people and technology."

PARC's cross-section of researchers examines all processes that lead to creation of the document. These include not only electrical engineering, solid-state physics, and other computer science disciplines, but also anthropology, psychology, and sociology.

"We are very interested in how to make people more effective problem solvers, how to streamline collaboration. How do you build a work environment that is high performance in the sense that it is incredibly motivating? How does technology enable that?" asks Dr. Brown.

Multimedia is itself transforming the definition of the document, says Brown. The effect of combining text, graphics, video, and audio images into a single unit changes the notion of what a document is. "We're looking ultimately at creating new media," says Brown. "We are now looking at building document structures that are so flexible that the way you want to understand something could then affect the way the document presents itself to you."

Elasticity, a means of presenting the document in alternative fashions, and transparency, in which interaction with the computer is virtually effortless, are the future according to PARC. "The truth is, tomorrow's interfaces you might not even recognize as such," says Brown. "If you see the interface, if you think of it as being an interface, you may already have failed because that means something is at odds; there is still a barrier."

Students and workers alike are embracing interactivity and multimedia as computers lose their mystique and are thought of as just another medium. Perversely, the entertainment sector of electronics, which Nolan Bushnell anointed with the highly successful Pong game, has lagged in successfully introducing new home entertainment concepts. Video games for the general population had faded in popularity by the early 1980s. By the end of the 1980s, video games were aimed almost exclusively at the teenage market. Years after the introduction of Pong, interactive home video was still in the testing stage. Marketers wondered if adults really wanted to get involved with interactive video. Did they want to participate in staging the video offering, or did they prefer to relax and be passively entertained?

The market for interactive video and virtual imaging may be undecided, but it is evident that in education and industry, interactivity represents an important breakthrough. Interactivity means the computer is no longer perceived as a remote temple of math, that it can be "talked to" as any other communication source. For the future interactivity will make the computer vastly more useful. And, as an alternative medium, the computer can be integrated in untold ways to produce new documents, new environments, and maybe even new ways of thinking.

■ The Computer As Knowledge Agent

A computer can be a high-speed implement for technical professionals or a dynamic medium in which to simulate a rain forest. It can also act as an agent on behalf of tomorrow's knowledge workers.

In the future one global network of information will exist to support a growing population of knowledge workers. To maintain some manageability of all this information, computers will be increasingly asked to perform functions that mimic the human brain. Without computers the world of the future would be unable to make sense of the overwhelming amount of data available.

Artificial intelligence and networking are twentieth-century inventions that have laid the foundation for future generations of knowledge workers.

Artificial intelligence (AI) has been in existence since 1956. Its first application, an expert system, was designed at Stanford University in 1965 by a renowned group of scientists: Joshua Lederberg, who won the Nobel Prize for his genetic research; Dr. Carl Djerassi, who invented the birth control pill; and Dr. Ed Feigenbaum, who codirects Stanford University's Knowledge Systems Laboratory.

Expert systems solve problems by accessing a body of knowledge culled from human experts, books, and other sources. In his book, *The Rise Of The Expert Company*, Dr. Feigenbaum explains that every expert system consists basically of two parts: a knowledge base and an inference engine. The knowledge base is comprised of both factual and heuristic (experiential, judgmental) knowledge. The inference engine manipulates and uses the information in the knowledge base to form a line of "reasoning," which is used to solve problems.

Feigenbaum's first system designed with his colleagues was the DENDRAL Project, an expert system for analytical chemistry which used data supplied by a mass spectrograph. "It was an experiment on how smart a program can be made if you give it a great deal of specific knowledge in a narrowly defined area," recalls Dr. Feigenbaum.

More than a quarter of a century later, Dr. Feigenbaum is still an active AI researcher. The soft-spoken professor and scientist believes the adoption of expert systems for commercial use "has been acceptably vigorous but inhibited by the fact that it has to grow along with, and integrate with, conventional software."

"There's also a bit of NIH [not invented here] resistance which has slowed acceptance in companies," Feigenbaum theorizes while puffing on his beloved pipe.

Early expert systems projects at Stanford focused on medicine and related fields. "Medicine turned out to be the quintessential field for expert systems because it has real expertise and it's not cut and dried or numerical. Medicine is experiential and subjective," Feigenbaum explains.

Since those early days, applications for expert systems have expanded beyond medicine. Recognizing that expert systems can be a productivity tool, IBM, Digital Equipment Corporation (DEC), and other major firms have incorporated AI into their work environments. By 1988 there were four dozen expert systems in use at various IBM sites.

According to Feigenbaum, workers need not fear that they will be made expendable by AI. He likes to cite the example of American Express, which uses an expert system to judge whether or not to authorize customer charges: "American Express has a very sophisticated system but it also has a rule that no one can be denied a charge solely by the machine. The final decision is made by a human . . . People don't want to give up their decision-making ability. They will keep the upper hand."

Feigenbaum's work and that of his colleagues has helped to establish AI as an industry in Silicon Valley. He is the cofounder of Teknowledge, an expert-system software company and a founding director of Intellicorp, a publicly held $25-million company that supplies software applications and training for expert systems.

Expert systems are slowly moving into new commercial applications. To gain more acceptance Feigenbaum says the systems will have to move out of their specialized-knowledge format to more generalized knowledge. This will require very large-scale knowledge bases, and the inputting effort is already under way. The goal, Feigenbaum says, is for future expert systems to be able to "reason" by analogy and eventually to utilize basic common sense.

Creation of knowledge bases won't be a problem in the long-term as AI technology progresses. "Computers will eventually be able to draw in their own knowledge and select what they need to know," Feigenbaum predicts. Greater and greater linkages of information, facilitated by networks, will make this possible.

Expert systems are the first commercially viable form of AI but not the only one. Feigenbaum notes that natural language understanding—the computer's ability to recognize continuous real-time speech—and computer-automated vision are other AI applications that will see wider acceptance in the future.

Aside from AI and expert systems, networking is one of the most powerful tools in the information world of the future. Integration of voice and data—as telephones, computers, and fax machines meld into a homogeneous system—is nourishing the rapid growth of network technology.

"The computer market in general is slowing but networking is growing 40 to 50 percent yearly," observes Morey Schapira, vice president of sales for Network General. One of the rising stars in networking, Network General became a public company in 1989 when it was three years old. It was named one of the hottest growth companies by *BusinessWeek*. The Menlo Park-based firm sells "The Sniffer" and "The Watchdog," diagnostic software for LANs (local area networks), which allow personal computers to communicate with each other and to share common resources, such as laser printers, at a given site.

Schapira says that networking is on a steep growth curve: "It's human nature. People want to talk to each other. Computers are now spending as much time communicating as computing."

Now that LANs are considered virtual commodities, the networking world is focusing on WANs (wide area networks) in which networks can talk to each other between sites. As Schapira explains, the most commonly used WANs are the phone company lines. A LAN in San Jose can talk to a LAN in Los Angeles through the communication link provided by phone lines. There are also private WANs, Schapira adds, that are built by companies such as Cisco in Menlo Park. In the future, LANs and WANs will merge into "one big happy network," Schapira says. LANs and WANs comprise one more step in the increasing global linkage of information.

As linkages grow, the issues of privacy and ethics will become more important, Schapira believes. In addition to diagnosing LAN problems, Network General's products can detect intruders on a network.

"In Silicon Valley the tradition has been to invent the technology first and then look at the impact of what we've done," says Schapira, who labels the phenomenon the "Frankenstein factor."

Privacy concerns may limit some linkages. But it is clear global linkages are the future. As voice and data blend and technology makes it possible to construct larger networks, humans will nurture their need to communicate by using more powerful communication tools.

■ The Second Revolution

Humans spent the last half of the twentieth century reaping the benefits of Silicon Valley's computer revolution, creating new ways of manipulating data by using the wondrous invention of the integrated circuit. In the twenty-first century a second revolution will sweep the world as humans conduct a full-scale effort at manipulating their own life matter.

Biotechnology, applied biological science, originated with scientists' research into how the human genetic structure works. Research projects revealed that DNA, or deoxyribonucleic acid, holds the blueprint for all living organisms. DNA molecules contain the hereditary instructions that determine a person's individual characteristics, such as hair color, and they also tell the body how to make proteins. Each cell in the human body contains a complete set of DNA. Scientists discovered that a specific portion of DNA could be isolated and cloned outside the human body. The cloning process required an environment that simulated the human body. Through the work of Stanford University professor Stanley Cohen, it became possible to combine a portion of human DNA with a host microorganism, such as bacteria, to simulate the human body's environment. This combining process, called gene-splicing, made it possible to produce recombinant DNA (rDNA). The use of rDNA has made possible the production of naturally occurring human substances, such as human insulin.

Virtually every biotechnology firm pays royalties to Stanford University, which holds the patent on Dr. Cohen's work.

By the end of the 1980s, biotechnology was a full-fledged global industry, having left the university research labs and become commercially viable. In 1989 United States sales of products based on rDNA exceeded one billion dollars. The first generation of successful firms includes Genentech, Cetus, Zoma, and Chiron. But owing to the extremely long R & D lead time for such products and lengthy federal agency approval cycles, the 1990s and beyond is considered the period when biotechnology will truly flourish. The twenty-first century will see a second generation of biotechnology firms emerge along with new products.

Biotechnolgy is impacting not only the fields of human therapeutics and diagnostics but also agriculture. Using the same principles of rDNA, it is possible to genetically alter crops and to produce new types of crop sprays. It is also possible to produce food from fruit and vegetable tissue cultures.

The ability to genetically engineer substances for human ingestion—either as food or therapeutics—has been the subject of ethical and political debate.

Whether a patient is a weekend jogger or world-class athlete, computer analysis of the client's physical
condition can help plan the next step
in rehabilitation or training. Photo
by Tom Tracy/The Photo File

Whether or not humans have
the right to alter life, or to clone
it, is a complex issue. Those who
advocate the industry's growth
believe society will gradually
come to accept genetic engineering as a way of life just as it
has other forms of technology,
such as the computer.

As a technological development, biotechnology is part of
a bigger story: the quantum
leap that life sciences—the entire spectrum of medical research and innovation—took
in the last decades of the twentieth century. Innovations such
as magnetic resonance imaging
(MRI), CAT scans, and the
ability to execute multiple-
organ transplants historically
changed the nature of medical
care and posed the possibility of lengthening the life span.

Life-science companies, biotechnology included, have clustered in the San
Francisco Bay Area from the beginning. Research conducted at Stanford
University and at the Berkeley and San Francisco campuses of the University of
California spawned the biotechnology industry and other life-sciences ventures.

"Biotechnology follows the same academic underpinnings as Silicon Valley,"
observes Joan Hamilton, San Francisco bureau chief for *BusinessWeek* and one
of a handful of American journalists with in-depth knowledge of biotechnology.

While the San Francisco Bay Area is a leading world center of biotechnology,
it does not have exclusive rights to the new industry. Biotechnology firms have
also clustered around Harvard, the University of Texas, and Baylor College of
Medicine. The industry also thrives in San Diego and Los Angeles, where the
highly successful Amgen is located.

Early biotechnology companies often chose to locate in South San Francisco
and the East Bay rather than in Silicon Valley. In the 1970s when the public
had a high anxiety level about the implications of genetic engineering, firms
found it advantageous to keep a low profile; many moved into older industrial
sectors, away from the high-profile glitz of Silicon Valley. Genentech, one of
the industry's most successful companies, chose a site in South San Francisco,
at the junction of Forbes and Point San Bruno boulevards. The windswept site
on the San Francisco Bay is part of the major industrial sector known as South
City, comprised of freight forwarders and other warehousing operations just
minutes away from San Francisco International Airport.

Genentech is considered the seminal company of the biotechnology
industry, as Fairchild Semiconductor was for the computer industry. During its
15-year history Genentech has introduced four of the first six genetically engi-

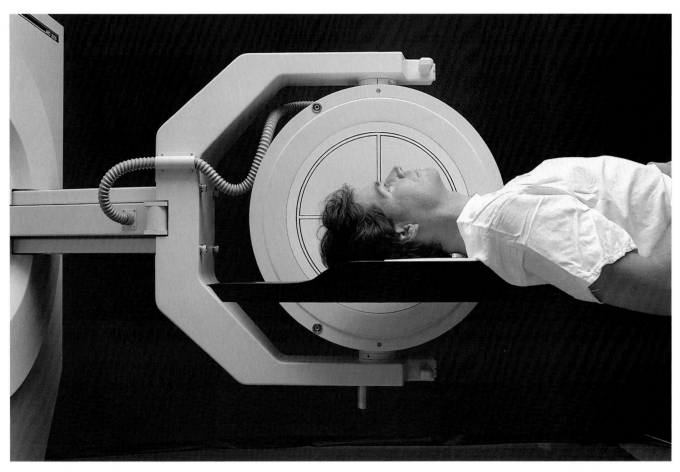

neered therapeutics on the market. In 1980 it introduced the biotechnology industry to Wall Street; its public offering was the industry's first. Investors have
done well by Genentech. In 10 years the company's worth grew from $3
million to its 1989 record level of $400 million.

Following a common practice of biotechnology and other life-sciences
firms, Genentech formed early strategic alliances with pharmaceutical
companies, licensing its technology to such giants as Eli Lilly. It continues to
collect royalties from pharmaceutical companies that produce Genentech-in-
vented rDNA drugs. Genentech itself directly manufactures two drugs:
Activase, a cardiac drug that dissolves blood clots, and Protropin, a human
growth hormone.

In 1990 Genentech successfully completed a merger with the Swiss pharmaceutical giant Roche Holding, in which 60 percent of Genentech was acquired. The
$2.1-billion deal allows Genentech to function as an independent company.

Such alliances with giant pharmaceutical companies provide needed capital
for life-sciences firms that have extremely high R & D expenses and that must
wait out the protracted development and approval cycles necessary to get a
drug to market. Genentech, for example, invests 40 percent of its revenue in
R & D. It currently has 12 products in human clinical trials that may be introduced during the 1990s. One of Genentech's proposed products, gamma inter-
feron, which it has trademarked as Actimmune, has wide-ranging potential for
treatment of life-threatening infections and for use in cancer therapy.

"Biotechnology will touch pharmaceuticals in every way as well as being an

Information on the medical condition
of patients can be gathered quickly
and painlessly through the use of sophisticated CAT scans. Early detection means quick treatment of many
disorders, often using new methods
and drugs researched and
developed in Silicon Valley. Photo by
Tom Tracy/The Photo File

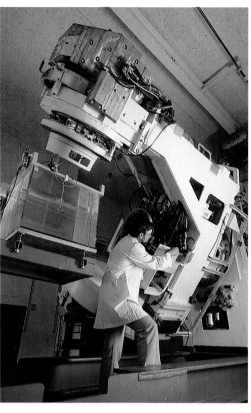

important research tool in the study of human development," says Gary Lyons, Genentech's vice president of business development.

The future will see "blockbuster drugs produced by biotechnology," Lyons believes.

For people the biggest advantage of taking an rDNA-produced drug versus a traditional synthetic chemical is that "you have a drug you know is safe because the human body produces it," Lyons explains. Being able to clone human-produced substances also eliminates supply questions. The pancreas of animals at one time was the only source of insulin for people. Now human insulin, produced by Genentech and licensed to Eli Lilly, accounts for more than 50 percent of the insulin market.

It's no longer a low profile for Genentech, a model of biotechnology success. "In just 15 years we've gone from idea to reality," says Lyons.

International pharmaceutical companies, seeing the lucrative markets opened by Genentech, are now aggressively pursuing their own market share. Genentech faces competition from other biotechnology companies and from the large pharmaceutical companies that are developing and selling their own rDNA products.

The Japanese have targeted biotechnology as a growth industry and have formed their own strategic alliances with United States companies, including Genentech. Under an agreement with Mitsubishi Kasei, Genentech is developing and marketing some of the Japanese company's pharmaceuticals.

In Japan, Kirin Brewery spent roughly $73 million in 1989 using gene-splicing to develop new beverages, vegetables, and drugs.

Commercialized rDNA products comprise just one facet of the biotechnology market. The twenty-first century is likely to see more wide-ranging developments in ultra-specific antibodies, which target a site in the body; in bioremediation, which uses bacteria to break down toxic substances, such as oil; and in biosensors, which can be used to probe all manner of environments, from the human body to packaged food.

The United States and Japan are already in a race for the biosensor market, the result of a perfect marriage between the principles of microprocessor miniaturization and biotechnology. The placement of biosensors within the human body will likely occur by the mid-twenty-first century.

To compete in the lucrative biotechnology market, the United States has relied in part on Silicon Valley for support technologies, particularly instrumentation, and for financial assistance in the form of venture-capital funding. While biotechnology is more a Bay Area than a Silicon Valley phenomenon, Silicon Valley has been involved from the start. For years David Packard has been a member of Genentech's board of directors. Hewlett-Packard has used the Genentech facility as a test site for instrumentation products.

Technology financiers played an important role in the birth of the biotechnology industry. Genentech's chairman of the board is Robert Swanson, a former associate of Kleiner, Perkins, Caufield & Byers, which gave seed money to his company. Swanson is credited with the early vision that such an endeavor could become profitable. Since then many of Silicon Valley's major venture-capital firms have joined the biotechnology market, seeing the potential for long-range payoff.

In Silicon Valley exploration into the entire life-sciences field is starting to pay off for investors. After years of painstaking R & D, ALZA Corporation, located on Palo Alto's Page Mill Road, is one firm that now realizes a profit. ALZA has pioneered new methods of drug deliveries as alternatives to the conventional pill or injection.

Named after its founder, Dr. Alejandro Zaffaroni, ALZA is a spinoff from Syntex, the pharmaceutical company where Dr. Zaffaroni was head of research. Technically ALZA has been a public company since its inception in 1968, when Syntex shareholders offered ALZA stock. A low cash-flow situation forced ALZA to become a wholly owned subsidiary of Ciba-Geigy from 1978 to 1982. It regained its independence and in 1983 recorded its first profitable year. In 1989 revenues totaled a record $93 million.

Just as Genentech has formed strategic alliances with pharmaceutical giants, so has ALZA. Among its product-development partners are Merck & Company; Sandoz; Pfizer; and Schering-Plough Corporation. ALZA has more than 40 drug-delivery products under development. Twelve products developed by ALZA are being sold, three of which the company markets directly.

ALZA's most commercially successful product has been Transderm-Nitro, a nitroglycerin skin patch that releases the chemical through the skin into the body. Marketed by Ciba-Geigy, the product has generated $300 million in worldwide sales. Transderm-Nitro provides an alternative to the traditional tablets taken by angina sufferers. The user applies ALZA's skin patch once daily, and it releases a uniform, steady dosage. It has some preventive value also, as opposed to the tablets that a person takes when an attack is already beginning.

ALZA pioneered transdermal products, commonly known as skin patches. The products consist of a drug encapsulated in a system of membranes. The drug flows at an even rate through the membrane, then through the skin and into the bloodstream. This method, ALZA says, is superior to injections or tablets, which usually start off with a high impact and then quickly taper off to ineffectiveness. A steadier rate also helps to eliminate side effects.

ALZA also has introduced a new form of tablet that works on the same principle of using a membrane to control the drug-release rate. The OROS system has been used by Pfizer Laboratories to produce Procardia XL, an angina and hypertension therapeutic, for the United States market.

Other forms of drug delivery are now in the development stage, according to Dr. Jane Shaw, who has been president of ALZA since 1970. "We are

Biotechnology makes great strides in the area of medicine and chemicals. Photo by Andrew Van Dis

researching ways of using electrical energy to move drugs across the skin," Shaw says. She expects the next generation of drug-delivery products to use the equivalent of ultraminiature batteries. These batteries would provide a low electrical current to "electro-transport" insoluble drugs across the skin.

Also in ALZA's future are bio-erodible polymers, new forms of membranes that can be placed inside the body and are designed to erode over time, Shaw explains.

Pharmaceutical giants now venturing into ALZA's technology will eventually become direct competitors. Ciba-Geigy, for example, has its own skin-patch R & D project, says Shaw.

The success of life-science companies such as ALZA and Genentech has inspired a closer partnership between industry, universities, and the public sector. In 1990 a new regional institute, the Bay Area Bioscience Center, was incorporated to serve as a clearinghouse for industry information and as an educational and training advocate. Directed by Fred Dorey the center is a spin-off of the Bay Area Council, a leading regional business group in existence for more than 40 years. Dr. Shaw; Ron Cape, chairman of Cetus; and Bill Terry, executive vice president of Hewlett-Packard, are members of the center's board.

According to Dorey, the Bioscience Center plans on being an active proponent of K-12 programs that teach subjects related to the life sciences. Since the field is so technically innovative, the educational system needs help in providing students with current material. High school and college level institutions also need to see life sciences as a new and rapidly growing employment market, according to Dorey. "We see a tremendous need for community colleges to add bioscience training to their curricula. There is going to be plenty of demand for an associate-degree-level person with some degree of scientific literacy," says Dorey.

Private firms such as Cetus have recognized the educational need and send out gene-cloning demonstration kits to high school biology and science teachers. Genentech funds an educational van that teaches gene-splicing.

Although it has a serious mission, the Bioscience Center retains a sense of humor. In its first edition of "Bay Area Bioscience Reports," its quarterly newsletter, the center quotes humorist Garrison Keillor: "They're breeding new dairy cows without legs. Legs just get in the way. Interrupt things. They're rectangular . . . Yes, sir, you can stack them up in rows in warehouses in the suburbs."

Genetically engineering cows is no longer a fantasy. Humans now possess the ability to manipulate all life forms. In the twenty-first century this ability will be put to use in human therapeutics, to identify new types of crops and new ways of fighting toxics.

Without doubt ethical issues will continue to arise as humans push closer to the very essence of being.

The Money Changers

Ask a venture capitalist to predict the future and the result will be laughter with a tinge of hysteria.

"Seeing even 10 years out in this business is something I would never do. I might predict a few months, based on fluctuations in the market now," responds Paul Ely, a general partner in Alpha Partners.

Savvy venture-capitalists such as Ely know that the cyclical boom-and-bust nature of Silicon Valley makes for a virtually unpredictable business future.

Since its emergence as a modern-day financing mechanism three decades ago—with investors Art Rock and Jack Melchor as pioneers—venture capitalism has gone through periods of abundant success and dismal failure.

In the early 1980s, IPOs (initial public offerings) were issued feverishly. Healthy stock valuations gave investors a high rate of return. "It seemed like everyone had a 30-percent ROI [return on investment]," Ely recalls. Then the boom cycle turned to bust. "Around 1985 great disillusionment set in," Ely remembers. The stock market crash of October 1987, "Black Monday," further killed any chances for IPOs.

Start-up companies simply had to wait out the cycle. By 1989 the climate heated up a little bit. Some IPOs were issued. "The extraordinarily high returns are a fact of history," Peter Wallace of Hambrecht & Quist notes. But the rate of return on the new IPOs remains comparatively attractive, Wallace says.

Venture capitalists still felt relatively bullish in 1990, but the consensus is that the business of financing technology has permanently changed. The climate in which they will operate in the coming decades will differ markedly from the boomtown early days. There are far more players in venture capital now, and a shakeout has already begun.

"The sheer amount of money and the number of practitioners has caused the business to be much more competitive," says Burt McMurtry, general partner in Technology Venture Investors. From the early days in the 1970s, when the venture-capital pool was as little as $100 million annually, the money pool has risen to a historical high of $5 billion. According to McMurtry the average annual pool is around $2 billion.

"Our industry is now overfunded," observes Grant Heidrich, general partner in the Mayfield Fund.

Where the venture capital comes from has radically changed from the early days of individual investors such as Art Rock. "Pension funds are now a big player in investments," declares Bob Wall, head of the investment-banking group for Cowen & Company, one of the top five "tech boutiques" in the business.

The fiscal power that pension-fund managers now wield has changed the culture of the venture-capital industry, Wall says. "There's more structure now than there has been in the past." So-called gatekeepers make up a new subculture of important players. Gatekeepers advise pension-fund managers on which venture-capital funds are worthwhile, Wall explains.

Venture capitalists in the future will have to resist the dampening effect these middlemen have on the industry, according to Wall. "Gatekeepers will result in a more conservative approach" to venture financing, Wall believes. "They do have a substantial influence on the industry. Some venture-capital firms have been forced into militating against the gatekeepers," says Wall.

One of the changes gatekeepers want to see is a uniform standard of reporting between venture-capital funds so that a common valuation of an investment exists. If the Mayfield Fund, Technology Venture Investors, and Alpha Partners were all to invest in New Company A, then there should be a common valuation, the gatekeepers believe. Wall says venture-capital firms are fighting this idea since each firm structures its deals differently and a common valuation is impossible.

Gatekeepers aren't going away, however. Their conservative influence will be a factor in the twenty-first-century venture-capital market.

Another major influencing factor in the investment market is the increasing number of American firms with foreign investors. This cross-pollination between America, the Pacific Rim, and Europe is creating a new breed of company with a global financial structure, observes Mike Nevens, a principal in the management consulting firm of McKinsey and Company. Nevens, who specializes in technology, notes that in Silicon Valley it's getting more difficult to find a major company without global financing ties. The Fujitsu-Amdahl alliance is illustrative of Silicon Valley's emerging global identity, Nevens says.

Foreign investors are attracted to Silicon Valley for the same reasons American firms are: the availability of a skilled work force, access to the R & D brain trust, and manufacturing expertise, Nevens explains.

The lines of distinction between companies' origins will continue to blur as more foreign investment money flows into Silicon Valley. Future generations of companies will be truly global in scope, presenting the basis for some change in public and trade policies.

The investment focus of venture capitalism is also changing. It now targets investments beyond computers. The emerging stars of the next century will be the entire range of life-sciences companies, including biotechnology firms. Most major venture-capital firms have already established life-sciences divisions. Technology Venture Investors has a biotech spin-off, Delphi Bioventures. Alpha Partners directs about one-third of its investments into medical technology. The Mayfield Fund aggressively invests in life sciences and was an original funder of ALZA.

Life sciences presents a challenge to venture capitalists, however, since its lengthy research cycles means it will take a long time to see a return on the investment. "These cycles may be longer than the life of a venture fund," notes Wall. "The total amounts of money needed by biotech start-ups, for example, is staggering. It's far more than the average computer company," he says. However, the rate of return on investments such as Genentech gives venture capitalists optimism about life sciences.

Biotechnology, life sciences, new technologies that enhance the field of medicine, targeted computer investments—these are parts of the equation for venture capitalism in the future.

Investments will be made in a more conservative culture. The days of brash individual investors and eccentric CEOs leading start-ups may be history. "I see the sharp-pencil guys taking over. That will certainly ruin the mystique of Silicon Valley," says Richard Carlson of Spectrum Economics. Jerry Sanders, president of AMD, typifies Silicon Valley in its carefree heyday, says Carlson. "Now it's scratch for survival," Carlson laments.

Silicon Valley may be a little duller, but it's still one of the most exciting places in the world, Carlson admits.

The Computer As Obsolete

"Mr. Watson, come here! I want to see you," Alexander Graham Bell said to Thomas Watson on March 10, 1876. Thus the first telephone transmission in the world began.

Just two years later a friend of Wilbur and Orville Wright, Cordy Ruse, built an automobile. Wilbur Wright laughed at the invention.

The telephone and the automobile are inventions that have reshaped the very nature of society. If there is one invention that has reshaped the way the world works, it is the integrated circuit invented by Robert Noyce. His 1959 patent filed while at Fairchild Semiconductor, the company he cofounded, paved the way for the beginning of computer technology.

Since Noyce's invention the computer world has been punctuated with wonderful innovations: the personal computer, faster and smaller chips, networking, color graphics, new operating systems.

What grand new innovation will take its place beside the integrated circuit in the history of the world? No mere mortal in Silicon Valley can foretell. Will it happen in the twenty-first century? Most likely the person with the answers hasn't even been born yet.

But as computer visionary Alan Kay likes to say, "The best way to predict the future is to invent it!"

6

Making It All Work

■ *Symbiosis*

When it comes to earning a living, people in Santa Clara County can basically be divided into two categories: those who work in the technology world—Silicon Valley—and those who serve Silicon Valley industry and its workers.

It is estimated that every engineer in Silicon Valley generates 25 other jobs. IBM's South San Jose operations—a disk-drive plant that employs 8,000 people and two nearby research centers with another 3,000 employees—offer a prime example of the technology lifeblood that feeds the county's economy. As the largest private employer in San Jose, IBM estimates that its San Jose operations and other Silicon Valley satellites generate an estimated one-billion-dollar economic impact on the county. This takes into account payroll, taxes, service and supplier contracts, medical fees, and employee buying power.

The "ripple effect" created by the technology industry stretches deep and wide into the economic fabric of the county. From PC board stuffers, chip set manufacturers, software developers, and graphics board manufacturers— whose efforts in part lead to a finished computer—to the sales reps, distributors, and packagers who market components, the business of Santa Clara County is umbilically tied to technology.

Computers have impacted industries from forestry to fisheries. Photo by Tom Tracy/The Photo File

Santa Clara County, with approximately 830,000 workers, is now a "one crop" economy, as described by Phil Kohlenberg, labor market analyst for the California Employment Development Department (EDD). The county's fortunes rise and fall with the boom-and-bust cycles of the technology industry. However, its bad times have historically been less harsh than the national experience.

Even in times of deep national recession, Santa Clara County has enjoyed relative immunity. The surging economic growth of its technology industry has protected it from hitting the depths of recession that

The once largely rural Santa Clara Valley has become a home for major corporations focused on high technology and computer development. Photo by George Hall/The Photo File

other regions of the United States have reached time and again.

The exception to this historical pattern occurred during the national recession that gained momentum in 1990 and continued into 1992. Santa Clara County's economic slowdown was "in sync" with the rest of the nation's, according to Kohlenberg.

A catastrophic occurrence, the outbreak of the Persian Gulf War on January 16, 1991, added another dimension to the recession. Silicon Valley defense contractors such as Lockheed, FMC, Trimble Navigation, and Raytheon, manufacturer of the Patriot missile which successfully downed Iraqi Scud missiles, were in a position to benefit from increased defense requirements.

The Persian Gulf War provided at least short-term stimulation to Silicon Valley's defense businesses. However, increased defense spending is not an overall antidote to a slow economy, says Kohlenberg. Personnel employed in aerospace and instrument manufacturing represent a proportionately small segment of the Silicon Valley work force compared to the total electronics sector. For the recession to truly end, the valley's general technology manufacturing has to regain momentum.

■ *Diminishing Returns*

Santa Clara County's new susceptibility to recession is the result of the technology industry's overall slowdown, which began during the mid-1980s. Technology's steady upward spiral simply stopped.

LEFT: Famous for its graphics software for Apple's Macintosh computer, Adobe is a member of the Santa Clara community with this corporate headquarters. Photo by Joseph Sohm/Chromosohm

BELOW: Sculpture that blends in with the corporate landscape adorns the grounds at Adobe Systems corporate headquarters. Photo by Joseph Sohm/Chromosohm

ABOVE: Once manufactured, computers are put to work throughout Santa Clara Valley tracking and recording data. Photo by Tom Tracy/The Photo File

RIGHT: Silicon Valley is home to developmental facilities such as Loral's Western Development Labs in San Jose. Photo by Joseph Sohm/ Chromosohm

RIGHT: At the heart of the work done in Santa Clara Valley is the manufacture of silicon wafers as performed by this Hewlett-Packard technician. Photo by Liane Enkelis

ABOVE: Product testing is often as crucial as the manufacturing process itself. Here a Xidex employee verifies that units are working properly before they are shipped to the customer. Photo by Tim Davis

RIGHT: San Jose is home to many technology companies, such as Cypress Semiconductor, located in the North 1st Street industrial corridor. Photo by Richard L. Kaylin

One of the most dramatic effects of this lag on growth is Silicon Valley's tremendous loss of semiconductor jobs. From September 1984 to September 1990, the number of Silicon Valley jobs in the semiconductor industry dropped from a peak of 120,700 to 85,500, the EDD reports. Japanese price competition was a critical factor in the decline.

The few modern Silicon Valley semiconductor firms that are on a growth curve, such as Cypress Semiconductor, owe their success to staying out of the commodity business. Cypress targets specific markets and produces avant-garde, high-performance products. One of its important growth targets is the RISC (reduced instruction set computing) chips market. RISC chips cut down computer-processing time, thereby making the specific application proceed more quickly.

One way to spruce up Silicon Valley sights is to add a bit of sculpture, as was done here at the Shoreline Technical Park in Mountain View. Photo by Joseph Sohm/Chromosohm

Semiconductor demand is generally regarded as symptomatic of the economy's state of being since chips are at the beginning of the technology food chain. Whether the computer system is a notebook computer or a mainframe, it depends on chips to run. When the chip industry is in decline, it simply means the computer industry isn't growing at a fast enough pace to deplete all the chips in production or inventory.

In order for new chips to be in demand, computers have to be in demand, and the truth is computers are far from reaching a saturation point in either American businesses or the home. "Real computer market penetration is about 20 percent in households and 50 percent in business," notes Richard Carlson, president of Mountain View-based Spectrum Economics.

Some semiconductor industry observers believe both the chip and computer businesses will be spurred by the retooling or replacement of aging computers. But Carlson cautions against too much optimism: "People aren't trading up computers as quickly as anticipated. The cost of business disruption is outstanding. To retool you have to buy components which are tricky, expensive, and cumbersome."

Carlson says Silicon Valley would benefit greatly from being able to market components in such a way that an "end user" could buy the products and integrate them into an existing system in a relatively painless manner.

"Silicon Valley has an unusual proportion of nerds talking to nerds, and they never talk to real customers," says Carlson. From the consumer perspective components need to be sold as packages. "There has also been a blockade at the retail end," Carlson says, with merchandising clearly missing the mark in customer contact, support, and comfort.

ABOVE: To maintain the sterile atmosphere of the "clean room" where components are assembled, technicians must dress in special suits and make sure no dirt or dust from outside can enter the working area. Photo by Richard L. Kaylin

RIGHT: Cypress Semiconductor founder and CEO T.J. Rodgers leads a successful chip company in San Jose. Photo by Richard L. Kaylin

Without an easier means of retooling computers available to the consumer, Silicon Valley will have to depend on the more difficult task of creating demand for new or replacement systems to fuel its economy.

■ State Of The Valley

The 1980s loss of semiconductor jobs in Silicon Valley in the short term was due to the vagaries of supply and demand, but the loss is part of a bigger story—the permanent exodus of technology production jobs from the region.

Rising stars such as Cypress Semiconductor look outside Silicon Valley when they want to add another wafer-fabrication facility. Cypress opened its first wafer "fab" in 1982 in San Jose, where its corporate headquarters is located in the Golden Triangle industrial sector on North 1st Street. But when he decided to open a second fab, Cypress CEO and founder T.J. Rodgers chose Round Rock, Texas, outside of Austin. Land costs for Round Rock are $18,000 an acre compared to $550,000 an acre for Silicon Valley, Rodgers says. Relatively lower labor costs, the absence of a state income tax, and the fact that there is no

sales tax on major capital equipment were other factors in his decision. "I can never see building another fab in California," Rodgers declares. For his third fab Rodgers chose to buy an existing facility in Bloomington, Minnesota, where water and energy costs are significantly less than California. He is already at work picking a site for a fourth fab.

It might seem challenging to find qualified semiconductor engineers in Bloomington, Minnesota. However, technology is such a pervasive part of the American economy now that qualified technical personnel live just about anywhere. Rodgers says it was quite easy to find skilled engineers for the Bloomington fab.

Silicon Valley does have a manufacturing future, Rodgers believes, but it will be predicated on the Cypress model: establishment of an R & D facility and corporate headquarters in the valley, with start-up manufacturing; expansion will occur elsewhere.

"The infrastructure here for start-ups remains unmatched," Rodgers says. In Silicon Valley the sheer multitude of companies that serve start-ups is virtually without parallel. "If I need equipment, I can get it delivered within the hour, and it's seven-day-a-week service," says Rodgers.

"There's a work ethic here like nowhere else. People have a dedication to technology" on all levels of the corporate ladder, Rodgers asserts.

In the twenty-first century Rodgers predicts Silicon Valley will continue to develop into a region of R & D and headquarters facilities. The next threat to Silicon Valley's economic health could be the movement of R & D to less expensive regions. Rodgers has already posed that challenge to Silicon Valley by establishing two design satellites in Mississippi and Texas.

■ The Coming Age

While manufacturing jobs in Silicon Valley may no longer enjoy the steep growth curve of the 1970s and early 1980s, more than 200,000 people—or about one-quarter of the work force—continue to be directly employed in electronics and aerospace manufacturing. Companies such as IBM, Hewlett-Packard, National Semiconductor, Lockheed,

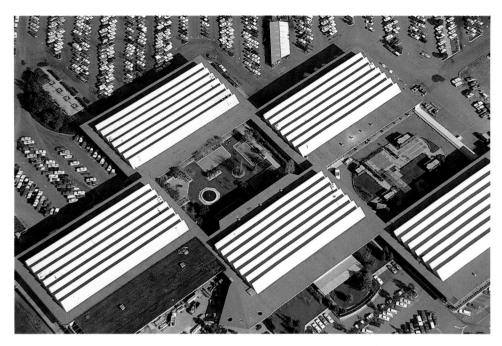

When seen from above, the Hewlett-Packard plant in the Santa Clara Valley begins to resemble one of the circuit boards it produces. Photo by George Hall/The Photo File

and FMC remain among the largest employers in Silicon Valley. The political climate in which these firms do business, however, has changed considerably since they opened their doors. A global concern for the environment has caused society to take a keener look at the effects of manufacturing. People now realize that the world is a closed ecosystem in which the waste products of manufacturing need to be limited, carefully handled, and disposed of with the least possible damage to human health and the environment.

In Silicon Valley industrial pollution became a dominant issue in the 1980s. New regulations created stricter rules for the use of both aboveground and underground storage tanks in order to more effectively prevent toxic-waste leakage. Regulations also significantly tightened controls on disposal of chemical and water wastes. Silicon Valley became one of the regions in the federal Superfund network of hazardous waste sites. More than 30 Superfund sites were named in the valley. According to the Superfund law the federal government pays for the cleanup of sites where a responsible party cannot be pinpointed. In cases where a private company can be identified, the firm must meet a schedule of cleanup, or the federal government can step in and perform the cleanup, for

Technicians suit up before entering specially prepared "clean rooms" where the initial steps of computer manufacture take place. Photo by Liane Enkelis

which it will send the company a steep bill.

Title III amendments, known as SARA-III (Superfund Amendments and Reauthorization Act), have also made industrial chemical emissions a matter of public record, giving firms an added incentive to be environmentally responsible. Firms are now required to publicly report pounds of pollution over a certain level which they emit into the atmosphere.

"SARA's really been effective in the valley," says Dr. Thomas D. English, director of environmental programs for the Santa Clara County Manufacturing Group (SCCMG). Since SARA, overall industrial emissions have been reduced by 62 percent, according to English.

It takes many steps to get computers produced and out the door to customers. One step is computer keyboard assembly as performed at the Hewlett-Packard plant. Photo by Liane Enkelis

Another area of environmental concern, solid waste disposal, remains a tricky problem for both industry and the consumer. Landfill input must be reduced 25 percent by 1995 under AB 939, authored by Assemblyman Byron Sher of Palo Alto. "The answer is to reduce by using less and recycling what you use," English says. "The driving force will be economics since landfill costs are extremely expensive."

For the future an emerging environmental issue is the reduction of toxic-metals runoff into San Francisco Bay. As the result of a successful suit by Citizens for a Better Environment and the Sierra Club, sewage-treatment facilities in Santa Clara County have been mandated to reduce metals runoff. Regulated Silicon Valley industry contributes 8 percent of the runoff. Therefore adequate reduction can only be achieved by approaching the general public, English explains.

 Taking Action

As a result of stronger environmental laws, major employers such as IBM-San Jose are now more closely regulated and monitored in all phases of the manufacturing process.

IBM, Hewlett-Packard, and other large manufacturers are meeting the challenge by improving waste-reduction processes in their plants and by researching new, nonpolluting manufacturing processes. They

LEFT: One of the original Silicon Valley giants is National Semiconductor, headquartered in Santa Clara. Photo by Joseph Sohm/Chromosohm

are also becoming leaders in chlorofluorocarbon (CFC) reduction. Both IBM and Hewlett-Packard want to completely phase out CFCs in their manufacturing processes by 1993, seven years before the deadline set by the Montreal Protocol International Treaty. "It's an unprecedented, remarkable effort," says English. CFCs are the major destroyer of the Earth's ozone layer. The continued commitment of firms such as IBM and Hewlett-Packard to eliminating CFCs is critical to global environmental health.

Until now IBM-San Jose has been using CFC-113 for precision cleaning of disk-drive parts, but the chemical is being replaced with a "sophisticated dishwasher," which uses old-fashioned soap and water for cleaning, according to Ray Kerby, former director of external and environmental programs.

CFC-113 is one of 3,800 chemicals used at IBM-San Jose. As technology has become more refined, the need for chemicals in the manufacturing process has risen accordingly. When IBM invented disk-drive technology, introducing the first magnetic disk systems for data storage in 1956, manufacturing processes were essentially mechanical and electrical. Since then the evolution to higher density and microminiaturization has demanded chemical processing. The head in a disk-drive assembly is now one-tenth the size of the head of a pin. Chemical processes are used to make the microminiature component, and chemicals are used to keep it free of dust particles and other substances.

For IBM and other technology manufacturers, the challenge is to comply with stricter environmental laws while producing competitive quality products.

"Our eventual goal is to use nonpolluting technologies so we can stay out of the regulations ballgame," says Kerby. Innovations such as the sophisticated dishwasher show how IBM is reducing toxic chemical use.

Closely watched IBM-San Jose, which has seven chemicals on the SARA-III list, has increased its own environmental monitoring. With Perkin-Elmer, IBM has developed ICAMS (Industrial Continuous Air Monitoring System). Based on Navy submarine technology, ICAMS monitors 450 locations at the San Jose complex. It can detect chemical concentrations in the air as low as one part per million and serves as an early-warning device should unusual levels occur.

In addition to air emissions IBM-San Jose has also been in the public eye for groundwater contamination. In 1979 chemicals were discovered in the soil and groundwater near IBM-San Jose's Cottle Road facility. Since then IBM has removed 70 underground storage tanks, and it continues a groundwater cleanup plan, which should be completed by the year 2000. The water is pumped out of the ground, cleaned of any chemical content, and then either used for landscape irrigation or for manufacturing. The state Regional Water Quality Control Board dictates that, as a conservation measure, the IBM water must be completely reused.

IBM recycles and reuses the water to the maximum extent possible. What cannot be reused is trucked to a Palo Alto commercial recycling facility, which separates the chemical elements and then sells it for other purposes. In a closed ecosystem there is no real "end" for the water; it reappears in other forms.

Technology firms—IBM is a classic example—have the twenty-first-century challenge of manufacturing progressively smaller and faster products while emitting minimal toxins into the environment. To be both environmentally sound and cost-effective, firms are researching means of using nonpollutant elements for manufacturing and of further reducing chemical and water waste. As Kerby says, staying out of the regulations game by using nonpollutants makes good sense both environmentally and economically.

■ Companies Of The Future

A new generation of companies is evolving in response to societal pressures to protect the environment. These companies help technology firms cut down on waste. Others are experimenting with new ways of manufacturing, substituting nonpolluting methods for old-fashioned toxic production.

Chemicals are recovered and recycled in the manufacturing process using machinery made by Alameda Instruments. While the machinery costs $600,000, a cost-benefit analysis shows it pays for itself within six months by offsetting chemical costs.

In San Jose the Zanker Material Recovery Systems company runs one of the most advanced full-service commercial recycling operations in the country. Zanker will even recycle entire buildings in addition to typical business by-products such as paper.

A good omen for the manufacturing environment of the future is Mountain View-based Catalytica, a specialist in catalytic process technology. A catalyst is a substance that initiates, accelerates, and controls the course of a chemical reaction without being changed itself. Catalytica's mission is to create less toxic, more energy-efficient manufacturing processes by introducing new, advanced catalysts. These new catalysts are created by molecular design, using computer simulation, 3-D graphics, and high-performance analytic instrumentation.

Catalytic process technology is an important step in cleaning up the manufacturing environment since the use of chemicals is so pervasive. When a person puts fuel in a car's gas tank, eats margarine or artifical sugar, wears polyester slacks, or takes penicillin, chemical processes using catalysts have been present. The worldwide value of products made from chemicals exceeds one trillion dollars.

Unfortunately the pervasive use of chemicals in manufacturing has created a host of environmental dilemmas. "It's an interesting paradox. Technology has created the problem, but it can also be the solution," observes Dr. James Cusumano, founder and chairman of the 17-year-old company.

Noxious emissions are among the most worrisome by-products of industry. By creating new catalysts Catalytica helps the energy, chemical, and petroleum industries reduce pollutants. One of Catalytica's successes is inventing a new catalytic combustion method for gas turbines that greatly reduces the emission of nitrogen oxide, one of the key ingredients in smog. The invention allows utility companies to produce electricity with virtually no nitrogen oxide emissions.

Catalytica was founded as a consulting and contract-research firm by Cusumano, who holds a Ph.D. in chemistry from Rutgers University; Dr. Ricardo Levy, a Stanford Ph.D.; and Michel Boudart, a Stanford professor of chemical engineering and a recognized world leader in catalysis. The three founders met while Cusumano and Levy were employed at Exxon Corporation in New Jersey and Boudart was an Exxon consultant. Catalytica took a new direction in 1983, switching to product development through joint ventures and technology licensing. In 1991 Catalytica will mark a milestone with its first commercial product release.

Taking the company public is a 1990s goal for Cusumano. Catalytica has received $55 million in venture-capital funding from the Mayfield Fund; Biotechnology Investments, an affiliate of N.M. Rothschild and Sons; Lubrizol Enterprises; and Koch Industries.

Catalytica has been a prolific research lab staffed by some of the best talent in the industry. It has 40 Ph.D.'s on staff and one celebrity: Dr. Henry Taube, a Nobel laureate in chemistry and the father of modern inorganic chemistry, works part-time at Catalytica. So far the firm has 14 joint-venture agreements and more than 170 registered patents, both domestic and foreign.

With catalysis representing a $5-billion global market with high growth potential, Catalytica seems to have found a profitable niche.

The companies of the future, Catalytica among them, marry the economic need to manufacture products efficiently with society's need to protect its environment. "I like to think of us as primary prevention. We can create processes which don't give you the problem," says Cusumano.

"The future will see a change in economics. We will be driven not only by market needs but also by environmental concerns," says Cusumano. "In the seventies the environmental movement was a whisper. In the eighties it crystallized. In the nineties it will be a roar."

■ Across The Spectrum

Of the approximately 830,000 persons employed in Santa Clara County, about 200,000 work directly in electronics and aerospace manufacturing. The approximately 630,000 remaining jobs are comprised of non-technology manufacturing positions, technology-related service industries, government, agriculture, and industries that serve the personal and social lives of Santa Clara County people.

The EDD estimates the county has about 215,000 service jobs, a category

Street vendors outside the Palo Alto post office add to the city's unique flavor. Photo by Gerald L. French/The Photo File

What was once chiefly farmland has given way to numerous computer-related industries, hotels, and conference centers. Some farming is still done on patches of undeveloped land throughout the county. Photo by Joseph Sohm/Chromosohm

which includes R & D and engineering firms and other subcontractors, health services, education, and hospitality. Retail jobs comprise the next largest job sector, with about 115,000 people. San Jose, Santa Clara County, and other governmental sectors generate about 88,000 jobs in the county. Non-technology manufacturing accounts for about 45,000 positions. Other job sectors include construction; transportation and public utilities; electronics distribution; and finance, insurance, and real estate. In addition there are about 3,000 persons employed in agriculture, the remaining vestiges of the Santa Clara Valley's original industry.

Through the 1980s and into the 1990s, there has been a shift in jobs from the manufacturing sector to the service sector to the point that there is almost an equal balance between the two. Silicon Valley's 1990-91 recession, however, affected service jobs as well. Many service sectors that would normally reflect growth either remained at the same level or declined. Recession became a two-edged sword: there was a decline in electronics; this decline meant a reverse ripple effect for service jobs, which essentially feed off of the technology industry. Since the technology industry is the county's economic lifeblood, when Silicon Valley manufacturing is in a slowdown phase, many other job sectors suffer, too.

Selling Affluence

A fluctuating economy and a national retrenchment in retailing has had its effect on Santa Clara County's retail trade. By the early 1990s certain shopping centers had emerged as clear competitive leaders while others struggled to find a niche they could serve.

One positive story was the beginning of a retail-district revival in San Jose's downtown.

ABOVE: The Stanford Shopping Center near the university campus and medical center brings an array of shops, including Macy's and Neiman-Marcus, to local residents. Photo by Gerald L. French/The Photo File

RIGHT: San Jose keeps pace with other shopping outlets with the extensive Valley Fair shopping center. Macy's, Nordstrom, and Emporium anchor the mall, which has an extensive dining facility on the upstairs level. Photo by Gerald L. French/The Photo File

This outdoor fountain greets visitors and decorates the landscape at Palo Alto's Stanford Shopping Center. Photo by Gerald L. French/The Photo File

Santa Clara County, with an amazing 130 shopping centers, ranks among the top five metropolitan areas in the United States in buying power. The proportionately high amount of well-paid Silicon Valley professionals creates a highly lucrative retail market. Total retail sales in the county are estimated at $11.6 billion.

In order of revenue the top five Santa Clara County shopping centers are Valley Fair, Stanford, Eastridge, Oakridge, and Vallco. Valley Fair, at the intersection of highways 280 and 880 in San Jose, is one of the prize gems owned by San Diego-based Hahn Company. The center recorded $347 million in taxable sales for 1989. Valley Fair underwent a major renovation during the 1980s, reopening as a two-tiered street of specialty stores anchored by Macy's, Nordstrom, and the Emporium.

"The typical Valley Fair shopper reflects this area's upward mobility and professionalism," notes Kaycee McKenzie, marketing director for the shopping center.

Farther up the peninsula is the county's second-biggest revenue producer: Stanford Shopping Center. Unlike Valley Fair, which is an enclosed center,

Stanford prides itself on its outdoors approach. Its 150 shops and 4 prestigious department stores are approached by a series of attractive walkways in a pretty village atmosphere. According to the center's management Stanford is committed to conserving the environment, with ecologically sound landscaping and recycling measures.

Eastridge and Oakridge malls cater to suburban families who live in the many subdivisions which dot the Evergreen and southern sections of San Jose. The sprawling Eastridge center, with more than 1.5 million square feet developed on 200 acres, serves as a community resource by hosting many special events. Eastridge also houses a large ice arena used for competition figure skating and hockey. Oakridge, part of Hahn Company's holdings, has more than 110 shops, 3 major department stores, and a six-screen theater complex.

Vallco Fashion Park in Cupertino changed its look during the 1980s, adding many specialty stores and freestanding displays. Competition from Valley Fair and Stanford Shopping Center prompted the center to redirect its marketing from a regional concept to one which focuses on Cupertino and surrounding communities.

Suburban malls such as Valley Fair drew shoppers away from city downtowns when they opened, many of them during the 1960s. For the 1990s, downtown shopping will reemerge as a market with a different tack.

San Jose now has its own downtown retail mall—the Pavilion—and independent retailers, notably Mosher's and Alta, which are leading a mercantile renaissance. These retailers are not competing with suburban malls. Their strategy is to cater to San Jose's growing downtown market.

Sunlight makes its way indoors at Vallco Fashion Park in Cupertino. Photo by Gerald L. French/The Photo File

The Pavilion is targeting four distinct customer groups: the downtown work force, San Jose Convention Center visitors, the large San Jose State University population, and the growing number of people living downtown. The Pavilion retail operations began rather shakily and it has since decided to focus on promoting its food and entertainment facilities. Last Laugh, a popular comedy club, is housed in the Pavilion. Several other entertainment venues are being added.

As San Jose's downtown population grows, so will the need for high-quality retailers. At the forefront of the urban revival are Mosher's—a classic menswear store located just a short walk from San Jose's landmark restaurant, Original Joe's, at 1st and San Carlos streets—and Alta, a sophisticated women's store that features original designs. Alta is located in a corner of the San Jose Fairmont Hotel.

LEFT: This familiar sign leads the way to the Old Town shopping area of Los Gatos, 12 miles south of San Jose. Once the heart of this suburban business community, the multi-level facility is home for a variety of restaurants and boutiques. Photo by John Elk III

FACING PAGE: San Jose's light rail system serves downtown business such as the Pavilion shopping center. The Fairmont Hotel dominates the background. Photo by Gerald L. French/The Photo File

For Ed Mosher, owner of Mosher's, being downtown means going back to his roots. A San Jose native and 1952 graduate of San Jose State University, Mosher opened his first men's clothing store in 1955, across the street from his alma mater. "I pioneered the Ivy League look in San Jose," Mosher recalls.

Through more than three decades of retailing, Mosher has left San Jose's downtown, been back, and left again, but he has always fervently believed San Jose could regain the splendor of its retailing heyday of the 1950s and 1960s. When shoppers fled the downtowns for malls, Mosher chose economic survival and followed them, opening in prestigious locations. He was the first tenant in Los Gatos' Old Town, he opened the first store in San Jose's Town & Country Village, and he was a tenant at Vallco for 10 years. At one time Mosher operated four stores in the county.

With San Jose's new downtown taking shape, Mosher moved back to his first love in 1986, opening his store at 315 South 1st Street.

Mosher thinks it's just a matter of time before more retailers open shop downtown. The city's plans to build more downtown housing will increase the number of young professionals who can shop locally. One downtown address already belongs to Mosher, who lives in an attractive condominium complex. A true urbanite, Mosher sold both his cars and walks to work each day.

"A new type of downtown shopping is happening all over America," says Mosher. "Malls will continue to be there for convenient day-to-day shopping. Our type of store is for the people living and working downtown, for the visitors who want a special gift, who are looking for unique merchandise."

By 1992 San Jose will be getting a second Mosher operation, with a different twist. Mosher has decided to indulge a lifelong love of the theater by opening Mosher's Backstage in San Jose's theater district. Patterned after Ted Hook's Backstage in New York City, Mosher's Backstage will be "an after-theater supper club where stars appearing in San Jose will come and be introduced," Mosher explains. By day his son Todd, a graduate of the California Culinary Institute, will serve California cuisine "with Italian overtones."

Mosher will have no trouble attracting stars to his supper club. Ted Hook, a fellow San Jose State University graduate who has danced in more than 450

Sculpture enlivens the Santa Clara Valley. This dynamic piece calls attention to the Silicon Valley Bank. Photo by Mark E. Gibson

movies and musicals, will work with Mosher on his club. Mosher, a frequent visitor to the New York theater, calls Ted Hook's "the main hangout for movie and theater people in New York." The same will most likely be said about Mosher's Backstage in years to come.

Mosher's and Alta represent the downtown merchants of the future. They add another dimension of choice for the Santa Clara County consumer.

In one of the nation's most affluent buying markets, shoppers have an abundance of choice, from glossy malls such as Valley Fair to the emerging San Jose retail district and established downtown village centers in Los Gatos, Saratoga, Los Altos, Palo Alto, and Mountain View.

■ *Money Managers*

Santa Clara County's affluence creates special demands on the more than 30,000 persons who make their living locally in the finance, insurance, and real estate professions.

Competition is particularly fierce in banking and real estate, both residential and commercial. With one of the highest per capita income areas in the nation, Silicon Valley is a financial plum everyone wants to pluck.

Silicon Valley customers demand more in terms of service and responsiveness, knowing they will get it. Those institutions that thrive, do so because they give above-average service.

The nature of the technology business also creates special opportunities. During the 1980s Silicon Valley experienced a passel of banking start-ups.

Spring brings out the splendor of the Municipal Rose Garden in San Jose's famed rose garden district, known for its wide streets and stately homes. Photo by Gerald L. French/The Photo File

While the start-ups carved out their respective niches, locally grown full-service banks began to compete more aggressively with the banking giants.

One of the most successful banking start-ups is Silicon Valley Bank, founded in 1983 by Roger Smith, a veteran Wells Fargo executive. To start Silicon Valley Bank Smith assembled a powerhouse of co-founders: the late Thomas J. Davis, Jr., of the Mayfield Fund venture-capital firm; Intel board member D. James Guzy; Intel executive Laurence R. Hootnick; Sigma Partners venture-capitalist J. Burgess Jamieson; and Larry Sonsini of Wilson, Sonsini, Goodrich & Rosati, a prominent Silicon Valley technology law firm.

From the beginning Smith was clear about his target: "I saw there was a banking void for emerging technology companies." He hedged his bet somewhat by adding commercial and real estate divisions, but the technology division remains the largest of the bank's operations.

While most banks chose genteel addresses, Smith opened Silicon Valley Bank in San Jose's North 1st Street industrial corridor. He let technology entrepreneurs know that he wanted to be part of the action.

Immediately Smith veered from traditional banking policy in order to attract his target customer. "Most banks would have a company be profitable for several years before they would lend money," says Smith, who serves as president of the bank. "We will loan companies money before they're profitable."

Smith's strategy has paid off well. By making early

Many commercial banks have a presence in downtown San Jose, the commercial and banking heart of Silicon Valley. Photo by Gerald L. French/The Photo File

commitments to technology companies, he has kept them as customers while they've grown. Chips & Technologies and Cirrus Logic are among his clients.

Silicon Valley Bank's growth curve is a venture capitalist's dream. Starting with assets of $5 million, the bank has reached $622 million in assets.

One of the reasons Silicon Valley Bank has been successful, Smith says, is because it is loyal to its customers who may be brilliant technically but are not well versed in finance and management. "In the banking business everyone wants consistency. We stay in there even through the rocky times. We're not cut and runners," says Smith.

From its original North 1st Street site, Silicon Valley Bank has grown to a total of five Silicon Valley locations and one in California's Orange County. In 1990 Smith opened the first out-of-state branch in Boston.

"We have obtained a certain pedigree. We are now nationally known for our technology expertise," says Smith.

Bank start-ups in Silicon Valley have been able to succeed, Smith believes, because the valley "doesn't care who your father was; it's what you can do. People are willing to take a chance on you. They want you to succeed. It's part of our entrepreneurial flavor."

Silicon Valley's start-up climate worked equally well for Phil Boyce. A fourth-generation native of Santa Clara County, Boyce spent his childhood picking prunes on ranches in Saratoga. He graduated from Los Gatos High School and San Jose State University. After spending almost a decade in the banking business he decided it was time to start one of his own.

Entrepreneurs barely 30 years old are the stuff of legends in Silicon Valley. In 1975, at age 31, Boyce wanted to start a community bank. He invested $68 to host a luncheon for 20 friends, 17 of whom invested in the fledgling Pacific Valley Bank.

His timing was perfect. The bank's history matched that of the technology industry. "Being the new imaginative kid on the block was great because the technology entrepreneurs were also the new kids," Boyce reminisces.

Boyce's notion was to have his bank become an integral part of the evolving Silicon Valley community: "We wanted to deal with people who made decisions locally, and we wanted to be involved in local business ourselves."

Pacific Valley Bank took off quickly. It ended its first full year with $18 million in assets and more than 4,500 accounts. In Silicon Valley's innovative environment Pacific Valley Bank pioneered in banking service. It introduced automatic teller machines (ATMs) to the county, opening the first ATM on-site at a technology manufacturer. The bank also developed accounting software for public administrators.

In 1987 the bank became Pacific Western Bank after merging with COBANCO. By 1991 the bank had 125,000 accounts and had topped one billion dollars in assets. Strategic acquisitions allowed the bank to expand into the Santa Cruz and Monterey markets.

Pacific Western Bank has grown to serve both general and high-technology accounts, becoming one of the leading retail banks in California and the largest independent commercial bank in Santa Clara County. "We've literally put thousands of customers in business over the years," says Boyce, counting among them a successful restaurant chain, a large HMO (health maintenance organization), three newspapers, and dozens of electronics firms.

The bank has done well because it emphasizes customer service, Boyce says. "We visit our customer companies. They don't have to come to us. And we structure our products according to what they need, not what we want."

In 1982 Boyce became chairman of the bank, opening the $30-million, 12-story Pacific Valley Bank building in San Jose. The building houses the bank's headquarters, main branch, and other prestigious firms. Boyce's baronial executive suite, graced with a sweeping view of downtown and appointed with beautiful art, befits a Silicon Valley mogul.

Throughout his bank's growth Boyce has stayed on course, remaining closely involved with the community. Bank directors sit on the boards of local companies. Boyce is personally credited with getting Silicon Valley's traditionally tight purse strings to loosen up a bit for charity. In 1981 Boyce launched the Pacific Valley Foundation. It was a breakthrough for local philanthropy, spurring other individuals and firms to underwrite charitable activities. The medically indigent and the arts are among Boyce's recipients.

Boyce also actively supports education. He is chairman of the president's advisory board of San Jose State University, a Santa Clara University trustee, and director of the UC Santa Cruz Foundation.

"I firmly believe in our business that we derive our strength from the community, and that we should put back into the community more than we take out," Boyce declares.

Not all banking start-ups during the 1970s and 1980s had as smooth a growth curve as Silicon Valley Bank and Pacific Western Bank. Others struggled to find a niche and survive as a 1980s shakeout tested the viability of some institutions.

California Business Bank, a 1982 start-up, experienced early, fast growth and then hit rock bottom during 1984 and 1985. Bad loans and heavy losses almost ruined the bank. Dick Conniff, a quiet and unassuming alumnus of Bank of the West, became president of California Business Bank in 1985 and is widely credited with saving the bank.

"We narrowed our focus and concentrated on building up assets. That basically saved us," says Conniff. California Business Bank has found its place in small, privately held businesses, professional firms, medical and dental practices, and nonprofit agencies. Bank assets for 1990 totaled $56 million. The bank has its headquarters on South Market Street in San Jose, in the high-rise district of downtown.

Conniff regards the 1990s banking market as "saturated and very competitive" and doesn't believe the battle is over for California Business Bank.

The national experience of savings-and-loan failures has created a "general distaste for banking," according to Conniff. This negative environment, coupled with a real estate slump, makes it tough for a small bank to do business.

However, Conniff is optimistic. In the long term Silicon Valley's normally robust economy will make it possible for regional banks such as his to survive, he says.

The banking start-up mania of the 1980s will not be repeated in the 1990s, according to Conniff. Mergers and acquisitions will continue a phase of banking consolidation. By the next century further polarization will result in basically two types of banks: small, "boutique" banks and larger, full-service ones, says Conniff.

Thomas Cunningham, Jr., is among the top real estate brokers in Santa Clara Valley. Photo by Gerald L. French/The Photo File

■ *The Real Estate Whirl*

When the real estate business is good in Santa Clara County, it's very good. But when it is bad, it's dismal.

In one of the most high-priced markets in the nation, real estate professionals can reap astronomical rewards when business is on the upswing. However, the cost of doing business in an affluent market is also high. When the market is flat, vacant commercial buildings built at premium prices become a financial albatross. Extravagant "spec" (speculative) homes sit empty, creating headaches for builders who have taken out loans against the eventual sale of the properties.

To win in the real estate game in Santa Clara County takes a seven-day-a-week commitment and nerves of steel. For the most part, real estate has paralleled Silicon Valley's cyclical economy. Firms that survive the down cycles work just a little bit harder and keep their overhead at a minimum.

Cunningham Associates, founded in 1968 by Thomas J. Cunningham, Jr., has weathered more than one business cycle. One of the top five commercial and industrial real estate brokerages in Silicon Valley, the firm has stayed "lean and mean" throughout its history, says Cunningham.

After more than two decades the firm has 18 salespeople and 7 support staffers. While other real estate firms have legions of salespeople and tremendous overhead, Cunningham Associates is a spare, highly productive organization.

Cunningham and his executive vice president, Ray Baker, spend 90 percent of their time helping their salespeople close deals. Aggressive young agents such as Regina Reilly work with Cunningham on major projects. "Our approach to

Great America Parkway is the headquarters to high-tech companies such as SynOptics. Photo by Michael O'Callahan

people has made us successful. We place a high value on the individual," Cunningham says.

In 1991 Cunningham and Reilly were at work on a significant project: marketing a 90-acre San Jose site owned by the Southern Pacific railroad and used as a switching yard. The site at Julian and 1st streets will most likely become an R & D complex with some retail activity, according to Cunningham.

R & D is a favorite bailiwick of Cunningham. His office is on the Oakmead Parkway in Sunnyvale, in the middle of an R & D district. To Cunningham R & D buildings represent the future, but there will be a difference. As land gets more scarce and even more expensive, buildings will move up instead of out. "We will see more density in R & D and manufacturing. Firms will go to multiple stories, either mid- or high-rise," Cunningham says. The one-story campus-style buildings of Silicon Valley's past are not necessarily its future.

Silicon Valley began the 1990s with 23 million square feet of vacant office space, the fallout of rampant overbuilding during the prior decade. By the mid-1990s the vacancies should be leased by industry, Cunningham says, but the experience has been a sobering one for developers. The "spec" building of the past is being replaced with "build-to-suits," says Cunningham. This relatively low-risk approach means firms will build for a designated tenant rather than build a structure and then hunt for a customer.

The surplus of office space has toppled some firms. Brokerage firms have left the market, Cunningham says.

A similar shakeout is occurring in the residential real estate market. The sleepy home-buying market of the 1989-91 period has caused those professionals with marginal success to reconsider their career options.

"There are two kinds of realtors: the ones who are usually very successful and the others who are just eking out a living," declares John Pinto, a San Jose realtor and former president of the San Jose Real Estate Board. "About 5 percent of the people do 95 percent of the business."

Pinto, whose firm grossed about $20 million in 1990, says real estate is still a good business to be in when the market is Silicon Valley. After all, says Pinto, it's more profitable to sell a home in Silicon Valley, with a median price

The extensive facilities of the Stanford Medical Center in Palo Alto help make Santa Clara Valley a prime location for medical research and high-quality health care, both public and private. Photo by Scott Loy/The Photo File

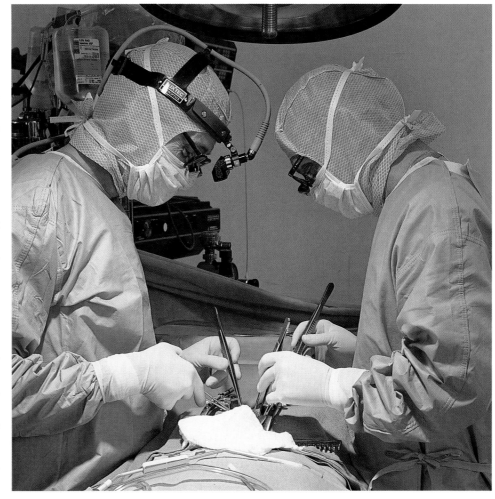

hovering around $250,000, than in Akron, Ohio, with a median price of $65,000.

"The real estate professional is a classic example of the American entrepreneur. You can be an immigrant. You can start with little. And if you really learn the business and work hard, you can make a six-figure income," says a smiling Pinto.

■ *The Healing People*

Silicon Valley's affluent, highly competitive market is a challenging one for banking and real estate professionals. The market is equally saturated and competitive in health care.

Even during the 1990-91 recession, when virtually all market sectors were flat, health-care jobs continued to increase in Santa Clara County. Roughly 41,000 professionals earn a living in health services.

The region's affluence attracts some of the finest physicians and other health-care professionals. "Absolutely the best medicine in the world is available here," says Bob Kirk, president of Health Dimensions, the parent corporation for several leading Santa Clara County hospitals.

A desirable market such as Santa Clara County also creates fierce competition among hospitals and health-care plan providers. Intense competition in some industries creates price wars to the benefit of the ultimate consumer. Unfortunately the reverse has been true in health care. While Santa Clara County may be an extremely competitive market, local industry has not been able to escape the national phenomenon of skyrocketing health-care costs.

The price of health care has risen a breathtaking 40 percent since 1988. Silicon Valley industry therefore contributes 25 percent of its net income to pay for health-care benefits.

Escalating health-care costs are a matter of serious concern for Silicon Valley employers, who see health care taking an increasing share of their profits.

To appeal to employers watching the bottom line, new health maintenance organizations (HMOs) have been created to offer an alternative to out-of-control costs. Health Net, a one-billion-dollar HMO with 800,000 California members, is actively courting more Silicon Valley business, says Henry Loubet,

Kaiser in Mountain View is one of several health maintenance organizations that help keep the county's residents healthy. Photo by Joseph Sohm/Chromosohm

the company's Northern California regional vice president.

Health Net presents Kaiser Permanente with its first real California competition in the HMO market. Kaiser, the nation's largest HMO, has 4 million members in California. While Kaiser also operates its own hospital system, Health Net is strictly an HMO with a network of physicians and clinical services. Kaiser, founded in 1940, owns about one-third of the Santa Clara County market. It is well entrenched as one of the usual health-care plan options offered employees. Health Net,

with 13,000 Silicon Valley members, is basically in the start-up phase locally. ESL and Hitachi are among the Silicon Valley companies who have added Health Net as an option.

An alternative form of health insurance, the HMO was the original concept of Henry J. Kaiser, the industrialist who, among his accomplishments, built the Kaiser Permanente Cement Corporation in Cupertino. The quid pro quo in an HMO is to trade choice for dollars. A subscriber cannot pick any doctor or hospital; the doctor must be with one of the HMO's medical groups. However, the cost savings are substantial, for both the employer and employee, who increasingly is asked to share the cost burden of a health-care plan.

Health Net controls health-care costs by prepaying a medical group based on the number of enrollees. "We do not use a fee-for-service-based system," Loubet explains. Since the medical group is not paid according to the number of patient visits, "it promotes efficiency and discourages frivolous, unnecessary visits," says Loubet.

"Managed care," a universal health-care industry anthem, is what the HMO achieves, Loubet says. The result is tighter control on inflation.

The least expensive way to take care of people is for them never to get sick in the first place. Silicon Valley, with its innovative youthful spirit, has embraced Health Net's "wellness" concept, says Loubet. The HMO works with employers on health-promotion programs, including how to stop smoking, stress reduction, and weight management.

"We want members to take responsibility for their own health," Loubet says. Health Net and Stanford University are studying 700 persons in the wellness programs to gauge the impact of such programs.

There are 30 million Americans enrolled in HMOs. During the 1980s HMOs grew rapidly while traditional private health insurers lost members. "HMOs are here to stay," says Loubet.

Health Net's main HMO rival, Kaiser, also competes in Santa Clara County's

The San Jose Medical Center is part of the network of medical facilities servicing the Santa Clara Valley. Photo by Richard L. Kaylin

The San Jose Medical Center is part of the network of medical facilities servicing the Santa Clara Valley. Photo by Richard L. Kaylin

saturated hospital market. Kaiser operates two hospitals in Santa Clara County: The Kaiser Permanente Santa Clara Medical Center serves more than 263,000 members while the Santa Teresa Community Medical Center in South San Jose serves 159,000 members. Kaiser also operates a satellite facility in Gilroy, and in 1991 it opened the new Mountain View Medical Office Building, consolidating its North County services and closing its Sunnyvale offices.

Kaiser's local hospital competitor is Health Dimensions. Founded in 1984 Health Dimensions became the nonprofit parent corporation for San Jose Medical Center and Good Samaritan Hospital. It also operates Samaritan Oaks HealthCare Center (formerly Mission Oaks), and in 1989 it opened South Valley hospital in Gilroy.

Health Dimensions' records for 1990 estimate its market share at about 22 percent and Kaiser's at 19 percent. The firm markets itself as the private alternative to Kaiser.

Since incorporating, Health Dimensions has become a health service entrepreneur.

RIGHT: The best available medical resources are available to children of the Santa Clara Valley with the opening of the Lucile Salter Packard Children's Hospital in Palo Alto. Photo by Gerald L. French/The Photo File

FACING PAGE: The Lucile Salter Packard Children's Hospital stands as a newly constructed symbol of Stanford's commitment to children's health care. Photo by Gerald L. French/The Photo File

Superior local medical facilities such as O'Connor Hospital serve Santa Clara Valley residents. Photo by Gerald L. French/The Photo File

Among the medical research facilities available at Stanford is the Beckman Center for Molecular and Genetic Medicine, headed by Nobel Prize-winner Paul Berg. Photo by Gerald L. French/The Photo File

It is in partnership with First + Care, a 17-location network of urgent-care treatment centers; it also operates several nonhospital medical services.

With health-care costs escalating "we are seeing inpatient care declining and more outpatient care," says Health Dimensions president Bob Kirk. Technological advances have made more outpatient treatments possible. Lithotripsy, a method of using sound waves to blast away kidney stones, is marketed by Health Dimensions through the Northern California Kidney Stone Center and a related mobile-unit division.

A national decline in inpatient activity will continue, Kirk says, further contributing to a surplus of hospital beds. The future is in adding new outpatient services and in using the managed-care approach of limited choice to control costs.

In northern Santa Clara County an important medical presence is Stanford University Medical Center, one of the world's leading teaching and research facilities. The center and its Children's Hospital have a combined 18 percent of the county market share. However, Stanford's market is really global. Its many specialty services bring in adult and child patients from around the world.

Stanford University Medical Center—which consists of several research centers, a 633-bed hospital, more than 100 specialty clinics, the School of Medicine, and the

Lucile Salter Packard Children's Hospital—conducts scientific research that will determine the nature of health care in the future.

In May 1989 Stanford opened the Beckman Center for Molecular and Genetic Medicine, named in honor of philanthropists Arnold and Mabel Beckman. Directed by Nobel Prize laureate Paul Berg, the Beckman Center is devoted to researching the causes of disease at the molecular level.

Stanford Medical Center has made medical history on many occasions. It pioneered recombinant DNA research, constructing the first rDNA molecule in 1972. The center was the site of the first kidney transplant in California in 1960, the first adult human heart transplant in the United States in 1968, and the first successful human heart and lung transplant in the world in 1981.

Scientific breakthroughs in the future could come from many of Stanford's research projects. The center is researching new immunization strategies against AIDS; new ways of improving survival rates of heart and lung transplant patients; the use of monoclonal antibodies to fight disease; new methods of treating arthritis; and noninvasive imaging techniques. Numerous other research projects are also ongoing.

In addition to Kaiser, Health Dimensions, and Stanford, other hospital providers in Santa Clara County are El Camino Hospital in Mountain View; O'Connor Hospital and Alexian Brothers, both in San Jose; Los Gatos Community Hospital; and Santa Clara Valley Medical Center (VMC), the county-run public hospital.

When patients don't have insurance, they normally turn to Santa Clara Valley Medical Center, which has about an 11-percent market share. As the county public hospital VMC treats all patients, regardless of their ability to pay. Even in affluent Santa Clara County, there are a startling number of uninsured patients. And the number is rising as health-care insurance becomes increasingly expensive. An estimated 10 percent of the population is uninsured.

VMC "is the safety net for uninsured patients," asserts Robert Sillen, the hospital's executive director. The hospital also is a major provider to Medi-Cal patients. Since the return on Medi-Cal patients is 60 cents for each dollar of actual expense, most hospitals in the county shun Medi-Cal business, according to Anne Moses, VMC's associate director.

"Community hospitals don't want our uninsured patients. So while they may have empty beds, VMC is at capacity all the time," Moses says.

The only publicly operated hospital in the county, VMC has been designated as the site for many specialty-care services. VMC and Stanford Medical Center serve as the region's two

specialty hospitals. VMC is highly regarded for its burn center, its rehabilitation center for spinal cord and head injuries, its Neonatal Intensive Care Unit, and its regional high-risk pregnancy program. With Stanford and San Jose Medical Center, VMC is also one of three regional trauma centers.

"Corporate America sends its clients to VMC for our specialty services," says Sillen. For corporate and industrial workers VMC opened the Repetitive Motion Institute to treat injuries caused by repeated, computer-related tasks. Silicon Valley's assembly-line workers, information processors, and others who use repetitive motion to perform their tasks are clients of the institute. As part of its service the institute will visit a workplace to evaluate its ergonomic level and to make suggestions for improvement.

As Silicon Valley's population demands more services, the budget pinch at VMC tightens further. VMC has established its own foundation to raise money in the community. One of its biggest future challenges will be the continuing search for funds to underwrite its service to the medically indigent. Sillen advocates a form of universal health insurance which he says will also work towards cost containment.

"The free marketplace doesn't work in health care," Sillen declares, noting that other major industrial nations have universal health coverage. The concept,

The reflecting pool at the *San Jose Mercury News* is often a celebration site because of the newspaper's many awards for excellence. Because of the high caliber of awards won in recent years, the pool has been dubbed Pulitzer Pond. Photo by Gerald L. French/The Photo File

according to Sillen, has been in existence for at least four decades.

"Business is getting tired of health-care costs. Only by having a regulated system can we contain industry growth and costs," claims Sillen.

Without question the quantum leap that health-care costs have taken is an issue Silicon Valley will be aggressively tackling in the future. The managed-care approach of limited choice will continue to have impact. Other options will undoubtedly surface as employers and workers resist further health-care expense.

The *Peninsula Times Tribune* staff helped celebrate at the May fete parade. Photo by Joseph Sohm/Chromosohm

■ Telling The Story

When Santa Clara County wants to get information about banking, real estate, or health care, it usually turns first to the *San Jose Mercury News,* its major metropolitan area daily, and then to the more than 150 other media outlets serving the county.

The county is served by a combination of locally owned media and nationally owned outlets. It also has the benefit of outlets originating from either the San Jose or San Francisco markets.

A rich selection of media is available: 4 metropolitan dailies, 2 suburban dailies, 54 weeklies and biweeklies, 28 television stations, 5 cable television systems, and 61 radio stations.

In daily newspaper competition the *San Jose Mercury News* is far ahead of the pack. The daily, winner of two Pulitzer Prizes, has close to a 60-percent market share; its Sunday paper climbs to 67 percent. About 332,000 people read the

The editorial offices of the *San Jose Mercury News,* a Knight-Ridder publication, are home to some of the region's top journalists. Photo by Gerald L. French/The Photo File

Mercury News' Sunday edition.

Ranking third in the nation in newspaper display-advertising linage, the *Mercury News* is also a moneymaker for its parent company, Knight-Ridder. Another major factor in the paper's financial success, according to George Owen, director of marketing services, is its classified advertising section. Silicon Valley industry creates an endless demand for employment ads.

Other dailies read by Santa Clara County residents include the *San Francisco Chronicle,* which has about a 10-percent market share, the *San Francisco Examiner,* the *Peninsula Times Tribune,* the *Oakland Tribune,* and the region's national competitor, *USA Today.*

Santa Clara Valley's prosperous readers have inspired publishing start-ups to serve specific markets. Among the most successful is the valley weekly *Metro,* founded in 1985. "Our readers first used *Metro* as a cultural guide. They now look to us as a forum for ideas; for political, thought-provoking articles as well," explains publisher David Cohen.

"*Metro* represents the emerging sense of a metropolis, those things that happen as the dream emerges: arts, entertainment, and major sports entities. The evolution during our first six years has been exciting," Cohen says.

Since its founding *Metro* has spun off a sister paper, the *San Jose City Times,* and purchased the *Los Gatos Weekly.*

The increasing multicultural diversity in the valley has spawned a number of ethnic media, which face special business challenges.

Hilbert and Betty Morales own and publish *El Observador,* the valley's largest Hispanic newspaper. "*El Observador* has survived 10 years," says Hilbert Morales. He sees the future of the paper depending on advertisers'

recognizing the marketing potential of the paper.

"The Hispanic press is a valuable resource for reaching the Hispanic audience. Our future depends on getting advertisers to see us as a cost-effective way to reach their potential markets," says Morales.

Santa Clara Valley's demographic diversity also creates a highly competitive, fragmented broadcasting market. Viewers can pick from San Francisco- and Oakland-based network affiliates, locally owned stations, ethnic media, and cable systems.

The only local major network affiliate is ABC's KNTV. The station's commitment to local news, billing itself as the San Jose NewsChannel, is a key reason for its success, according to general manager Stewart Park.

"There's a tremendous appetite for local news," Park says. "While San Francisco media will always be committed to a broad scope of the Bay Area, we're free to focus 100 percent of our resources and energies on covering San Jose and Santa Clara County."

Public-broadcasting aficionados in the valley have the luxury of being able to tune in to both KQED in San Francisco and KTEH in San Jose. News of Silicon Valley is now being generated from KTEH, with the "Silicon Valley Report," produced by John Crump, and the Mike Malone talk show.

Silicon Valley workers who spend long hours commuting on the local freeways can choose from dozens of radio stations, from the easygoing San Jose-based KBAY, with newscaster Lissa Kreisler, to the country-and-western favorite KEEN, KBAY's sister station, to contemporary music favorites such as KWSS, KARA, and KEZR.

The well-educated, affluent Santa Clara Valley market can satisfy its thirst for information with an abundance of media choices.

Surging Ahead

Santa Clara County is expected to continue as a choice market for the region's many service businesses. More than a quarter-million jobs are expected to be added by the year 2005, according to the Association of Bay Area Governments. These new workers will demand more services. Since many workers will be highly skilled and educated, it is likely Silicon Valley's buying power will remain robust. Retail, entertainment, and cultural amenities are in a position to benefit as the valley surges ahead.

7

Taking Pleasure in the Arts

■ *San Jose: Where The Medicis Play*

In the great cities of the world, one facet that is always present is an exuberant cultural life. As the next century unfolds, San Jose will begin to reach world-class status as Silicon Valley's city of the future becomes a Bay Area mecca for the arts.

Until the late 1970s the arts in San Jose were in a moribund state. For culture, citizens of San Jose and neighboring communities would go to "the city," as they affectionately called San Francisco. Old-line families in the seaport city continued the tradition of noblesse oblige and supported the opera, ballet, and other arts. At the same time San Jose, as the rest of Silicon Valley, was creating a new definition for itself. Development in technology, commerce, and land was the priority of the day. The arts would have to wait.

The decade of the 1980s saw San Jose arouse from its cultural sleep and nurture an unprecedented growth in the arts. As San Jose's skyline took shape and Silicon Valley became a mature business market, the valley's executives looked outward and began to aggressively support the arts. Money from the vast fortunes made in technology companies trickled into arts budgets. Deficit-ridden arts companies began to discover their own modern-day Medicis. A new tradition of noblesse oblige was being born in Silicon Valley.

The arts come to life on the stage of San Jose's Center for the Performing Arts. Theatergoers enjoy Broadway shows, classical dance, and popular performances of all types. Photo by Gerald L. French/The Photo File

San Jose reaped the benefits. A city which never had had a classical opera company now had a truly fine one in Opera San Jose. Legitimate theater became established with the emergence of the San Jose Repertory Company. Cleveland and San Jose became partners in

209

RIGHT: Villa Montalvo in Saratoga has excellent gardens for strolling. Behind the main building is an amphitheater that hosts one of the leading summer music festivals in the area. Photo by Andrew Van Dis

FACING PAGE TOP: Sculptures such as this are found on the grounds of Saratoga's Villa Montalvo. Besides the music festival annually held on the grounds each summer, the main building is occasionally the site of musical master classes with visiting musicians such as pianist Dave Brubeck and others. Photo by Andrew Van Dis

the San Jose Cleveland Ballet. The San Jose Civic Light Opera broke national records with 32,000 subscribers, the largest paid subscription base of any musical theater company. And the San Jose Symphony doubled its number of subscribers, ending the decade with a record fund-raising year. For the first time in history, Silicon Valley residents really had a cultural choice. It was no longer necessary to go to San Francisco to enjoy high culture. San Jose was becoming "the city."

It is a dizzying time for the arts in San Jose. There are now more than 80 recognized arts groups in the city. Art—in all forms—is flourishing. The exquisite dancing of San Jose Cleveland Ballet's star, Raymond Rodriguez, is a counterpoint to the bawdy melodrama of the Opry House Theater in San Jose's historic Old Almaden district.

On a typical fall Sunday afternoon in San Jose, the families of Silicon Valley can be seen strolling past the dancing fountain in Plaza Park across from the Fairmont Hotel. They enjoy the golden sunshine as they walk to the Montgomery Theatre where a new play is previewing at the San Jose Repertory. Some will continue down San Carlos Street to the new full-length production of the San Jose Cleveland Ballet. Afterwards they'll have supper at Eulipia, San Jose's bastion of modern cuisine, or perhaps just a glass of champagne in the Fairmont's beautifully appointed lobby.

The Medicis of Florence and Tuscany would have been proud.

◼ The Arts: Bigger And Better

From its nascent state San Jose's arts community will blossom into a full-fledged metropolitan cultural center during the twenty-first century. And San Jose's "arts czar," Dan McFadden, is leading the way.

A testament to San Jose's commitment to the arts is City Hall's establishment of the Office of Cultural Affairs headed by McFadden. His office supports growth in the arts by working with the San Jose Redevelopment Agency to construct new municipal arts facilities, promoting city-sponsored arts events, acquiring more than $4 million worth of art for public places, conducting an arts education outreach to more than 50,000 students, and coordinating special events such as the annual "Christmas in the Park" outdoor spectacular, which draws thousands of people to San Jose's downtown.

"One of the primary functions of our downtown is to serve as an entertainment and cultural center. We're pleased that the arts are absolutely thriving here," says McFadden.

By the year 2020 city officials plan to have their own versions of Broadway and Off Broadway in San Jose's downtown. Work is already in progress to increase the number of professional performing facilities from two to six. San Jose's major performing arts groups struggled for space during the 1980s boom, effectively playing musical chairs between the 2,700-seat Center for the Performing Arts (CPA), a round European-style theater designed by disciples of architect Frank Lloyd Wright, and the quaint, drafty 37-seat Montgomery Theatre, completed in 1932. Hit performances at the San Jose Repertory couldn't be extended due to the space crunch, and both Opera San Jose and the San Jose Symphony suffered from stage and acoustic limitations.

By tripling the number of theaters, Opera San Jose and the San Jose Repertory will find permanent new homes, and emerging performing arts companies

such as San Jose Stage Company and City Lights will have room to grow and cultivate their own audiences.

New space will also serve the city's three dozen multicultural arts groups, a reflection of San Jose's growing ethnic diversity.

Taiko, the Japanese drum corps, and the Los Lupenos De San Jose dance company are dazzling groups that will benefit from the additional booking dates that will open up as the city expands its facilities.

As Voltaire said, "All the arts are brothers; each one is a light to the others." San Jose arts are fueled by the visions of local arts entrepreneurs, people who fortunately have the administrative and business savvy to put these visions into practical applications.

"We also worry about budgets and the bottom line. It's just that our business happens to be entertainment," declares Stewart Slater, executive producer of the San Jose Civic Light Opera, known locally as the CLO. The 57-year-old company had its best decade during the 1980s with Slater in charge, breaking records in subscriptions and attendance. Clearly the CLO has the right formula. Slater and artistic director Dianna Shuster mix fresh local talent with more seasoned Equity actors and put them in crowd-pleasing shows such as the *Pirates of Penzance, Guys & Dolls,* and *Dreamgirls.* And the audience keeps coming back, to the tune of an 84-percent renewal rate for season tickets.

While the Center for Performing Arts will continue to be CLO's home base, Slater wants to add smaller shows to the repertoire when the city opens up new performing arts facilities.

As part of a growing downtown center for the arts, San Jose's Montgomery Theater serves as the home of the San Jose Repertory Company. Each year the company produces a season of classical and contemporary works that bring a range of theatrical experiences to local audiences. Photo by Gerald L. French/ The Photo File

Slater is committed to making CLO relevant for the 1990s and beyond by adding new and younger audiences to the subscription base and by working with local arts magnet schools to use the CLO as an educational resource. "San Jose has a growing ethnic majority so we in the theater need to overcome any language barriers. Arts education is the best means of accomplishing this," Slater says. In 1990, to target the younger audience, he produced *Jesus Christ Superstar*, a play with a modern score. Slater updated the production for the 1990s. "We're not a museum theater. We view each piece as a new piece. We must be relevant to the modern audience."

San Jose opera lovers are grateful for Irene Dalis, who after 20 years as a major star with the Metropolitan Opera, singing mezzo-soprano, returned to her native San Jose. Dalis settled down to the pleasant task of conducting the

opera workshop at San Jose State University, her alma mater. She discovered a tremendous number of talented young singers with plenty of energy and no place to professionally perform. Dalis fixed that by founding Opera San Jose in 1984.

"People here do believe in young talent. We've never had a deficit and have enjoyed gradual growth," says Dalis in her trademark throaty voice.

From day one Dalis has been clear about her goal. "Our motto is 'We don't import stars. We export stars.'" In less than a decade Dalis brought Opera San Jose into the inner circle of premier performing groups in the city, staging ambitious full-length operas such as *La Boheme* and *La Traviata* and producing the world premieres of two operas: *Hotel Eden* by Henry Mollicone and *West of Washington Square* by Alva Henderson.

During the 1990s Dalis will expand the Resident Artists Program, begun during the 1988-89 season and patterned after European models. The year-round program grooms promising singers for lead roles by subsidizing them while they work full-time on their opera careers. By the mid-1990s Dalis would like an ensemble of 10 in the program.

Dalis awaits Opera San Jose's move to a planned 1,600-seat theater, which will allow for bigger audiences and greatly improved acoustics. Opera San Jose will share the facility with other groups.

Ballet in San Jose has been nurtured by the ultimate balletomane, Karen Loewenstern, who founded the San Jose Cleveland Ballet in 1985. "Ballet is my favorite art form, and I was tired of having to go to San Francisco to see it," Loewenstern says.

A true "Medici," she is the wife of ROLM cofounder Walter Loewenstern. Her connections among Silicon Valley's affluent enabled Loewenstern to raise the start-up money to fund her vision and to promote continued corporate sponsorship of the ballet company.

As the third such co-venture in the nation, San Jose Cleveland Ballet married the San Jose market to the 15-year-old Cleveland Ballet, creating a bi-city company. Residing permanently in Cleveland, the corps de ballet maintains a rigorous travel schedule in order to perform a complete season in each city.

Every ballet company has a "look," and San Jose Cleveland Ballet's definitely comes from its cofounder and artistic director Dennis Nahat, a former principal dancer with American Ballet Theatre and the Joffrey Ballet, and a former Broadway choreographer.

His stamp of Broadway theatricality, combined with a genius for storytelling in dance, and the upbeat liveliness of the young corps, add up to a pleasurable experience for his audiences.

Nahat was able to attract his former dance partner, prima ballerina Cynthia Gregory, to join the company as a permanent guest artist. Gregory has enraptured audiences in lead roles in *Coppélia* and *Romeo and Juliet.*

For the 1990s and beyond Loewenstern's goal is to double the ballet company's subscription base, which totaled a respectable 4,500 in just four seasons. She also plans to produce an independent *Nutcracker* production. Corps dancers will be chosen locally while the principal dancers will come from Cleveland. In order to accommodate two cities, San Jose's *Nutcracker* has appeared early in the season, around Thanksgiving. *Nutcracker*s are traditional

San Jose Cleveland Ballet demonstrates the grace and beauty that is the trademark of the fine dancers of the company. Courtesy, San Jose Cleveland Ballet

moneymakers for companies so better San Jose booking dates closer to Christmas will bring in higher revenue by being able to appeal to the holiday spirit at its peak.

By the mid-1990s the company will open a full-fledged ballet school in San Jose, similar to the School of Cleveland Ballet, for which Nahat also serves as artistic director.

If music be the food of love, then the San Jose area has had a 112-year-long love affair with the San Jose Symphony, one of the oldest symphonies in the United States. But the love affair really intensified in the 1970s and 1980s during the reign of internationally prominent maestro George Cleve. "George really built the symphony musically. When he took over it was a semiprofessional group. Now we are a significant orchestra," says Douglas N. McLendon, symphony president.

Cleve will leave the San Jose Symphony during the 1992 season to pursue a career as an international guest artist. It will mark the end of his 20th year with the orchestra, and the search is in high gear for a replacement of equal caliber.

Silicon Valley audiences love the symphony's Masterworks Series, which showcases classical music, and its Pops Series, which features such favorites as Henry Mancini, Peter Nero, and Doc Severinsen. The symphony performs at both the San Jose Center for the Performing Arts and to constant sell-out crowds at Cupertino's Flint Center in northern Silicon Valley.

In the early twenty-first century, the San Jose Symphony plans to achieve major United States symphony status, with a $15-million operating budget and

a lengthened performance schedule, which will allow musicians to work full-time, year-round. It's an ambitious goal for the symphony, which entered the 1990s with a $4-million budget, but McLendon believes it can be done: "Success breeds success, and the word is out that the symphony's good, the music's good." With the CPA and Flint Center selling out, McLendon fervently wishes that a new, acoustically perfect 3,000-seat concert hall will eventually be built. Such a hall is mentioned in the City of San Jose's facilities plan for the year 2020.

If there's an arts Santa, he'll not only grant the wishes of the opera and symphony but also that of the San Jose Repertory Company. San Jose Repertory plans to move out of the Montgomery Theatre by the mid-1990s, ideally to a permanent new 600-seat facility. Both the short- and long-term changes will enable the repertory to extend hit shows such as the blockbuster "1940's Radio Hour."

Founded in 1980 by Jim Reber, San Jose Repertory embodied the lightning growth of arts in that decade, its subscriber base growing from 1,000 to more than 10,000. Now into its second decade the repertory is also ready to expand its theatrical vistas.

With an available year-round theater, the San Jose Repertory can develop new plays in a workshop environment and work cooperatively to share the theater facilities with important out-of-town groups, such as El Teatro Campesino.

▇ *Life In The Land Of Woz*

It is the year 2010. A seven-year-old girl, accompanied by her parents, skips lightly along Woz Way—named in honor of Apple Computer cofounder and philanthropist Steve Wozniak—en route to the Children's Discovery Museum of San Jose. There she'll walk down the museum's Main Street, encountering the sights and sounds of city life. Visiting the interactive exhibits she'll stop to blow bubbles in "The Laundryworks." In "The Factory" she'll learn how to

ABOVE AND FACING PAGE: San Jose's Children's Discovery Museum allows visitors hands-on experience with a wide range of objects and tools. Kids can play with real fire trucks and police cars, grind corn with a stone grinding wheel, or slide down a sewer-pipe slide. Above photo by Gerald L. French/The Photo File; facing page photo by Michael O'Callahan

ABOVE AND FACING PAGE: One of the most wonderful attributes of Santa Clara Valley is its mixture of industry with the arts. Fantastic and beautiful sculptures often grace the headquarters of many of Silicon Valley's greatest high-tech companies, proving that business and pleasure can mix. Photos by Joseph Sohm/Chromosohm

make a finished product on a working assembly line. Then in "The Waterworks" she'll work with water wheels and real canal locks to understand hydraulics and energy sources. Later, after a ride on one of the historic trolleys operating in downtown San Jose, followed by a picnic lunch in the beautiful Guadalupe River Park, where the museum is located, the family will walk to the other end of Woz Way to visit the Tech Museum of Innovation. There in "The Garage" —named to commemorate the humble beginnings of so many Silicon Valley start-ups—she and her parents will look at a close-up of the integrated circuit and learn about the impact it made on Silicon Valley and the world. In the CAD/CAM exhibit she will use computer-assisted design to create her own special bicycle. At day's end the family agrees it has been an enriching experience for all.

The 1990s are bringing not one but two sparkling new museums to Silicon Valley: Children's Discovery Museum and the Tech Museum of Innovation. Although stylistically different, both honor the creative mind and the discovery of knowledge, the impetus for Silicon Valley entrepreneurship and invention. The Tech Museum of Innovation will provide historical perspective, and, at the same time, it will update displays to keep current with ever-changing technology. Children's Discovery Museum gives children a window to the larger world, offering a wealth of hands-on experiences to learn about the arts, humanities, science, and technology.

Another one of San Jose's fine examples of business combined with art is seen here. Photo by Mark E. Gibson

The 42,000-square-foot Children's Discovery Museum opened in June 1990. A 1995 completion date is expected for the Tech Museum of Innovation, which has a "garage" exhibit currently open to the public as a teaser of things to come. Both facilities have been designed by Mexico City architect Ricardo Legorreta, noted for his dynamic angular designs.

■ *A Visual Feast*

After the isolation of a computer cubicle and the linearity of the computer screen, the Silicon Valley worker craves color, form, a stimulation of the senses. An antidote can be found in two major art museums: the Triton Museum of Art in Santa Clara and the San Jose Museum of Art. Silicon Valley's 1980s arts explosion infused both museums with new energy and purpose. Dynamic new directors took charge, each bringing a different arts perspective. Both have successfully conducted major new capital-construction campaigns.

Bill Atkins spearheaded the campaign and construction of the Triton's spectacular new 22,000-square-foot building, a cool white blend of modern and neoclassical elements. Silicon Valley pioneer David Packard and Santa Clara attorney Austen D. Warburton contributed major construction gifts.

The oldest public art institution in Silicon Valley, the Triton was founded in 1965 and was originally situated in San Jose. Soon after, it moved to its current site on Warburton Avenue just down the block from Santa Clara City Hall. For years the Triton consisted of a series of separate wood pavilion structures that gave the museum a campus-like feel. Today the new building stands as a monument to the future, supported by technology giants such as Hewlett-Packard, Apple, Intel, and Fujitsu.

The Triton's permanent collection includes nineteenth- and twentieth-century American painting, Native American art, and a growing number of works on paper by California artists. Atkins will continue this eclectic approach, adding to it an emphasis on multicultural artists. He has already featured contemporary Hispanic and Asian-American artists in major shows.

Michael Danoff arrived at San Jose Museum of Art with a mission to bring the museum into focus by concentrating on "the art of our time." With a new 42,000-square-foot addition, which opened in May 1991, doubling the museum's size, there is now space enough to concurrently stage larger exhibitions and show some of the permanent collection.

"Being in touch with contemporary art allows people to be in touch with the spirit of our time," said Danoff, who resigned as museum director in 1991. A controversial director during his tenure, Danoff's aggressive approach did score a few hits. He secured the prestigious 1989 museum showing of works by Jasper Johns and Robert Rauschenberg from the Anderson Collection.

The San Jose Museum of Art features contemporary art that brings residents in touch with today's newest art expressions. Photo by Gerald L. French/The Photo File

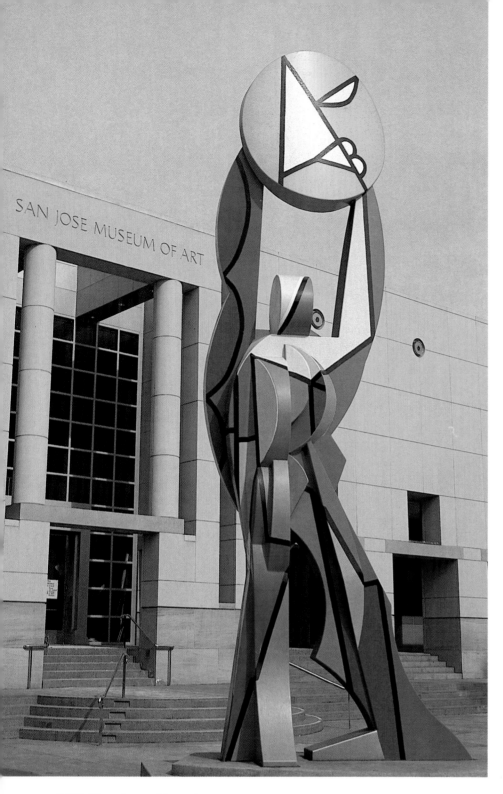

ABOVE: This modern sculpture outside the San Jose Museum of Art
lends visual interest to downtown.
Photo by Gerald L. French/The Photo
File

RIGHT: The Rosecrucian Museum in
San Jose is part of a large complex
featuring artifacts from Egypt. The
museum houses mummies, model
pyramids, and other displays. Photo
by Ernest Braun/The Photo File

LEFT: The Fairmont Hotel dominates the cityscape of downtown San Jose. Just outside the main entrance is Plaza Park with its walk-through fountain which delights children who visit the park. Photo by Kerrick James

FACING PAGE: The richly appointed lobby of the Fairmont Hotel is a feast for the senses. Photo by Gerald L. French/The Photo File

San Jose Museum of Art, while only 22 years old, has ties to the history of San Jose's downtown. Its original structure, recorded in the National Registry of Historic Landmarks, was built in the 1890s for use as a post office.

Today a visitor can walk from the museum across Fairmont Plaza, site of a new 18-floor luxury office building, to the elegant Fairmont Hotel that graces South Market Street. And perhaps there's time for a visit to nearby St. Joseph's Cathedral, a gloriously reconstructed church with a resplendent copper dome that glistens over downtown. In 1990 St. Joseph's was dedicated as the official home of the Catholic Diocese of San Jose by Bishop Pierre Du Maine.

Having viewed collections at the San Jose Museum of Art and the Triton

ABOVE: The California History Museum is another feature of the DeAnza College campus in Cupertino. Photo by Gerald L. French/The Photo File

FACING PAGE BOTTOM: This museum on the Santa Clara University campus, named for benefactor Isabel de Saisset, holds American, European, and Oriental art. A special collection features artifacts of California Native Americans that predate the Catholic missions. Photo by John Elk III

Museum of Art, the peripatetic art seeker can go commercial gallery hopping in Saratoga, Palo Alto, Los Gatos, and downtown San Jose. Everything from fine art to Nagel posters is on display. The romantically inclined might visit the annual Valentine Invitation Exhibition at the San Jose Institute of Contemporary Art, for which modern artists create some surprising interpretations of love.

University- and college-affiliated art viewing offers another option. Stanford University has a fine art gallery and the renowned Rodin sculpture court. Santa Clara University's De Saisset Museum and DeAnza College's Euphrat Gallery often have interesting exhibitions that are open to the public.

All these attractions add up to a visual feast of pleasure for the senses.

■ *North County Moves To The Beat*

If musical notes could take form, the air over Highway 101 and Interstate 280 would be crowded with clefs emanating from Flint Center in Cupertino, Shoreline Amphitheatre in Mountain View, and the Mountain Winery in Saratoga.

North County, the home of Hewlett-Packard, NASA Ames Research Center, and Apple Computer can count music as one of its most popular products.

Years ago, when she was belting out songs, Vicky O'Brien made lifelong friends with such celebrities as Joel Grey. O'Brien, who holds a doctorate in education, has put her contacts to use as the tireless executive director of Flint Center.

The walls of O'Brien's office are lined with colorful posters of Flint Center productions and its many guest celebrities, among them Grey. "Flint Center is busy 220 days out of the year, with rehearsals and entertainment. I try to see every production," says O'Brien. Shows at the acoustically perfect Flint Center range from new-age synthesist composer Kitaro to virtuoso violinist Itzhak Perlman to Lorna Luft's tribute to her mother—Judy Garland.

ABOVE: This combined facility in Mountain View acts as a center of the community, housing both local government offices and a performing arts center. Photo by Joseph Sohm/Chromosohm

While Flint Center is internationally known for its acoustics, it also hosts many nonmusical events such as the sell-out Celebrity Forum, in which famous people speak about their lives and careers. Cary Grant, Beverly Sills, Henry Kissinger, and Ted Koppel have held court in past years. Flint Center has another interesting sideline. Its attractive 2,571-seat theater is often used by Apple Computer for stockholders' meetings and by other Silicon Valley firms such as Atari.

The center opened its doors in 1971 and is named in honor of Calvin C. Flint, the first superintendent of the Foothill-DeAnza Community College District. The district operates the center, which is located on the campus of

A focal point for performing arts of all kinds is the Flint Center on the DeAnza College campus. Internationally known speakers and performers appear regularly on its stage. Photo by Gerald L. French/The Photo File

DeAnza College. O'Brien says that future plans call for a new reception hall to be built in front of the center and for the main lobby to be expanded.

In the 1960s the late Bill Graham made history with his fabled Fillmore West in San Francisco. For the twenty-first century Graham built a rock temple, Shoreline Amphitheatre, adjacent to Mountain View's Shoreline Park.

Shoreline has the biggest tent in the world. *San Francisco Chronicle* architecture critic Allan Temko describes the tent: "Visible for miles across the Peninsula shorelands, as tall as a 20-story building and nearly twice as wide as a football field, this two-masted tent shares the scale and technical audacity of NASA's wind tunnels and the mammoth dirigible hangars of nearby Moffett Field."

The tent arcs over Shoreline's sunken stage and most of its 7,250 reserved seats. The huge lawn that skirts the reserved area seats another 12,750.

Opened in 1986, this $20-million architectural tour de force is a cooperative venture between Graham and the City of Mountain View, which contributed an $8-million start-up loan. Apple Computer cofounder Steve Wozniak and oil heiress Ann Getty were private backers.

In every way Shoreline is a class act. Musicians like to play at Shoreline because of its sophisticated sound system, which equalizes the quality of sound for those on the lawn to that heard by those in the seats closer to the stage. Artists also enjoy Shoreline's long list of other technical and guest amenities. The audience loves to come to Shoreline for far above average food, the friendliness of Shoreline's staff, and the fact that every seat in the amphitheater is a good seat. Large video screens placed around the amphitheater provide a crystal-clear view of performers. All concession stands also have video monitors so no one will miss a beat.

"We want to take a Disneyland approach, to make the whole experience of coming to Shoreline a fun and comfortable one," says general manager Bob Dagitz.

Due to Graham's stature in the music world, rock megastars made the Shoreline a tour stop. Bruce Springsteen, Madonna, Diana Ross, Elton John, Rod Stewart, and Neil Diamond have performed on Shoreline's stage.

Although firmly established as a premier place for rock concerts, Shoreline will expand beyond rock in the coming years, according to Dagitz. "We want to do ethnic festivals, to offer classical music, and to do other events that are meaningful to our local community."

Across the valley from Shoreline, on the terrace of Mountain Winery

Shoreline Amphitheatre's massive twin tents and stage have hosted such rock superstars as Rod Stewart and Bruce Springsteen. Photo by Joseph Sohm/Chromosohm

(formerly Paul Masson) in the Saratoga hills, couples can sit at a table sipping a glass of wine and enjoying a California nouvelle cuisine dinner. They can revel in the dazzling view of the valley's city lights below, then, as night settles in, walk to the winery's concert area to spend the next few hours under the stars, listening to the vocal and musical mastery of such greats as Ray Charles. Life doesn't get any better than an evening at the Mountain Winery.

Now in its 34th season the winery's Paul Masson Summer Series of concerts sells out months in advance. Loyal Silicon Valley audiences return each year to hear such fine performers as Miles Davis, Chuck Mangione, Joan Baez, Smokey Robinson, George Shearing, and Mel Torme.

Concerts are held in a charming outdoor amphitheater, whose backdrop is

Ray Charles is one of many musical legends who have created an evening of unforgettable magic at the Mountain Winery in the Saratoga Hills. Courtesy, Paul Masson Collection

RIGHT: A quartet of musicians practices in scenic quietude at the Mountain Winery. Courtesy, Paul Masson Collection

FACING PAGE: Perhaps the leading summer music festival in Silicon Valley is held at the Mountain Winery in the hills above San Jose. Photo by Gerald L. French/The Photo File

the ivy-draped facade of the winery, built in the early 1900s by Paul Masson himself. With 1,000 seats the amphitheater provides an intimate setting and evokes a highly personal camaraderie between the artist and audience.

The Play's The Thing

TheatreWorks in Palo Alto has always taken chances during its 22-year history—Shakespeare set to new music; multicolored popcorn for a playful audience; horror; medieval fantasy; peace-movement messages. And the chances have paid off. TheatreWorks is now the preeminent theater company in North County, with devoted subscribers coming from as far away as Santa Cruz and Sacramento. Every year drama critics give TheatreWorks kudos for its inventive approach to the classics and its skillful production of new works.

BELOW: TheatreWorks delighted audiences with this production of *You Can't Take It With You*. Courtesy, TheatreWorks

In 1970 Robert Kelley, fresh from Stanford University's undergraduate creative-writing program, started the Youth Workshop in his hometown of Palo Alto. In those irreverent post-hippie days, Kelley's group staged original works, many of them musicals, some of them written by Kelley. The Youth Workshop became a hit from its first production, and in 1975, with an eye on the future, Kelley changed its name to TheatreWorks.

Although his face is a little more craggy and his hair a little thinner than in those early days, Kelley's inventive energy continues to burn brightly. As

ABOVE: If something can be cooked with garlic, it will be found at the Garlic Festival in Gilroy. Here fresh meat is prepared and served with the pungent herb. Photo by Mark E. Gibson

RIGHT: International cooking is the order of the day as woks are used to prepare dining treats at the Gilroy Garlic Festival. Photo by Mark E. Gibson

FACING PAGE: The arrival of spring receives a traditional May Pole welcome in this Los Altos backyard celebration. Photo by Renee Lynn

it heads towards its third decade, TheatreWorks is as fresh as ever.

"We want to continue to support new writers and to introduce new plays to our region," says Kelley. "And we are still the only people doing new musicals in the Bay Area." To encourage new works Kelley has started an annual playwright's competition with cash awards.

By the next century Kelley plans to put TheatreWorks in a new theater that seats 600 to 700 and expand its 7,200-person subscription base.

TheatreWorks has already outgrown the 400-seat Lucie Stern Theatre in Palo Alto, where it performs half its season. The remainder is staged at the Burgess Theatre in Menlo Park.

■ Life is A Festival

From May to October in the Santa Clara Valley, outdoor festivals sprout as plentifully as the valley's beautiful mustard seed in early spring—a reminder of the valley's agricultural history.

At the beginning of the twentieth century, Santa Clara Valley was known as the

"Valley of Heart's Delight." The lush valley floor produced cherries, apricots, wheat, wine grapes, corn, hay, walnuts, and a long list of other edibles.

As Santa Clara Valley approaches the twenty-first century, most of the valley floor is now used for housing and industry. But valley residents still love to honor its agricultural roots with celebrations of food, wine, and art.

The Gilroy Garlic Festival has become internationally famous for its yearly celebration of southern Santa Clara Valley's most popular product. There's french-fried garlic and even garlic ice cream for the adventurous.

Virtually every city has its

ABOVE: The grounds of Ridge Winery in Cupertino lend themselves nicely to outdoor dining. Photo by Renee Lynn

RIGHT: California is noted for its wines, and dozens of communities throughout Northern California and Santa Clara Valley have local wineries. This harvest is from the Page Mill Winery in Los Altos Hills. Photo by Renee Lynn

art and wine festival. Sunnyvale, Mountain View, Los Altos, Palo Alto, and Milpitas all offer a sampling of ethnic foods, local wines, and dozens of arts and crafts booths.

For kids a wondrous event is Sunnyvale's "Hands-on-the-Arts" festival. Each year 10,000 kids and their families participate in this two-day performing and visual arts extravaganza. A major participant is Sunnyvale's Community Theatre Center, a nationally recognized young people's theater.

Perhaps the one event that most closely mirrors the valley's agricultural past is the annual Santa Clara County Fair. For food devotees nothing beats the fair's homemade strawberry shortcake, sausage sandwiches, and fresh corn-on-the-cob. Newcomers and old-timers alike visit the exhibition halls to see who baked this year's best pie or grew the best tomato. And the many educational exhibits offer a chance to learn about agriculture and home arts.

From the 10 acres of livestock exhibits to the intricate square-dancing performances, the fair is good old-fashioned country fun.

There's a midway for those who'd like to beat the odds at darts or ring tossing. And evening brings concerts by popular singers and bands.

The Santa Clara County Fair is in its 47th year, and as long as there's a 4-H Club, it'll be around.

■ *City Lights*

When the sun dips behind the Santa Cruz Mountains, a couple might catch some jazz at J.J.'s Blues Cafe in Mountain View after dining on modern French cuisine at Chez T.J. Others might walk along Sunnyvale's historic Murphy Avenue, stopping to sample the famous chicken salad at Tao Tao.

Silicon Valley has a great love of food and music, as does the rest of the San Francisco Bay Area region. Virtually every type of American and ethnic cuisine is available in the valley's hundreds of restaurants. And in Mountain View and San Jose, many of these restaurants are just a few beats away from good live jazz or popular music.

"Jazz and blues are really taking off in Silicon Valley," says San Jose Jazz Society president Sammy Cohen, who has observed the recent proliferation of clubs. Cohen has brought in such notables as Dave Brubeck and Dizzy Gillespie to perform at free San Jose concerts.

For those who like to dance off their dinner calories, there are three dozen valley dance clubs, ranging from hard rock to ballroom dancing.

To laugh away workday woes the valley now has more than a half-dozen first-rate comedy clubs where rising stars can try out their routines.

The hard-working people of Silicon Valley can relax by participating in a wealth of arts and entertainment adventures.

During a local Cupertino festival, youngsters promote the coming of soccer's World Cup to the U.S. Photo by Joseph Sohm/Chromosohm

ABOVE: Even the smallest members of the community find a place in Cupertino's annual May fete parade. Photo by Joseph Sohm/Chromosohm

FACING PAGE: A costumed firedog named Sparky is part of an annual Cupertino spring celebration, and one of the local ladder trucks is always a crowd pleaser. Photo by Joseph Sohm/Chromosohm

8

Being a Sport

■ *Playtime in Santa Clara Valley*

D uring the winter months there is a curious increase in the number of business travelers to the Santa Clara Valley from certain parts of the United States. These harried business people fly into San Jose or San Francisco International airports seeking respite from week after week of freezing temperatures, ice, snow, and sleet. And they find it.

"Here we have one of the most ideal climates in the world," says Glenn Trapp, a meteorologist for the National Weather Service. The Santa Clara Valley is in a Mediterranean climate region that extends from Los Angeles to San Francisco, encompassing the California coastline, explains Trapp. "Basically it's a two-season climate. We have a well-defined rainy season from October 15th to April 15th and summer the rest of the year," Trapp notes. In winter mean temperatures hover in the 50s and in the summer, in the 70s. Humidity varies from 67 percent in January to 51 percent in July. What that all means, says Trapp, is that most of the time the climate is relatively mild. Santa Clara Valley rarely has to endure the extremes of heat, cold, or humidity so prevalent in most of the United States.

Technically Santa Clara Valley's paradisiacal climate is due to a subtropical high-pressure ridge that sits over the region, Trapp says.

The valley's Mediterranean climate is complemented by majestic redwoods, breathtaking mountaintop vistas, trout-silvered creeks, and lush evergreen forests.

Propelled by warm breezes, these board sailors glide through the waters at Shoreline Park, enjoying a growing sport that is fast and fun. Photo by Patty Salkeld

■ *A Separate Place*

During the twentieth century, as the Santa Clara Valley economy prospered, land became an in-demand commodity. Industrial parks and housing tracts sprouted to keep apace of commercial growth.

ABOVE: Easy access to wilderness is prized by Santa Clara Valley residents, who fortunately do not have to travel far to escape the day-to-day pressures of city life. Photo by Andrew Van Dis

LEFT: The immense size of California's redwoods must be seen at close range to get the full impact of these natural wonders. Photo by Andrew Van Dis

A rose garden adds decoration to the grounds of the Mission of Santa Clara de Asis located on the Santa Clara University campus. Photo by Gerald L. French/The Photo File

By the early 1970s the Santa Clara County Board of Supervisors and other governmental leaders feared that Silicon Valley workers would have no place to play and recreate unless some of the valley's land was preserved. Citizens voiced the same concern, and a national environmental movement further increased the public's awareness of land as a nonrenewable precious commodity.

As the concept of "open space" took hold, Santa Clara Valley voters in 1972 approved a charter amendment allowing for tax dollars to be used for parks acquisition and development. The board of supervisors then began buying thousands of acres for parkland. Today the Santa Clara County Parks System encompasses 40,000 acres and includes 29 separate regional parks.

In 1972 a second ballot measure also responded to citizens' desire for open space. Voters in the valley's northern cities and in neighboring San Mateo County approved the creation of the Midpeninsula Regional Open Space District, a tax-supported public agency. The district now owns more than 25,000 acres in the foothills and baylands and operates 26 open space preserves.

Balancing the need for open space with the demands of commercial growth continues to be a challenge in the Santa Clara Valley. In September 1985 the

Santa Clara County Board of Supervisors convened the Preservation 2020 Task Force. Chaired by Supervisor Dianne McKenna the task force looked at remaining available open space in the county and constructed a master preservation plan. As a result of the plan recommendations, Supervisor McKenna led a campaign to support a ballot measure that would create a new open space district to complement the Midpeninsula Regional Open Space District. The new agency would acquire land in the remainder of the county outside Midpeninsula's domain. The ballot measure achieved an impressive 63 percent of the vote, just short of the two-thirds vote needed to pass since it carried with it a $25 property assessment.

■ *Nature's Ways*

The banks of Vasona Lake, one of the county's most popular parks, shimmer in the morning sunlight. A jogger passes under a shady tree. Doug Gaynor, director of Santa Clara County's Parks and Recreation Department, admires the view from his Los Gatos office window: "We're pleased that people in the Santa Clara Valley place an emphasis on a high quality of life. They know that a good parks system is a part of that quality."

Since 1972 when the parks ballot measure was passed, Santa Clara Valley voters have consistently supported the county's efforts to maintain and acquire open space. Those efforts will continue through the 1990s. Santa Clara County plans to add up to 20,000 more acres of parkland by the end of the decade, according to Gaynor.

Part of the new lands will be used by the county to link into the planned Bay Area Ridge Trail, a cooperative project between local and county governments

in the region. By the late 1990s a cyclist or hiker will be able to travel the hills ringing San Francisco Bay without having to leave open space. "The views from the ridge will be gorgeous," promises Gaynor.

A similar project is the planned Bay Trail, which will link Santa Clara County parkland with other park properties to form a continuous trek along the waterline of San Francisco Bay.

The two magnificent new bay trails, when completed, will be a fitting complement to Santa Clara County's many parks, which already offer a wealth of recreational options. Park activities include power boating, camping, fishing, skeet and trapshooting, swimming, horseback riding, hang gliding, sailing, and archery. "We try to provide something for everyone," Gaynor notes.

Santa Clara County operates three types of parks—reservoir, mountain, and urban. "Regardless of where you live, there's a county park nearby," says Gaynor.

Each of the county's 29 parks has its own distinct character and purpose. One of the largest and most popular reservoir parks, seven-mile-long Anderson Lake in the southern part of the county near Morgan Hill, gives water sport lovers a year-round chance to boat and fish. Hiking enthusiasts often enjoy the four-mile trail along the lake's western shoreline.

Joseph D. Grant Park and Mt. Madonna Park are two of the county's spectacular mountain parks. Located in the Diablo range in eastern Santa Clara

ABOVE: Upholding the rowing traditions of equally famous schools in the East, these members of the Stanford crew team hold their own in intercollegiate competition. Photo by Andrew Van Dis

FACING PAGE: Whether it is a long-distance ride or just a day trip, bicycle touring remains a popular outdoor activity in the Santa Clara Valley. Photo by Andrew Van Dis

FACING PAGE, INSET: The outdoor lifestyle afforded by the year-round mild climate in the Santa Clara Valley allows for a variety of recreational activities. Mountain biking is proving increasingly popular throughout the area. Photo by Tim Davis

Valley, the mammoth 10,000-acre Grant Park is the largest of the county parks. Grant Park has been a working cattle ranch since the late 1880s. Since much of its land continues to be leased for cattle grazing, the park retains an Old West flavor that delights the hikers and equestrians who travel its 40 miles of trails. Grant Park is a favorite of picnickers who enjoy lunching under the park's many large oak trees. Eventually Santa Clara County plans to open a small museum at the ranch to honor the valley's Indian heritage.

Groves of California's famous redwood trees grace Mt. Madonna Park, tucked in the Santa Cruz mountain range, the dividing mountain range between Santa Clara Valley and the popular coastal counties of Santa Cruz and Monterey. Many consider Mt. Madonna to be the most awe-inspiring of all the county parks. From certain vista points it is possible to see the Pacific Ocean. Mt. Madonna is a place for quiet reflection, for camping near a stand of redwoods, or a romantic picnic for two. Parents like to bring their children to see the rare miniature white fallow deer that call the park home.

Two Santa Clara County urban parks, Santa Teresa Park and Ed R. Levin Park, offer a favorite California sport—golfing. Situated midway between Morgan Hill and San Jose, Santa Teresa Park's main attraction is its lush 18-hole public golf course, open seven days a week. A restaurant, bar, driving range, and putting green give golfers everything they need for a day of fun. In the springtime the park's abundance of beautiful wildflowers draws hikers and equestrians to its trails.

Nestled in Santa Clara Valley's eastern foothills, Ed R. Levin Park, named in honor of the former Santa Clara County supervisor, has many attractions in

ABOVE: The sport of crew is not just for men anymore, as this women's shell demonstrates. Photo by Andrew Van Dis

FACING PAGE: These wetsuit-clad board sailors brave a brisk morning and hit the water and wind of Shoreline Park. Photo by Renee Lynn

addition to its 18-hole Spring Valley Golf Course. During winter months the park's Sandy Wool Lake is stocked with trout. The park also features hang gliding and hot air ballooning. It is the site of special events such as the Silent Air Show and the Society for Creative Anachronism.

■ *Midpeninsula Retreat*

High in the hills above Cupertino, Fremont Older, a prominent San Francisco newspaper editor, and his wife Cora once owned some of the most beautiful land in Santa Clara Valley. In the early twentieth century their gracious home was the scene of glittering parties attended by the Bay Area's most prominent citizens. Today the Fremont Older property is protected as an historical preserve by the Midpeninsula Regional Open Space District. The Older's home is listed on the National Register of Historic Places and is open to the public for specially scheduled group tours.

Since its establishment in 1972 the district has acquired 26 preserves such as the Fremont Older estate, giving busy Silicon Valley workers a much-needed natural retreat. The wonder of it is that all of these lands are just a 30-minute drive from many of Silicon Valley's industrial campuses.

None of the preserves have ballfields or barbecue pits. A safe haven for wildlife, preserves are meant to be a place in which to commune with nature. A hiker can take pleasure in listening to the wind rustle through a grassy hillside.

The most popular district retreat is Rancho San Antonio, a 1,000-acre preserve in the foothills above Los Altos. Rancho San Antonio's landscape is varied, from oak-shaded creekside settings to grassy meadows high above the Santa Clara Valley floor. A main attraction is the working Deer Hollow Farm, which contains ranch buildings dating back to the turn of the twentieth century.

■ *Shoreline Park*

A bronze-breasted, ring-necked pheasant struts proudly across the road, undaunted by the nearby automobile. It is February, and the mating season is under way at Mountain View's Shoreline Park. Being a polygamous male the pheasant happily "struts his stuff" to attract a few hens.

Nearby the predatory loggerhead shrike, a cousin to the songbird, perches above the San Francisco Bay shoreline, peering out from the black mask around his eyes. Known as "the butcher," the shrike will soon swoop down upon its prey.

At Shoreline the pheasant and shrike have plenty of

LEFT: The chance to observe and photograph Great White Egrets like this is one reason the land in Palo Alto next to San Francisco Bay has been turned into a wildlife refuge. Photo by Tim Davis

FACING PAGE: Getting in the last flight before calling it a day, this hang glider pilot soars across the California landscape. Photo by Eric Luse

neighbors since the park, at the southern mouth of the San Francisco Bay, is part of the Pacific Coast flyway for migratory birds. Close to 200 species of birds have been sighted at Shoreline, a tranquil wildlife sanctuary operated by the City of Mountain View. It is a favorite spot for the Santa Clara Valley Audubon Society and bird-lovers throughout the region.

"Oh, look. There's a Great Egret!" says Ginny Kaminski, Shoreline's volunteer coordinator, as she points to the majestic white bird standing on a nearby grassy knoll. A former environmental education teacher, Kaminski's eyes are trained to spot the many species that inhabit the park. She notes that the Great Egret is a regular resident of the Charleston Slough, which winds through 53 acres of the park. A former Leslie Salt pond, Charleston Slough is reverting back to marshland. It represents the city's ecological goals for the rest of the 800-acre park. "Historically all the water around here was natural marshland. We're trying to restore things back to their natural state," explains Kaminski.

Shoreline Park is a tour de force of municipal ingenuity. Its history began when the baylands in Mountain View were used as the dumping ground for San Francisco's and other communities' garbage. Rather than let the garbage just sit there, the City of Mountain View took the approach that the landfill could be a usable resource. During the 1970s it used the refuse to raise the lower elevations of the landfill by 15 feet, providing an adequate base for development. Mountain View then used more than $17 million it had collected in dumping fees to build Shoreline on top of the landfill. It opened the park in 1983. Since one of the by-products of a landfill is methane gas, the city began another revenue-generating program by recovering the gas and selling it to utilities as an energy source. The successful program generates funds that are used for the continuing operation of Shoreline.

At Shoreline bird-watching is only one of many recreational options. The park's 50-acre saltwater Shoreline Lake, fed by the Charleston Slough, is used extensively by sailors and windsurfers who enjoy the winds coming in from the bay. For golfers there's a par-72, 18-hole golf course designed by Robert Trent Jones II. Walkers, joggers, and bicyclists enjoy the seven miles of paved trails on the park's north shore.

In 1990 Mountain View added another chapter to Shoreline's history by restoring the Rengstorff House. A German-born immigrant, Henry Rengstorff

LEFT: Jet skiing has become popular as yet another way to achieve speed on the water. The sport's popularity has led to professional competitive events. Photo by Andrew Van Dis

FAR LEFT: Wildlife abounds in Santa Clara Valley, a place that is often thought of as substantially urban. However, areas such as Shoreline Regional Park are near and provide the opportunity to see animals, such as this burrowing owl and nearly 200 other species of birds, in their natural habitat. Photo by Renee Lynn

BELOW: Shoreline Park volunteer coordinator Ginny Kaminski dons period costume for a tour of the Rengstorff House.

was a wealthy landowner and rancher. In 1867 he commissioned an opulent home befitting his family's prominent status in the community. Rengstorff's home was later moved by the City of Mountain View from its original address on Stierlin Road to a temporary location near Shoreline and finally to its permanent location near Shoreline Lake. The home is a rare example of early Italianate architecture and is open to the public as a showcase of Mountain View's early history.

■ Fun Just Around The Corner

California serves as a national model for leading the active life. One of the reasons is that its cities consider parks and recreation amenities to be an important part of their service to the public.

In Santa Clara County virtually every city—from Gilroy in the south to Palo Alto in the north—offers a diverse list of activities, from tap dancing, beer making, and a sushi workshop, to t'ai chi, samba dancing, and tennis.

Sunnyvale is a sterling example of a city committed to recreational opportunities for its residents. It won an "All-American City" award for its beautifully designed parks and innovative recreational programs directed by Katherine Bradshaw Chappelear, superintendent of recreation. Illustrative of Sunnyvale's unique approach is its school/park cooperatives in which the city works with schools to preserve open space adjacent to a school site. Sunnyvale's Columbia School/Park cooperative won the 1986 Environmental Award from the California Parks and Recreation Society. Schoolchildren and neighborhood residents share use of a swimming pool, soccer fields, tennis courts, basketball and volleyball courts, and children's play structures.

To respond to the needs of two-career families, Sunnyvale runs an "After School Pals Program" for K-6th grades. The children learn arts and crafts, participate in sports and games, and on occasion take field trips or see a movie.

Sunnyvale's attractively designed Community Center complex opened in 1973. Situated on 22 acres of prime land in the heart of the city, the complex

contains a multipurpose recreation center, a 1,500-person capacity gymnasium, the 200-seat Performing Arts Theatre, and the nearby Creative Arts Center and Gallery.

Each year more than 187,000 San Francisco Bay Area schoolchildren and their families visit the Performing Arts Theatre to attend performances by the California Theatre Center. Janlyn, a professional modern dance company, and the Sunnyvale Community Players also share the theater space.

The miraculous discovery of art occurs time and again at the Gallery Education Program. Students from all over the Bay Area visit an art gallery—often for the first time. Later they participate in a hands-on art project. Coming from many cultures, these children share the universal joy of experiencing art firsthand.

■ Oasis In The City

During the 1990s one of the most aggressive new parks and recreation projects under way in Santa Clara County is the $100-million Guadalupe River Park, a landmark intergovernmental effort that will develop three miles of waterfront

One of the unique features of San Jose's Kelley Park is the Japanese Friendship Garden. The walkways in this part of the park reflect Japanese taste and design. Photo by Gerald L. French/The Photo File

along the Guadalupe River in San Jose's downtown.

When completed Guadalupe River Park will be a verdant getaway for city dwellers and workers. Its pattern of riverwalks will be reminiscent of San Antonio's riverfront pathways.

"Right here, in the middle of downtown San Jose, we will have this beautiful park," says Bob Ryan, project manager and a member of the City of San Jose's Redevelopment Agency. Santa Clara County government, the Santa Clara Valley Water District, and the U.S. Army Corps of Engineers are partners in the project along with the City of San Jose.

"Commercialism will be kept to a minimum" in the park, notes Ryan. "We're taking a low-key approach." The main purpose of the park is to serve as a greenbelt of open space in the downtown commercial zone. Defined by I-280 at the southern end and I-880 in the northern, the park will skirt San Jose's major cultural and sports centers. It will be used by families as a place to stroll or have a picnic before seeing a concert or visiting one of San Jose's museums, and by office workers as an alfresco dining spot.

Urban greenery such as the Guadalupe River Park is an important part of San Jose's overall parks-and-recreation agenda for the 1990s. The city maintains more than 3,000 acres of parkland containing 124 neighborhood and regional parks. This includes several themed cultural gardens which honor the city's ethnic diversity. During the 1990s the city will develop two new gardens. A Mexican Cultural Garden will be developed on the East Side, which has a large Hispanic population. A Vietnamese Heritage Garden is

planned for a five-acre site along Coyote Creek near Capitol Expressway in San Jose.

"We recognize cultural diversity as the strength of our community," declares Bob Overstreet, director of recreation, parks, and community services. "Gardens provide a medium in which to interpret our cultural heritage to the rest of the community," he explains.

The Chinese Cultural Garden in the Overfelt Gardens on McKee Road and the Japanese Friendship Garden in Kelley Park pay tribute to two of San Jose's Asian cultures. A focal point of the Chinese garden is a 30-foot bronze and marble sculpture of Confucius, a gift from the people of Taiwan. Okayama's Korakuen Park is the inspiration for the Japanese garden, which observes the traditional balance of religion, nature, and symbolism. The garden is a testament to the "sister city" relationship between San Jose and Okayama.

■ *The Sporting Life*

Silicon Valley proved it wanted to play in the majors in June 1988 when San Jose voters approved the construction of a $100-million sports arena at the intersection of Santa Clara and Autumn streets near the city's downtown. The arena vote threw down a symbolic gauntlet: Silicon Valley had entered the national competition for professional sports franchises. Just as the valley had tired of going to San Francisco for culture and developed an arts mecca of its own, it was now ready to take charge of its own sports market.

After the arena vote professional sports fever ignited in Silicon Valley. As a result San Jose now has the "Sharks," a National Hockey League (NHL) expansion team, which will become the flagship team at the arena. The City of San Jose and local entrepreneurs are also wooing Bob Lurie, owner of the San Francisco Giants pro baseball team, to move his team from Candlestick Park to San Jose. A November 1990 ballot measure asking Santa Clara voters to approve the team's move to their city failed. Subsequently, in 1991, San Jose announced a campaign to bring the Giants to its city. San Jose already has a Giants Class A farm team, the San Jose Giants, who play at San Jose Municipal Stadium.

Due to open in the fall of 1992, the San Jose arena is a futuristic concept by architects Sink, Combs, and Dethlefs, who designed Denver's McNichols Arena. The four-story structure's modernistic stainless steel facade is punctuated by a 100-foot-tall glass-enclosed gallery entrance, adding high drama to the design. A completely covered facility, the arena is designed for multipurpose use. With a maximum seating capacity of 20,000, it can accommodate hockey, basketball, boxing, wrestling, and gymnastics. The City of San Jose expects the arena to host about 160 events yearly.

The Sharks "add marquee value" to San Jose at a time when it is becoming a nationally prominent city, says Dean Munro, former chief of staff to Tom McEnery, San Jose's former mayor. Munro is now executive director of the arena and the new San Jose Sports Authority.

San Jose's market demographics make it a perfect spot for expansion teams, according to Munro. "There are 2.5 million people within a 30-mile radius of the arena. The greater San Jose area is the richest in the country in terms of median household disposable income. Plus we have an incredible enthusiasm for professional sports," Munro says.

Entrepreneurs Howard Baldwin, former owner of the New England Whalers, and Morris Belzberg, retired CEO of Budget Rent-A-Car, worked with Munro to bring the expansion team to San Jose. Their dream is to sit in the owner's box at the first Sharks game at the arena during its 1992 inaugural season.

Besides the arena, San Jose has a major new facility for university sports and community use: the new $36-million Events Center at San Jose State University. The Events Center is a modernistic 129,000-square-foot facility. Its facade is influenced by the "mission style" architecture, reminiscent of the Santa Clara Valley's early mission settlements.

"We're a multipurpose resource for the community," says Judy Hermann, Events Center public relations director. The Events Center can seat 4,600 persons for athletic events and 6,000 for concerts. It also contains the largest outdoor pool in Northern California, a 4,000-square-foot weight room, and a 4,000-square-foot aerobics room. Students and faculty share use of the Events Center with local residents. San Jose State University's Spartan basketball team is the main tenant of the arena section.

The new recreational center on the San Jose State University campus is the home for both college and professional sports. Elsewhere in the complex are racquetball courts, a gym, and a weight room. Photo by Gerald L. French/The Photo File

Weekends bring Santa Clara Valley residents to the public parks for family events and company functions. Kelley Park in San Jose bustles with activity on this occasion. Photo by Gerald L. French/The Photo File

■ *Softball By The Sea*

In the 1950s the usual after-work sport of husbands was hoisting a few drinks at the local watering hole. In the 1990s husbands can often be found pitching a game at Twin Creeks Softball Complex in Sunnyvale. And increasingly their wives might be up at bat.

"We thought softball would be a fad, but it's lasted and continues to grow every year," says Dave Collishaw, Twin Creeks general manager and a former player with the San Diego Padres.

Twin Creeks, the world's largest softball complex, opened in April 1983. Businessman Ray Collishaw, Dave's father, decided to develop a playing facility after he learned that there were more than 5,000 softball teams in the Santa Clara Valley with no place to play. Local parks and recreation departments couldn't meet the growing demand. Collishaw leased 62 acres of county-owned land on the San Francisco baylands in Sunnyvale and built the $7-million complex.

With 10 softball fields Twin Creeks is now a year-round host to more than 4,000 teams playing an impressive 20,000 games. Each year some 800,000 people visit the complex. There are tournaments almost every weekend.

Twin Creeks is one of the elite complexes qualified to host the national championships of the United States Slo-Pitch Softball Association. "We regularly hold the nationals. People come from all over, and it's good for business in our local community," says

Collishaw. Every year Twin Creeks also hosts the San Jose State University women's fast-pitch invitational tournament.

As Twin Creeks looks ahead, the trend is towards increasing the number of coed teams and adding well-rounded family activities, says Collishaw: "Coed teams are often sponsored by companies. They now represent about a quarter of our players. And we're also finding more husband and wife duos." Twin Creeks plans on adding children's entertainment shows and miniature golf as family attractions.

The 14,000-square-foot Twin Creeks clubhouse is the social hub for families and singles. Downstairs features the large Dugout restaurant while upstairs has the Bullpen sports bar and a nearby disco.

Plans at Twin Creeks call for putting in a driving range and adding a concert area for musical entertainment during tournaments, says Collishaw. Twin Creeks is adjacent to the planned 170-acre Baylands Park to be developed by the City of Sunnyvale. The combination of Twin Creeks and Baylands Park will make the baylands a major Bay Area recreational destination.

■ At The Club

As the thwack, thwack of tennis balls resounds in the background, Gordon Collins, general manager of Courtside Tennis Club, sits at a patio table, warmed by the Los Gatos sunshine. A former Pebble Beach tennis pro, Collins has spent more than a decade managing the quintessential California sports club.

In a picture-perfect setting at the base of the Santa Cruz Mountains, Courtside is everything a club should be: cozy, friendly, intimate, and—above all—fun. Courtside has been voted one of the top four tennis clubs in the nation by the U.S. Tennis Association. Tennis luminaries such as Arthur Ashe, Vic Braden, Jack Kramer, and John McEnroe have conducted tennis clinics at the club.

"As one of our members said, this is their Shangri-La. The club is a little haven. It's a nice, clean environment in the prettiest club setting in the valley," says Collins.

Developed by local businessmen Jim Compton and Ken Camp, Courtside opened in 1977 and has stayed true to its concept as a low-key club with limited membership. Its list of amenities is impressive: 21 tennis courts (including 4 indoor courts), 4 racquetball courts, a full workout room, pool, spa, and clubhouse.

The club now has a nursery. "We're becoming more family oriented. Our members who are starting families like to bring in the kids, too," Collins says. The club runs a summer tennis program for 300 kids and also offers swimming lessons, aerobics, and racquetball.

Courtside is one of more than four dozen health clubs in Silicon Valley, ranging from specialty-clubs such as Royal Courts for racquetball to Gold's Gym, a popular weightlifting spot. Clubs also vary from private, members-only facilities to community-oriented facilities such as the Central YMCA in San Jose and the Page Mill YMCA Fitness Center in Palo Alto. For people who just like to swim or work out, Silicon Valley has a number of Ys that fit the bill.

Those with more sumptuous tastes and budgets can choose from a number of private clubs. Two of Silicon Valley's most prestigious are Decathlon Club in Santa

Clara and the San Jose Athletic Club, both owned by Western Athletic Clubs. During 1989 and 1990 San Jose Athletic Club was extensively renovated. Its mix of amenities and services represents what people want in fitness training now, according to Sandy Carver, director of public relations. Treadmills, LifeCycles, rowing machines, and sophisticated Cybex equipment are part of the club's total workout program. Massage services and fitness and grooming clinics are also offered. Both Decathlon and San Jose Athletic Club have restaurants and lounges for after-workout relaxation.

"Fitness in the nineties is a complex issue. The next generation of athletic clubs will be clubs that can respond to multiple member needs," Carver says.

An assortment of club options are also available for Silicon Valley golfers who can play year-round due to the region's mild climate.

Silicon Valley has a number of plush country clubs with beautifully manicured golf greens. At Los Altos Golf & Country Club, membership entrance fees have ranged as high as $70,000. Popular private clubs include Almaden Golf & Country Club and San Jose Country Club in San Jose and La Rinconada Country Club in the Los Gatos Hills.

Public golf courses, where green fees average from $15 to $20 per round, are in high demand, particularly on weekends. Santa Teresa Golf Club in southern San Jose and Palo Alto Municipal Golf Course are especially busy spots.

■ *Much To Do*

Santa Clara Valley, a land of temperate climate and awe-inspiring landscape, is an active person's Eden, overflowing with recreational options.

There's lots to do in town, but occasionally wanderlust will strike. Santa Clara Valley residents are fortunate to live within a day's travel of some of the world's most beautiful playgrounds. Residents love to drive "over the hill" to Santa Cruz and other Pacific Coast beaches, or northeast to Lake Tahoe's skiing and gambling resorts. Or they head north to the redwood forests and beaches in Marin County. Wine country lovers, within a matter of hours, can be enjoying an oaky Chardonnay in one of the Napa/Sonoma region's many wineries.

Indeed Santa Clara Valley, a natural paradise, is part of the greater paradise that is California.

■ Future Perfect

This valley has always had a magic to it, a mystical hope for a better life. I'm constantly amazed at the level of success people have been able to attain here...The American dream, the California dream, has really been the San Jose experience.
—Tom McEnery, mayor of San Jose, 1982-90.

We've been downtown believers for two decades. It's been interesting and pleasing to see the models and plans turn into concrete and glass.
—Curt Wright, who started the advertising agency Battenberg, Fillhardt & Wright in a garage in Berryessa in 1969 and moved to downtown San Jose in 1970.

San Jose is a renaissance city. It is the Florence of the future.
—Ed Mosher, who opened his first retail store in downtown San Jose in 1955.

There's less ego in Silicon Valley than 15 years ago. Very few companies now are named for people. It's a realization that they won't own the whole piece of the pie.
—Roger Smith, founder of Silicon Valley Bank.

The next century will be the Century of Global Transactions. Driven by the technology engine, it will create opportunities for new and old nations, both big and small . . . The term foreign country *will vanish from our lexicon. This world is not so distant. It is being created today by thousands of business enterprises while we speak.*
—Regis McKenna, founder of the international high-technology marketing/consulting firm, at the International Technopolis Conference, May 1990. McKenna, Regis Mckenna, Inc.

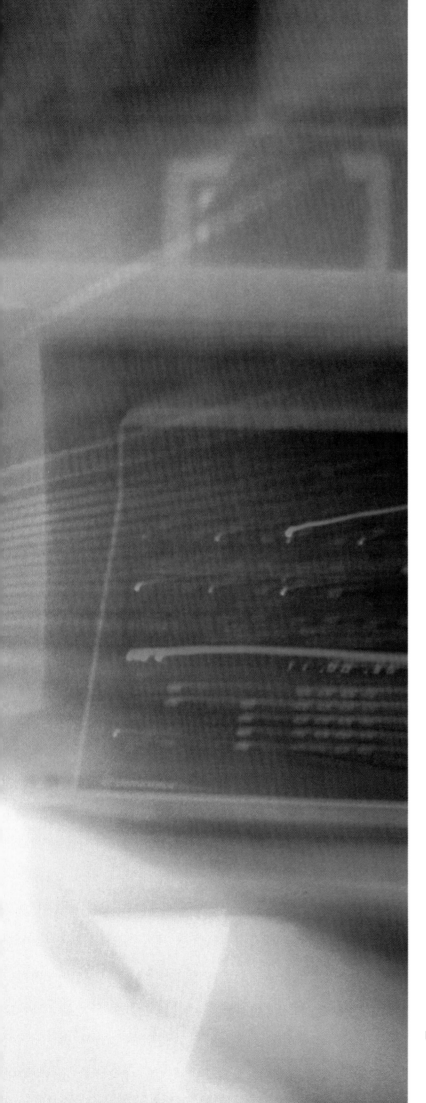

Networks

Silicon Valley's energy, transportation, and communication providers keep power, people, and information circulating inside and outside the area.

Photo by Richard L. Kaylin

Santa Clara Valley Water District

Silicon Valley residents just reach for the tap and out it flows—the clean, safe water they depend on. But how many of them ever stop to think about how that water gets to that tap? Or where it comes from? Or how it is made safe to drink? Though many people may never give it a thought, for the employees of the Santa Clara Valley Water District, the care and keeping of the water supply is a major part of their job. But that's not their only responsibility.

The valley is blessed with hundreds of miles of creeks that meander through the country, but in times of heavy rains these meandering creeks can become torrents of raging water that threaten lives and property. Protecting the valley's residents and businesses from flood devastation is the other job of the Valley Water District.

The Santa Clara Valley Water District is a local public agency responsible for Santa Clara County's water supply and flood control needs. The agency's history began in 1929 with the formation of the Santa Clara Valley Water Conservation District. The conservation district built eight dams and a raw–water distribution system to capture winter flows and use them to recharge the underground water basin.

The Santa Clara County Flood Control and Water Conservation District was formed in 1951 with responsibility for flood control. This district was also charged with treating and distributing drinking water imported from outside the valley.

In 1968 the two districts merged under the direction of an independent elected board of directors. The agency's present name, Santa Clara Valley Water District, was adopted in 1974.

In November 1987 the Gavilan Water Conservation District merged with the valley agency. The merger helped to integrate the operation of imported water with water from local reservoirs, as well as better coordinating operations and eliminating double taxation. The merger also brought additional reservoirs and groundwater recharge facilities under the Valley Water District's operation, and added nearly 4,500 groundwater production wells.

Today the Santa Clara Valley Water District manages three drinking–water treatment plants, three pumping stations, a hydroelectric plant, hundreds of miles of improved creeks and rivers, 18 percolation facilities, and an extensive in–county water distribution system connecting sources of imported water, local reservoirs, and water treatment facilities. These facilities and district programs provide Santa Clara County with high–quality drinking water and protection from flooding.

In the 1980s the Valley Water District assumed a progressively larger role in protecting drinking–water quality for Santa Clara County residents. The district strengthened existing groundwater protection programs, introduced new programs to correct groundwater contamination, and took steps to improve the quality of local and imported surface water.

Despite efforts to alert Santa Clara County residents to the need to protect local water quality, the disposal of motor oil, radiator antifreeze, solvents, and other hazardous materials along creeks and in storm sewers continues to be a problem. The district, in cooperation with the county and 13 cities, has developed programs to control these problems in order to provide greater protection of streams, creeks, and critical groundwater recharging facilities.

After consecutive years of below–average rainfall, low reservoir carryover, and declining groundwater levels, the drought became the district's top priority in the late 1980s. In 1989 the district organized an in-house drought task force. The task force wrote a comprehensive drought plan that became a reference for other water agencies throughout the state.

Significant relief from demand on the local groundwater basin came in 1989 with the completion of two major links in the district's water distribution system: the $50–million Santa Teresa Water Treatment Plant and the $22.6–million Snell pipeline. The Snell pipeline is 9.7 miles long and delivers treated water from the Santa Teresa plant to pipelines operated by the San Jose Water Co. and the city of San Jose Municipal Water Co.

Located in the Santa Teresa hills above Almaden Valley, the Santa Teresa Water Treatment Plant (the largest single facility project in the district's history) is expected to meet the water treatment needs in the north and central county areas through the year 2020. Water comes to the plant from the federal Central Valley Project San Felipe Division via the San Luis Reservoir located 12 miles west of Los Banos in Merced County, as well as from local reservoirs. The plant is capable of producing up to 100 million gallons of treated water a day for distribution to growing communities in Almaden Valley and other areas of San Jose.

Though the Santa Clara Valley (as most of the rest of the state) has been plagued by drought conditions in recent years, flood protection is still a real concern. The valley floor is a natural floodplain that has been covered by floodwaters many times. Between 1888 and 1988 the county experienced 21 major floods. Three serious flooding events occurred in the five–year period from 1982 through 1986 alone.

As the countywide flood protection agency, the Valley Water District builds flood control projects to reduce the potential for damage and danger from such flooding. But the district also strives to preserve the natural qualities, scenic

District reservoirs provide a means of capturing local rainfall for recharge underground.

beauty, and recreational uses of the valley's waterways. The district prefers flood control methods that have minimal impact on the environment, such as floodplain management, earth levees, or gabions, and revegetation projects that foster development of natural bird and animal habitats. The district also encourages cities and the county to require creekside developers to separate their developments from creeks and roadways, using loop streets or cul–de–sacs wherever possible.

Educating the public on water issues remains one of the district's priorities. In addition to co-operating with local media, the district works to educate Santa Clara County students about water quality and supply, the district's flood control programs, and the importance of water conservation. The district's school programs include student workbooks for elementary students, films for all ages, teacher workshops, facility tours, and classroom presentations.

As the county heads toward the next century, the Santa Clara Valley Water District continues its effective management of the water supply and flood control needs of county residents.

Drinking–water treatment plants, such as the Santa Teresa Water Treatment Plant in south San Jose, provide the district with a facility for treating surface water.

BT North America Inc.

BT North America Inc. is one of the world's premier suppliers of telecommunications products and services. Headquartered in San Jose, the company has been providing its expertise and leading-edge technology to a worldwide business market for more than 20 years.

The scope of BT North America's offerings underscores its commitment to serving its worldwide customers now and into the future. The company's wide range of products and services include voice and data value-added networks, business equipment, data communications products and services, applications, and integrated trading systems, among others.

At the heart of BT North America's Global Network Services (GNS) is the TYMNET Global Network, one of the largest international value-added communications networks in the world. TYMNET was designed around a flexible software-based architecture which provides a full spectrum of networking options and features, inherent security and reliability, extensive protocol support, and more locations and transmission speeds than any other network. With more than 4,500 nodes (communications processors) worldwide, TYMNET facilitates millions of business transactions every day.

In countries not covered directly by the TYMNET network, BT North America has established special relationships with local operating telecommunications administrations. Because these adminstrations use TYMNET equipment and technology, customers can still obtain the same superior level of service.

And remaining countries can still access BT North America's GNS through gateways either owned or managed by the company's parent organization, British Telecommunications, plc.

BT North America's videoconferencing products are another example of the company's ability to provide customers with the latest in global communications capabilities. The company's recently introduced "videocodecs" allow users to integrate video, voice, and data signals for fully interactive conversations.

Electronic Data Interchange (EDI) is one of today's most sophisticated methods of interbusiness communications. BT North America EDI Net is a premier EDI service which transfers documents from application to application, across industries, and in standard format.

BT North America's electronic transaction services are among the most advanced in the world, encompassing complete point-of-sale programs for financial and retail industries. The company processes more than 400 million such transactions annually from more than 160,000 merchant locations and delivers services to 600-plus banking institutions.

The company also offers the industry's most comprehensive line of messaging services, which comply with established international communications standards.

Other BT North America products and services include the Concert network management system, which allows interface with systems from other suppliers and gives customers a unified view of their networks; LAN Interconnect/Frame Relay capabilities, which accommodate the evolving requirements of international telecommunications; and virtual private network services, which enable customers to link their networks to overseas virtual networks.

BT North America is a wholly owned subsidiary of British Telecommunications, plc., one of the world's largest telecommunications organizations, with more than $23 billion in annual revenues and offices in more than 30 countries. BT, as the parent company is generally known, employs a staff of approximately 226,000 worldwide.

BT North America employs a U.S. staff of 1,600 and manages approximately 3,000 worldwide.

Aris Helicopters Ltd.

Whether threading two–ton vent shafts into seven–story buildings, delivering vital organs for transplant operations, replacing a community water tank destroyed in the 1989 Loma Prieta earthquake, or lifting an injured horse out of an isolated canyon, it's all in a day's work for the experienced staff at Aris Helicopters Ltd.

Aris was founded in 1972 by Stephen and Nancy Sullivan. Steve, a former U.S. Army pilot who flew helicopters in Vietnam, was working for a civilian flying service when he and his wife decided to strike out on their own. After combing the country for a promising market, they set up shop in Santa Clara County with their first two–passenger helicopter.

Today the Aris Helicopter fleet is one of the largest in Northern California. Headquartered at the San Jose International Airport, the firm maintains satellite offices in Los Angeles and Sacramento. And, with several different models of aircraft at its disposal, Aris' operation is highly diversified, providing a wide range of contract services to clients throughout the western United States.

These services include Air Medevac, emergency personnel transport, fire fighting, search and rescue, geological and seismic surveying, offshore transport, and news photography. As acknowledged experts in the fields of precision "sling" or aerial crane operations and "back country" or remote–site work (specialties requiring the greatest pilot skill), Aris is California's largest supplier of helicopter support for construction com-

An Aris "Lama" helicopter fighting a wildfire.

panies, environmental studies, seismic crews, and government agencies.

Aris' services are also popular for surveying commercial real estate. Representatives of restaurant or service station chains, for example, sometimes need to inspect several locations in traffic–choked communities in a single day. They often turn to Aris for the unique perspective and quick point–to–point transportation that a helicopter can provide.

That quick access is at the heart of Aris' personnel and cargo transport service. Whether an executive is needed at a last–minute corporate meeting down the coast or a maintenance engineer is heading into the Santa Cruz mountains to repair a damaged power line, Aris Helicopters has the ability to move key personnel—and equipment—wherever they are needed, quickly and safely.

Aris is staffed by a crew of seasoned pilots—most of them hold Airline Transport Pilot certificates and are Certificated Flight Instructors. Flight training is an important facet of Aris' operations. Aris instructors have trained students from NASA, the California Highway Patrol, the California Department of Forestry, and even the Federal Aviation Administration as well as pilots from 24 different countries.

Aris Helicopters Ltd. has grown up with the Santa Clara Valley. As the need for quick, safe, economical transportation continues to grow, Aris will continue to meet those needs.

From flight training to executive transport—Aris' diverse fleet in action.

American Airlines

American Airlines first established its hub terminal at the San Jose International Airport in December 1988. It was the airline's sixth hub and it served some 18 West Coast cities, as well as its Chicago and Dallas/Fort Worth hubs. Today American serves Silicon Valley from a newly expanded, $21-million hub terminal with a total of 130 flights a day to 27 cities.

American opened the new, 102,000-square-foot terminal facility in October 1990. The new terminal includes 11 gates with jet bridges and spacious new facilities for its regional airline partner, American Eagle.

In March 1991 American began nonstop service between San Jose and Tokyo, Japan. The route will soon be flown by the new 245-seat McDonnell Douglas MD-11 aircraft. The MD-11, powered by three General Electric engines, is a quiet, stage-3 aircraft with a range of 6,800 miles.

The San Jose-Tokyo route, awarded to American by the U.S. Department of Transportation in 1990, was a crucial development for the Silicon Valley business community, making San Jose an important West Coast gateway for travel and shipping to the Pacific Rim. The route underscores American's strong commitment to its San Jose hub and its belief in local industry's ability to support long-haul, international flights.

The new Tokyo service is American's second nonstop service to Japan. The airline has been serving Tokyo from its Dallas/Fort Worth hub since 1987.

The first regularly scheduled flight of what was to become American Airlines was considerably shorter than the 5,154-mile San Jose-to-Tokyo trip. It was made on April 15, 1926, by Charles Lindbergh, who flew mail for a small airline in a DH-4 biplane from St. Louis to Chicago. That airline and about 85 others were consolidated in 1929 and 1930 into an airline called American Airways, the immediate forerunner of American.

In 1933 American began flying the 18-passenger Curtiss Condor, the first U.S. sleeper plane. With the introduction of the Condor, flight attendants made their first appearance on American.

American Airways was reorganized in 1934 and became American Airlines. That year, the company introduced the Air Travel Plan, one of the industry's first sales promotion programs and the predecessor of today's credit travel. American flew the world's first commercial DC-3 two years later on a trip from Chicago to New York. The DC-3 was built to American's specifications and became the workhorse of the air for many years, including valiant service during World War II.

In 1947 American introduced the fully pressurized DC-6, offering sleeper flights between New York and Los Angeles. During the 1940s American also entered the airline catering business with a subsidiary called Sky Chefs. And by the end of the decade, the company was the first airline with an all-postwar fleet.

During the 1950s American pioneered nonstop transcontinental service in both directions

A DC—10—30 Luxuryliner.

across the United States with the DC-7. And on January 25, 1959, with the Boeing 707, American became the first airline to offer coast-to-coast jet service.

American was also one of the earliest airlines to computerize. In the 1960s the company teamed with IBM to introduce its Semi-Automated Business Research Environment (SABRE), the world's largest privately owned, real-time computer network. During its development, many of the features that are now standards in the travel business were introduced by SABRE: invoice/itinerary, car and hotel bookings, unbiased flight schedules and displays, and fare quotations and automatic pricing.

American gained its first Caribbean routes through a merger with Trans Caribbean Airways in 1970. Four years later the company introduced one-stop automated check-in 1974. And it invented Super Saver fares in 1977 to stimulate discretionary travel.

The 1980s saw American welcome its 500-millionth passenger. In 1984 the company ordered 67 Super 80 aircraft and placed options on 100 more for the largest single aircraft purchase in U.S. history. Two years later employment at American topped 50,000 for the first time and the company announced a merger agreement with AirCal, helping to establish an American presence on the West Coast.

Six regional airlines operate under the American Eagle name, providing convenient transportation for people in thousands of smaller towns as well as feeding passengers to American Airlines flights.

Today American Airlines has seven hub terminals, including Dallas/Fort Worth, Chicago, Nashville, Raleigh/Durham, San Juan, and Miami. These hubs serve some 184 cities nationally and internationally with more than 2,200 departures per day. As of this writing, more than one billion passengers have flown on American Airlines and its predecessors.

American Airlines has been widely recog-

A 747-SP Luxuryliner.

nized for excellence throughout its history by its customers and its industry. The company was named the number-one airline in the world in 1987 by North American Frequent Flyers in a survey conducted by the International Foundation of Airline Passenger Associations. American came in first among the major airlines in eight of the first nine U.S. Department of Transportation dependability reports. Its first and business class food service on the Dallas/Fort Worth-Tokyo route won the International Flight Catering Association's coveted Mercury Award in 1988. This is the top award for in-flight food service.

American was named the favorite airline of frequent-flying readers of *Advertising Age* magazine in 1987. *Business Week* magazine chose company president Robert L. Crandall as one of 1988's best U.S. managers. And that same year, The Gallagher Report named Crandall one of the year's top 10 managers in U.S. business.

In 1990 The Minority Economic Resources Corporation selected American to receive its MERC Corporate Partnership Award for significant public commitment to the legacy of Dr. Martin Luther King, Jr. *Black Enterprise* magazine named American one of the top 50 companies in the U.S. offering career opportunities for blacks.

And American was named the best U.S. airline in all categories by the Zagat Survey, a national survey effort that ranked all airlines in 1990.

Locally, American's San Jose flight attendants and cabin services personnel won the City of San Jose Mayor's Award for 1990 called "Breaking New Ground," recognizing environmental achievement in industry for its innovative employee-driven recycling program. The California Department of Conservation also honored the airline's San Jose recycling program with its Recycling Achievement award for 1990.

A crew diligently checks the cockpit to ensure that the plane performs at a first-rate level.

Empire Broadcasting, KARA—KLIV

An aerial view of the KARA–KLIV complex. In the fore-ground is the old KLIV building and in the rear are the new quarters for both stations.

From left: John McLeod, vice president of programming; Vincent Lopopolo, executive vice president; and Robert Kieve, president, in front of KARA's automation equipment.

With the proliferation of adult contemporary music stations throughout the Bay Area, the competition for the celebrated "AC" music listener aged 25 to 54 is vigorous, to say the least. But in Silicon Valley, KARA 105.7 FM has managed to consistently attract a sizable chunk of that affluent, educated audience.

KARA, and its sister station, KLIV 1590–AM, are owned and operated by Empire Broadcasting Corporation. Formed in Rochester, New York, in 1967 by president Robert Kieve and others, Empire first purchased

KLIV on July 1, 1967, acquiring KARA five years later.

KARA's programming mix of "oldies" from the 1960s and 1970s reaches close to 200,000 people every week. In addition to its strong listenership in the 25 to 49 age range, a significant number of "spill–over" listeners aged 50 to 54 and 18 to 25 tune to the station daily.

KLIV, which offers music from the 1940s, 1950s, and 1960s, targets adults over age 45—people who are attached to the music they grew up with.

Though they are known primarily for their music, KARA and KLIV make regular use of their full–time news staff. KARA provides news reports every hour during morning and afternoon drive times, special traffic updates during key commute times, and regular weather reports throughout the day.

KLIV provides news 24 hours a day, with local updates every half hour during morning and afternoon drive times, and South Bay traffic reports three times per hour during the morning and afternoon commutes.

The long tenure of many of the staff members of the Empire Broadcasting team is unusual, if not unique, in the radio industry. Program director John McLeod has been with the company since its creation in 1967. Kim Vestal, the KARA morning disc jockey, has been calling the South Bay to rise and shine since 1980. And Jane McMillan, the KLIV morning host, has been on the local airwaves for seven years.

Empire demonstrates a strong commitment to the South Bay communities it serves. When, for example, the San Jose City Council decided it could no longer afford to publish its weekly agenda in the local newspapers, KLIV offered to broadcast the agenda at no charge, which it still does, several times every week. KARA also broadcasts the agenda of the Santa Clara City Council.

It's certainly not surprising, then, that the presence and influence of KARA and KLIV continue to be felt throughout Silicon Valley.

KBAY/KEEN

In 1946, before the electronics revolution created Silicon Valley, radio service to the then largely agricultural communities of Santa Clara County was extremely limited. In fact, San Jose only had one radio station.

But that was also the year George Snell, Floyd Farr, and George Mardikian decided that San Jose would be a good place to get into the radio business. Today the two radio stations they founded, KBAY 100.3–FM and KEEN 1370–AM, are among the foremost broadcasting entities in the Bay Area.

Radio KEEN was the first to go on the air. The station's first broadcast began at 8 p.m. on June 21, 1947, and was marked with a gala grand opening of its Hotel De Anza studios. More than 5,000 people attended the celebration. Three live orchestras, several soloists, and the San Jose Municipal Band performed. Local officials, including California Lieutenant Governor Goodwin J. Knight and San Jose Mayor Al Ruffo, gave speeches. And Highway 101 in front of the hotel was closed to allow dancing in the street.

The De Anza was the home of KEEN (and later of KBAY) for more than 27 years. The station has moved several times in the intervening years and is now located at 399 North Third Street in Campbell.

In KEEN's early years, its programming followed traditional AM radio formats: popular music, news, sports, and public affairs. But in 1953, in a bold move, the owners changed the station's format to country and western. To support the change, they brought in big–name disc jockeys such as Cottonseed Clark, Foy Willing, Cactus Jack, and Red Murrell. The new format caught on quickly, and today KEEN is known as one of the top country music stations in the United States.

But KEEN's founders were not only interested in AM radio. They kept their eyes on FM broadcasting from its early days. In the early 1960s they perceived that no other Bay Area FM station was offering an easy–listening musical format, and they moved to fill that market niche.

In 1963 KEEN–FM went on the air. Its transmitter, located on Loma Prieta Peak, 4,000 feet above sea level, gave the station wide coverage. In fact, the high power and great height of the transmitter combined to produce one of the strongest signals in Northern California. Today KBAY–FM (as KEEN– FM came to be called) is the most listened to radio station in Santa Clara County. From as far south as King City, to north of Marine, and east to Yosemite, more than 350,000 listeners tune in to the station each week.

Farr and Mardikian died in the late 1970s. Snell maintained his involvement in the stations until his death in July 1991. His two sons have run the stations since 1980. Steve Snell is the general manager of KBAY, and his brother, Christopher, is the general manager of KEEN. Both are general partners in the enterprise, and together they continue to strive to meet the needs of their ever–growing Silicon Valley audiences.

From left: Christopher Snell, the late George Snell, and Steve Snell in front of the KBAY/KEEN offices/studios.

MIX 106.5 KEZR

Broadcasting from the geographical center of San Jose's downtown redevelopment project, radio station KEZR is in a unique position—literally—to serve its Santa Clara County audience. And since the station became locally owned and operated on August 9, 1976, Mix 106.5 has held a leading position among the area's adult contemporary music listeners.

KEZR's format is music intensive, with a strong commitment to presenting news and other information that affects San Jose and the Bay Area. The station is owned by Alta Broadcasting Company, a locally based, privately owned corporation founded by two brothers, John and Jim Levitt.

The Levitts have a long history and strong ties to both the broadcasting business and the San Jose community. In 1928 their father, Joe Levitt, settled in San Jose, where he opened a radio and record store called Coast Radio. The store was located on First Street, on the downtown site where the Federal Building now stands.

Joe Levitt first became involved with local broadcasting through radio station KQW. KQW

was the first commercial radio station in the United States to broadcast music. Joe Levitt sponsored a live musical program at the station in which he himself sang and promoted his store.

In 1948, after serving in World War II, Joe Levitt returned to San Jose and applied for his own broadcaster's license. His station, KXRX, was one of the earliest AM stations on the air in the city.

Both John and Jim worked in their father's station while they were growing up, later pursuing other interests. But in 1976, recognizing growing opportunities in FM radio, the two brothers joined together and purchased their own station, KEZR.

A year and a half later, Joe Levitt sold his station and retired. John and Jim, who had been renting space at their father's station, moved the station to North First Street, where it stayed for the next 11 years. KEZR began broadcasting from its downtown San Jose location on May 15, 1989.

Within a few years of its founding, KEZR became the number-one local station in its demographic group in both ratings and revenues. The station's early format was on the soft side of what was then called progressive rock. Today its format continues to follow its baby–boom audience with 1980s–based adult contemporary programming.

Over the years KEZR has consistently remained among the leading FM stations in Santa Clara County. One of the forces behind the station's success has been its strong and committed sales organization. Much of its sales staff has been with the station for more than 10 years (a rare thing in the broadcasting industry). And as a locally owned station, KEZR is able to establish many long–term relationships with its advertisers.

But almost as important to KEZR's success has been the Levitts' commitment to the community in which they live. From sponsoring Good Samaritan Hospital's annual 10K run, to lending on–air personalities to emcee the local United Way campaign kick-off, KEZR has proved to be a tireless supporter of local organizations and events.

Mix 106.5 KEZR's colorful vans are seen all around San Jose and the South Bay promoting the station and its commitment to the community.

San Jose International Airport

In 1945 James M. Nissen and a group of local businessmen leased some Santa Clara Valley farmland from the City of San Jose. There they built a hangar, an office building, and a single runway—one of the region's first municipal airports.

San Jose International Airport's KidPort in Terminal C provides interactive exhibits with an aviation theme so that young travelers can expend energy before a flight.

Less than 50 years later, that little airfield has grown into one of the busiest commercial airports in the world. Today the San Jose International Airport serves more than 7 million passengers a year with nonstop flights to cities throughout the U.S., Canada, Mexico, and Japan.

Owned and operated by the City of San Jose, San Jose International is the principal air facility serving the Silicon Valley and the South San Francisco Bay and Monterey Peninsula areas (a region with a population of 2.5 million). No taxpayer funds are used to operate the airport; it is a self-sustaining operation supported with revenues from user fees and federal grants.

San Jose International is a downtown airport located two miles from the center of the city. It is served by all of the major domestic carriers, as well as one international carrier, and it offers a growing network of nonstop and direct flights daily.

San Jose International contributes significantly to the region's international business activities. It was recently designated American Airline's West Coast hub, and, with its March 1991 inaugural flight to Japan, it now serves the so-called "technology corridor" between Boston, San Jose, and Tokyo. By the end of the century, more than 14 million passengers a year are expected to use the airport.

To better serve this growing number of customers, San Jose International is currently undergoing a $516-million expansion. This expansion project will provide for a total of three terminal buildings, the first of which—a 16-gate terminal—was completed in 1990.

And despite its increased air service, sound levels around the airport should actually decrease during the next decade. San Jose International has had an active notice mitigation program in place for several years. In fact, the airport was the first in California to receive state approval and certification for a fully operational airport noise monitoring system. In addition, the airport restricts the hours of scheduled commercial airline

operations, has spent $75 million to acquire homes and relocate residents south of the airport, and continues to insulate homes surrounding the airport for better sound control.

San Jose International is served by Alaska, American/American Eagle, America West, Continental, Delta, Mexicana, Northwest, Skywest, TWA, and United airlines. Its all-cargo carriers include Emery, Federal Express, Airborne, and United Parcel Service.

The airport is also a provider of general aviation services with two first-rate, fixed-based operators, ACM and the San Jose Jet Center, providing service to general aviation users. Aris Helicopters and Air One provide helicopter services at the airport.

San Jose International Airport continues in its dedication to providing a gateway to the Silicon Valley and the South Bay by ensuring safe, efficient, and attractive facilities that provide first-rate service to the community with a staff committed to the highest standards of customer satisfaction.

10

Professions

Silicon Valley's professional community brings a wealth of insight and service to the area.

Photo by Mark Snyder/The Photo File

Fenwick & West

Above: International expert Henry W. West was the president of the Asian subsidiary of a well-known high technology company before joining Fenwick & West.

Right: Joel Riff and David Hayes compare the screen displays of two computer programs for possible copyright infringement.

Below: Fenwick & West has three managing partners: Edwin N. Lowe, Edmond C. Gregorian, and Henry W. West.

Fenwick & West is recognized as one of the premier intellectual property law firms in the world. This reputation is based on the Firm's expertise in recognizing, solving, and advising on legal issues related to interests of high technology clients doing business in California and the world. This service is provided by Fenwick & West through its offices in Silicon Valley and Washington, D.C.

Fenwick & West's diverse client base ranges from *Fortune* 500 companies and well-known international business concerns to entrepreneurial start-up companies. Through its clients the Firm is frequently positioned at the leading edge of developments in law and business. Many of the Firm's attorneys have engineering and other technical degrees as well as law degrees. Indepth understanding of the technology enhances Fenwick & West's attorneys' ability to provide insightful, innovative, and creative solutions to clients' legal problems. Several of the Firm's attorneys are nationally recognized experts on

technology-related legal problems such as computer and software rights; technology development; maintenance and protection through knowledge and use of patent, copyrights, trademark, and trade secret principles; international licensing; acquisitions; mergers and joint ventures; and complex technology litigation. Attorneys within the Firm regularly consult internationally on marketing and distribution plans and programs, financing techniques, and sources and tax planning issues.

On the investor side, Fenwick & West represents the largest public venture capital fund group

Bruce W. Jenett and Jacqueline A. Daunt listen to Dr. George P. Koo of International Strategic Alliances, Inc.

transaction, and litigation services for clients of any size.

Many of the lawyers in the Intellectual Property Group have technical degrees, including advanced degrees in engineering, computer science, mathematics, and physics. This technical background enables the Firm to provide some of the most sophisticated service available anywhere in the world relating to protecting proprietary rights, including trademark, copy-

Left: William A. Fenwick, Litigation Practice Group leader, contemplates a search and analysis strategy for a case's data base.

Below: Internationally recognized tax expert James P. Fuller confers with German tax authority Jurgen Killius.

in the United States. The Firm has been ranked among the eight most influential venture capital law firms in the United States by *Venture* magazine. However, not all of the Firm's clients are technology-based. For example, Fenwick & West has represented Robert Trent Jones, Jr., in the development of golf courses in more than 20 countries, including the first golf course in the Soviet Union. The Firm also represents the American Electronics Association, the largest U.S. electronics trade association.

The Firm's Intellectual Property Group is divided into six practice areas: copyright, patent, trademark, licensing, export control and customs, and antitrust. Working with the Corporate and Litigation groups, the Intellectual Property Group provides counseling,

right, maskworks, trade secret, and patent protection. In response to legal trends relating to patentability of computer software, the Firm's patent practice is a fast-growing area of the business.

The Firm's Corporate Law Group provides legal assistance for public and privately held companies. The group's practice covers the entire spectrum of business organizations. Typical involvement includes day-to-day advice as well as general or special counsel. As issues develop, the attorneys use their knowledge of a company's technology, marketplace, and management to make recommendations about

attraction and retention of key employees, national and international marketing and distribution techniques, acquisitions, mergers, capital structuring, capital programs to support approved company objectives, and advice on all phases of company management and operation.

The Tax Group at Fenwick & West has an international reputation and represents more than 50 *Fortune* 500 corporations as well as major foreign entities. The Tax Group focuses on worldwide tax planning for international transactions, joint ventures, mergers and acquisitions, and major tax litigation matters.

The Firm's International Practice Group is significantly involved across the breadth of Fenwick & West's activity. Given the technology emphasis of the Firm and the worldwide pattern of technology development, use, and transfer, all elements of the Firm are involved in varying degrees in international transactions. As a consequence, Fenwick & West represents some of the largest foreign technology companies in development, acquisition, and licensing of technology, both in-bound and out-bound; acquisition or merger of U.S. and foreign companies; joint ventures for manufacturing of complex products both in the United States and aboard; copyright, patent, and trademark matters; tax planning; and litigation. Through its Washington, D.C., office, the Firm also handles international trade, export control, and Customs matters.

Litigation is another major practice area of the Firm. Services to clients, both domestic and foreign, cover a wide range of issues. Much of the litigation or alternative dispute resolution has a broad technology focus. The Firm's litigation attorneys are active in all types of business disputes, including copyright, patent, trademark, and other technology-related matters. The Firm has also represented clients in arbitration and other alternative dispute resolution practice, and several of its attorneys have served as arbitrators in high technology cases.

Fenwick & West's practice areas include:

Alternative dispute resolutions
Copyright
Corporate law
Corporate partnering
Employee benefits
ERISA law
Immigration
Intellectual property
International transactions
International and domestic tax
Litigation
Mergers and acquisitions
Patents
Securities and antitrust law
Trademarks
Technology licensing
Venture capital

At an "all hands" meeting before an initial public offering, Fenwick & West corporate attorneys David Healy, Barry E. Kramer, Gordon K. Davidson, Gail E. Suniga, and Scott P. Spector review the prospectus.

Pictured here are some of the patent attorneys in Fenwick & West's Intellectual Property Group. Front row, left to right: Kenneth M. Kaslow, partner; Albert C. Smith, partner; Edward L. Radlo, partner. Back row, left to right: Dennis Fernandez, associate; Francis Lewis, associate; Greg Sueoka, associate. Patent attorneys not pictured are David L. Hayes, partner, and associates Stuart P. Meyer, John S. Ferrell, and Kenneth Leffler.

Ernst & Young

In Silicon Valley's early years—as a community of entrepreneurs looked to the future and created a new wave in the high–tech industry—the people of Ernst & Young's South Bay office decided that their success for the future meant developing special resources to serve high–tech companies. Ernst & Young became one of the first major accounting firms to recognize the special needs of technology–based companies, and over the next 20 years it became the leading professional services firm serving high–technology companies.

Today Ernst & Young is the market leader in virtually every segment of the high–technology industry—computers and peripherals, semiconductors, software, telecommunications, and life sciences—and its client roster reads like a "Who's Who" of electronics and biotechnology. Ernst & Young's San Jose and Palo Alto offices serve one–third of the "revenue ranked" top 100 companies, and they serve more than 40 percent of the 50 fastest growing companies in Silicon Valley. Nearly a third of all public companies in the valley also depend on Ernst & Young for their accounting, auditing, and management consulting services. Demonstrating its commitment to Silicon Valley, more than 85 percent of Ernst & Young's South Bay practice is dedicated to high–technology clients.

In addition to being the preeminent professional services firm in Silicon Valley, Ernst & Young is the leading integrated services firm in the United States, employing some 24,000 people in more than 100 cities. Internationally, Ernst & Young has representatives in more than 600 cities in 100 countries.

Based upon a philosophy of integrated service—where the needs and requirements of each client are met with a combination of skills and capabilities customized to the clients' unique business issue and environment—Ernst & Young has consistently met the changing business needs of high–tech companies by helping them face the classic challenges of financing, managing, commercialization, globalization, and rapid technological innovation. Ernst & Young's high–tech teams include professionals with extensive industry–specific backgrounds in finance, tax, accounting, manufacturing, management, and systems. They also provide knowledgeable support in regulatory matters relating to the FDA, USDA, EPA, and other government agencies.

Ernst & Young advises high–tech companies in accounting and tax practices, planning, and compliance. Its industry professionals are up–to–date and knowledgeable about the accounting and financial reporting techniques and requirements unique to technology–based companies. Ernst & Young professionals also conduct efficient, quality audits, and they provide guidance for tax compliance and planning.

When a high–tech company looks for venture capital, public or private equity, debt capital, or strategic alliances, the seasoned professionals at Ernst & Young help high–tech companies determine their best financing alternatives and assist in their effective implementation. They help large and small high–tech companies achieve their goals through strategic partnering, and they can also help with mergers and acquisitions, corporate alliances, joint ventures, and other types of business combinations.

Clients also benefit from Ernst & Young's worldwide network of professionals serving high–tech and other manufacturing businesses in Eastern and Western Europe, the Soviet Union, and the Pacific Rim. Ernst & Young's people can

help with decisions about the forms of organization most advantageous for companies with international operations, and its consultants can assist in planning international tax strategies, currency and reporting, custom and duties, market entry options, and transfer pricing.

Ernst & Young has also developed a premier consulting capability to help high–tech companies become world–class manufacturers. Design for manufacturing, total quality management, and just–in–time processes address key areas of manufacturing where know–how can help companies achieve lower costs while maintaining quality. And through its international practice, Ernst & Young can help companies understand the complexities of offshore manufacturing and how to appropriately set up and manage operations in foreign countries.

The firm's actuarial, benefits, and compensation groups consist of professionals in all aspects of actuarial analysis, benefits, and compensation. Their executive compensation consultants review and advise on many facets of compensation packages for executives and directors, including base salary, annual and long–term equity–based incentives, and comprehensive employment agreements. Their services cover all stages of a project, from design through administration, and can help develop a comprehensive and efficient benefits and compensation program to support a company's business objectives.

Ernst & Young information systems specialists work with major companies in every high–technology segment, creating information strategies from clinical trials management and analytical

data management to distribution and after–sale service. Its professionals also consult on networks and communications, technical systems, and data base software.

The entrepreneurial spirit that drives Silicon Valley inspires Ernst & Young's San Jose and Palo Alto practices. The firm grew with the valley, helping many high–technology companies get started and stay on course. Ernst & Young professionals continue to support entrepreneurs in the preparation and evaluation of plans and projections. They help management address increasingly complex issues and new challenges by providing consulting support in areas such as strategic business planning and management systems development and implementation. And they also help companies establish performance measures and provide systems to track results.

Ernst & Young professionals understand industry issues, seek creative solutions, and serve as management advisers. Through personal attention and technical experience, the firm continues to be the preeminent provider of quality professional services for high–tech companies in Silicon Valley.

Ernst & Young supports excellence through its exclusive sponsorship of the U.S. Olympic Committee's Job Opportunities Program, a program to help athletes gain work experience while training for the Olympics.

The entrepreneurial spirit—so prevalent in Silicon Valley—is recognized and honored through Ernst & Young's Entrepreneur of the Year Award, presented annually to executives in young high–technology businesses.

Frank, Rimerman & Co.

Frank, Rimerman & Co., Certified Public Accountants, was founded in 1949 with the belief that a firm builds a reputation for quality two ways: from the expertise of its people and from the level of service it provides.

Today Frank, Rimerman & Co. is the largest locally owned accounting firm in Silicon Valley. With offices in Menlo Park and San Jose, the firm provides audit, accounting, tax, litigation, and management consulting services to a wide spectrum of area businesses and individuals.

From the firm's founding, the people at Frank, Rimerman & Co. have had a clear vision of the kind of firm they wanted to create: one in which a group of talented professionals could offer together more than they could offer as individuals, and one in which those individuals would stimulate excellence in each other.

As a locally owned firm in a competitive major marketplace, they have had to be better.

This is why they developed a strong commitment not only to their clients, but also to the profession. Few firms in the United States can equal the role they have played in determining the future course of the profession. Most recently, the firm's managing partner, Tom Rimerman, was elected

chairman of the 300,000-member American Institute of Certified Public Accountants, the national professional body of CPAs in the United States.

Frank, Rimerman & Co.'s membership in the Firms Division of the American Institute of CPAs is an additional indication of their commitment to service excellence. This voluntary organization requires stringent quality control standards, personnel training programs, and regular peer reviews (during which an outside CPA firm evaluates the firm's compliance with quality standards).

In addition, as a member of The American Group of CPA Firms (TAG), an association of independent firms with affiliations throughout the world, Frank, Rimerman & Co. is serving clients with business operations in 49 states and 21 foreign countries. TAG provides its members, and their clients, the strength and service of an international organization, and the resources of specialists in virtually every industry. This involvement has added great depth to firm personnel and, as a result, client services.

In the pursuit of its vision the firm has developed individuals that deliver the technical expertise of the very largest firms with the personal touch of a small firm.

While Frank, Rimerman & Co. emphasizes traditional accounting functions, it also provides a broad range of management consulting services, from computer systems consulting to special studies to enhance profitability and customer service.

Frank, Rimerman & Co. is also regularly called upon to assist law firms, the courts, and other clients by providing expert testimony in complex litigation matters.

Though locally owned, Frank, Rimerman & Co. provides services to major corporations and is also there for smaller companies and individuals. Many accounting firms do not know how to talk to the kinds of entrepreneurs who built Silicon Valley, but Frank, Rimerman & Co. was cast in the very same mold. The firm understands the special needs of start-ups and expanding businesses and has helped companies grow into large, publicly traded concerns.

Frank, Rimerman & Co. also believes it has a responsibility to the local community. Members of the firm have served as officers and directors of many of the valley's most significant nonprofit programs and organizations, such as The Community Foundation of Santa Clara County, KTEH Public Television, Peninsula Community Foundation, San Jose Museum of Art, San Jose State University, University of Santa Clara, San Jose Symphony, Children's Health Council, and Lucille Salter Packard Children's Hospital at Stanford, Junior Achievement of Santa Clara Valley, Peninsula Center for the Blind, Technology Center of Silicon Valley, and many more.

Berliner, Cohen & Biagini

It's been nearly 30 years since Sanford A. Berliner first began practicing law in San Jose. Back then the city—about one-third its present size—was generally considered a bedroom community for the new high–tech companies sprouting up to the north. But to San Berliner, it was ". . . a place where things were happening . . . a community where a person could have an impact."

Few locally owned law firms have had as much impact on the communities of Silicon Valley as Berliner, Cohen & Biagini. The firm San Berliner founded in 1969 with law–school classmate Sam Cohen is today the largest business law firm in San Jose.

From its early days headquartered in the Bank of America building on First Street in downtown San Jose, the firm's goal was for Cohen to develop a strong litigation practice and Berliner a sophisticated real estate practice.

That strategy has proved to be a successful one. In 1975 Berliner, Cohen started an expansion that has continued ever since. By the end of that year the firm had almost 10 lawyers on staff. Over the next few years the firm expanded to 20 attorneys, eventually outgrew its facilities, and moved to the Union Bank Building on the corner of Almaden Boulevard and San Fernando Street.

Today, with more than 50 attorneys and 12 full–time paralegals and assistants, Berliner,

Sam Cohen (left) and Stan Berliner.

Cohen occupies 52,000 square feet in the new Ten Almaden Office Building.

The firm specializes in commercial litigation; real estate and commercial transactions; land use, environmental, and public law; tax law; and corporate and general business law. Because of its size, expertise, and experience, the firm provides quality legal services promptly and efficiently to meet both the routine and extraordinary needs of its clients.

Berliner, Cohen represents a wide variety of clients, ranging from some of Silicon Valley's largest corporations to new ventures and start-ups to leading real estate developers in the Bay Area and private real estate investors. The firm's clients also include banks, software developers, medical clinics, mortgage banking companies, municipalities, and other public agencies.

The firm's real estate department represents lenders, developers, owners, and investors in all facets of commercial, industrial, and residential real estate. This area of the firm's practice is highly sophisticated and involves transactions throughout California and in many other areas of the United States.

The department's practice includes property sales, acquisitions and exchanges, development, leasing, conventional and creative financing, developing and structuring complex joint venture arrangements and redevelopment projects, and private syndication of real estate interests.

Though Berliner, Cohen has been involved in major real estate transactions throughout the state, it is best known locally for its pivotal role in San Jose's downtown redevelopment effort. It was San Berliner, acting as a liaison between the city and developers, who sealed the deal that brought the Fairmont Hotel to the eight-square-block San Antonio Plaza. Many believe it was this deal that actually got the downtown project off the ground.

In addition to its real estate department, the firm's land use, environmental, and public law department handles specific real property issues for both the private and public sectors relating to the land development process. Berliner, Cohen represents private clients in zoning and land use matters and in administrative and regulatory proceedings at the state and local level (including proceedings related to toxic waste disposal and other environmental matters). The firm also serves as special counsel to many municipalities and other public agencies in an advisory capacity as well as in the trial of environmental, condemnation, and land use matters.

Berliner, Cohen's well-known real estate department is backed by a solid, well-respected litigation department. Sam Cohen, one of the top litigators in Santa Clara County, is a frequent lecturer on trial practice and techniques, and is a special master on the complex business litigation panel of the Santa Clara Superior Court.

The firm's litigation practice encompasses a broad range of civil matters, including general business disputes, trade secrets, wrongful discharge, creditor's rights in bankruptcy, securities, real estate, construction, toxic contamination, landslide, and subsidence, as well as professional malpractice defense, white-collar criminal defense, and complex matrimonial dissolutions. The firm also has an extensive appellate practice.

The firm's corporate practice is remarkably diverse. It covers a wide variety of privately held and publicly traded corporations, including electronics and computer companies with domestic and international operations, software companies and software developers, commercial banks and other financial institutions, title companies, and manufacturing and construction companies. The corporate department offers expertise in federal and state securities matters, commercial loans, creditors' rights, distribution and purchasing agreements for products and commodities, partnership agreements, and a full range of technology licensing and protection transactions.

Berliner Cohen's tax practice embraces the full range of federal, state, and local tax issues. The federal tax practice includes all aspects of real estate transactions, tax controversy matters with the Internal Revenue Service, corporate tax planning, executive compensation (including qualified employee-benefit plans), and corporate acquisitions and reorganizations. On the state and local level, the tax department handles income, sales, use, and property tax problems, including reassessment and transfer tax issues. In addition, the tax department provides estate planning and probate service.

Berliner, Cohen & Biagini continues to devote considerable attention and effort to the recruitment and training of its able and highly motivated professional staff. Known for its relaxed and collegiate atmosphere, the firm emphasizes mutual respect and recognition of skills and strengths in others, and promotes a team environment where professionals can excel.

The firm boasts several prominent alumni, including Superior Court judges John Flaherty and Conrad Rushing, and Municipal Court Judge Jamie Jacobs-May.

Hoge, Fenton, Jones & Appel, Inc.

The law firm of Hoge, Fenton, Jones & Appel was first established in Monterey in 1952 by two prominent Bay Area trial attorneys. The firm's founders, J. Hampton Hoge and Lewis Fenton, believed in setting high standards for the delivery of legal services, and as the firm grew, its reputation for the highest professional standards grew with it.

In the nearly four decades since its founding, the attorneys at Hoge, Fenton have continued to practice the philosophy and principles of its founders, setting an exceptional standard for

client service throughout California. Today the firm comprises more than 80 lawyers delivering quality legal representation from offices in Monterey, San Jose, and San Luis Obispo.

Hoge, Fenton has long maintained a reputation for handling litigation matters in a competent, creative, and efficient manner. Building on its early expertise in litigation, the firm has expanded its practice into a number of other areas, including securities, tax and estate planning, land use, environmental law, and contract and agreement negotiation.

Organized into departments which address a wide variety of contemporary legal issues, the firm serves a broad spectrum of corporate, government, and individual clients. A sampling of problems addressed by Hoge, Fenton attorneys includes: A *Fortune* 500 company sued for trade-name infringement; a major Japanese electronics firm accused of unfair competition and pirating semiconductor technology; former shareholders in a leveraged buy-out sued for misrepresentation; and a real estate development firm desiring to build a resort complex in an environmentally sensitive coastal area.

Hoge, Fenton prides itself on providing objective advice based on a careful evaluation of what clients seek to achieve and how best to accomplish those goals. This client-partnering process involves developing a friendly and responsive working relationship. By understanding the client's business, Hoge, Fenton believes it can give prompt, economical advocacy without compromising the quality of its work.

The core of Hoge, Fenton's practice is litigation, real estate, insurance coverage, corporate, and estate

The offices of Hoge, Fenton, Jones & Appel are located next to St. Joseph's Cathedral in downtown San Jose.

Hoge, Fenton, Jones & Appel
has maintained a reputation
for handling litigation matters in a competent, cre-
ative, and efficient manner.

planning work. Recently, the firm has aggressively expanded its range of services to include the environmental area.

Hoge, Fenton's trial attorneys handle a broad range of major litigation in federal and state courts. Although these litigators principally practice throughout California, they appear with increasing frequency in courts throughout the country. In addition to court actions, Hoge, Fenton's advocates are also experienced in arbitration, mediation, and other forms of alternative dispute resolution.

Hoge, Fenton enjoys a formidable reputation in the areas of business litigation and casualty work. This practice group handles casualty matters for a broad range of clients, from major insurance carriers to various self-insured parties. They are experts in the fields of personal injury, construction injury, and property damage claims.

The firm's construction litigation practice takes an interdisciplinary approach to construction litigation through a unique combination of its knowledge of the many dynamics of design and building. Attorneys working in this area utilize abilities in land use, real estate transaction, and trial law, and expertise concerning environmental and toxic materials.

In the land use area, Hoge, Fenton attorneys address all issues related to governmental ap-

proval of residential, retail, office, industrial, and resort projects. They have represented clients regarding rezoning, variances, special use permits, assessment appeals, condemnation proceedings, and subdivision and site plan approvals. Based in the Monterey office, the group's practice includes presentations at public hearings and public meetings, negotiations with public officials, drafting of zoning amendments, and representation in court proceedings.

Hoge, Fenton attorneys represent owners, developers, and insurers on a wide variety of environmental issues, including groundwater use and pollution, open space preservation, lender and broker liability analysis, and defense of environmental criminal prosecutions. The environmental practice also addresses coverage analysis in litigation, and regulatory compliance and enforcement at the federal, state, and local levels.

Contamination of the environment has become a major problem leading to the enactment of complex laws and regulations at all levels of government. Ignorance of these mandates cannot only be environmentally damaging, but also financially devastating to the responsible party. Hoge, Fenton's environmental law department helps its clients minimize the potential environmental hazards and their financial inability exposure.

Ireland, San Filippo & Company

When T.W. "Bill" Ireland started his own certified public accounting practice in San Jose in 1975, he had few clients, no partners, and an office consisting of a desk in a hallway. Today, with nine partners, four offices, and more than $7.5 million in annual sales, the firm he founded, Ireland, San Filippo & Company, is one of the leading professional service organizations in the Bay Area.

Ireland, San Filippo is a full–service accounting firm exclusively serving the closely held corporations—usually owner–managed enterprises—that make up the vast majority of Silicon Valley businesses.

"We have always and will always focus on entrepreneurial companies," says the firm's founder. "It's the kind of work we find most satisfying, so that's what we concentrate on. We understand the business needs of entrepreneurs and we know how to help them to make their organizations become what they want them to become."

Ireland, San Filippo combines the efficiency and organizational strength of a large, departmentalized organization with the accessibility of a local accounting firm. Distributing the work load among four departments frees the firm's partners to focus on personal client contact.

The firm's Business Services works exclusively with clients' internal accounting staff, assisting them in closing month–end financial statements. This group works to ensure that clients' internal records are kept satisfactory and up to date. The firm's partners constantly monitor this information so they can alert clients to negative trends before they become irreversible.

The firm's Audit Review Group generates traditional, year–end financial statements and prepares corporate and partnership tax returns. Tax preparation for the individual business owners is handled by the partners. (Because all of Ireland, San Filippo's clients are entrepreneurs, the corporation is just an extension of the individual. The individuals underneath those corporations are the firm's real clients.)

This frees the firm's Tax Department for what is called "heavy tax" work; that is, tax research on such things as the tax ramifications of liquidating a corporation, merging organizations, estate planning, and sales and property tax issues. The Tax Department also provides the most efficient and timely representation of the firm's clients on audits and correspondence issues.

Ireland, San Filippo's Management Advisory Service Group (MAS) performs consulting services relating to business valuations, claims loss, and other forensic accounting services.

It helps clients with the critical task of establishing a business plan. This group helps clients manage their resources more effectively with forecasting and projection tools. By setting up goals and budgets and taking a hard look at bottom lines, overhead, and money spent on capital expenditures, clients get the kind of feedback that keeps them on track toward their goals.

The group applies its expertise in computer systems analysis to clients' needs. Specifically it

Planning and development sessions are an integral part of assisting Ireland, San Filippo & Company clients in their success.

identifies software needs unique to the client and/or industry. The department stays abreast of changes in software relating to the construction, manufacturing, and distribution industries. Additionally, the department focuses on general ledger, word processing, spreadsheets, and network software options. From software to hardware, from mainframes to networks, the MAS Group helps clients sift through the many alternatives.

Entrepreneurs have a sixth sense about their own businesses. But as any business evolves, it eventually reaches a level where it just can't be managed from the gut. The firm's MAS group helps clients establish organizational tools that safeguard their growing businesses and help them manage them more effectively.

In response to the needs of its many construction industry clients, Ireland, San Filippo has also established an affiliated company, The Complete Service Bureau. This company offers a payroll service and tax reporting for a range of companies, and job–costing analysis for construction industry clients.

This departmentalized organizational structure gives the professionals at the firm the room they need for personal growth. By keeping departments small but growing through the opening of more, rather than larger, offices, the firm provides career opportunity for its people while maintaining its ongoing one–on–one involvement with the client.

Ireland, San Filippo was one of the first local accounting organizations to effectively utilize computers. In fact, in the early 1980s, the firm wrote its own sophisticated, professional accounting software package called Staff Accountant. Although not currently marketed, it still provides Ireland, San Filippo with a competitive advantage, since most accounting firms still rely on manual spreadsheets.

Adapting computers early to its operation has helped Ireland, San Filippo meet its commitment to timely delivery of quality services. Today "timeliness" is the firm's watchword. For example, while typical accounting firms—even large national organizations—manage to file only a small percentage of their clients' returns on time, routinely settling for extensions, at Ireland, San Filippo 95 percent of all returns are filed on time.

But timeliness means more than making filing deadlines. It means the firm's highly skilled professional staff is readily available to its clients. They are, in fact, just a phone call away. And since providing ongoing advice to its clients is part of Ireland, San Filippo's quality service, there's no charge for phone calls.

In actual practice, however, it is the firm that does most of the calling. Ireland, San Filippo strives to meet with clients a minimum of once a quarter. During these one-on-one client meetings, the firm's partners help clients focus on critical business issues which are typically overlooked by entrepreneurs busy with day-to-day responsibilities. This ongoing focus helps entrepreneurs develop strategic planning unique to their needs and ambitions.

The firm's professionals perform most of their work on the clients' premises. This frees them from the distractions of their own offices and allows them to work more efficiently because the answers to their questions are close at hand. It also facilitates personal contact and better rapport with clients.

Ireland, San Filippo & Company serves its clients from four Bay Area locations: San Jose, Palo Alto, San Carlos, and San Francisco.

Ireland, San Filippo & Company emphasizes communication with its clients. It works closely with each client on a regular basis to plan for individual and business needs.

In order to be accessible to its clients, Ireland, San Filippo & Company has strategically located its offices away from congested downtown areas and close to major freeways.

KPMG Peat Marwick

Above: The firm is committed to quality client service. Each of Peat Marwick's offices has developed a quality service council, a cross-functional team that includes members from every department and level within each office to identify and address client service issues. Photo courtesy of Doug Menuez

When KPMG Peat Marwick first opened its San Jose office in 1952, Santa Clara County was a rural agricultural community with only a hint of its future as a major metropolitan area and center for high technology.

Since that time Peat Marwick has grown with the valley and has played an important role in the development of its business infrastructure and community culture. As a result, Peat Marwick has a strong commitment to the economic vitality of Santa Clara County, serving clients in high technology, financial services, real estate and construction, state and local government, health care, and a variety of other industries.

Although Peat Marwick has been in Santa Clara County for four decades, the firm's roots go back to turn-of-the-century New York. In 1897 Scottish-born accountants James Marwick and Roger Mitchell joined forces to become Marwick, Mitchell & Co. In 1911 Sir William B. Peat, head of his own distinguished British accounting firm, met Marwick while traveling from England to the United States on an ocean liner. Legend has it that by the time the ship arrived in New York, the two had reached an agreement to combine their practices.

This "hands across the sea" philosophy has continued throughout the firm's history with a long tradition of international scope and expertise. The firm *thinks* globally. Over the years, Peat Marwick has linked much of the business world by developing international accounting standards and coordinating its multinational audit, tax, and consulting capabilities. Locally, multinational Bay Area clients call upon Peat Marwick's international capabilities in the Asia Pacific Region, European developments, and international trade and customs.

So it is not surprising that Peat Marwick is the local leader among the major accounting firms in serving companies with Far East subsidiaries and parents. "With more than 100 Japanese clients in the Bay Area, we have many Japanese-speaking professionals in the San Jose office, including the partner in charge of the Northwestern Region Japanese Practice," says Daniel M. Healy, managing partner of the San Jose practice. "This is just one example of how we use our resources to satisfy clients' special needs."

Extending beyond the traditional accounting, audit, and tax functions, the firm's management consulting services are equally out of the ordinary. For example, Peat Marwick calls upon two other established Silicon Valley firms as strategic alliances: Regis McKenna Inc., the well-known marketing and communications consulting firm to high technology companies; and Pittiglio Rabin Todd & McGrath, one of the world's leading operations management consulting firms for technology-based organizations.

The firm's specialization in targeted industries—the concept that each client is part of a dynamic market that requires services tailored to special needs and goals—is a response to marketplace demands. "Clients choose service providers best prepared to solve business problems specifically related to their industry," says Healy. "The networking of Bay Area professionals and their knowledge has allowed us to provide quality specialized services to many industries, including high technology, financial, government, agribusiness, and the complex health care industry. With four major Bay Area offices—San Jose, Palo Alto, Oakland, and San Francisco—we can pool our resources to bring our best talents to the marketplace."

These talents and resources are also brought to the community—Peat Marwick is one of the largest supporters of the area's cultural, artistic, service, and charitable organizations. "Ingrained in our corporate culture is the philosophy that we must give back to the community that has sup-

ported us for so long," says Healy.

With the merger of the prestigious European firm Klynveld Main Goerdeler in 1987, Peat Marwick is part of the largest of the "Big Six" public accounting firms, with 75,000 employees located in 802 offices in 123 countries. Through its affiliation with KPMG, the combined firm has a dominant share in 13 of 22 critical markets worldwide. The firm boasts more than 180,000 clients, representing every facet of the world economy—commercial, financial, educational, and governmental.

What drives this organization? According to Healy, it's the belief in quality service. The firm's client service strategy emphasizes strong relationships with client senior management and a high level of partner involvement with every client, regardless of size, industry, or location. The firm stresses comprehensive training, investing a significant portion of its annual budget in training its personnel.

One of the telling indicators of Peat Marwick's commitment to quality is the involvement of clients in the quality process. Each client receives a questionnaire annually, allowing them to provide feedback on such critical areas of service delivery as responsiveness, communication, technical support, value of services, satisfaction, and performance. "What matters is not how well we think we are serving our clients, but how well our clients think we are serving them," explains Healy. "The quest for quality is everywhere. Not only here at Peat Marwick, but at our clients' and throughout businesses worldwide. We demonstrate to our clients that we care—that we make quality our business."

KPMG Peat Marwick is the leader among major accounting firms serving Japanese multinational companies, providing accounting, tax, and management services to approximately 3,500 Japanese businesses in Japan and around the world. In San Jose, Peat Marwick has more than 10 bilingual professionals serving more than 100 Japanese practice clients. Pictured from left to right are Yoshio Honda, senior vice president of the Information Systems Group, Fujitsu America, Inc.; and Hiro Yoshihara, partner in charge of the Northwestern Region Japanese Practice of KPMG Peat Marwick. Photo courtesy of Doug Menuez

Left: The high technology sector is one of the principal industries designated for global priority in the 1990s by the firm. In the Bay Area, Peat Marwick is dedicated to serving and enhancing high technology, which includes supporting The Tech Museum of Innovation, an interactive exhibition that allows people to see, experience, and understand the technology that affects them. Pictured are exhibition explainers Roy G. Hayter and Stanley B. Halper describing microcomputer chip circuitry to audit partner Mary Pat McCarthy, a member of The Tech Museum's board of directors.

Ropers, Majeski, Kohn, Bentley, Wagner & Kane

Silicon Valley and the Bay Area have many capable attorneys. But in the specialized area of litigation and arbitration, the reputation and experience of one firm clearly stands out: Ropers, Majeski, Kohn, Bentley, Wagner & Kane.

The strong reputation of Ropers Majeski is based on the firm's thorough understanding of the trial process. According to a recent survey, Ropers Majeski has tried more jury cases to conclusion than any other law firm in California.

By providing succesful, quality trial work, the attorneys of Ropers Majeski have established a reputation for excellence. The firm's prominence in litigation is also demonstrated by the number of its members elected to the American College of Trial Lawyers and the large number of firm partners admitted to the prestigious American

Board of Trial Advocates. The firm is also represented in the International Academy of Trial Lawyers. In 1989 the American Board of Trial Advocates named founding partner Eugene J. Majeski Trial Lawyer of the Year.

Majeski, along with Harold Ropers, now deceased, founded the firm in Redwood City in 1950. At that time the area was still largely agricultural, filled with vegetable fields and prune orchards. Silicon Valley was scarcely a dream.

The two San Francisco attorneys, however, saw an opportunity for a litigation firm in the region. Ropers and Majeski built their early reputation in trial work. Their great success in this area developed relationships with corporate clients that are still strong today.

Ropers Majeski has experienced dramatic growth since its founding. Today, with 150 attorneys, it is the second–largest law firm on the Peninsula, and maintains the largest group of litigators in Northern California.

Specializing in civil and commercial litigation and appellate work, Ropers Majeski conducts a full–service practice, including corporate law, real estate, insurance matters, probate, and trusts and estates. The firm's broad practice also includes business and construction contract negotiations and litigation, government regulatory representation, employment matters, products liability, and intellectual property matters.

The firm's practice spans many industries, including aerospace, construction, engineering, financial institutions, and high technology.

Ropers Majeski has one of the largest appellate departments in California (larger than any other law firm in the Bay Area). With more than 25 years experience, the department is prepared to represent clients in the state and federal appellate courts, the California Supreme Court, and the U.S. Supreme Court.

The firm not only handles appeals that are generated by its own litigation departments, but also advises clients on the viability of appeals in cases tried by other law firms. Many law firms refer matters to Ropers Majeski's appellate department when their own firms do not have the appropriate appellate capacity.

The Appellate Department includes six partners. Robert F. Kane, a former ambassador to Ireland during the 1980s and a former justice of the district court of appeals, is one of these partners.

The chairman of the Appellate Department, Michael J. Brady, with many years of appellate experience, authors the firm's Summary of California Appellate Decisions. Indexed and updated every three months, the summary is an ongoing work that condenses appellate developments in all areas of commercial and casualty litigation. The summary is a popular and well-known professional publication circulated to many general counsels' offices.

The firm is also active in environmental law and litigation—an area of increasing importance to Silicon Valley companies. Ropers Majeski is currently engaged in two of California's largest environmental lawsuits: the Aerojet Sacramento litigation and the Stringfellow toxic litigation in Southern California. The firm offers assistance for environmental matters that arise from contract, permit, compliance, land use, and litigation.

In addition to representing clients in both state and federal courts on these issues, Ropers Majeski has an interest in cases presented to state and federal environmental agencies and local land-use regulators.

In the future, successful resolution of environmental problems and disputes will be vital to the survival of Silicon Valley companies. Ropers Majeski is prepared to meet those challenges.

The Business Law Department represents clients in contract disputes, intellectual property rights matters, organization or reorganization of

Left: Richard M. Williams, a senior partner in the San Jose office, reviews the court findings with his client, Richard G. Bell, General Counsel of Watkins-Johnson.

Below: Mary L. Scharrenberg offers advice to her clients on how to avoid litigation in employment matters.

business entities, and employment matters. Clients range from national conglomerates to emerging technology companies to individual enterprises. Representative clients include California Micro Devices, Intel, Stanford Hospital, Toys 'R Us, and the Watkins-Johnson Company.

In an effort to keep its clients informed on significant developments in California law, Ropers Majeski conducts annual seminars throughout the United States. These seminars discuss the most significant case law and statutory developments of the past year. They focus on any new directions in which California law is moving.

Brooks, Stednitz & Rhodes Accountancy Corporation

(From left) Gordon Brooks, Bob Rhodes, and Jack Stednitz are the firm's founding partners.

Brooks, Stednitz & Rhodes Accountancy Corporation (BS&R) is one of Santa Clara County's leading certified public accounting firms. Ranked by the *San Jose Business Journal* among the top 25 accounting firms in the Bay Area, BS&R offers its clients a number of services, including tax preparation and consulting, computerized data processing, compilation and review, auditing, litigation support, accounting consultation, and peer review.

The firm was originally established as a partnership in 1970. The partners, Jack Stednitz and Bob Rhodes, were CPAs who had been practicing in San Jose for a number of years, working at the local offices of a Big Eight accounting firm. That same year Stednitz and Rhodes were joined by Gordon Brooks, who was an established local CPA and a partner in another local firm.

Brooks, Stednitz & Rhodes was incorporated in 1973. Dean Burdsall became a principal of the corporation in 1974, Bob Johnston in 1977, and Patricia Ford in 1990.

The firm has grown steadily since its founding and currently maintains a client base of some 1,300 companies and individuals. The companies it serves are generally small- to medium–size businesses (no publicly traded corporations) though many of the firm's individual clients are key executives of larger corporations. Some of the firm's

(From left) Partners Bob Johnston, Patti Ford, and Dean Burdsall.

clients have been with the firm for more than 30 years, often spanning generations of businesses and families.

BS&R serves a number of industries including nonprofit, wholesale and retail, trade, services, manufacturing, and communications. Over the years the firm has developed a strong presence and expertise in construction, serving a number of local companies and individuals in that industry. The firm also serves many clients in the medical professions, as well as several local law firms.

BS&R maintains one office in San Jose, from which it serves clients primarily in Santa Clara, San Mateo, Santa Cruz, Monterey, and Merced counties, with only a few clients located outside of these areas.

Tax planning and return preparation accounts for approximately half of the firm's services. Audited, reviewed, and compiled financial statements, accounting system consultations, quality reviews, and computerized data processing constitute the other half.

Growing up with the high–technology companies of Silicon Valley has allowed BS&R to take advantage of computer technology to increase the quality of its productivity and improve its client services. Procedures that once took four or five days can today be completed in hours—and with greater accuracy than ever.

But the professionals at BS&R recognize the difference between the tools of their trade and the services they provide. Rather than just sending out numbers, they sit down with the companies and individuals they serve and help them understand what the numbers mean—to their families, their businesses, and their futures.

And rather than developing a business clientele that is "CPA dependent," BS&R prefers to serve its business clients in a way that leaves them free to conduct their daily affairs without having to pick up the telephone or plug into their accountants' computers.

This philosophy of service—of setting up effective accounting systems and operating as an extension of the company—is really what Brooks, Stednitz is all about. It's a philosophy of helping, and it has served the firm, and its clients, well.

BS&R is known for the quality of its people. Its staff of 23 includes 17 professionals and one paraprofessional. The firm provides its people with excellent training opportunities, from in–house staff training to off–site programs for continuing professional education.

BS&R has been a member of the California Group of Accounting Firms (CalGAF) since 1980. CalGAF is an affiliation of CPA firms from Santa Barbara to Santa Rosa that share management experience and develop coordinated, assocation–wide staff training programs. Through CalGAF, BS&R increases its resources and broadens its professional reach.

The firm's five principals are well known and respected both in the local community and the accounting profession. Retired principal Gordon Brooks has been a practicing CPA since 1957. He was a partner in a local San Jose firm prior to joining Stednitz and Rhodes, where he worked extensively with local small businesses. He has served on the governing council of the AICPA.

Jack Stednitz, also a founding principal, was born in Lincoln, Nebraska, but moved to Palo Alto at an early age. He is a graduate of the University of California at Berkeley, where he received B.S. and M.B.A. degrees. He began his accounting practice with Arthur Andersen & Co. in 1956.

Bob Rhodes began his accounting career after completing his education at Sacramento State University. He joined Arthur Andersen in 1961, where he met Jack Stednitz. He is also a founding partner, and, in addition to serving a large clientele, he serves as managing partner of the firm.

Dean Burdsall, one of the firm's two audit and accounting principals, joined the firm in 1971 and became a partner in 1974. He is a graduate of Pasadena College and formerly worked as an auditor for Peat, Marwick, Mitchell and Co. He serves on the AICPA Private Companies Practice Section Peer Review Committee.

Bob Johnston has been a principal at Brooks, Stednitz since 1977. After graduating from Chico State University, he was employed for several years by Arthur Andersen in that firm's auditing department. He is also an audit and accounting

A staff meeting in the firm's conference room.

principal, and he performs reviews on most financial statements prior to their release.

Patricia Ford joined the firm in 1985 and became a principal in 1990. Her specialty is tax preparation and consulting. She is a graduate of Santa Clara University and has earned an M.S. degree in taxation.

The entire staff of Brooks, Stednitz & Rhodes is active in a wide range of local community service organizations, including local Rotary clubs, the Sierra Club, the Red Cross, Second Harvest Food Bank, Junior Achievement, and Executive Women International. The firm's staff is also active in professional organizations, including the American Institute of Certified Public Accountants, CSCPA, and the Santa Clara County Estate Planning Council, among others.

BS&R's reception room.

Skjerven, Morrill, MacPherson, Franklin & Friel

Skjerven, Morrill, MacPherson, Franklin & Friel is a Silicon Valley–based general practice law firm with a strong focus on intellectual property law. Established in 1976, Skjerven Morrill maintains offices in San Jose and San Francisco, and serves both domestic and international clients with more than 40 attorneys and patent agents.

Skjerven Morrill is particularly well qualified to represent clients in the high–technology industries of Santa Clara County. In fact, many of the firm's attorneys have had extensive high–tech industry experience. For example, one of the firm's founders, Richard H. Skjerven, served as vice president, general counsel, and secretary of American Microsystems; Alan H. MacPherson served as general patent counsel and director of patents and licensing for Fairchild Camera and Instrument Corporation; and Richard Franklin served as director of Fairchild's corporate legal department.

Skjerven Morrill's client list includes some of the most prominent high–tech companies: Ad-

vanced Cardiovascular Systems, Inc., LSI Logic, Advanced Micro Devices, Cetus, NEC, Cirrus Logic, Xilinx, Zilog, Raychem, Ampex, and the Stanford University Office of Technology and Licensing.

Skjerven Morrill's intellectual property practice encompasses the procurement, enforcement, and licensing of patents, trademarks, copyrights, and maskwork rights. The firm's attorneys advise clients on the patentability of inventions, prepare and prosecute patent applications—both in the United States and overseas—and advise clients on questions of validity and infringement of patents.

The firm's attorneys also counsel on all aspects of technical know–how and trade secrets. Its licensing practice frequently deals with sophisticated, state–of–the–art hardware and software where Skjerven Morrill's familiarity with the involved technology is uniquely valuable.

The firm's trademark practice involves its attorneys in the determination of trademark, service

mark, and trade dress availability, the preparation and prosecution of applications to register trademark rights in the United States and abroad, and the counseling of clients concerning the selection, use, and enforcement of trademarks, as well as counseling concerning the trademark rights of third parties.

Skjerven Morrill attorneys register and enforce copyrights, and counsel clients on clean room procedures and on the scope of copyright protection vis–a–vis the rights of others.

The firm's maskwork practice has evolved from its very early participation in congressional hearings in mid–1970. The result of those hearings, the Semiconductor Chip Protection Act, became law in November 1984. The firm continues to provide counseling with respect to the creation and enforcement of maskwork rights, as well as dealing with claims of third parties with respect to such rights.

Skjerven Morrill is unique among intellectual property firms in that it also provides its clients with a broad range of business law and litigation services. From review and preparation of all forms of general business agreements to formation and financing of corporations and partnerships, mergers, and acquisitions, from real estate leases to international joint ventures, the firm maintains an active corporate and commercial law practice.

While Skjerven, Morrill, MacPherson, Franklin & Friel specializes in litigation involving complex and emerging technologies, it also handles a broad range of business litigation, including contract disputes, partnership and corporate dissolutions, and real estate matters. The firm regularly represents both plaintiffs and defendants in state and federal trial and appellate courts, in commercial arbitration and mediation proceedings, and before administrative tribunals such as the Patent and Trademark Office, the Customs Service, and the International Trade Commission.

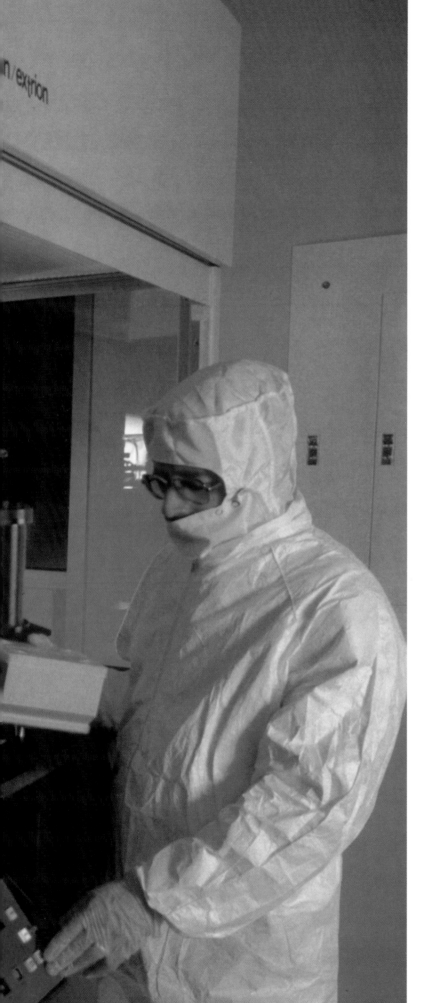

11

High Technology and Manufacturing

Silicon Valley is a mecca for flourishing high-technology manufacturing and research and development industries.

Photo by Liane Enkelis

Conner Peripherals, Inc.

Conner has been called the most successful high-technology start-up company of the 1980s. That is high praise, indeed, especially when one considers that the San Jose-based disk-drive manufacturer did not even begin shipping its first products until 1987. But in that year, Conner set an American business record for first-year growth, posting sales of more than $113 million. And that remarkable growth did not stop there. Just two years later, with sales of $700 million, the company joined the ranks of the *Fortune* 500, making Conner the fastest-growing manufacturing start-up in American history. In 1990 Conner posted sales of more than $1.3 billion.

Today Conner is one of the leading original equipment manufacturers (OEM) suppliers of high-performance, 2.5- and 3.5-inch hard disk drives. As devices that physically store and retrieve computer data, hard disk drives represent critical components in today's computer systems. Conner supplies this critical component to a customer base that includes leading American, Asian, and European computer systems manufacturers.

Conner Peripherals was founded in 1986 by Finis F. Conner and John P. Squires. Conner was an almost legendary figure in Silicon Valley (having founded two highly successful disk-drive firms), when Squires (who also had two disk-drive companies to his name) approached him in 1985 seeking to launch his new 3.5-inch disk drive. Though at that time most disk drives were 5.25 inches in diameter, Conner and Squires foresaw the enormous current popularity of small personal computers and correctly predicted that the smaller drives would soon be in great demand.

Conner continues to direct the company today as chairman of the board and chief executive officer. Squires continues his efforts as executive vice president of research and development and chief technical officer. In addition to the foresight of Conner and Squires, one of the keys to Conner Peripherals' phenomenal success is the company's innovative product-development strategy. Unlike traditional manufacturers who design drives, build them, and then work to sell them to prospective customers, Conner sells product ideas to customers then designs and builds its drives to meet specific customer needs.

Using this strategy Conner readily anticipates shifts in market demand, and so the firm builds drives that fulfill the needs of customers and, ultimately, end users, faster than its competitors. In fact, Conner's timely response to demands for innovative data-storage solutions has set the product standard for the industry.

This tremendous drive toward innovation not only enables Conner to serve a broad base of existing customers, it allows the firm to effectively penetrate new and emerging markets. For example, Conner has played a leading role in the development of "notebook" computers (full-function computers that fit into a briefcase and weigh less than seven pounds) by introducing new disk-drive families for this exciting new breed of personal computer. Besides traditional computer markets, these new drives may have future uses in such nontraditional applications as facsimile machines, automotive guidance devices, and laser printers.

In this way Conner serves all personal-computer market segments with multiple products. Laptop computers, for instance, have evolved into serious business systems because of the performance and power of Conner's innovative 3.5-inch disk drives. Portable computer applications of Conner's low-power, high-performance drives have helped usher in a new era of small, powerful systems. Conner's desktop customers enjoy such performance and design advantages as fast data access and throughput, a choice of system interfaces, low power consumption and ruggedness, and the broadest product line in the industry. And Conner's advanced microcode-based disk-drive design is perfectly matched with the high-performance requirements of workstations and other advanced systems.

But it is not just its products that have made Conner Peripherals an industry leader. The depth and experience of Conner's management team is

Conner offers a complete family of high-performance, 2.5-inch disk drives for the new generation of battery-operated notebook computers. These products store up to 680 million bits of information and weigh just 6 ounces.

Conner Peripherals, Inc., corporate headquarters, located in San Jose.

unequaled in the industry. And it is that depth of experience that has steered the company through its meteoric growth.

Conner's senior management team has an average of more than 20 years of business experience with high-technology companies. William J. Almon, president and chief operating officer, joined Conner after spending nearly 30 years with IBM; William J. Schroeder, vice chairman, was cofounder, president, chairman, and chief executive officer of Priam Corp.; C. Scott Holt, executive vice president of sales and marketing, was vice president/sales and marketing for Microscience International Inc., and later, for Seagate; and Carl W. Neun, senior vice president and chief financial officer, was vice president for Plexus Computers and held various executive management positions at Shugart Corp. including vice president of marketing and sales.

As one might expect, Conner executives and employees are extremely hard-working, dedicated, and focused on their company's continuing growth and success. But they are not so focused that they ignore the community in which their company thrives. In fact, from Conner's founding, contributing to local charities has been a vital part of the firm's corporate culture.

But unlike some corporations that tend to throw money at charitable groups and let it go at that, Conner prefers to form ongoing relationships with the organizations to which it gives. The company works with some 40 local charities, including the Valley Medical Center Foundation, the Valley Institute of Theatrical Arts, Athletes and Entertainers for Kids, and the local chapter of the American Cancer Society, among others.

At least half the members of Conner's execu-

tive staff play significant roles on local charitable boards, and the company promotes an active volunteer program that makes Conner employees available for everything from answering telephones to staffing special events.

Conner has business operations around the globe, including headquarters, domestic manufacturing and development operations in San Jose; international manufacturing facilities in Scotland, Singapore, Malaysia, and Italy; and research and development facilities in Longmont, Colorado. The firm also has sales offices located in Boston, Los Angeles, San Jose, Minneapolis, Dallas, Tokyo, Taipei, Seoul, Singapore, London, Paris, and Munich. Conner employs more than 10,000 people worldwide.

Conner Peripherals is one of the leading original equipment manufacturers (OEM) suppliers of high-performance, 2.5- and 3.5-inch hard disk drives.

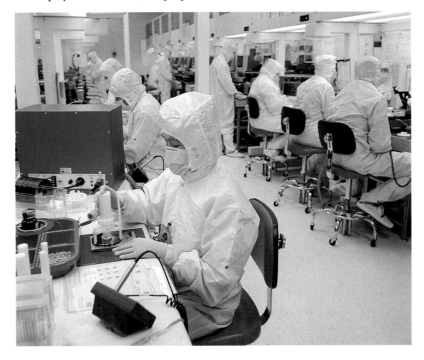

California Micro Devices

When the founders of California Micro Devices (CMD) established the company back in 1976, they didn't have a large operation—just a small, four-man laboratory in Sunnyvale without glamorous technology. But what they and their predecessors did have was a strong belief in themselves and their products and an equally strong determination to build a quality company.

In the first decade of CMD's existence, that determination pushed the now Milpitas-based concern into the ranks of the leading electronics firms in the nation. Today CMD is a growing, $35-million operation with two facilities totaling 110,000 square feet and more than 200 employees working together to produce some of the highest quality products in the industry.

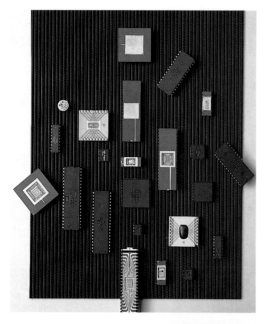

Founded without venture capital backing, CMD focused its early efforts on the development and production of so-called "thin film" technology. Thin film refers to a layer of metal, often no more than a molecule thick, used to make precision microelectronic components. The particular technology that CMD used was originally developed by Bell Laboratories in the early 1970s. At that time, however, few companies recognized the promise of the new technology and most were unwilling to put their resources into its development.

But at CMD, people saw the tremendous potential of thin films and were excited about its possibilities. With few resources, the company began using thin films to produce passive electronic components for unique, precision, high-reliability applications such as aircraft guidance systems, satellites and space sensors, and military weapons systems.

Because thin film components were initially used in such precision devices, the technology acquired an early reputation as an elite—and expensive—process, best suited to those limited applications.

But CMD refused to allow this perception to limit its constant search for new thin film applications. Today the company's Thin Film Division produces a wide variety of products including thermal printheads (used in facsimile machines, cash registers, and ticket printers, among others), inkjet printheads (used in less expensive, laser-quality printers), and magnetic heads (used in disk drives for data storage).

CMD's Thin Film Division enjoys a reputation for the highest standards of quality as evidenced in the products the company produces. For example, CMD resistors that were originally selected for application in the U.S. space program had a design life of five years. Yet 10 years later, these components are still operational, allowing continued use far beyond their projected life span.

To produce these quality products, the Thin Film Division utilizes one of the best-equipped facilities in the world. Located at the company's

Above: Typical CMD products.

Right: Wafer fabrication.

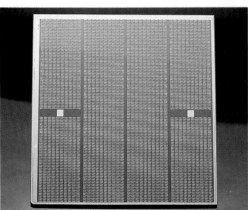

In 1990 CMD commenced BiCMOS process development for fabrication of integrated circuits for the mass storage industry and in 1991 developed thin film recording devices for the same industry—resulting in a unique combination offering products for complete on-board signal processing capability for the disk drive industry.

While commitment to research and development is vital to CMD's continued technological leadership, the company's strength as a business lies in its dedication to customer support and satisfaction. As an example, CMD's Thin Film Division has developed more customized network designs than any other company in the industry.

The company's emphasis on quality and cutting-edge technology, coupled with strong customer support, has paid off in consistent growth. Today, CMD operates two state-of-the-art facilities—a far cry from its original small lab.

CMD's 40,000-square-foot Milpitas facility houses the Thin Film Division—and includes the most competitive and flexible wafer fabrication facility in the world. The company's Tempe operation consists of a 50,000-square-foot semiconductor plant with a full design center that has telecom microcircuit engineering and manufacturing capabilities and an additional 20,000-square-foot test and fabrication facility.

However, an even more important ingredient in CMD's recipe for success is its people. The staff at CMD is made up of a remarkable group of people—remarkable not only for the quality of their work but for the diversity of their individual backgrounds. Highly skilled people representing many races and nations come together at CMD, where one can find a work environment that offers opportunities for ongoing learning and encourages personal and professional growth; in short, a place where a person can excel.

With its history of steady growth (the company more than quadrupled in its first 10 years), rigid quality standards, dedicated people, and strong commitment to research and development, California Micro Devices will remain a leader in the development and manufacture of high-performance microelectronic components well into the future.

California Micro Devices is located at 215 Topaz Street, Milpitas, California, 95035.

corporate headquarters in Milpitas, California, the facility makes innovative use of lasers as well as a wide variety of materials and deposition systems to create different characteristics for very demanding applications.

In 1987 CMD expanded its operations further with the acquisition of the Microcircuits Division. Based in Tempe, Arizona, the Microcircuits Division is CMD's semiconductor manufacturing arm. The division's manufacturing and test facilities offer many capabilities including advanced BiCMOS and CMOS processing technologies, along with high-quality telecommunications, data communications, and microprocessor products for a variety of applications.

CMD's leading-edge communications technology is found in a host of products including telephones, central office switching equipment, facsimile machines, credit card verification systems, and mobile cellular radios. The division also supplies key components for personal computers, modems and add-on boards, disk drive controllers, and monitors, along with providing foundry and test services to original equipment manufacturers.

Anthem Electronics, Inc.

The electronic components distribution industry is one of the most competitive in the high-tech arena. But even in this highly competitive environment, Anthem Electronics, Inc., stands out as, in the words of industry analyst Kidder, Peabody & Co., "the class operation."

Forbes magazine also holds the company in high esteem. In 1990 the magazine honored Anthem as one of the best 200 small companies in America.

Since its founding 23 years ago, Anthem has consistently outgrown its industry, becoming the fastest growing and most profitable electronics distributor in the United States today.

Anthem Electronics is the country's fifth-largest distributor of semiconductors and the largest distributor of leading-edge disk drives. The company has distinguished itself in the $9-billion market for domestic distribution of semi-

Peyton L. Gannaway, president and chief operating officer (left) and Robert S. Throop, president and chief executive officer.

An artist's rendering of Anthem Electronics' new building.

conductors and peripheral products by becoming a specialist, focusing on a relatively small number of product lines (27 lines vs. more than 100 from its major competitors). The company's largest product lines include National Semiconductor, Advanced Micro Devices, Cypress Semiconductor, and Texas Instruments for semiconductors, and Seagate, Maxtor, Conner Peripherals, and Hewlett-Packard for disk drives.

Value-added programs are the fastest-growing business segment in the distribution industry. Anthem has invested heavily to achieve a strong market position in this area. The company has developed sophisticated value-added services that assist customers in reducing costs, improving asset turns, increasing product quality, and enhancing time to market. These services include kitting, turnkey manufacturing, subsystem integration, programming, testing, and special inventory management programs.

Anthem has established a business unit called Eagle Technology. Eagle is responsible for the manufacture and marketing of Novell adapter boards and other proprietary and licensed connectivity and related products. Eagle has the exclusive rights to manufacture and market Novell's Ethernet network interface cards worldwide.

The focused strategy of Anthem has clearly withstood the test of time. The present goal is one of superior execution. To that end, Anthem has a major ongoing program aimed at improving the execution of every aspect of the business.

To maximize success, the company must have excellent people and excellent processes. Anthem's goal is to have a staff of excellent people who are highly capable and highly motivated. To achieve this goal the company must recruit, train, and manage well. Central to this program is training. Anthem has invested heavily in training with courses covering sales, general management, technology, product management, and quality. Learning has become part of the culture at Anthem.

Excellent people must be provided effective processes in which to work. Anthem has initiated a total quality program with the goal of improving the effectiveness of all of its processes. Everything is examined to assure that is done in the most timely, accurate, effective manner possible. Process improvement is an unending, continuous activity.

Anthem Electronics, Inc., is committed to doing all that is necessary to maintain the position as an industry leader and a "Company of Choice."

Becton Dickinson Immunocytometry Systems

Medical science has come a long way from the days when a binocular microscope was considered a high-technology cellular analysis tool. Today a veritable convoy of truly advanced systems aid researchers in their quests to unlock the secrets of cell biology. Leading that convoy and providing unprecedented insights into the nature and cause of disease at the cellular level is Becton Dickinson Immunocytometry Systems (BDIS).

BDIS, the San Jose-based Division of the Diagnostic Sector of Becton Dickinson and Company, pioneered the development of cell-sorting technology. BDIS flow cytometers (cell analysis instruments), computer software, and monoclonal reagents (which permit the recognition and tagging of unique immune cells) help physicians and researchers to isolate, characterize, and analyze immune cells in blood and tissue.

BDIS was formed from the merger of two Becton Dickinson operations: the FACS Systems Division and the Monoclonal Center.

The FACS Division was formed in 1975, when Becton Dickinson introduced the first commercially available fluorescence-activated cell sorter, or FACS. Using a powerful argon laser, the BDIS FACS brand cell sorters were the first to discover and define many previously unknown human blood cells. One of the first BDIS FACS is a featured exhibit in the American History Museum of the Smithsonian Institution in Washington, D.C.

Today, approximately 2,200 FACS-brand flow cytometers—more than any other type available—are used in basic scientific research, clinical research, and in clinical laboratories around the world. In fact, BDIS is the market leader in producing and developing instruments that facilitate the diagnosis, monitoring, staging, and definition of immunocytological diseases and in studying characteristics of human cancers.

With the advent of monoclonal antibody technology in the mid-1970s, Becton Dickinson formed its Monoclonal Center. This organization was established to develop monoclonal antibody reagents for use in its flow cytometry systems and to conduct basic immunology research.

These two organizations were consolidated in 1984 under the aegis of BDIS. This consolidation has produced a team effort focused on fully integrating product development, manufacturing, and marketing.

In 1989 the two organizations were brought together under one roof in BDIS's new 300,000-square-foot facility on Qume Drive. The new facility sits on 22 acres and houses some 150 research scientists, engineers, and biomedical research and software development professionals.

BDIS is a truly international organization. With 60 percent of its sales outside the United States, it has facilities in Europe, Japan, Canada, and Singapore and a worldwide sales and service support network.

Though a relatively young organization, BDIS benefits from the maturity and established resources of its parent corporation. Based in Franklin Lakes, New Jersey, Becton Dickinson and Company is a leading, diversified transnational medical technology corporation with sales of more than $2 billion and more than 19,000 employees at 74 locations in 20 countries.

Since its founding in 1897, Becton Dickinson and Company has been responsible for a number of medical technology industry firsts, including the first blood pressure instruments, the first two-piece scalpel, the first ACE bandage, the first all-glass syringe, and the first disposable plastic syringe.

Top: The Becton Dickinson facility site in San Jose.

Above: The FACScan, one of the company's primary products.

Northern Telecom

When Northern Telecom established its first Santa Clara Valley facility in 1974, the operation had 20 employees, produced only a small-business communications system, and had virtually none of the growing PBX (private branch exchange) market.

Since that time, Santa Clara Valley has become Silicon Valley, and Northern Telecom's Meridian 1 and its predecessor the SL-1 have emerged as the world's leading business communication systems, with almost 50,000 systems installed in more than 70 countries worldwide.

Northern Telecom is the leading global supplier of fully digital telecommunications switching systems, providing products and services to telephone operating companies, corporations, governments, universities, and other institutions worldwide. Northern Telecom has 49,000 em-

ployees and in 1990 had revenues of $6.8 billion. In addition, in the first quarter of 1991 the company acquired STC PLC, a leading United Kingdom telecommunications firm with 14,000 employees and 1990 telecommunications revenues of approximately $1.6 billion.

The company operates manufacturing plants in Canada, the United States, the United Kingdom, Malaysia, the Republic of Ireland, France, the People's Republic of China, and Australia. Research and development is conducted at 21 of these facilities, as well as by Bell-Northern Research Ltd., a subsidiary that operates R&D facilities in seven locations: two in Canada, three in the United States, and two in the United Kingdom.

Northern Telecom manufactures a wide range of telecommunications equipment for telephone companies, private corporations, educational institutions, government agencies, hospitals, offices, and residences. Its products include telecommunications switching and transmission systems, data communications networks, fiber-optic cable and equipment, wire and cable, telephones, outside plant hardware, and other equipment for public and private communications networks.

To maintain its competitive advantage as a leader in the development and application of digital and optoelectronic technologies, Northern Telecom invested $774 million, or 11.4 percent of revenues, in research and development in 1990.

Northern Telecom maintains two facilities in Santa Clara Valley. The manufacturing facility in Santa Clara opened in 1979 with 600 employees. Due to rapid increase in product demand, the plant was expanded in 1981 and again in 1984; the facility now encompasses 350,000 square feet. The plant employs about 1,200 people in the design, manufacturing, and marketing of Northern Telecom's Meridian 1 business communication systems. More than 500 people work in direct manufacture of Meridian 1 digital voice and data communications systems, Meridian digital telephone sets, and other associated telecommunications equipment belonging to the Meridian 1 product line. The Santa Clara facility supplies products for the United States and Pacific Rim markets.

Evolution of the Meridian 1 is the responsibil-

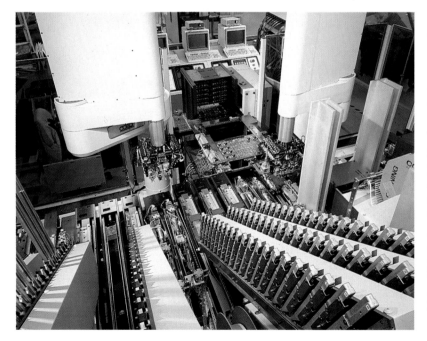

ity of the scientists and engineers at Northern Telecom's research and development facility located in nearby Mountain View. More than 400 employees work in the Mountain View facility.

Another manufacturing facility, in San Diego, produces large-scale integrated circuits for use in Northern Telecom products manufactured globally. Northern Telecom is one of the few telecommunications corporations in the U.S. to produce large-scale integrated circuits primarily for its own consumption.

The company employs approximately 4,000 people in California, and about half live and work in the Bay Area.

Northern Telecom is known as a technology leader in the industry. In 1976 Northern Telecom was the first telecommunications equipment manufacturer to announce the development of a fam-

ily of fully digital switching equipment. Today it is the leading global supplier of fully digital telecommunications switching systems with more than 73 million lines of its Meridian business communications systems and DMS switching systems in service or on order in more than 80 countries.

Most recently the company was first in the industry to commit to development of a full line of fiber-optic and communication systems products. Fiber World is the company's vision and statement of commitment to this next generation network architecture. Fiber-optic-based products will become the foundation and technology platform for the high-speed communications networks of the next century.

Northern Telecom has also been recognized for its commitment to the environment. The company embarked on a corporate-wide program in 1988 to eliminate all chlorofluorocarbon (CFC) usage by 1991, a goal years ahead of national and international mandates. In fact, the Santa Clara facility succeeded in eliminating all CFCs from its manufacturing process by December 1990.

CFC solvents are chemicals that are used throughout the electronics and telecommunications industries. These solvents deplete the protective ozone layer that shields the planet from the sun's harmful ultraviolet radiation as well as contribute to changes in global climate. They account for approximately 16 percent of ozone-depleting chemicals worldwide.

Northern Telecom has been recognized by the U.S. Environmental Protection Agency as an industry leader in reducing CFC solvent consumption and has played an important role in several worldwide projects related to stratospheric ozone protection.

Responding to the evolving needs of the marketplace has been the driving force for innovation at Northern Telecom. And in the spirit of innovation that permeates Santa Clara Valley, the company is ready to provide powerful and effective means to communicate vital information in the emerging global economy of the next century.

Above: Meridian 1 Communication Systems provide voice and data switching for 30 to 10,000 communication ports, meeting the needs of small, medium, and large organizations.

Top: Personal safety comes first!

Far left: Northern Telecom's Santa Clara facility is a showcase for just-in-time (JIT) manufacturing methods. Pictured here are Kan-Ban boxes, part of the computerized JIT parts supply system.

Left: Another human resources innovation is Northern Telecom's adoption of skill-based pay, a system of compensation motivating the manufacturing employee's acquisition of multiple skills. Operation of the PC-Autoloader is pictured here.

United Technologies Corporation's Chemical Systems Division

As demand increases to place U.S. satellites into precise orbits, NASA and the space industry continue to depend upon United Technologies Corporation's Chemical Systems Division's (CSD) high-performance space motors. Two powerful CSD ORBUS motors provide the thrust for the Inertial Upper Stage. Here the Magellan spacecraft is being released from the Space Shuttle's cargo bay with CSD's ORBUS motors preparing to propel its precious cargo on a trajectory to Venus. CSD's IUS motors have also successfully sent the Galileo probe on its journey to Jupiter and the Ulysses probe to study the sun.

Hidden in the foothills of the Diablo mountain range, about 15 miles southeast of San Jose, the highly skilled, dedicated professionals of The Chemical Systems Division of United Technologies Corporation (UTC) are hard at work. This UTC Division is fulfilling a vital role in this country's aerospace and defense industry, and it is leading the way in every facet of modern rocket propulsion technology.

UTC's Chemical Systems Division is a leading rocket, hybrid rocket, and ramjet development and production company with facilities and research capabilities second to none. The division's 5,200-acre Metcalf Road operation was established in the late 1950s when UTC first began producing the five-segment, 250-ton solid propellant rocket motors used in pairs as the booster stage for the Air Force Titan III-C launch vehicle.

Today the division uses its one-million-square-foot facility to produce advanced propulsion systems for a wide range of defense and space programs. It has pioneered the development and production of segmented Titan solid-propellant boosters for the launching of Voyager and Viking unmanned space vehicles, and for Department of Defense communications/surveillance satellites. Its current boosters for Titan are configured in five-and-one-half and seven segments for the Titan Commercial and the Titan IV, respectively.

The Titan IV and the Titan Commercial are the latest in a long family of Titan vehicles that stretches back over 25 years. UTC is extremely proud of the performance of these vehicles, which have become the workhorses of U.S. Air Force unmanned, heavy space launches.

The division has also produced more than 50 Algol III-A motors for the Scout launch vehicle. This larger, more powerful first stage motor has now flown with 100 percent success on the last 30 of Scout's 112 flights.

Two of the division's ORBUS space motors power the Boeing Aerospace Inertial Upper Stage which keeps highly sophisticated satellites delivered into space by the Space Shuttle in geostationary orbit. Additional ORBUS motors provide this so-called "orbital transfer propulsion" for commercial satellites and different upper-stage programs such as the Transfer Orbit Stage, Intelsat VI, and other series of satellites.

And the division's booster separation motors have become a vital component in every Space Shuttle launch—they separate the solid rocket boosters from the Shuttle orbiter.

The division also remanufactures third-stage motors for all Air Force Minuteman III missiles. It produces booster motors for the Navy's Tomahawk cruise missiles, and is developing the booster for the Advanced Standard Missile to be used in the vertical launch system. Both of these systems employ thrust-vector control.

Currently, the division's third stage for the Trident D-5 fleet ballistic missile is being flight tested. When introduced to the fleet, it will help provide this country's defense with unsurpassed range and accuracy.

The division's systems propel the Air Force BLU-106/B Boosted Kinetic Energy Penetrator submunition tactical missile, which targets and immobilizes enemy airfields. And it produces the hybrid propulsion system for the Air Force Firebolt target vehicle, which is designed to simulate supersonic enemy missiles and high-performance aircraft.

One of Santa Clara County's oldest and largest employers, UTC's Chemical Systems Division employs some 1,500 people. The vast majority of the division's employees work at its main facility, south of San Jose. But about 150 work in downtown San Jose, and another 200 work at California's Vandenberg Air Force Base and the Kennedy Space Center in Florida where they conduct launch services primarily for the department of the Air Force.

The division is an active member of the chambers of commerce of the communities of Gilroy, Morgan Hill, and San Jose, as well as a proud member of the Santa Clara County Manufacturers Group. Most of the division's employees reside in Santa Clara County and are active in local churches and civic organizations. The division itself is a longtime supporter of community organizations such as the United Way and Parents Helping Parents. The division also supports local Scouting organizations by making its property available for camp-outs. Division employees also teach introductory business courses to high school students through Junior Achievement.

UTC's Chemical Systems Division is part of the newly formed Government Engines & Space Propulsion Division (GESP), headquartered in West Palm Beach, Florida. The SP&S organization also includes United Space Boosters, Inc., in Huntsville, Alabama, and the liquid propulsion unit of Pratt & Whitney's Government Engine Business in West Palm Beach.

Headquartered in Hartford, Connecticut, UTC is about the world's 15th-largest corporation with $22 billion in sales in 1990, and 190,000 employees in 50 countries around the world. Some of its more recognizable products include Pratt & Whitney aircraft engines, Carrier air conditioning, Otis elevators, Sikorsky helicopters, and Hamilton Standard aircraft propellers and space support systems for the space program.

Though the division is an important defense contractor, its principal product, the Titan solid rocket booster, is widely used in launch systems for other than defense purposes. For space explo-

ration, earth resources intelligence gathering, and the deployment of sophisticated satellites used for television, radio, and telephone communications which link the world, Titan technology is currently unsurpassed.

So as the world moves cautiously toward peace, the products and technologies of UTC's Chemical Systems Division will continue to be in high demand.

Focusing on a long and robust future, UTC invested approximately $140 million in capital improvements in its Chemical Systems Division facility during the late 1980s. From a state-of-the-art ammonium perchlorate grinding apparatus, to the latest computer management software, the division has the resources to maintain its leading role in solid rocket fuel production and development well into the next century.

As of July 30, 1991, UTC had signed a letter of intent to merge CSD with the Atlantic Research Corporation, a division of Sequa Corporation of New York City.

The Commercial Titan Launch Vehicle is powered by CSD's two five-and-one-half segment solid rocket motors, which lifts the entire vehicle for the first two minutes of flight.

Tandem Computers Inc.

When major corporations first began using computers to handle their business operations in the late 1960s, few could have predicted how vital these systems would become. Today, whether it is a high-level securities trade or an ATM withdrawal, an international bank transfer or an automobile registration renewal, online transaction processing (OLTP) computer systems have become essential tools for doing business.

And the company that pioneered the technology that makes OLTP possible is Tandem Computers Incorporated.

Founded in 1974 by a group headed by current president and chief executive officer, James G. Treybig, Tandem Computers produced the

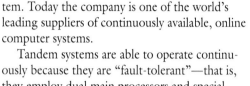

world's first fault-tolerant, OLTP computer system. Today the company is one of the world's leading suppliers of continuously available, online computer systems.

Tandem systems are able to operate continuously because they are "fault-tolerant"—that is, they employ dual main processors and special operating software that keep the system operating if any single point of failure should occur.

Without this fault-tolerant system, devised by Treybig and pioneered by his company, true online transaction processing is not cost-effective.

Tandem systems also employ a unique multiprocessor computer architecture that makes expandability possible. Unlike other computer systems, each processor added to a Tandem system provides a full processor's worth of performance. Tandem systems can be connected in networks with equipment from other vendors to provide a single computing resource. Tandem also offers a fault-tolerant system based on the industry-standard UNIX operating system.

The same parallel architecture that provides Tandem systems' continuous availability prevents bottlenecks common in systems with shared memory storage. In a Tandem system, as transaction volume and complexity increase, the work is redistributed throughout the system, preserving split-second response times.

Since it shipped its first computer in May 1976, Tandem has become a *Fortune* 500 company serving banking, manufacturing, telecommunications, retail, and other industries around the world.

More than 30 of the world's largest stock and futures exchanges and over 60 securities firms run on Tandem systems. Tandem systems run ATMs, point-of-sale networks, and other enterprises where hundreds of business transactions must be processed each second and recorded instantly. Tandem computers process each transaction as it occurs, with exceptional speed and reliability.

Large retailers use Tandem systems to approve credit requests, ensure adequate merchandise distribution, and retrieve store sales data electronically.

Hundreds of firms in production-intensive indus-

Right: Tandem is a *Fortune* 500 company serving financial services and banking, manufacturing, telecommunications, retail, and other industries around the world.

Below: Tandem headquarters is in Cupertino, California, in the heart of Silicon Valley.

Above left: Tandem maintains a world-class benchmarking facility in Cupertino to demonstrate its products' competitive advantages.

Above: TNN, the Tandem Television Network, which ranks as one of the largest television networks in the world, is one of Tandem's many innovative communication tools.

tries such as automobiles, aerospace, electronics, pharmaceuticals, and food manufacturers use Tandem computers to integrate their operations. Applications in these industries include shop-floor control, work-in process tracking, collection and analysis of quality-control data, and inventory management, among others.

More than 300 banks—50 of those among the largest in the world—count on Tandem systems. Tandem is also the system of choice for more than half the nation's largest electronic funds transfer networks.

More than 70 telecommunications companies worldwide, including all seven of the U.S. regional Bell operating companies, call on Tandem systems for such applications as network management, information gateways, and service order entry systems.

Tandem systems are also used by governments around the world for such applications as communications, logistics, manufacturing, welfare eligibility and delivery systems, and public-safety records management.

In 1988 *Fortune* magazine named Tandem's distributed data base management technology among the "100 products that America makes best."

Headquartered in Cupertino, California, in the heart of Silicon Valley, Tandem Computers maintains some 70 U.S. sales offices, with more than 40 sales offices outside the country. Tandem is a truly global organization with subsidiaries thoughout Europe, Asia, Australia, and South America. The company's manufacturing plants are located in facilities in Northern California; Austin, Texas; Guadalajara, Mexico; and Neufahrn, Germany. Tandem employs more than 10,000 people worldwide.

Tandem maintains its leadership and continued growth through strategic partnering with companies that provide services or products that are complementary to Tandem systems. The company's merger with Ungermann-Bass, Inc., for example, provided strong, enterprise-wide networking capability.

To strengthen the company's leadership in data security, Tandem merged with secure transaction systems leader Atalla Corporation, enhancing security offerings for the company's entire product line.

And strengthening its position in telecommunications, Tandem merged with Integrated Technology, Inc. (renamed Tandem Telecommunications Systems, Inc.). Tandem also works closely with third-party vendors to supply software solutions to its customers.

But throughout its development, Tandem's most important partners have always been its people. Early on, the company's founder, James Treybig, established a corporate culture based on his own strong values of respect for the individual. While Tandem seeks out the best and the brightest in the industry, the company also provides them with the tools and opportunities they need to do their best work. The company not only encourages open communication between all departments and all levels of management, Tandem uses such innovative devices as its own corporate television network to facilitate that communication and create a community.

But Tandem also endeavors to create a balanced environment, encouraging its employees to become involved in their communities and to take regular sabbaticals to pursue other interests.

Since the 1970s Tandem Computers Incorporated has been designing computer systems that work the way business really works. The online, NonStop® architecture Tandem pioneered has been both a force for change and a tool to manage it. In the 1990s, as businesses become even more global and up-to-the-second information becomes even more critical, Tandem will continue to set the pace as Silicon Valley's leading online computer systems company.

Loral Corporation

Loral Corporation is one of the largest defense electronics and space communications companies in the world. A $3-billion, *Fortune* 200 firm, Loral serves all branches of the U.S. military and such civilian government agencies as NASA and the National Oceanic and Atmospheric Administration, as well as major international telecommunications and broadcast services providers and other regional customers.

Headquartered in New York City, Loral maintains over two dozen divisions in cities across the country, from Akron, Ohio, to Sarasota, Florida. But most of Loral's 26,000 employees can be found in divisions located in California—with the greatest concentration of these in the Silicon Valley area.

Loral's local divisions include: Loral Western Development Labs and Loral Rolm Mil-Spec Computers in San Jose, Space Systems/Loral in Palo Alto, Loral Space & Range Systems in Sunnyvale, Loral Fairchild Imaging Sensors in Milpitas, and Loral Randtron Systems in Menlo Park.

Western Development Labs (WDL) is a pioneer in microwave communications and one of the world's principal total systems contractors. WDL has a distinguished performance record and demonstrated capability in the high technology areas of satellite communications; terminals; advanced communications and switching systems; and command, control, and high-speed information systems.

Loral Rolm Mil-Spec Computers designs and manufactures rugged mil-spec 16- and 32-bit super mini and super microcomputers that perform complex processing tasks for command and control. The division also produces 3D workstations using CISC and RISC technology, as well as operating systems, compilers, and real-time and development software.

Space Systems/Loral produces space systems and subsystems for NASA, the U.S. Department of Defense, and international and regional customers. Since 1960 this division has produced more than 85 highly capable communications and weather satellites, logging more than 14 billion miles and representing about 20 different types of satellite systems, as well as some 200 satellite ground terminals to support a full range of space missions.

Loral Space & Range Systems is a major communications systems development contractor, providing operations and maintenance, training, and logistic support for the Air Force Satellite Control Network. It is supplying and integrating new generation equipment at 17 Automated Remote Tracking Stations worldwide, including the Air Force Systems Command's Consolidated Space Test Center (known locally as "The Blue Cube.")

This division serves and supports Air Force satellite programs of the highest national priority, maintaining the technical integrity of its networks,

Loral Space & Range Systems simulation and training business includes realistic electronic combat threat simulators at Defense Department training ranges and range management systems, which provide measurement, debriefing, and control capabilities.

Loral Space & Range Systems, a major command, control, communications, and intelligence (C3I) contractor to the U.S. Defense Department, is supplying and integrating updated equipment at 17 automated remote tracking stations worldwide for the Air Force Satellite Control Network.

and guarding against risks ranging from loss of vital program data to loss of a satellite itself.

Loral Fairchild Imaging Sensors is a leading supplier of visible and infrared focal plane arrays and sensors using platinum silicide charged-coupled device (CCD) technology for a variety of defense applications in reconnaisance, surveillance, and guidance. Its CCD sensors have also been supplied to France's SPOT Image Corporation for use in both commercial and environmental satellite remote sensing applications.

Loral Randtron Systems, which supplies the characteristic rotodome antenna for the U.S. Navy's E-2C aircraft, designs and produces advanced microwave antenna assemblies for electronic combat and airborne early warning. In addition to the TRAC-A for the E-2C, the division supplies the multi-channel rotary joint for the U.S. Air Force's E-3A airborne warning and control system (AWACS) aircraft.

These six divisions, together with the company's other divisions, create the vast array of complementary defense electronics technologies that have given Loral its industry leadership position. These technologies support vital requirements for the national defense in several core activities, including: electronic combat; reconnaissance and surveillance; simulation and training; tactical weapons/guidance; command, control, communications, and intelligence; and space systems.

ELECTRONIC COMBAT

Loral has long been a leading supplier of some of the most advanced radar warning systems available. Radar and missile warning, radar and infrared jammers, expendable countermeasures; these and other sophisticated electronic warfare systems supplied by Loral served U.S. pilots in the Persian Gulf during Operation Desert Storm, adding considerably to their combat edge.

Loral's concept of "aircraft self-protection" goes beyond traditional systems and builds on the company's expertise in other areas. Because Loral has assembled the sensor technologies, processing, and countermeasures that go into forming an integrated electronic combat system, it can now fuse those disparate systems into 360 degrees of aircraft self-protection.

Loral is also moving to apply electronic self-protection systems to tanks and other armored vehicles. The company's Missile Countermeasures Device for main battle tanks and fighting vehicles, for example, jams guidance on air- or ground-launched anti-tank missiles.

COMMAND, CONTROL, COMMUNICATIONS, AND INTELLIGENCE

The precise coordination of air and ground combat operations demonstrated during Operation Desert Storm gave the world a glimpse into command, control, communications, and intelligence (C3I) at its best.

Loral's advanced C3I technology successfully executed these operations with systems permitting real-time intelligence, reconnaissance, targeting data, and communications across all echelons of command. By integrating its C3I systems with its wide variety of supporting land, airborne, and space-based sensors and command posts, Loral has created a truly unified battlefield.

Antenna components for the next-generation INTELSAT VII telecommunications satellites undergo trials inside Space Systems/Loral's (SS/L) new Compact Antenna Test Range, a huge anechoic chamber at SS/L's Palo Alto facility. SS/L produces space systems and subsystems for NASA, the U.S. Defense Department, and international and regional customers.

Loral's supporting role for the Air Force Satellite Control Network has also allowed military planners to rely on round-the-clock, space-based, real-time support to military operators. And its Maneuver Control System permitted commanders of ground forces to know where their troops—and enemy forces—were at all times.

But Loral recognizes that future battlefields will have to be even more highly integrated. To that end, the company has developed the technological linkages that will make such integration possible. For example, Loral's C3I technologies can be combined to support a communications-rich environment, enabling the transfer of combat

Loral Randtron Systems anechoic radar lab in Menlo Park, California, enables extremely accurate testing and evaluation of leading edge antenna design and fabrication concepts.

Inside the "Blue Pumpkin," a thermal/vacuum testing chamber which can accommodate an entire satellite, Space Systems/Loral puts its satellite's electronic components through a battery of tests to assess how they will actually operate in space.

information, intelligence, and command orders at unprecedented speeds, accuracy, and volume.

Loral's integrated systems will give the overall battlefield "picture" even greater clarity by combining satellite-based, position-locating systems with the company's core display and processing capabilities, thus enabling rapid transfer of high-quality color imagery, maps, and graphics of local terrain, weather, and intelligence information to all appropriate users.

RECONNAISSANCE AND SURVEILLANCE

Tomorrow's battlefield will be unified through the application and integration of advanced electronics and software in a sensor-rich environment unlike any in history.

Loral's imaging sensors for reconnaissance, tactical strike missions, and smart weapons turn night into day with infrared focal plane arrays. They use precision electro-optics to see from miles away, or synthetic aperture radar to penetrate clouds and smoke.

By combining sensors with an aircraft's electronic combat system, Loral has made it possible for a pilot to detect and deceive approaching missiles. Sensor applications in space will eventually enable us to detect intercontinental ballistic missile launches—allowing our nation to stop them in flight—or monitor and measure the earth's sometimes violent weather patterns.

Loral technologies—such as its silicon charged-coupled devices, platinum silicide, and mercury cadmium telluride focal plane arrays—are driving the development of tomorrow's sensor-rich defense systems. And the company continues to make significant advances in image processing, stereo displays, target recognition, and in designing sensors that do not need bulky cooling equipment, as well as research into making component material more uniform, efficient, and sensitive.

TACTICAL WEAPONS/GUIDANCE

During the war in the Persian Gulf, terms like cruise missile guidance and "smart" bombs entered the nation's vocabulary. The war showed just how advanced tactical weapons have become over the last two decades. Loral's optics, processors, targeting, and guidance technologies enabled missiles, like the Tomahawk, Maverick, and Sidewinder, as well as laser-guided munitions, to rack up impressive scores in the gulf. Meanwhile, a new generation of smart weapons has been taking shape at Loral. These weapons include those that recognize and counter different types of advanced threats.

One such weapon, the Short-Range Anti-tank Weapon (SRAW), will place a shoot-down, top-attack tank killer into the hands of infantrymen. SRAW's accuracy, resulting in a high hit probability, makes it a force multiplier, and its fire-and-forget operation is essential for today's increasingly lethal battlefield.

The next-generation, short-range, air-to-air missile being developed by Loral, the AIM-9R Sidewinder, will be able to acquire its target from greater distances and lock on despite countermeasures, thanks to new digital electro-optical imaging guidance development.

Other brilliant weapons, employing Loral sensors, will be deployed in space, eventually orbiting the earth and providing unblinking protection from ballistic missiles.

Sensors, processing power, advanced algorithms—Loral technologies that give today's weapons their smarts, will allow them to meet even more demanding requirements tomorrow.

SPACE SYSTEMS

Around the world, there is a growing demand for more capacity in modern telecommunications, accurate weather forecasting, and space science technology that is not less powerful than that which sparked the Industrial Revolution. Loral meets these growing demands with a firm foundation of satellite programs and a strategic international partnership built to capitalize on these emerging new space-based requirements.

Loral is a space systems provider for the International Telecommunications Satellite (INTEL-SAT) Organization for international telephone traffic; the National Oceanic and Atmospheric Administration, whose Geostationary Operational Environmental Satellite (GOES) will monitor the earth's weather patterns; the Space Communications Corporation of Japan (the Superbird communications satellite); and NASA.

But Loral has gone beyond assembling the tools of the pure satellite maker. Tomorrow's space systems will be loaded with sensors, requiring a complete understanding of how sensors and platforms work together. And because these sensors will capture such a prodigious amount of data, a systems approach as to how to process, store, and distribute that data will be essential.

Loral's mastery of space communications and remote sensing technologies, coupled with its expertise in developing the nation's mission control centers for manned space flight at Johnson Space Center and supporting unmanned space flight at Goddard Space Flight Center, will ensure its success in such an environment.

SIMULATION AND TRAINING

Loral is the number-one simulation and training company in the country. A complete training systems house, Loral has capabilities ranging from computer-based instruction to simulation, instrumented range management, and support services.

The scope of Loral's contractor pilot training is truly impressive. The company employs more than 300 former military aviators to conduct classroom

and simulator training at 11 navy bases. Every navy student pilot is trained by Loral.

And force-on-force air and ground training using Loral's MILES laser-based systems and pilot training on Loral-managed instrumented ranges continue to be the ultimate tests of unit combat skills and tactics.

In 1990 the U.S. Air Force selected Loral to develop, operate, and support a family of weapons systems trainers and mission rehearsal devices, in addition to providing computer-based training, traditional classroom instruction, and courseware development for Special Operations Forces aircrew training.

Over the past two decades, the Loral Corporation has moved steadily into the forefront of the defense electronics industry. Loral will continue developing the solutions demanded by the ever-changing defense environment, supplying the technologies and systems expertise that will meet or exceed the requirements of the future.

Loral Western Development Labs in San Jose, California, designed and developed a basic satellite communications ground terminal for use in the Defense Satellite Control System that is simple to operate, easy to maintain, and rapidly deployable.

Novellus Systems Incorporated

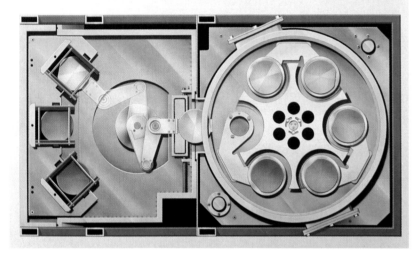

Above: A cut-away view of the Concept One-W CVD system illustrates the system's unique multistation, sequential deposition design.

Right: The Novellus process development laboratory is designed to closely simulate conditions in customer fabrication facilities.

Novellus Systems, Inc., manufactures, markets, and services advanced, automated semiconductor fabrication systems. Novellus' systems provide semiconductor manufacturers with solutions to bottlenecks in the implementation of both mature and emerging integrated circuit (IC) designs, and the company is at the leading edge of designing processing equipment for the next generation of semiconductor manufacturing plants.

These systems, called Chemical Vapor Deposition (CVD) systems, are used to deposit high-purity, thin metal films on wafers during the process of fabricating ICs.

Though recent trends in semiconductor processing system design have been toward single-wafer processing chambers, Novellus' initial system, the Concept One, is based on a sequential batch processing chamber design, which is unique in its ability to deposit the highest-quality film layers with high throughput.

The system's design allows semiconductor manufacturers to tailor processes for optimum on-the-wafer results without serious impacts on throughput. This has contributed to the superior characteristics of all the dielectric film processes available for the Concept One, including doped

and undoped silane oxides, nitride (UV and oxynitride), and TEOS.

The Concept One system was introduced in 1987 and is widely regarded as a leader in the market for systems that deposit dielectric films used as insulating layers in semiconductor devices. The viability of the design has been proven by its performance in the fabrication lines of many of the world's major semiconductor manufacturers. As of this writing, more than 200 Concept One systems are in operation around the world.

The Concept One-W, introduced in 1990, is based on the same simple design approach that contributes to the proven reliability of Concept One. Novellus' newest system deposits blanket tungsten metal films (W is the symbol for tungsten). Tungsten is increasingly used for contact/ via filling and interconnect applications in advanced semiconductor devices.

The Concept One-W addresses a number of problems associated with blanket tungsten deposition. It deposits smooth, uniform films with the

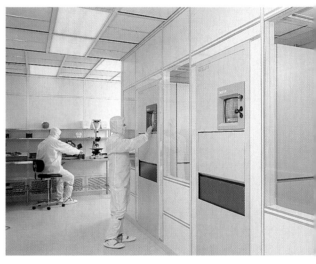

step coverage required in the production of advanced devices, and solves the particle problems caused by backside tungsten deposition by combining vacuum wafer clamping with a unique gas exclusion technique. This approach actually prevents tungsten from depositing on the wafer backside. And it eliminates the need for frontside mechanical clamping of the wafer, which creates particles where the clamp contacts the wafer. The new system also eliminates the need for time-consuming etching of the backside of the wafer in order to remove the film.

The Concept One-W extends into a new process area, the sequential deposition design architecture introduced in the company's Concept One system. A key benefit of the sequential

deposition design is the ability to produce highly uniform film thickness with high net throughput across a broad range of process conditions.

Another feature that has been extended to the Concept One-W system is the in situ plasma cleaning of the process chamber. This in situ plasma process cleans the chamber automatically after each batch, therefore eliminating particle problems and downtime caused by the build up of tungsten within the process chamber.

Novellus R&D and manufacturing facilities are designed with customer productivity in mind. Process development and customer demonstrations are conducted in a sub Class 10 clean room with six to-the-wall system positions. This applications lab is designed much as an actual semiconductor manufacturing area is, facilitating process development under customer-like conditions.

Novellus was the first company to actually manufacture CVD process equipment in a clean-room environment. This practice allows Novellus' customers to move new systems into clean room fab areas much more quickly than was previously possible, and to operate them with a minimum of contributed particles.

Novellus was also the first to perform an actual deposition as part of its final testing procedure. This extra step greatly reduces the need for the company's field service personnel to make last minute adjustments in the customer's fab area during systems installation.

In the future, because operating personnel and the general clean room environment are large sources of device-killing contamination, semiconductor factories will be highly automated. This factory automation will require the integration of process steps that have widely varying cycle times and process conditions. The ability to match the throughputs of these various process steps is critical—and the Novellus approach to process chamber design is ideal for the automated integration of the fab line.

Since its founding in 1984 Novellus has experienced strong and consistent growth. A venture capital start-up, Novellus made its initial public offering in 1988, making it the first semiconductor capital equipment company in four years to go public. By 1991 the company's annual sales exceed $50 million.

Headquartered in San Jose, Novellus opened a second facility there in 1989 to accommodate its expanding product development, training, and domestic sales efforts. The firm's international presence was also increased that year with the establishment of a new subsidiary in Japan, a branch office in Korea, and the expansion corporate offices in the United Kingdom.

Novellus was one of the founding companies in the Modular Equipment Standards Architecture (MESA) Group, an industry-wide group that developed standards to enhance the productivity and competitiveness of the semiconductor equipment industry and its customers. MESA has received the support of many equipment companies and key semiconductor manufacturers, and has now become a part of Semiconductor Equipment and Materials International (now called MESC). Novellus is committed to the development of systems that conform to MESC interface standards.

Novellus Systems, Inc., continues its commitment to serving the worldwide semiconductor manufacturing market through its subsidiaries and sales and support offices throughout the world.

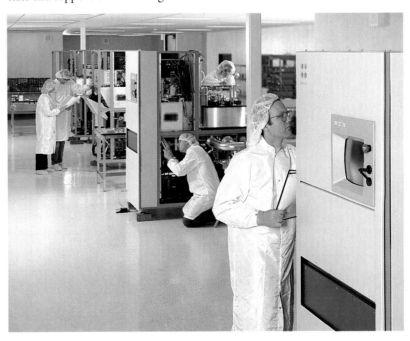

Romic Chemical Corporation

For almost 30 years Romic has transported and recycled industrial solvents and other chemicals.

Each weekday trucks carrying hazardous wastes pull into Romic Chemical Corporation's 14-acre resource recovery facility. And each day they leave with recycled chemicals that reduce customers' liability at the same time they promote resource conservation and environmental protection.

For almost 30 years Romic has recycled and reclaimed chemical wastes from Bay Area industries. About half of the East Palo Alto company's customers are electronics firms.

In addition to electronics companies, Romic customers include aerospace, paint, printing, and automotive industries. The company serves businesses as small as the local dry cleaner, as large as Silicon Valley semiconductor manufacturers, and as innocuous as the food industry.

Most of the chemicals the firm recycles are solvents: thinners, cleaners, degreasers, and similar products. Romic also processes paints, antifreeze, oils, and the universal solvent, water.

"When people hear the words 'hazardous waste,'" says company founder Mike Schneider, "they usually think of pesticides or radioactive material from a huge industry. But virtually every home and business in this country generates hazardous waste."

Hazardous wastes are defined by federal and state laws as wastes that may pose a risk to health or the environment if improperly managed. In the home, they include such commonly used products as medicines, cleaners and polishes, paints, automotive products, pet supplies, fertilizers, pool chemicals, and hobby supplies—to name just a few. In industry, almost every manufacturing process, including production of food and clothing, generates some type of hazardous by-product.

Twenty-four hours a day, seven days a week Romic recycles chemicals that are no longer useful to industry because they contain water, dirt, oil, or unwanted chemicals. The company processes these wastes in a number of ways, including:

• Distillation, which removes impurities from solvents, allowing them to be resold for industrial use.

• Alternative fuels blending, which produces a fuel that is shipped to cement kilns and burned in place of oil, natural gas, or coal.

• Water treatment, which removes small amounts of solvents and other chemicals from wastewater.

Off-site destructive incineration is also available for that portion of the waste that is not recyclable.

Customers have two options when they send their wastes to Romic. One is custom tolling, in which chemicals are segregated, batch processed, reclaimed, and returned to the generator. Many

customers prefer this closed-system
method. Others, however, do not want
or need the recycled product back. For
these customers, wastes are received and
recycled, then sold on the market to
secondary users.

Romic has several affiliate companies
on-site. Research and development
firms are currently developing technologies for reducing air pollution from automobiles, removing chemicals from
groundwater, and recovering metals
from wastewater. Antifreeze Environmental Service Corporation recycles antifreeze from cars and trucks. California
Solvent Recycling specifically services
small-quantity generators. Romic also operates a
second recycling facility in Chandler, Arizona.

Still a family-owned com-
pany, the Romic commitment
to environmental protection
and customer service is
handed down from Mike
Schneider to his son, Peter.

Romic's state-certified laboratories are critical to its
operations. All wastes are
analyzed prior to shipment,
and again once the shipment
arrives on-site. Samples are
also drawn and analyzed
during several stages of
processing and before the
recycled product is re-
turned to industry.

ROMIC'S HISTORY

Schneider founded Romic Chemical Corporation
in 1964. An 11-year veteran of the chemical business, he invested his family's savings and took over
a local specialty chemical company. But instead of
making chemicals, he focused his efforts on the
company's recycling and reclamation capabilities.

That proved to be a profitable move. Starting
with $100,000 in sales at the end of his first year,
Schneider built his company into a $25-million
corporation. Still family-owned and -operated,
Romic offers its customers the technical and financial advantages of a large corporation along
with the service-oriented spirit of a small business.

Romic's growth has been consistent and
compatible with that of the high-tech industries
that gave birth to Silicon Valley. In fact, the company's earliest recycling efforts were undertaken
at the request of the valley's oldest electronics
firm, which was seeking a way to reclaim the
methyl alcohol used as a final rinse in clystron
tube manufacturing.

Later, Romic began recycling paint solvents and soon counted every major paint and coating manufacturer among its customers. Eventually paint coating evolved into more sophisticated products containing epoxies. Romic's processing capabilities also had to evolve to keep pace with the new challenges repesented by these technical advances.

As industry waste disposal regulations became more stringent and environmental concerns grew, more high-tech industries sought Romic's services. Many of them were involved in the manufacture of magnetic recording tapes, which used sophisticated solvents. These companies sought to improve profit margins through reclamation. Although the new chemicals were more complicated to process, Romic was more than a

distillery. The company employed a process called fractionation, which is still used today to reclaim chemicals to specification grade.

Romic played a very important role in development of both the coatings and the electronic industries. And the firm remains a leader in the recycling industry because it consistently produces products that meet the specifications of new chemicals. This provides customers with significant savings in material costs. In addition, recycled products are exempt from the "feed stock" tax applied to virgin chemicals.

Romic's state-of-the-art facility is renown in the industry for its ability to reclaim more difficult waste streams. This is particularly true of the new specialty blends being introduced

in the market today to replace ozone-depleting solvents containing HFCs and CFCs.

PROCEDURES AND OPERATIONS

Romic customers complete detailed profiles that explain what their waste consists of, how it was created, and its physical and chemical characteristics. Laboratory technicians at Romic then analyze a sample of each customer's waste chemicals. This analysis determines whether Romic can accept the waste and how it should be processed to recover the maximum amount of product.

Hazardous wastes must be transported by a licensed hazardous-waste hauler. Romic has a fleet of trucks, tankers, roll-off and van trailers licensed to transport hazardous wastes. Romic drivers are trained to handle such materials, operate special equipment, respond to emergencies, and prevent spills or accidents.

They are also adept at checking and completing manifests and other paperwork associated with hazardous waste transportation. The company must comply with transportation regulations of the California Highway Patrol, the U.S. Department of Transportation, and the California Department of Health Services. Romic trucks are routinely inspected by all three of these agencies.

Romic also has a thorough inspection and preventive maintenance program of its own. The

program and the care with which the company selects and trains its drivers is the reason Romic has an exemplary safety record. In fact, in the company's nearly 30-year history, no Romic driver has ever had a spill on the road. The company's safety record is two times better than the average for truck drivers and four times better than the average for automobile drivers.

Like its drivers, the Romic facility must meet exacting standards and is built with environmental protection in mind. All processing and storage areas are built on six or more inches of concrete surrounded by "secondary containment structures." If, for example, a tank ruptured, any resulting spill would be contained, pumped out, and cleaned up.

Many solvents are recovered at Romic through distillation, using thin-film evaporators and fractionation columns to obtain the highest yields and specifications. This process is simple, proven, and does not require chemical reactions or dangerous conditions.

But some of the chemicals brought into Romic's facility cannot be reclaimed through distillation. Either there's too little product that can be recovered, the technology isn't available, or the cost is prohibitive.

But many chemical wastes that are not recyclable still have a high energy value. When mixed to certain specifications, they can be substituted for fuel. Romic's alternative fuels are shipped to specially permitted cement kilns in Southern California or out of state. Using these oil and solvent wastes as fuel preserves natural gas, oil, and coal and eliminates the necessity and liability of managing these wastes in a less preferable manner.

Most people don't think of water as a solvent, but it is actually the most universal solvent in the world. And it, too, can be reclaimed for reuse. Water reclamation has become increasingly important in recent years for a number of reasons. Recent droughts have created a water shortage in California; industry, in its efforts to use water-based products instead of more hazardous ones,

is using more water and creating greater amounts of wastewater; and water reclamation is better for the environment than disposal.

Romic's water treatment system operates similarly to those at sewage treatment plants. The wastewater that goes into Romic's system comes from a number of sources, including rinsewater from manufacturing processes, water extracted during recycling, even rainwater that falls on the facility.

Romic uses a great deal of water during recycling, so reusing as much of this reclaimed water as possible cuts costs and conserves this precious resource. In fact, by recycling treated watewater, Romic has reduced its fresh water usage by more than 50 percent—some 7 million gallons per year.

Romic Chemical Corporation plays an important role in managing chemical wastes in the western United States. Recognizing the importance of not only managing, but reducing hazardous wastes, Romic continues its efforts to improve its operation and seek solutions to environmental problems.

Top: Romic operates on a 14-acre site located in East Palo Alto.

Above: At one time Romic recycled solvents exclusively. However, as regulations became stricter and more industries began replacing chemicals with water-based products, greater volumes of wastewater were generated. Today, more than a third of the company's business consists of wastewater, treated in this water treatment unit before being recycled on-site.

Heuristics Search, Inc.

Since two young electronics engineers first set up shop in a Palo Alto garage some 50 years ago, Santa Clara County has become the eye of a veritable technological tornado. But it wasn't merely technology that stirred the storm that created Silicon Valley. It was people—highly skilled, talented people.

Helping Silicon Valley's high-technology companies find the people they need to keep from being swallowed by that storm is the specialty of Heuristics Search, Inc.

Heuristics Search is the largest professional recruitment firm specializing exclusively in the placement of software development engineers in the United States. Founded in 1979 by current president Elizabeth Patrick, Heuristics serves a broad spectrum of companies from start-ups to multinationals. The firm's established reputation

and proven recruitment approach attracts the kinds of professional technical talent its client companies need to be successful in their highly competitive industry.

Unlike most placement companies, Heuristics is a management consulting firm that customizes its services to meet the specific needs of its client companies' individual software managers.

"It's our job to provide the right technical talent for the company," says Elizabeth Patrick. "The client's manager in charge of the project often knows best what technical expertise he or she needs for both present and future projects. The personality that will best fit in with the group and management style is also important. By working closely with the managers, we learn what they need to get their goals accomplished."

In the hiring formula the chemistry between the hiring manager and the candidate is critical. The requirements for a particular staff opening simply don't tell the whole story—and neither do resumes. Each candidate brings a personality and lifetime of experiences and expectations to the job.

"Our business is based on relationships," says Patrick. "Our goal is to establish a mutually satisfying, long-term relationship in which each party utilizes the strengths and talents of the other."

In their efforts to find the most qualified candidates, Heuristics' recruiting professionals review more than 50 resumes each week and personally interview an average of 40 individuals to select

fewer than 10 candidates for final presentation. Each recruiter makes a concerted effort to acquaint selected candidates with the philosophy and goals of the client company.

"Since the largest percentage of our candidates are currently employed," says Patrick, "any suggested opening must be a logical career step, something that they are excited about, will enhance their careers, and get them where they want to go."

Heuristics provides client companies opportunities to make presentations showcasing their organizations to help the firm's recruiters better understand their needs. Client companies also have the opportunity to use the firm's offices for off-site interviews of candidates. This ensures hiring managers an efficient selection process in a quiet, professional atmosphere, away from disturbances encountered back at the office.

Heuristics' ongoing, aggressive advertising keeps the firm in constant touch with the entire market. The firm's salary surveys are extremely accurate because they are drawn from a large population of computer scientists. And because the firm continuously attracts new potential candidates, client companies avoid the expense of running their own recruitment advertising.

"There is a relentless interviewing and market research process ongoing at this company," says Patrick. "We maintain a continuous dialogue with the market. It's this networking process that allows us to respond so quickly to our clients' needs."

Rather than find candidates only in response to an opening (a process that can take two or three months), Heuristics is in constant touch with the skilled technical people required to staff even the toughest software project. To ensure the highest recruiting power for a client, Heuristics' staff of account executives work to serve the firm's clients as a team.

"We are here to make sure our clients get the best possible service from this company as a whole," says Patrick. "Our team concept is vital to the kind of service we offer. In other words, if one of our account executives is representing you as a client, so is every other person in this company."

Heuristics takes its "team" philosophy seri-

ously. Rather than assigning a single representative to each account, the firm assigns a team of people so that clients have a consistent interface with the organization. And Heuristics' highly trained staff works as hard as the companies they serve—and they often set the pace.

Heuristics is also dedicated to supporting the local quality of life. The firm supports, among other organizations, the San Jose Cleveland Ballet, the San Jose Symphony, and San Jose public television.

Heuristics Search, Inc., is a company with a strong appreciation of Santa Clara County and the growth of the region's high-tech industries.

"We have prospered because local industries have prospered," says Patrick. "We want to contribute back to Silicon Valley the highest value we can. The productivity of the local high-tech industry is important to us, and we believe we are contributing to the success and the technical excellence of this valley, for our candidates, for our client companies, for everyone involved in local innovation and excellence. We do our part to make sure that everyone we serve has the tools they need to be excellent in this competitive industry."

Above left: Heuristics' team approach assures clients success in hiring.

Above: Heuristics is the largest professional recruitment firm specializing exclusively in the placement of software development engineers in the United States.

Sunrise Technologies, Inc.

Lasers. Most of us have seen them only in science fiction movies. The word conjures up images of the future, of narrow beams of light firing through space. But lasers have actually been with us for a long time—since 1960, in fact. And thanks to the pioneering work of companies like Sunrise Technologies, Inc., lasers are in wide use today in a variety of medical applications ranging from oral surgery to the treatment of glaucoma.

Sunrise Technologies is one of the world's leading suppliers of sophisticated medical laser systems. Founded in 1987, the company develops, manufactures, and markets solid-state lasers and related products from its Fremont, California, headquarters. The company's products are currently in use throughout the United States, Italy, France, the Netherlands, Germany, England, Canada, Japan, Australia, Mexico, and many other countries.

The company's founders, Arthur Vassiliadis, Ph.D., David Hennings, and Joe Shaffer, recognized the tremendous potential for the medical application of laser technology. The medical use of lasers involves the controlled application of heat to hard or soft tissue. A laser device fires a coherent beam of light that is partially absorbed

when applied to animal or human tissue. This absorption process converts the light to heat, thus altering the tissue.

Lasers currently perform such delicate medical tasks as treating the retina of the eye, clearing plaque from the arteries of the heart, cleaning out herniated disks, and dissolving kidney stones. Lasers have become the accepted treatment for many retinal diseases, prolonging vision and saving sight for hundreds of thousands of patients a year around the world. And, largely because of the research and development efforts of Sunrise Technologies, lasers in dentistry are now generating enthusiastic interest.

Sunrise researchers first applied their expertise in pulsed lasers and fiber-optic delivery systems to the development of a viable portable system for dental applications. They knew that application of lasers in dentistry would involve the use of the technology on hard tissues, such as tooth enamel, dentin, and bone, as well as soft tissues in many areas in the mouth. And while water-cooled drills and local anesthetics were the

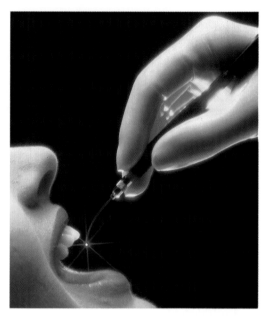

traditional means for reducing heat and pain experienced by the patient, Sunrise was out to create a better solution.

In December 1988 the company announced the completion of its new dental laser instrument, the dLase 300. This device is able to vaporize tooth decay, cut dentin and cementum, and seal dentinal tubules, while eliminating the pain associated with many of these procedures.

The dLase 300 can also be used to cut periodontal soft tissue, the procedure needed for single-tooth gingivectomies. Using this dental laser makes these procedures not only painless, but bloodless as compared to conventional cutting with a scalpel.

Before Sunrise began to explore potential laser applications in dentistry, the technology was used only experimentally in this field. As a result of the combined research and development efforts of Sunrise and the company's marketing partner, ADL, compact, reliable, low-cost laser systems are currently in use by dentists.

In May 1990 the company received clearance from the U.S. Food and Drug Administration to market the dLase 300 for soft-tissue dental procedures. As of this writing, approval for use of the

system for hard-tissue dental procedures is still under investigation.

The use of lasers in ophthalmology (the branch of medical science dealing with diseases of the eye) is not new. In fact, more than 90 percent of ophthalmologists use lasers in their practices. A major application for lasers in ophthalmology is photo-coagulation, a procedure that treats retinal detachment, stops fluid leakage, and coagulates vessels within the eye. Lasers are also used to treat conditions of the eye related to diabetes and aging, retinal tears, macular and vascular disease, and glaucoma.

Sunrise's second product, an ophthalmic system known as the gLase 210 Holmium laser, received FDA clearance for commercial sale in December 1990. The gLase 210 performs a filtering procedure which lowers the pressure in the eyes of glaucoma patients, and may be a medical breakthrough in the management of glaucoma.

The gLase 210 has made a filtering procedure much simpler and only minimally invasive. The procedure can be performed in an office in an outpatient environment, and studies have shown that patients experience an immediate drop in interoccular pressure that is maintained post-operatively. And because the procedure causes little trauma, it can easily be repeated.

Sunrise has developed a third product—a high-power Holmium laser system for surgery and many other specialty applications such as in orthopedic surgery. Finally, Sunrise is preparing to launch a major program directed at correcting all refractive errors through the use of a non-invasive approach using infrared lasers to change the curvature of the cornea.

Sunrise experienced excellent growth during its first few years and continues to explore exciting new applications for its products. The company has a staff of more than 65 employees and is growing rapidly, working with medical experts to generate products that fill genuine needs. Sunrise

made its initial public offering in 1989, and in the calendar year 1991 will ship more dental and medical laser systems than any other company in the world.

Sunrise Technologies was recently ranked by the *San Jose Mercury News* among the top 20 medical products and equipment companies in Santa Clara County. The company was also named one of the *San Francisco Chronicle*'s top five "Rising Stars" two years in a row.

Sunrise Technologies, Inc., continues to pursue its goal of expanding the potential medical applications for solid-state lasers. The company remains at the forefront of this exciting technology, exploring laser wavelength and striving to create new delivery systems for all medical specialties.

Left: Sunrise researchers have developed three portable laser systems, pictured here, for dental, ophthalmic, and surgical applications.

Below: Dr. Terry Myers treats a patient with a Sunrise Technologies dental laser system.

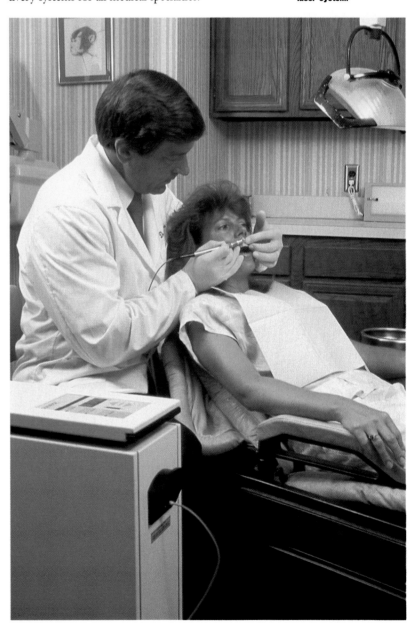

S-MOS Systems, Inc.

S-MOS Systems, Inc., has achieved something few Silicon Valley semiconductor manufacturers have been able to accomplish: the successful integration of American marketing and engineering with Japanese production prowess.

Founded in 1983 by current company president Daniel S. Hauer (a 30-year veteran of the semiconductor industry), S-MOS designs, develops, markets, and contract-manufactures custom, semicustom, and standard integrated circuits (ICs) for desktop computing, embedded systems (including industrial control), computer peripherals, and communications.

And through its affiliation with Seiko Epson Corp., S-MOS is backed by one of the world's most advanced CMOS IC manufacturers. CMOS stands for Complimentary Metal Oxide Semiconductor. This advanced technology produces chips that consume less power and generate less heat, a crucial advantage in building ever-denser circuits. Seiko Epson has been manufacturing CMOS ICs since 1969, and CMOS application-specific ICs (ASICs) since 1981. Seiko Epson is part of the Seiko Group, famous for Seiko and Epson products.

At its corporate headquarters in San Jose, S-MOS maintains a large research and development facility. This R&D center is where the company develops new hardware and software technologies to keep pace with advancements in process technologies. The company's rapidly evolving process technology has made S-MOS/Seiko Epson one of the most advanced CMOS semiconductor suppliers in the world.

S-MOS' products include ASICs—both gate arrays and standard cell—and standard products, including chip sets, LCD drivers and controllers,

Dan Hauer, president of S-MOS Systems.

S-MOS Systems' offices at 2460 North 1st Street in San Jose, California. Photo by Larry A. Brazil

floppy disk controllers, SRAMs (medium and fast, up to one megabyte), mask ROMs, and four-bit microcontrollers.

Typically, the company's customers are large *Fortune* 500 original-equipment manufacturers—the primary market for its products being high-volume North American desktop computer manufacturers. But S-MOS is diversifying its product base to include industrial and consumer markets.

The S-MOS organization is divided into four business units: the Standard Products Group, ASICs and Support Tools, Contract Manufacturing (foundry services), and Board Level Products.

In the area of standard products, S-MOS offers static random access memories (SRAMs), mask read only memories (ROMs), and module-level product SRAMs, including one megabit, 256K, 64K, 16K, and 4K, all targeted toward nonvolatile storage applications requiring battery back-up, such as portables, laptops, and hand-held computers. The company has faster versions and a BiCMOS process currently under development.

S-MOS offers a wide variety of CMOS mask ROMs, from 64K to 4Mbit featuring very fast access times. And prototype turnaround is typically between seven and eight weeks.

The company also provides a variety of liquid crystal display (LCD) drivers and controllers, including video-LCD interfaces and graphic LCD controllers.

S-MOS markets products for data storage applications such as data separators for floppy disk drives and hard disk drives, and cache controllers.

In June 1990 the firm introduced The Dragon: two graphics chip sets that combine a graphics controller, a color palette, and a VGA-LCD interface specifically designed for laptops. The Dragon supports up to 64 shades of gray and color and is compatible with most graphic standards, including VGA and EGA.

S-MOS' four-bit microcontrollers, though overshadowed by the more glamorous 32- and 16-bit controllers and processors, are still in great demand because of their low power requirements, which extend the life of the power source—especially important for portable equipment.

The company's fundamental approach to its ASICs and support tools product group is to provide software tools and hardware cells that address system-level integration needs.

All S-MOS gate arrays comprise cells that functionally emulate standard logic, further integrating discrete function and breadboards to the gate array level.

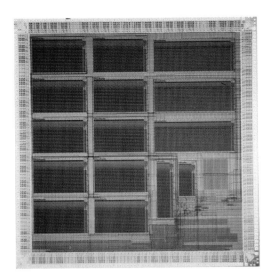 

The company utilizes a variety of design workstations in the development of its ASICs and support tools, including Sun, Daisy, Mentor, Viewlogic, VALID, and PC-based systems running FutureNet CAD or Viewlogic software.

S-MOS' CMOS gate array products are built with design rules ranging from 3 to .8 microns. The firm's first gate arrays were introduced in October 1988.

The company's Design System (SDS) is an open-system design package for the PC and Sun workstations. SDS options available on the PC include Logic Array Design System (LADS), NavNet, OrCAD, Viewlogic, Futurnet, and S-MOS utilities.

S-MOS' Logic Array Design System runs on a wide range of computers, including IBM PCs and PS/2 models, and 32-bit workstations from such companies as Sun, Intergraph, Daisy, and Mentor. S-MOS offers LADS to its customers for design of ASIC and compiled-cell products.

S-MOS also provides silicon foundry services and wafer fabrication, assembly, and test services through Seiko Epson. S-MOS first established its contract manufacturing services in 1986. Today the firm has four-, five-, and six-inch wafer lines available. An additional six-inch line is being added, which will be capable of producing wafers using sub micron and BiCMOS process technology.

Established in 1989, the company's assembly services consist mainly of packaging, primarily flat pack and small outline packaging. And S-MOS' test service, from wafer sort to final test, was begun in early 1990.

S-MOS' newest product area, Board Level Products, is coming out of a new business center which was established in 1991 by S-MOS. It is headquartered at the company's ASIC design center in Raleigh, North Carolina. The new division uses S-MOS' existing sales channels to offer advanced board-level design packaging, subsystem manufacturing, and test and assembly on a turnkey basis. Its customers will have a heavy focus on application-specific boards and modules for desktop, laptop, and portable and notebook computers for small personal communications products such as pagers, cellular phones, and for handheld instrumentation—all of which will use ICs either from S-MOS or from other vendors according to customer need. Typical volume for these products can range from 5,000 units for large, complex designs to 500,000 a year for simpler designs.

Key board level technologies offered include multilayer (to eight layers) for pin through hole (PTH), surface-mount technology (SMT), and a PTH-SMT mix; double-sided SMT; three lines between pins now, up to five lines under development; tape-automated bonding (TAB); chip-on-board (COB); chip-on-flex (COF); automatic assembly of 0.5mm-pitch Quad Flat Pack (QFP).

Due to its variety of services, S-MOS is also a product development and business partner, serving many of the functions of an IC integrator. The company often works with customers to develop products from concept to mass production. Customers can enter the product development process at any stage, from front-end or back-end design of an ASIC, to the purchase and manufacture of a chip set or other standard product.

S-MOS markets its products through a direct sales force and comprehensive network of distributors. In addition to its San Jose headquarters, the company operates branch offices in Boston, Chicago, and Raleigh, North Carolina. And the firm recently opened a Canadian design center in Vancouver, British Columbia.

S-MOS Systems, Inc., is a privately held company. As of this writing, the firm's annual revenues are projected at $137 million with 220 employees.

Above left: The SLA10000, part of S-MOS Systems' new ASIC series.

Above: The SED1702 LCD driver from S-MOS Systems, with 160 segment drive outputs.

Advanced Cardiovascular Systems

The Silicon Valley is widely known as the birthplace of a multitude of high-technology innovations that have revolutionized modern life. Yet, while the very words "high technology" summon images of computers, satellites, and assembly line robots, few associate this mecca of invention with medical technology.

But Santa Clara County is, in fact, the home of one of the most innovative medical device developers in the industry: Advanced Cardiovascular Systems, Inc.

Advanced Cardiovascular Systems is the world's leading designer and manufacturer of therapeutic medical devices used in the treatment of atherosclerotic disease of the coronary and peripheral arteries. The company was founded in 1978 by two talented cardiologists, Drs. Ned Robert and John Simpson, and a seasoned Silicon Valley entrepreneur, Ray Williams.

Drs. Robert and Simpson first learned of a revolutionary technique for treating coronary artery disease—called percutaneous transluminal coronary angioplasty—in the late 1970s. The technique was invented by Swiss cardiologist Dr. Andreas Gruentzig and involved the use of a tiny balloon to open narrowed arteries in the heart.

Coronary artery disease, which results from

The corporate headquarters of Advanced Cardiovascular in Santa Clara.

the gradual buildup of fatty deposits called plaque within the arteries that supply blood to the heart, affects millions of people each year. The condition often results in chest pain and can lead to heart attacks. Prior to the mid-1960s, treatment for the disease consisted of managing a patient's symptoms and increasing the pumping efficiency of the heart with medications.

With the development of coronary bypass surgery—a procedure in which surgeons form new conduits of blood flow by "bypassing" the area of blockage—the mortality rate of those suffering from coronary artery disease was decreased. But open-heart surgery is extremely

traumatic for the patient and requires four to six weeks of recuperation.

Dr. Gruentzig's technique seemed to hold the promise of eliminating, in many cases, the need for this kind of invasive procedure.

Drs. Robert and Simpson, then fellows at Stanford, were so inspired by Dr. Gruentzig that they set out to design their own coronary angioplasty device.

In 1978, with the approval of Stanford University Hospital, the two cardiologists successfully completed their first coronary angioplasty procedure, using a catheter of their own design, at the Palo Alto Veterans Hospital. Later that year, with the help of Williams, they founded the company that is today Advanced Cardiovascular Systems, Inc., to pursue their pioneering research. In March 1982 the new company received approval from the U.S. Food and Drug Administration to market its first device: the Simpson-Robert Coronary Dilatation Catheter.

The catheter technology developed by Robert and Simpson has added an important alternative to medication and traumatically intrusive surgeries for the treatment of coronary artery disease. The Simpson-Robert dilatation catheter utilizes a small, plastic, inflatable balloon which is positioned within the coronary artery across the area of blockage. Once in position, the balloon is inflated, stretching the arterial wall, cracking and compressing the area of obstruction, and reestablishing a pathway for blood flow through the narrowed artery.

Coronary angioplasty procedures are much less traumatic for patients, both physically and financially. They can be performed with only local anesthesia, require a week or less of recuperation, and cost 50 to 75 percent less than bypass surgery.

By 1984, close to 59,000 coronary angioplasty procedures were being performed annually in this country. Projections for the 1990s indicate that approximately 500,000 such procedures will be performed on a vastly expanded patient population, which will include those not successfully treated with medication alone, as well as those unable to tolerate the trauma of open-heart surgery.

Today, after years of rapid and steady growth, Advanced Cardiovascular Systems has become a recognized world leader in the development of medical devices used in the treatment of coronary artery disease.

"Our phenomenal success," says CEO Jim Harper, "has been guided by some basic principles: to offer products that have lasting value to the customer; to hire and train the best people

The company's 225,000-square-foot manufacturing facility is located in the Temecula Valley and is currently being expanded with an additional 270,000 square feet.

we can find; to pay for performance; and to expect continuous improvement."

Since its founding, Advanced Cardiovascular Systems has offered the most diversified and innovative coronary angioplasty product line available, providing physicians with an effective and versatile alternative to coronary bypass surgery. The company's commitment to this life-enhancing and lifesaving procedure has fueled its rapid growth, while enabling many of those suffering with coronary artery disease to enjoy a significantly improved quality of life.

The rapid growth and financial stability of the young company eventually brought it to the attention of Eli Lilly and Company. Lilly, an international corporation that develops, manufactures, and markets pharmaceuticals, medical instruments, diagnostic products, and agricultural products, acquired Advanced Cardiovascular Systems in 1984—with beneficial results for both organizations.

As part of Lilly's MDD or Medical Devices and Diagnostics division, Advanced Cardiovascular Systems is a research-intensive operation with more than 1,600 employees, a significant number of which are engaged in the company's ongoing R&D efforts. The company's engineers and scientists work on both basic and applied research projects designed to identify and evaluate innovative medical products.

The company's corporate headquarters in Santa Clara houses its R&D and sales and market-ing departments, its support staff, and its corporate administration group. Santa Clara is also the location of the company's pilot manufacturing facility, which produces prototypes for clinical studies and tests manufacturing processes.

The company's 225,000-square-foot manufacturing facility is located in the Temecula Valley, 60 miles north of San Diego. The facility is currently being expanded with an additional 270,000 square feet. The company also maintains an additional R&D facility in Basingstoke, England.

Advanced Cardiovascular Systems' world-class manufacturing operations utilize Just-In-Time manufacturing techniques and problem-solving teams across all manufacturing functions. Through these practices, the company quickly addresses manufacturing issues, reduces lead time, and produces the highest quality products and services.

To help physicians meet patient's varying needs, the company has developed a diverse product line, including perfusion systems, rapid exchange systems, and over-the-wire systems. All of the company's dilatation catheter systems are designed with PE 600® Balloon Material and MICROGLIDE® Coating, which facilitate positioning the balloon across the area of obstruction, promoting less traumatic dilatation.

But Advanced Cardiovascular Systems does more than simply develop and manufacture the most technologically innovative products available. Because of the evolving nature of coronary angio-plasty technology (the average product life cycle is

10 to 12 months), the company has also established an innovative program of clinical education.

From technical needs to continuing education, the company offers its customers comprehensive support, with the ultimate benefit of the patient in mind. Results have shown that the time and energy the company spends on clinical implementation planning helps practitioners perform coronary angioplasty procedures safely, simply, and more successfully.

Advanced Cardiovascular Systems' clinical field force comprises dozens of individuals worldwide who provide technical and educational support for coronary angioplasty practitioners. Each "clinical specialist" has extensive cardiac catheterization laboratory experience so that he or she can provide on-site technical information and educational support.

To enhance their own expertise, the company's clinical specialists keep current with the latest technology by attending numerous conferences and by observing coronary angioplasty procedures in cardiac cath labs around the world. Further interactions take the form of hands-on workshops and in-service seminars in which the company's clinical personnel work one-on-one with staff members and physicians. This process encourages an extensive exchange of ideas, techniques, and information.

Advanced Cardiovascular Systems also offers a continuing education program which includes in-service seminars and local symposia. The goal of this program is to provide educational resources that continually meet the needs of both physicians and cath lab staff members. The company is committed to providing educational services of value in a partnership with its customers which will culminate in exceptional patient care.

Throughout the rapid, worldwide growth in the use of angioplasty procedures, Advanced Cardiovascular Systems has led the way in developing new concepts into products. Since September 1988 the company has converted over 90 percent of its product catalog to new and improved devices. In 1989 it was the first medical device company in the United States to receive simultaneous U.S. Food and Drug Administration approval of two unique dilatation catheter designs. Also in 1989 the company launched more new products than all other dilatation catheter companies combined. In 1990 ACS was voted Innovator of the Year by the international Product Development Management Association. Previous winners of this award include Hewlett-Packard Company and Merck & Company.

Future development of product concepts will depend on solving current clinical problems and challenges. To provide direction for future product development, the company has established an advisory board made up of leading cardiologists.

In 1988 Advanced Cardiovascular Systems created its first division: Peripheral Systems Group. Headquartered in Mountain View, Peripheral Systems Group specializes in the research and development of angioplasty technology for non-coronary applications. Its mission is to take the company's technology into applications outside the heart, striving to eliminate the need for invasive surgery wherever possible.

Devices for Vascular Intervention in Redwood City is a sister operation. Founded by ACS founder Dr. John Simpson in 1984 and acquired by Eli Lilly in 1989, this company is developing catheter systems that cut, capture, and remove plaque from diseased blood vessels. In September 1990 the U.S. Food and Drug Administration approved for market release a new device designed by the company which removes plaque from arteries of the heart.

Advanced Cardiovascular Systems owes its success and leadership in the medical device industry to the contributions of many individuals. The company rewards those contributions with recognition of accomplishments, pleasant and stimulating working conditions, open communications, competitive compensation, and one of the most comprehensive benefits packages in the country.

The company also supports its belief that its people are its greatest asset through its commitment to their professional growth and development. The company's commitment to employee development manifests itself in ongoing technical and professional training programs, as well as through the active encouragement of cross-functional moves.

Advanced Cardiovascular Systems' goal has always been to provide safe, cost-effective therapeutic approaches and treatments to coronary artery disease. The company's commitment to investing in research and development and in quality manufacturing, along with its responsiveness to dedicated health care professionals, has enabled it to develop therapeutic solutions of enormous value and benefit.

The future of the rapidly growing medical device industry is an exciting one. Advanced Cardiovascular Systems will continue to play a leadership role in that industry, bringing dynamic and innovative products and services to the marketplace and its ultimate customers, the patients.

Trimble Navigation Ltd.

Below: Transpak is a portable, "personal" GPS receiver that puts the power of GPS right in your hand. In the future everyone will have a receiver like this.

Bottom: NavTrac GPS is a new marine product that converts navigation into a form everyone can understand. Just follow the "roadway" displayed on the system's large graphic screen.

Bottom center: Navigator is the first GPS receiver for general navigation. It includes the removable Nav Data card—a complete data base of aviation information.

Bottom right: TRIMPACK, a military version of Transpak. Rugged and powerful, it's living proof of the robustness of GPS.

In Silicon Valley, cutting-edge technological innovation is the order of the day, almost commonplace. But even in this mecca of high-tech it's hard to imagine a company developing products that could change our lives as fundamentally as the invention of the telephone.

Yet at Trimble Navigation in Sunnyvale, that's exactly what they're doing. Founded in 1978 by former Hewlett-Packard employees, this visionary company is a world leader in the development of commercial satellite-based navigation and position data products.

Why visionary?

"When Alexander Graham Bell invented the telephone," explains company president and co-founder Charles R. Trimble, "I'm sure he had no concept of the vastness of the changes he was setting in motion. But his invention answered such a basic human need—the need to communicate— that the telephone system is today an essential utility like the water system, the electric power grid, highway systems, railroads, natural gas pipelines, air service, and broadcasting.

"But we understand that the system that we are accessing and developing products for has become, in effect, another utility; one that answers another basic human need: the need to know where you are and where you're going. And we also understand that it is going to change our infrastructure in fundamental ways."

Trimble's new utility— called "positioning"— has been made possible by the combination of two new technologies. The first is the NAVSTAR Global Positioning system, or GPS. This government-funded system of 24 satellites (21 plus three in-orbit spares) was developed by the Department of Defense at a cost of more than $10 billion. (As of this writing, 15 satellites have been deployed. Full deployment is scheduled for 1992, with launches approximately every 60 to 90 days.)

The other new technology that is making Trimble's new utility possible is the GPS receivers themselves. Trimble Navigation designs, manufactures, and markets these receivers, which are sophisticated electronic instruments for determining precise geographic location. Since 1981 the company's products have been bringing GPS to ships, aircraft, surveyors, private cars, fleet vehicles—even individual hikers and foot soldiers. The company pioneered the first commercially available GPS system in 1984 and its hand-held TRIMPACK became the primary navigational positioning device for Operation Desert Storm in 1991.

The company has defined and currently serves five markets: survey and mapping, marine navigation, military systems, aviation navigation, and tracking systems, and Trimble's pioneering efforts to bring GPS technology to marine navigation has redefined accuracy.

Applications for Trimble's GPS Survey Systems are almost limitless. Government and private surveyors are using the company's systems for everything from recalculating the height of mountains to monitoring movement of the earth's crust.

In 1988, in a joint project involving three major universities and the Japanese government, Japan created a nationwide network of receivers—called the Japanese Earthquake Monitoring System—which continually monitors crustal movement. Japan chose to build this network around 25 of Trimble's 4000SD receivers.

And Trimble GPS systems are being used to survey one of the largest and most complex public works projects on the East Coast: the Third Harbor Tunnel that will go under Boston Harbor.

Trimble's new "kinematic survey" system provides an order of magnitude improvement in pro-

ductivity. Using this system, the surveyor can walk the perimeter of a given site and automatically record the position data for later analysis. (The surveyor doesn't even need to be a trained geodesist.)

The company has also developed navigation and tracking systems for delivery fleets, ships, airplanes, and automobiles, as well as hand-held units for use by individuals. Trimble's Pathfinder is a portable GPS data-gathering system designed for collecting the positioning information used in geographic information systems, such as resource mapping, municipal utility management, and rough surveys. And use of Trimble's survey systems isn't limited to determining position. Real-time motion can be measured as well.

While Trimble's Sensor group is striving to miniaturize the technology of GPS for individual use, the company's Systems Division is developing the technology to link individual GPS sensors into large-scale networks.

By linking GPS sensors with each other and by combining these systems with communications networks, management of whole fleets of individual vehicles will be possible.

Trimble's Systems Division is currently working on a NASA contract to apply the concept of a multi-station GPS networking system as the emergency back-up landing and guidance system for the Space Shuttle. The company is also developing systems for the Department of Defense, the National Oceanic and Atmospheric Administration, and the Coast Guard, as well as a wide variety of private users.

For example, the U.S. Coast Guard is exploring the use of a Trimble GPS system in wide-area tracking of oil tankers to increase

safety by allowing monitoring and coordination of tanker traffic. The Canadian Coast Guard in Vancouver has successfully demonstrated a Trimble GPS tracking system to provide more effective coordination and response of hovercraft in search-and-rescue operations. An oil survey company is using Trimble 4000 series Locators and Delta-Nav software system to provide position data with two to five meter accuracy to the offshore oil industry. And, a major metropolitan transit authority is exploring the installation of a Trimble GPS tracking system for its buses to increase safety and scheduling efficiency and reduce maintenance costs.

Because of the commitment of Trimble Navigation to the development of "positioning," for the first time in history, the world will soon have an absolute, and universal reference for where things are—a reference accessible to everyone. It's impact will be global, from streamlining mapping and surveying to reorganization of property law and the inventorying of resources; from safer air travel to the personal convenience of in-care maps and locations data bases. Like Bell's invention, Trimble's new utility is changing the world.

Trimble Navigation is headquartered in Sunnyvale and employs some 800 people, including 200 research and development engineers. The company has sold more GPS receivers than all its competitors combined and enjoys sales nearing $130 million. The company has sold more than 25,000 units containing GPS receivers and is currently the worldwide sales revenue leader for commercial GPS products. With a clear technological lead in what is expected to be a $4 billion industry by the middle of the decade, the company made its first public offering in July of 1990.

Below: NavGraphic II is the most direct navigation tool ever created. GPS information is translated into an image of your boat moving on an actual NOAA chart. This system represents the complete integration of computer, CD ROM, and GPS technologies.

Bottom left: Geodetic Surveyor is the most accurate GPS surveyor ever developed. It is capable of locating any point on Earth to within five millimeters. GPS is revolutionizing surveying and is giving people a much more accurate picture of the shape of the world.

Bottom right: Pathfinder is a portable GPS data-gathering system. It is useful for collecting the positioning information that is used in geographic information systems such as resource mapping, municipal utility management, and rough surveys.

Pyramid Technology Corp.

Since it first emerged as a pioneer of commercial open systems computing in the early 1980s, Pyramid Technology Corporation has led its industry in bringing high-performance open systems to the commercial marketplace.

Founded in 1981, Pyramid today is an international company with a major presence in Europe and the Asia-Pacific region. It operates a direct sales and support organization dedicated to providing computing solutions for specific industry markets. Its manufacturing and distribution partners include such companies as AT&T, Nixdorf Computer AG, Olivetti, Control Data, Electronic Data Systems, Andersen Consulting, Sharp, and Hyundai.

With an installed base of several thousand systems worldwide, Pyramid's products have been field proven in the demanding real-world environments of customers such as DHL Worldwide Express, which uses Pyramid systems to operate its global package tracking system; and Oracle, which employs Pyramid systems for both production and development applications. Pyramid systems are also used by the Internal Revenue Service and all regional Bell operating companies around the country.

Pyramid's systems are based on the UNIX computer operating system and a data processing technology known as Reduced Instruction Set Computing (RISC). While many of the com-

pany's competitors focused on developing small, multi-user systems, Pyramid addressed the needs of users of data processing systems with hundreds or thousands of users. Pyramid was one of the first companies to offer UNIX systems for commercial applications in these large computing environments.

Pyramid introduced the industry's first open commercial RISC systems in 1983. Since then the company has continued to enhance and define both the UNIX operating system and RISC technology for mainframe-class commercial applications.

Pyramid also pioneered the first commercial symmetric multi-processing (SMP) systems. SMP harnesses the power of multiple central processing units (CPUs) for mainframe-class throughput. Pyramid's SMP architecture allows systems to share workloads evenly across processors, and balances CPU performance with high-performance input/output and memory subsystems.

The company's MIServer line is the industry's broadest line of RISC-based, open-system servers. Ranging from entry-level office systems to systems that support more than 2,000 users, the MIServer line is scalable to meet the needs of an entire corporation.

Early in the company's evolution, Pyramid realized that relational data base management systems (RDBMS) represented another new technology which would bring major changes to the commercial data processing marketplace. For this reason Pyramid has tuned its system architecture, operating systems, and data base systems themselves to support large numbers of concurrent users accessing large amounts of data at very high speeds. So it's no surprise that Pyramid has become the premier open system data base server.

Pyramid currently supports more than 20 different data bases, including Oracle, Sybase, Ask Ingres, Informix, and Unify. The company has pioneered open systems performance features that overcome the storage limitations inherent in many UNIX implementations. And the systems administrator can fine-tune the data base and the MIServer system for particular applications. This rich, full-

featured open systems environment is the product of years of experience enhancing UNIX for the commercial market. Today Pyramid is in a unique position to quickly incorporate the latest advances in UNIX technology into its systems.

Pyramid is in the vanguard of two of the fastest growing segments in the commercial data processing marketplace: off-loading many traditional mainframe applications in the rapidly emerging client-server computing model; and delivering a new threshold of UNIX performance that allows current users to migrate their UNIX-based investment to systems capable of serving much larger and more demanding tasks.

For connectivity and interoperability, Pyramid supports virtually every major communications protocol. MIServer systems connect with mainframes, minicomputers, workstations, and personal computers, allowing the exchange of data throughout an organization, and, accordingly, the

most efficient use of computing resources.

UNIX is becoming a dominant force in the data processing world because users today are demanding greater freedom of choice in the systems they buy. They want standards that allow them to make changes which preserve their substantial investments in applications software. And they want systems that allow them to take advantage of the latest changes in technology.

But being in the forefront of technology and providing standards isn't enough. Users today are asking for solutions. They want to work with companies that understand their individual problems and how to solve them.

Pyramid pays close attention to these customer needs. Because over 90 percent of Pyramid hardware sales involve a major data base, Pyramid has taken a leadership role in working with its data base partners, creating a separate division to assure customers of well-integrated data base solutions on Pyramid systems.

In addition, Pyramid's fully staffed international customer service division makes its accumulated expertise with large open systems available to customers as a strategic resource. Extending well beyond traditional telephone hotline and on-site support, the division offers a wide range of customized professional, consulting, and educational services to help customers achieve maximum return on their system investments.

Pyramid Technology Corporation has been ranked among the top 100 Bay Area companies by both the *San Francisco Chronicle* and the *San Jose Mercury News*. The firm is widely considered one of the fastest growing computer companies in Silicon Valley. Based in Mountain View, Pyramid operates sales and support offices throughout the United States, the Asia-Pacific region, and Europe.

Above: All seven Regional Bell Operating Companies (RBOCs) use Pyramid systems. Their high-performance commercial features easily handle the massive data bases used in planning telephone services for millions of subscribers.

Below: Trading and dealing, portfolio management, commercial lending, and retail branch automation are just a few of the areas where Pyramid systems help financial service providers reduce costs while increasing competitive advantages.

Borland International, Inc.

When Philippe Kahn first came to the United States in 1982, it was not to start a business, but to find a job with one of Silicon Valley's high-tech companies. But that job never materialized, and a year later the 31-year-old French mathematician founded Borland International, Inc.

Headquartered in Scotts Valley, Borland International is today one of the nation's leading microcomputer software manufacturers. European headquarters are in Paris, with international subsidiaries throughout Europe and the Pacific Rim. The firm has developed and marketed high-performance office automation tools to more than 8 million personal-computer users worldwide.

The son of a mechanical engineer, the company's founder grew up in France, where he

Borland's family of PC software products.

Pascal has become the most popular of all software development tools.

Encouraged by its success with Turbo Pascal, Kahn's new company broke into the business software market in 1984 with Sidekick, a personal organizer for microcomputer users. Sidekick was phenomenally successful and other successful products followed.

Borland's Paradox was the first relational data base with true multiuser, multitasking capabilities. Its QBE (Query By Example) system is now the standard interface for querying relational data bases. Paradox uses Borland's VROOMM (Virtual Runtime Object-Oriented Memory Manager) technology to make maximum use of whatever hardware it's running on—from older 8088-based machines to the most powerful 486 systems.

Quattro Pro, Borland's high-end spreadsheet program, also uses VROOMM to pack more features into a spreadsheet package requiring only 512K of memory. Quattro Pro won virtually every award and product comparison given by trade publications and software users. Quattro Pro offers users more tools to better analyze and present data, allowing them to make decisions faster than ever.

In October 1991, Borland completed the acquisition of Ashton-Tate Corporation. Borland's goal is to combine its object-oriented technology and unsurpassed level of customer satisfaction with Ashton-Tate's strong international presence and large user base. The end result will be new, innovative products from Borland that give computer users unprecedented power to access and manipulate data.

earned a doctorate degree in mathematics from the University of Nice. Kahn also studied in Zurich under Niklaus Wirth, the computer scientist who developed the original Pascal programming language.

With the founding of Borland, Kahn introduced Turbo Pascal, a new programming language that he developed with the help of some European colleagues. While some competitors were selling similar products for about $600, Kahn priced Turbo Pascal at $49.95.

Despite the price, initially Kahn couldn't find a distributor to carry his product, and so he relied on mail-order sales generated by an ad in a computer magazine. The ad, written and designed by Kahn, produced about $100,000 worth of orders the first month. Since its development, Turbo

Today Borland International employs more than 1,950 people worldwide. Borland's success can be attributed to technology leadership. The company is a pioneer in object-oriented programming, the recognized future of software programming. It is also a market-leader in programming tools for the Windows operating platform. Borland's products are marketed through a national sales organization, subsidiaries, and leading domestic and international resellers. The company's products are available worldwide and translated into many different languages.

Network Equipment Technologies, Inc.

Network Equipment Technologies, Inc. (N.E.T.), develops, manufactures, markets, and services advanced communications products that enable information-intensive organizations worldwide to interconnect and deploy wide-area networked applications over public and private transmission services.

Years before N.E.T. was founded in 1983, the rising volume of critical business applications (such as funds transfers) that ran on public communications networks (such as AT&T and MCI) had forced high-volume users to move to private networks. But because of their limited capacities, these early networks became expensive and unreliable.

In 1983 AT&T began offering circuits of much greater speed known as T1 lines, creating an opportunity for big corporations to design private "utility networks." But the communications equipment available at that time was simply not powerful enough to perform all the functions required by large, private utility networks.

The need had arisen for a new generation of network equipment, and N.E.T. was founded to fill that need. The company's flagship product, the IDNX (Integrated Digital Network Exchange) was introduced in 1984. The first of its kind, the IDNX today enables organizations to build wide-area networks that map all forms of communications—data, voice, video, image, and facsimile—to the best transport mechanism—public or private transmission—based on business priorities.

In addition to the IDNX product line, N.E.T. offers a broad range of communications resource management products, including access products for linking remote company locations around the world, internetworking products for consolidating a company's local-area network communications, and broadband networking products for high-bandwidth communications.

As of this writing, more than 4,500 of IDNX systems have been shipped to a total of 346 N.E.T. clients. While most of these clients are large banks, financial institutions, airlines, retail chains, and government agencies, many of the *Fortune* 500 and 1,000 manufacturing

and service companies are beginning to recognize the importance of developing information-driven strategies to maintain or increase market share.

N.E.T.'s service operations are as well known and respected as its products. In their book, *Total Customer Service: The Ultimate Weapon*, William H. Davidow and Bro Uttal site the company's service infrastructure as "the biggest reason for N.E.T.'s success."

N.E.T.'s Technical Assistance Center operates 24 hours a day, utilizing the industry's most advanced tools to diagnose each problem, dispatching a field service engineer within minutes of the original trouble report. Since N.E.T. maintains its own cadre of trained field service personnel in 60 cities worldwide, the company's response time is two hours to the client's site, rather than the industry standard of four hours.

Because the company invested early in its service infrastructure, N.E.T. is able to keep its switches working more than 99.99 percent of the time, with virtually no downtime.

But service at N.E.T. really starts with product design. The quality of N.E.T.'s products are so

N.E.T. wide-area networking products are used by leading organizations worldwide to reduce corporate communications costs and to take advantage of new video, image, data, and voice applications that help them respond to new business opportunities and maintain competitiveness.

high, in fact, that the editors of *Fortune* magazine named the IDNX one of its "100 products America makes best."

Headquartered in Redwood City, N.E.T. employs approximately 950 people worldwide. The company operates sales and service offices in the United States and Canada, and sales subsidiaries in Europe and Asia.

Acknowledged as the leader in the domestic marketplace, N.E.T. is expanding its sales to organizations throughout Europe and other international markets and is moving aggressively to address the needs of the carrier market as well.

Intel Corporation

Gordon Moore (right) and
Andrew Grove (left).

To say that Intel Corporation revolutionized the electronics industry is an understatement. From creation of the world's first microprocessor to development of a host of peripherals, microcontrollers, and advanced integrated circuits (ICs) and systems, Intel has been an industry pioneer throughout the evolution of Silicon Valley.

Intel was founded in 1968 by Robert N. Noyce, Gordon E. Moore, and Andrew S. Grove. All three men were already well-known electronics industry innovators. Noyce, a Ph.D. from MIT, was co-inventor of the integrated circuit. Moore, a Ph.D. chemist from Caltech, made some of the basic discoveries that led to the IC and other developments. And Grove, a Ph.D. from the University of California, Berkeley, played a critical role in developing and implementing Metal Oxide Semiconductor (MOS) technology.

The Intel i486 microprocessor.

Starting with 12 employees, the founders of Intel set out to pursue the potential of integrating large numbers of transistors into silicon chips. Their efforts eventually yielded the technology that allowed the development of the modern personal computer.

Intel originally flourished as a supplier of semiconductor memory for mainframe computers and minicomputers. Today the company is a leading supplier of microcomputers, which comprise the largest, fastest-growing segment of the computing market.

Intel is, and always has been, a company shaped by an unyielding commitment to technological innovation. Nowhere is this commitment more

A clean room where manufacturing is done.

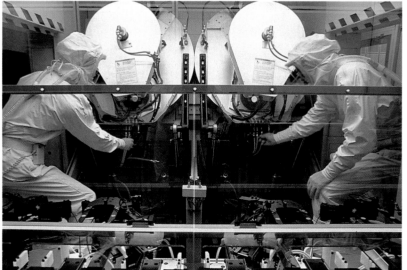

clearly seen than in Intel's research and development efforts. Despite the cyclical nature of the electronics business, the company's R&D budget has climbed every year since its founding.

The fruits of that investment are some very advanced, leading-edge products. Microcomputers based on Intel technology can be found in thousands of applications ranging from personal computers and automobiles to automated machine tools and military systems.

Most of Intel's customers are original-equipment manufacturers who incorporate its components, modules, and systems directly into their own products.

In addition to microcomputers, Intel's enhancement products for personal computers are sold through a network of more than 2,000 retail computer stores. The company also sells scientific computers and systems-interconnect products directly to end-users.

Founded by scientists and engineers, Intel is a company whose innovative nature is an integral part of its corporate culture. For example, Intel was the first Silicon Valley company to offer its employees sabbaticals—eight weeks paid leave every seven years in addition to their regular vacations.

The company also offers progressive compensation programs, an employee cash bonus program, and a highly successful stock option program (with some 6,000 participants as of this writing).

But more important, Intel strives to maintain an open working environment that promotes ready communication between all levels and departments, and in which individuals are given opportunity and responsibility.

Intel Corporation is an international company employing some 24,000 people throughout the United States, Europe, and the Far East, and with an annual sales volume of approximately $4 billion.

EXAR Corporation

In a community driven by high-technology innovation, EXAR Corporation stands at the forefront of Silicon Valley's semiconductor industry. As one of the area's leading analog semiconductor companies, EXAR is a well-established manufacturer of mixed signal application-specific integrated circuits (ASICs).

Founded in 1971, EXAR designs and manufactures custom, semi-custom, and application-specific standard products for ASIC users. While many of these products serve communications and microperipheral markets, EXAR also focuses on consumer markets. Applying its unique analog and Analog Plus design expertise, the company also supplies product solutions for users in automotive, medical, and industrial markets.

EXAR Corporation has long been a pioneer in analog semi-custom integrated circuit (IC) design. In 1971 the company assembled a multitude of uncommitted IC components on a single die, or master chip, which could be easily interconnected according to customer specifications. This first commercially available analog semi-custom IC could be produced at a fraction of the cost of a conventional custom IC, with a turnaround time of only a few weeks. EXAR's master-chip approach also affords design engineers the ability to make quick, economical design changes and to easily convert semi-custom chips to full custom ICs.

The company has successfully completed more than 1,000 custom and semi-custom programs and continues to expand its product offerings in this area.

In addition, for more than 12 years, EXAR Corporation has supplied the telecommunications and data communications markets with a range of products, including PCM line interfaces and repeaters, speakerphone circuits, modem ICs, modem filters, and UARTs.

EXAR also manufactures an extensive line of industrial, instrumentation, interface, and special-function circuits. These include PLLs, VCOs, timers, function generators, op amps, CMOS analog SCF, voltage regulators, tone decoders, and display drivers.

EXAR has long maintained a policy of making use of product synergy in the development of new products. For example, the company's strong relationship with hard disk drive manufacturers lead to its development in 1988 of a series of standard hard disk drive ICs.

EXAR's majority stockholder is Rohm Co. Ltd. of Kyoto, Japan, which owns 32 percent interest in the company. In 1971 EXAR was the first established Japanese subsidiary in Silicon Valley, as well as the first Japanese subsidiary to begin semiconductor manufacturing in the United States and the first Japanese subsidiary to complete a successful initial U.S. public offering, in August 1985.

Using its systems and mixed-signal design expertise, EXAR offers total system solutions in silicon for modern manufacturers.

Headquartered in San Jose, California, EXAR employs some 575 people. The company maintains three fabrication facilities: one in San Jose (62,500 square feet); another in Sunnyvale (20,000 square feet); and a third in Santa Clara (24,000 square feet). EXAR's sales and distribution offices are networked worldwide.

Heading into the 1990s, EXAR Corporation is striving to enhance its own in-house application standard product line, while continuing to provide ASIC designs with quick turnaround times, easy design changes, high integration, and low cost.

Mixed-signal and VLSI chip with analog, digital, and EEProm.

The Tech Museum of Innovation

Can you picture a 23-foot double helix made entirely of telephone books? Or a nine-foot-square "microchip" that calculates the day on which your birthday will fall in the year 2020? How about a robot that draws your portrait?

Anything is possible with today's technology, and The Tech Museum of Innovation wants to ensure the public can experience the very latest in a striking way.

Housed in a 17,000-square-foot facility, The Tech combines interactive exhibits, hands-on labs, and special programs to give people a better understanding of Silicon Valley innovations.

The Tech, serving as a prototype for a planned facility 10 times its size, covers six areas of technology: space, microelectronics, biotechnology, robotics, high-tech bikes, and materials. Not only is The Tech an educational experience, but it also

was ranked by travel experts as one of the top 10 new U.S. tourist attractions of 1990—just one month after its November opening.

"Our approach is different from a traditional science museum," says Peter Giles, The Tech's president and chief executive officer. "We focus on advanced technologies being developed in Silicon Valley. And we focus on the real-world uses of those technologies."

The Tech tapped educators and high-tech experts to help develop the exhibits, labs, and public programs—a strategy used by the museum for its other projects, including an annual lecture series called Tech Talks and the Technology Challenge. Such collaborative efforts are the cornerstone of its mission.

"We want to bring today's technologies directly to people's hands, and in a fun and interesting way show how Silicon Valley innovations influence our lives," Giles says. "The best way to do this is pull the many resources of this region toward a common goal."

In addition to technical know-how, The Tech has also received generous financial support from the City of San Jose, more than 300 corporate supporters and many thousand individual members.

The Tech began its first programs in 1987 with temporary exhibits and the Tech Talks series. That same year it started classroom outreach with Project Mindstorm, which brought media tools into a San Jose elementary school, and Laser-Links, which offers high-tech computer equipment and teacher training to high school science classrooms in Palo Alto.

"Our bottom line goal is to inspire middle and high school students to seek careers in science and technology," Giles emphasizes. "We want to propel the natural curiosity that most people have as youngsters into more serious lifelong interests."

However, The Tech's public programs and interactive exhibits aren't just for youth. "We can all afford to learn something about the way our world works. Technology has a tremendous impact on our lives, but most people know little about it," Giles says. "The Tech is a place where anybody can get firsthand involvement with these amazing innovations."

Like the many Silicon Valley start-ups which began in garages, The Tech will grow, moving into a new 170,000-square-foot facility by the mid-1990s. The museum will be located adjacent to the Children's Discovery Museum, and expand on The Tech's tradition of providing hands-on interactive experiences.

American Electronics Association

When it was founded in 1943, the American Electronics Association (AEA) was simply a rallying point for a small group of California companies seeking a more equitable share of government contracts. Today AEA has evolved into the nation's largest electronics trade association and a leader in the movement to foster U.S. industrial competitiveness.

Unlike other more vertical associations, AEA represents a cross section of U.S. electronics and information technology companies across the nation. Keeping its membership broad-based allows AEA to be a more effective voice for the U.S. electronics industry as a whole, engaging in activities that strengthen U.S. companies' competitive position in markets throughout the world.

With headquarters in Washington, D.C., and at the Techmart building in Santa Clara, AEA's growing membership includes more than 3,400 companies nationwide, with some 1,000-plus members based in Silicon Valley.

AEA member companies come from such high-technology fields as electronic data processing, including all types of computers, hardware and software, semiconductors, telecommunications equipment, medical instrumentation, and defense electronics.

Although AEA member companies include the giants of the industry, more than 70 percent are dynamic smaller firms that will shape the industry of tomorrow. And all AEA members, large and small, are entitled to a wide range of programs and services designed to expand their business development opportunities, including, among others, AEA's exclusive compensation surveys, high-tech financial conferences, innovative management programs, international marketing support, and up-to-the-minute industry information and publications.

As part of the largest high-tech network in the United States, AEA members regularly meet industry peers, competitors, and customers through meetings and networking events at AEA's 18 regional councils.

And, perhaps most important of all, through their membership AEA member companies have a powerful voice in government on both the state and national levels. In Washington, AEA lobbyists affect decision makers on such important industry issues as capital formation, federal procurement, international trade, science and technology education, and human resources.

And, unique in the electronics industry, AEA maintains an active presence in 10 key state capitals throughout the country, with the goal of creating a network of industry executives active and informed on the critical state issues facing the industry.

Associate membership in AEA is open to professional organizations that provide service to electronics companies. American universities and colleges offering engineering and technical education are also eligible for associate membership.

The association employs a support staff of 130 people in 15 offices across the country and offices in Tokyo and Brussels.

Since its founding the American Electronics Association has been the voice, both at home and abroad, of the U.S. electronics industry. As America enters the twenty-first century, that voice will continue to be heard loud and clear, strengthening the competitive position of electronics companies in markets throughout the world.

The American Electronics Association's theme of "Strength Through Unity" is the inspiration for this original photography by Mason Morfit.

Xerox Palo Alto Research Center

Multimedia technologies are being explored to facilitate collaborative work practices.

Experiments in Thin Film Semiconductors, such as laser-recrystallized silicon, are done by using a high-powered, ultraviolet laser.

In 1970 Xerox Corporation established a second major research center to complement its Webster, New York, facility. The new research center would expand the firm's role beyond reprographics and into information handling and communications. It would provide the technologies for the company's future office information products. It would, in the words of then president Peter Mc-Colough, lay the research foundation for Xerox scientists to become the "architects of information" for the business office.

Today the Xerox Palo Alto Research Center (PARC) is a laboratory of the future in which the workplace of the future is being developed. PARC occupies a 200,000-square-foot facility in the Stanford University Industrial Park in Palo Alto. The site was chosen because of its close proximity to a major research university (Stanford), which would help attract outstanding technical talent,

and because Santa Clara County was fast becoming the center of the microelectronics industry.

"There's a sense of adventure in this valley," says Dr. John Seely Brown, vice president, PARC. "There's a willingness here to think the unusual. It is a place where people can really think out of the box."

PARC founders believed that modern information technology would be built on both the information sciences and the physical sciences. In keeping with that idea, PARC is staffed with approximately 250 world-class research professionals whose disciplines range from computer science to psychology, microelectronics to programming languages, and network architecture to linguistic theory.

"It is truly a cross-disciplinary environment," says Frank Squires, former vice president of research operations at PARC, and one of the center's founding managers. "But all of the researchers at PARC have a common goal: making systems habitable and helping people and organizations to become more effective in the work environment."

Toward that end, PARC researcher activities involve computer science, artificial intelligence, imaging devices, electronic materials, document processing, and composition and publishing systems.

These research activities are spread across five laboratories housed at the Palo Alto facility. They include the Computer Science Laboratory, the Electronic Documents Laboratory, the Electronics and Imaging Laboratory, the Electronic Materials Laboratory, and the Systems Sciences Laboratory. A sixth, affiliate lab, EuroPARC, located in Cambridge, England, deals with human/computer interface and systems design and extendibility.

"In one way or another," says Brown, "all our research here is focused on the document. But that statement can be a little misleading if taken too narrowly. The document is actually the interchange medium for people to work together. Organizations function today because of the document and the technology that surrounds it, creates it, stores it, and modifies it."

The technology developed from PARC research has fundamentally changed the way people relate to each other in the modern workplace. It has, in fact, changed the way modern businesses operate.

For example, PARC had a prototype laser printer in operation by 1973. By 1977 the Xerox 9700 electronic printing system was released into the marketplace. This work developed into basic printing technology and has become a multi-billion-dollar business for Xerox Corporation.

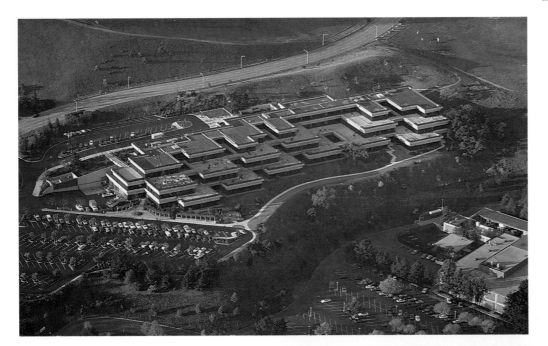

PARC researchers were also the first to develop the concept of the local area network, or LAN. The resulting Ethernet became such a widely used LAN that it is now the industry standard.

Even the personal computer was conceived at PARC. From research conducted at the Palo Alto center, Xerox developed and marketed the 8010 professional workstation. These interactive personal workstations featured multiple windows, a "mouse" pointing device, iconic user interfaces, bitmap graphics and architecture, WYSIWYG (what you see is what you get), and the Ethernet-linked services of file systems and printers.

In addition to research that Xerox applies directly to the development of its own products, PARC research has led to the formation of entirely new enterprises. Basic materials and device research on solid-state lasers, for example, began at PARC in 1971. This work led to a joint venture in 1983 between Xerox and Spectra Physics, which resulted in the formation of Spectra Diode Laboratories, Inc., (SDL) a world leader in high-power, solid-state lasers.

But SDL is not the only new enterprise spawned by PARC research. Synoptics Communications, Inc. (fiber-optic networks), Cipher Data Products (optical disk storage devices), and ParcPlace Systems (Smalltalk software standards) all are organizations which spun off from research done at PARC.

PARC is one of three Xerox research centers that constitute the Xerox Corporate Research Group. Research efforts at the Webster Research Center, located in Webster, New York, are concentrated on marking technologies (xerography, inkjet) for light/lens and electronic copying, electronics and software for electronic printers, display technology, and materials research. To the north of the Webster center, in Toronto, is the Xerox Research Centre of Canada, where materi-

als research and materials processing for xerography, inks, and paper are studied. Like these other Xerox research centers, PARC's role is to generate ideas for new products and businesses, but also to provide the company with a source of technical leadership.

"We're not technologists just for technology's sake," says Brown. "This is no ivory tower. We do some of the farthest out research in Silicon Valley, but we do it in the service of making people more effective. And to do that effectively, we maintain a rich dialogue between not only researchers, but all parts of the organization: sales, service, marketing, and development. We realize that it is only through working with other parts of the company that we can succeed as developers of technology in response to real human needs."

The Xerox Palo Alto Research Center continues to strive to accelerate technological advances and, by transfer to the product divisions, ensure that innovative development remains the principal cornerstone of Xerox Corporation.

Varian Associates, Inc.

It is almost impossible to talk about Silicon Valley without mentioning the name Varian in nearly the same breath. Varian Associates, Inc., has played a vital part in the development of Santa Clara County's high-technology industries for more than 40 years.

Headquartered in Stanford University's Palo Alto Research Park, Varian is a diversified international electronics company that designs, manufactures, and markets high-technology systems and components for applications in worldwide markets.

The company was founded in 1948 by a group of Stanford University researchers for the purpose of developing commercial applications for two areas of invention: the klystron microwave tube (invented by Russell Varian with the help of his brother Sigurd in the 1930s), which would later spawn a new microwave industry, and the principle of nuclear magnetic resonance (first demonstrated by professors Felix Bloch and William Hansen), which would lead to fundamental advances in molecular research.

Today, with more than one billion dollars in sales, Varian designs, manufactures, and markets products and support services for communications, defense, medical, environmental, industrial, and scientific applications. And in virtually all of its product areas, Varian continues to be a key player, if not the leader, in that field.

Varian has manufacturing sites in Arizona, California, Massachusetts, and Utah, as well as five foreign countries. The company employs approximately 10,000 people in these facilities and in its network of nearly 100 sales and service offices that serve customers worldwide.

At first glance, Varian might seem to be a conglomeration of unrelated businesses. But at the company's core are certain fundamental technological strengths that serve as the foundation for all its activities. In recent years the company has taken steps to focus on these core technologies.

"Historically," says company chairman and chief executive officer J. Tracy O'Rourke, "Varian has been in and out of more businesses than most other Silicon Valley companies. But what we are striving for today is a more balanced and sharply focused operation."

Though the company has pared down its activities, Varian's major product lines still cover a broad spectrum of markets, including electron devices, analytical instruments, semiconductor process equipment, and medical therapy equipment.

Varian's first product was the klystron vacuum tube—a device that revolutionized radar communications. Today, without Varian tubes and components, most major U.S. defense systems could not function. These critical devices provide the radio frequency energy needed for radar, communications, missile guidance and control, and electronic countermeasures. For example, the U.S. Navy's AEGIS class cruisers, the latest surveillance ships designed to protect an entire aircraft carrier fleet, each use almost 400 Varian tubes.

Varian components and equipment are also key to commercial radio and television systems, as well as to early warning radars that safeguard the United States. And Varian components and equipment are critical to secure the power behind signals beamed skyward to satellites, across difficult terrain, or to close-in receivers at frequencies resistant to eavesdropping.

Varian's expertise in vacuum tube technology has made the company particularly well qualified to build linear accelerators. Applying its linear accelerator technology, the company supplies major defense and aerospace contractors with the world's most powerful commercial X-ray source. The system produces X rays of large impervious castings, such as solid rocket motors, munitions, and vessels destined for use in nuclear power plants, to help ensure that they are flawless.

The company also pioneered the development of linear accelerators for medical applications. Physicians, chemists, physicists, and other scientists depend on Varian products for diagnosing and treating disease.

From analyzing the composition of pharmaceuticals and fine champagne to monitoring pollutants in soil, air, and water, Varian instruments perform a wide range of tests with pinpoint accuracy. Photo by Jim Karageorge

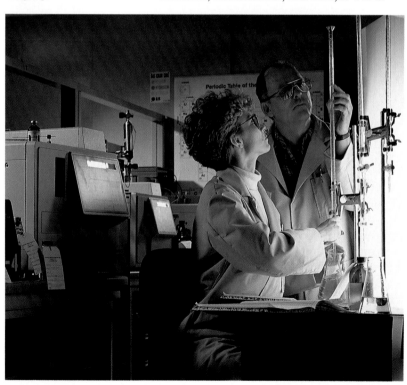

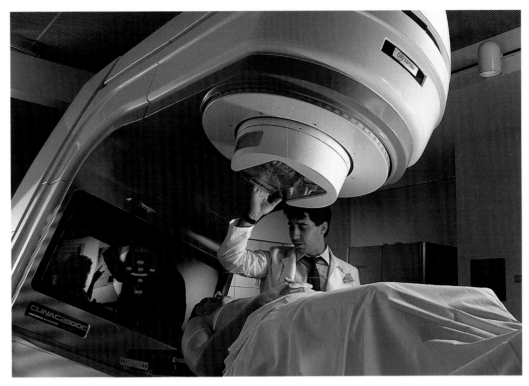

Varian pioneered develop-
ment of linear accelerators
for radiation treatment of
cancer and is the leading
manufacturer of these and
related systems used to
speed patient treatments
and treatment planning.
Photo by Jim Karageorge

And the company has become the leading manufacturer of systems that provide radiation therapy for cancer victims. More than 1,700 Varian radiotherapy systems help clinics and hospitals around the world treat more than 54,000 patients each day.

Varian is a major manufacturer of X-ray tubes for mammography, computerized tomography, and for routine diagnostics. Through innovative approaches and close customer coupling, the company has developed tubes that improve the picture quality of mammography X rays, thus allowing physicians to more accurately detect tiny cancerous lesions in the breast.

Varian was the first company to apply the theory of nuclear magnetic resonance (NMR) in a commercial application to study the structure and composition of molecules. The company's expertise in this field is unequaled. With 200 NMR patents to its credit, Varian has won worldwide renown for supplying the key analytical instrument—an NMR spectrometer—for molecular research.

In the field of quality control, Varian analytical instruments serve in myriad applications. From checking the composition of a wonder drug to detecting pesticide residue on produce, Varian products are reliable workhorses that produce accurate results time and again.

Varian instruments perform thousands of similarly sophisticated analyses in many other industrial applications. For example, the petrochemical industry relies on the company's equipment for analyzing crude oil to determine its basic components and thus the appropriate refining process. The mining industry employs Varian equipment in a similar application, while the chemical, food processing, and cosmetics industries look to Varian for the tools they need in research and development and quality control of everything from pesticides to breakfast cereal to perfume.

Varian's broad range of industry-standard semiconductor manufacturing equipment has secured a reputation as the most sophisticated in the industry. In fact, every major manufacturer of semiconductor chips from Japan to Germany counts on Varian systems for round-the-clock fabrication of these sophisticated devices.

As the key supplier of semiconductor manufacturing systems, Varian engineers work side by side with customers to surmount technological hurdles and develop breakthrough processes or "recipes" for chip manufacture. In the area of contamination control, for example, Varian has made significant advances in the way its systems handle wafers and thus reduced the chance of foreign materials damaging device performance.

Applying basic scientific principles to the needs of the world is Varian's strength. With its lean organization, its flexible, fast-response factories, and its unbending dedication to quality, Varian Associates, Inc., is organized for excellence well into the next century.

Westinghouse Electric Corporation, Marine Division

The Westinghouse Marine Division in Sunnyvale is a place rich in Santa Clara County tradition. It occupies the site of the former Joshua Hendy Iron Works, which became Sunnyvale's first industrial resident in 1907. At this site in the heart of Sunnyvale, 8,000 people were employed during World War II, working three full-time shifts to meet the nation's wartime ship propulsion needs.

The Marine Division purchased the Hendy Iron Works in 1947 and has since been a key player in the evolution of the U.S. Navy's surface ship and submarine fleets, as well as its strategic missile systems. The Marine Division is the world leader in the development and manufacturing of propulsion systems, main reduction gears, shipboard turbine generators, and launching equipment.

More than 2,400 employees work at the Marine Division's 1.2-million-square-foot facilities. In addition to engineering and computer centers, the facilities house some of the largest and most advanced computer-aided manufacturing equipment in the United States. The Marine Division's high-tech manufacturing equipment consists of the most precise gear grinding and measuring processes available. The Marine Division has invested heavily in its environmentally controlled Integrated Gear Manufacturing Center and its Steam Test Facility for production and testing of state-of-the-art main propulsion systems. This equipment enables the Marine Division to produce huge steam turbines and reduction gears with microscopic levels of precision. Westinghouse builds 50-ton systems with the precision of a fine watch.

The mission of the Westinghouse Marine Division is to achieve high levels of customer satisfaction and financial performance by transforming innovative technology into reliable, cost-effective systems through a Total Quality approach. For the last 35 years, the division's business base was primarily composed of two defense-oriented segments—Marine Machinery,

Above: The original Joshua Hendy Iron Works buildings were constructed in 1907.

Right: Nimitz-class aircraft carriers, such as the Carl Vinson (CVN-70), rely on eight Westinghouse ship service turbine generators for critical electrical power.

and Missile Launching and Handling. In the future, the division will be expanding these defense-oriented businesses by applying its considerable expertise in launching marine machinery and supporting technologies to closely related commercial markets.

MARINE MACHINERY

No manufacturer has served the U.S. Navy longer or better than Westinghouse. In 1912 Westinghouse delivered the first geared steam tur-

bine ever installed aboard a Navy ship. Since then, Westinghouse has pioneered and refined many of the industry's major technical advances, from the world's most powerful ship's service turbine generators to the world's quietest propulsion systems in the fleet.

Westinghouse technology has been setting the standard for naval propulsion machinery since the early part of the century. In the 1950s the company developed the propulsion system for the world's first nuclear-powered ship, the submarine *Nautilus.* Westinghouse also supplied the geared steam turbines for the *Enterprise,* the navy's first nuclear aircraft carrier. These powerful steam turbines have continued to drive the 89,600-ton carrier since 1961.

During the 1970s Marine Division engineers enhanced the performance and dependability of the company's main propulsion systems, such as those for the navy's Tarawa-class amphibious assault ships. Because of the outstanding performance of this system, the Marine Division adapted the same design for use in the navy's Wasp-class amphibious assault ships.

In the Spruance-class destroyer program, the Marine Division met the navy's challenge to reduce propulsion system noise. Using its innovative design and precision manufacturing techniques, Westinghouse produced machinery which performs better than specified by the navy and set a new standard for quiet surface ship machinery.

The division's success in the Spruance-class destroyer program made Westinghouse the obvious choice for the navy's next gas turbine-driven ships, the Kidd-class guided missile destroyers.

This technology led to the design of a similar system for the Ticonderoga-class cruisers, which at more than 9,000 tons are the largest gas turbine surface combatant ships in the fleet. As with the destroyers, these cruisers are among the most quiet in the navy.

In addition, several classes of aircraft carriers, including the *Midway* and *Enterprise,* are equipped with Westinghouse systems.

Westinghouse is the only navy supplier currently in production of submarine propulsion systems for the navy's Los Angeles-class and Seawolf-class submarines. This latter system is the quietest and most powerful main propulsion system ever developed at the Westinghouse Marine Division.

More than 300 propulsion systems and main reduction gears are now in service on navy ships. Today, the Marine Division is pioneering the advanced design and manufacturing methods twenty-first century marine propulsion systems will require. Westinghouse has and will continue to set the standard for noise performance in the future. The Marine Division continues to advance the state-of-the-art in supporting technologies such as materials and structural dynamics.

The Marine Division also sets the standard in the development and manufacture of ship's service turbine generators (SSTG). For more than 60 years, Westinghouse has been building SSTGs, which supply power for critical defense systems such as radar, sonar, communications, and weapons control. Without this vital source of power, most ships simply could not function.

Westinghouse SSTGs serve a broad spectrum of navy ships, from frigates to the largest nuclear carriers and submarines. For the Nimitz-class nuclear carrier, for example, the Marine Division

Above: Westinghouse Marine Division submarine propulsion systems are the most powerful and most quiet in the Navy.

Left: Cruisers in the Ticonderoga class are powered by Westinghouse Marine Division main reduction gear systems.

Above: Precision manufacturing in facilities such as the Integrated Gear Manufacturing Center allows Westinghouse systems to run extremely quietly.

Right: New advances, including the use of composite materials as well as steel, provide weight savings and durability to customers in the construction of specialized equipment.

More than 2.5 million hours of operating time are logged each year on Westinghouse Marine Division-built machinery. Many of the company's main reduction gears show little wear after 25 years at sea. And Westinghouse turbine generators manufactured before World War II are still hard at work.

As a result of its tradition of technical leadership in marine and heavy machinery, the Marine Division has developed a mechanical and materials engineering capability that is second to none. And, in addition to its own internal expertise, the Marine Division is able to draw upon the Westinghouse Science and Technology Center, one of the world's foremost private research and development organizations.

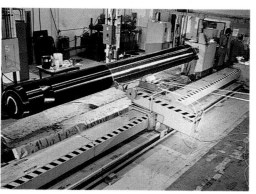

MISSILE LAUNCHING AND HANDLING SYSTEMS

Based on this wealth of experience in mechanical systems, the Marine Division has become a leader in the field of Missile Launching and Handling (ML&H) technology as well. The Marine Division's trademark of technical excellence has resulted in launching systems for the Navy's Fleet Ballistic Missile (FBM) program of unparalleled reliability. The division has developed, produced, and supported launching systems for all four generations of FBMs—Polaris, Poseidon, Trident I, and Trident II—and, during the 35-year history of this program, there has never been a failure of the Westinghouse systems in more than 600 operational submarine launches. That is a record of 100 percent reliability.

As a result of the Marine Division's involvement in the FBM program, it has developed a solid base of launch technology that has formed the foundation for the second segment of the division's business base. In 1975 the division was awarded a contract by the U.S. Air Force to develop a launching cannister for the MX missile, now called the Peacekeeper. The overall program, called Peacekeeper in Minute Man Silo (PIMS), is currently in the third production buy.

developed SSTG units with the world's highest power rating—enough power for a city of 75,000 people. And for the most numerous of all navy surface combatant ships, the frigates of the Knox class, the Marine Division manufactured 138 SSTG units. Today there are approximately 450 SSTGs in service on navy ships and submarines.

The Marine Division's turbine generators, like its propulsion equipment, are among the quietest rotating machinery ever built—quiet enough to fulfill the requirements of the Trident submarine program.

To the casual observer, the design of Westinghouse SSTG units and its marine propulsion systems may look like a simple arrangement of blades, gears, and shafts. But the development process for this extremely sophisticated equipment requires expertise in dozens of highly-specialized technical disciplines, ranging from sciences such as thermodynamics to practical manufacturing technologies such as welding and precision machining.

Marine Division engineers integrate these disciplines using sophisticated Westinghouse-developed computer programs and can simulate rotating turbine blades, meshing gear teeth, and stationary supporting structures. With these sophisticated analytical tools, Marine Division engineers readily overcome the technical challenges they regularly face. They identify and analyze individual sources of gear noise and vibration—something that was once impossible without the use of scale operating models.

Over the years Marine Division machinery has compiled an impressive record of reliability.

The follow-on to the PIMS program is the Rail Garrison Missile Launch Car program, which made the division a system level contractor. This program is currently in the full scale engineering phase.

The third major program in the ML&H segment is the submarine Cruise Missile Launcher program which began in 1980. After a comprehensive development effort, the program entered production in 1986. The division recently completed production of the 300th system.

For future systems the Marine Division is developing and refining high-tech composite materials that will provide weight savings to its customers, while maintaining durability and quality.

TOTAL QUALITY

The Marine Division strives to deliver the top level of performance in all of its programs, and has established Total Quality (TQ) as the foundation on which all its operational business activities are conducted. The Marine Division's position as the preeminent supplier of marine propulsion and ML&H systems is the result of the Total Quality transformation of its technically competent organization with a long heritage of engineering and manufacturing excellence into a broad-based business organization.

The Marine Division's TQ program was designed to encourage maximum employee participation at every level. The centerpiece of the division TQ program is Continuous Process Improvement (CPI), which consists of four elements: Quality Improvement Projects; CPI Training; workplace application of CPI techniques; and automation of the division's program management system.

COMMUNITY INVOLVEMENT

The Westinghouse Marine Division also recognizes the needs of the community. The Marine Division's community relations program places special emphasis on youth and education, especially with respect to minority or disadvantaged groups, as well as environmental concerns and the support of employee volunteerism in these areas and in cultural organizations where there is a significant benefit to the local community.

Employees are encouraged to participate in Westinghouse's corporate gift matching program, whereby their gifts to eligible organizations are matched by the corporation.

The Marine Division has been actively involved in Junior Achievement for the past 30 years and is a charter sponsor of the Sunnyvale Little League.

Historically, Westinghouse has supported the United Way of Santa Clara County. Marine Division employees have often been recognized with the United Way's Platinum Award—the highest recognition given to an employee group by the United Way.

The Westinghouse Marine Division holds memberships in the Sunnyvale Chamber of Commerce, the Clean Water Task Force, and the Santa Clara County Manufacturing Group, all active and influential groups in Silicon Valley. The Marine Division is also a member of the Technology Center of Silicon Valley.

The Westinghouse Marine Division has been an integral part of the local community for more than 40 years. Its involvement in and support of community activities, combined with its leadership role in supplying the nation's defense systems, makes the Marine Division an important part of the valley's history, as well as its future.

The Marine Division developed the launching cannister for the MX/ Peacekeeper missile.

Dionex Corporation

Dionex provides solutions for applications ranging from environmental analysis to biomedical research with an array of sophisticated separation technologies including capillary electrophoresis, ion chromatography, HPLC, and supercritical fluid separations.

Dionex Corporation is a Silicon Valley-based, high-technology company that develops, manufactures, sells, and services sophisticated analytical instruments with a broad range of applications, from evaluating a community's drinking water to helping medical researchers find the causes of disease.

Founded in 1975 and headquartered in Sunnyvale, Dionex was the first company to market ion chromatography systems. These systems and their related products isolate and identify the components of chemical mixtures.

Dionex chromatography systems are used extensively in environmental analysis and by the life science/biotechnology, chemical, petrochemical, power generation, pharmaceutical, and electronics industries. The company's customers include many of the largest industrial companies worldwide, as well as government agencies, research institutions, and universities.

Environmental monitoring represents the largest market for Dionex's chromatography systems—an area in which the company is recognized as a worldwide leader. In fact, Dionex's method for analysis of acid rain is the only chromatographic method approved by the United States Environmental Protection Agency. As part of a nationwide effort to create a comprehensive picture of region-to-region pollution caused by acid rain, the Illinois State Water Survey uses a Dionex chromatograph to monitor more than 10,000 water samples each year from 200 locations around the country. California waste treatment specialists use Dionex equipment to measure the nitrate content in wastewater dis-

charged into the San Francisco Bay. And the City of San Diego Water Utilities Department uses Dionex systems to evaluate drinking water for more than one million customers.

In addition, Dionex chromatography systems are used to monitor the raw materials, production processes, and outgoing wastewater at chemical manufacturing facilities. The company also works closely with the power industry to help ensure the smooth operation of nuclear and fossil fuel plants.

Dionex technology is also being used to solve the problems of biological researchers. Applying a variety of techniques, including liquid chromatography and capillary electrophoresis, Dionex bioseparations products analyze major classes of biological compounds (including carbohydrates, amino acids, nucleic acids, and proteins), helping researchers to understand diseases ranging from arthritis to AIDS.

At Children's Memorial Hospital at Northwestern University in Chicago, for example, researchers are using Dionex bioseparation instruments to find the cause of glaucoma, an eye disease that affects millions of people worldwide.

The company's supercritical fluid separations technologies provide new methods for chemical analysis and are currently used by major industrial and academic institutions around the world in quality control, environmental monitoring, product evaluation, and research and development.

One of the world's largest consumer products manufacturers, Proctor & Gamble Company, uses Dionex chromatography systems at its corporate R&D centers in Cincinnati, Ohio, to analyze the chemical composition of a variety of health care products. Based on the information provided by Dionex systems, Proctor & Gamble can adjust the formulation of its products to make them more appealing to consumers.

Dionex Corporation maintains regional offices throughout the United States, as well as subsidiaries in Canada, France, Germany, Japan, The Netherlands, and the United Kingdom. International sales represent more than half of the company's sales revenues.

ALZA Corporation

Palo Alto-based ALZA Corporation is an innovator in the medical field, pioneering the therapeutic systems approach to drug therapy. The company's unique technologies are designed to administer drugs on a controlled basis and to maintain appropriate drug concentrations in a patient's body throughout treatment. Unlike conventional forms of drug administration—including tablets, eye drops, and injections—therapeutic systems deliver drugs at a steady ongoing rate or in a predetermined pattern over extended periods of time.

ALZA was founded in 1968 by Alejandro Zaffaroni, Ph.D., who was formerly president of Syntex Research, a subsidiary of Syntex Corporation. Dr. Zaffaroni's objective in leaving Syntex to form ALZA was to develop technologies for controlling the rate and duration of drug therapy. Attesting to the value of the company's efforts, over 2,000 patents have been issued or are pending worldwide on ALZA inventions. Today, ALZA is the acknowledged world leader in the development and testing of therapeutic systems.

Company developments are directed at both human and veterinary applications. In human health care, ALZA's therapeutic systems include oral osmotic tablets providing controlled drug release; skin patches allowing 1-to-7-days of continuous therapy; polymer fibers placed between teeth and diseased gums for up to 10 days of targeted site-specific therapy; 7-day wafers inserted under the eyelid to treat ocular conditions; and lightweight pumps to provide intravenous therapy for ambulatory patients. Among the veterinary applications are implantable osmotic systems, ruminal pumps, and injectable systems.

When combined with drugs these therapeutic systems can significantly improve the outcome of therapy, expand the treatment indications, and even open up entirely new opportunities for medical therapy. They can reduce unpleasant or harmful drug side effects, while preserving or enhancing beneficial drug actions. In addition, they simplify therapy, thus increasing patient compliance with treatment regimens.

ALZA works in collaboration with many of the major pharmaceutical companies in the world on the development of new products. Today, a number of client/ALZA-developed products are being marketed worldwide. Perhaps most well known is Transderm-Nitro® (nitroglycerin), marketed by Ciba-Geigy. This once-a-day patch looks much like a small adhesive bandage, attached to the patient's skin and typically worn hidden under clothing. However, it provides the cardiovascular patient with vital drug therapy: a consistent flow of nitroglycerin to treat and prevent angina attacks.

Other well-known ALZA developments include Procardia XL® (nifedipine), a controlled-release tablet for the treatment of both angina and hypertension; Transderm Scop® (scopolamine) marketed by Ciba-Geigy, a skin patch to prevent motion sickness; and Volmax® (albuterol sulfate) tablets for relief of bronchospasms in patients with asthma, marketed by Glaxo. ALZA's first product was Ocusert (pilocarpine), a thin wafer which is inserted under the eyelid and gradually releases pilocarpine into the eye to treat glaucoma. Another early ALZA development was Progestasert (progesterone), an intrauterine contraceptive system that releases progesterone directly into a woman's uterus for its contraceptive effect.

While ALZA continues to develop therapeutic systems, the company is also expanding its own manufacturing and marketing efforts. A large-scale manufacturing facility in Vacaville, California, now serves as the company's primary source of supply, and ALZA is building the necessary infrastructure to comarket the Actisite® Periodontal Fiber with Procter & Gamble.

Because of the notable success of ALZA's innovative approach to drug delivery, therapeutic systems are expected to have a significant worldwide impact on the quality of drug therapy in the years ahead.

Below: In-vitro drug release rates from OROS systems are measured.

Bottom: A rotary die-cutting press executes the final step in manufacturing Transderm Scop patches for motion sickness prior to packaging.

LSI Logic Corporation

The L64700 family of high-performance video compression processors provides a complete solution for still-image and full-motion video (FMV) applications that will be used in products such as electronic cameras, digital copiers, digital desktop video on personal computers, video-conferencing and digital cable/satellite television delivery systems. The L64700 devices are the newest members of LSI Logic's growing portfolio of digital signal standard products.

LSI Logic Corporation, a 10-year-old Silicon Valley firm, enters the 1990s as a company that has undergone a dramatic transformation in the last decade—from a single product entity serving a niche market to a *Fortune* 500 firm serving the worldwide electronics market with a diversified product portfolio.

Over the past 10 years, the electronics industry has seen radical changes in technology and marketing. Tiny microprocessors now pack the punch of the older room-sized mainframe computers, and older desktop personal computers are the size of notebooks. Getting a product to market rapidly and in high volumes now are virtually everything. Many companies dread these changes, but LSI Logic thrives on them.

That's because LSI Logic's proprietary software tools help companies create products in "real time" to get them to market fast. The software tools are essential because they can be used to create customized products that can be changed quickly to adapt to new customer preferences and changing industry standards.

Think of the software as a word processing program that allows authors (in LSI Logic's case, engineers) to write a manuscript (design a chip or system). The company then acts as a publisher to print (manufacture) the book (chip). In recent years, LSI Logic also has become an "author," by using its own software tools to design standard chips aimed at a number of high-growth markets such as workstations, personal computers, consumer electronics, multimedia, and telecommunications.

LSI Logic virtually created the $10-billion market for application-specific integrated circuits (ASICs), chips customized to handle specific applications. Today, the company has parlayed its broad ASIC experience into a leadership position in gate arrays, standard cells, RISC microprocessors, video compression circuits, chip sets, and graphics products.

When LSI Logic was formed, no one could have guessed the profound impact it would have on the world's electronics and computer industries. Today, the ASIC industry represents more than 10 percent of total semiconductor sales worldwide, and the ASIC design methodology—which allows companies to rapidly and accurately design all types of semiconductors—has changed the face of the electronics industry.

A few of these ASIC chips can replace entire circuit boards crammed with dozens of simpler standard chips. With fewer and more powerful chips, customers can reduce the size of their computers, improve the reliability of the system, lower costs, and reduce the inventories required.

LSI Logic, with revenues of approximately $650 million in 1990, is among the nation's fastest growing public companies. Revenues have nearly doubled every two years since the company was founded and are expected to hit one billion dollars by 1993. The company employs more than 4,000 people worldwide.

The company was established in January 1981 by four cofounders led by Wilfred J. Corrigan, former chairman and chief executive of Fairchild Camera & Instruments. The company's shares are now publicly traded on the New York Stock Exchange (Stock Symbol: LSI).

LSI Logic operates 38 design centers and seven factories, and conducts business in 14 countries. Manufacturing facilities produce submicron circuits on six-inch wafers in CMOS technology that are sliced and housed in high-pin-count ceramic and plastic packages. The company's current lineup of products include:

• Application-specific integrated circuits (ASICs), gate arrays, and standard cells. Customized by customer engineers, these circuits contain up to 200,000 usable gates or 800,000 transistors.

• MIPS and SPARC 32-bit reduced instruction set computing (RISC) microprocessors, including stand-alone processors, embedded processors, modules, chipsets, and peripheral circuits. The company is the only firm with the license to produce both the MIPS and SPARC microprocessors.

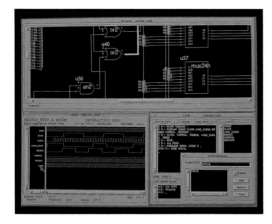

- High-performance digital signal processing (DSP) products for video compression and floating-point processors used in high-speed calculations.
- Application-specific standard products (ASSPs), chipsets, graphics, and multimedia products for IBM and IBM-compatible personal computers.
- Concurrent Modular Design Environment (C-MDE) and Silicon 1076 VHDL software design tools.

LSI Logic's products are geared to industries in which time-to-market is critical. Computers, which once had useful lives of about three to five years, now typically become dated after one year. Some leading-edge companies introduce new computers every few months in a bid to incorporate the latest advances in technology.

In this new operating environment, time-to-market is critical, and so is time-to-volume—the time it takes to accelerate production to supply the large quantities of chips necessary to satisfy the global volume requirements of customers. To satisfy both time-to-market and time-to-volume requirements of customers, LSI Logic has developed an integrated approach that weaves together its proprietary software design tools and the manufacturing infrastructure necessary to:

- Rapidly design circuits.
- Accurately produce working prototypes within a few weeks of the completed design.
- Ramp production in global factories to get the customer's products to market fast and in high volumes.

The company's primary markets include the computer, telecommunications, high-end consumer electronics, and defense/aerospace industries. Within the computer segment, the company focuses on workstations and personal computers. LSI Logic's chips are also found in video cameras, compact disc players, airplanes, radar systems, and telephones. Leading customers worldwide include Sun Microsystems, Digital Equipment, IBM, Compaq Computer, Matsushita, Hyundai, and Goldstar. LSI Logic

has completed more than 11,000 circuit designs for its customers.

LSI Logic is a "glocal" company—a global company that thinks local. In a novel approach, the company has formed affiliates in Japan, Europe, and Canada to help penetrate those markets by acting as local companies. The United States accounts for approximately 60 percent of revenues, with the remainder coming from Europe, Japan, and Canada. By the middle 1990s, LSI Logic expects to generate 50 percent of sales from outside the United States.

LSI Logic is the world's largest manufacturer of CMOS gate arrays and a leading producer of standard cells. To put its leadership position in perspective, LSI Logic has more revenues in gate arrays than all other U.S. competitors combined.

The ASIC market, which was nearly $4 billion in 1990, is expected to grow to nearly $18 billion in 1994, according to market researcher Dataquest, Inc. In other key markets, LSI Logic is the U.S. and worldwide leader in the 32-bit RISC market, and also is among the top three producers of chipsets and graphics products for the IBM-compatible personal computer market.

Looking ahead, LSI Logic is extremely well positioned to capitalize upon the growing electronics business—the largest and fastest growing industry in the world.

Left: The LCB007 series of cell-based ASICs from LSI Logic contain up to 200,000 equivalent logic gates—or 800,000 transistors. This combination of submicron technology and the packing densities needed to integrate a system on a single chip makes it possible to shrink the size and increase the power of computers.

Far left: LSI Logic's ASIC design toolsets enable customers to meet their time-to-market deadlines. The Concurrent Modular Design Environment® (C-MDE™) system includes powerful applications that help engineers navigate each step of ASIC design, from design capture, simulation and verification, floorplanning and packaging, to layout and test. This methodology can handle it all, from the simplest to the most complex designs.

Left to right: George D. Wells, president and chief operating officer, and Wilfred J. Corrigan, chairman of the board and chief executive officer.

Beckman Instruments, Inc.

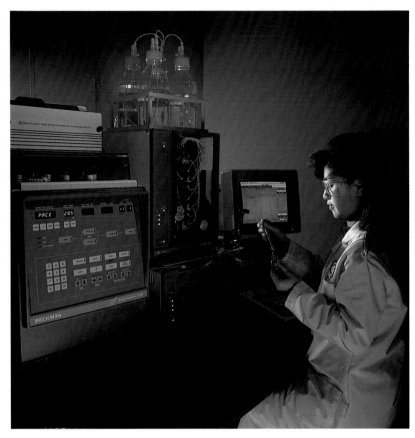

struments help physicians make rapid diagnoses on critically ill patients. In clinical laboratories throughout the world, Beckman diagnostic systems and analyzers are among the most popular products with the technologists who perform analytical tests on patients' blood and other body fluids.

Medical applications of Beckman diagnostic equipment include diagnosing diseases of the heart, kidney, bone marrow, thyroid, and other related ills.

Headquartered in Southern California, Beckman Instruments maintains 37 facilities worldwide and operates in more than 120 countries. With some 7,300 employees worldwide, Beckman Instruments has a solid sales, service,

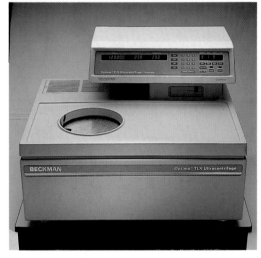

When Dr. Arnold O. Beckman put together his first simple "acidometer" back in 1935, he hardly thought of himself as an inventor of high-technology equipment. The assistant chemistry professor was only trying to measure the acidity of lemon juice.

But Beckman's device (the first pH meter) placed him and his new company, Beckman Instruments, Inc., at the center of a revolution in electrochemical instrumentation that today continues to open new worlds in science and medicine.

Beckman Instruments is a company dedicated to the life science laboratory. The firm develops, manufactures, and markets automated systems and supplies used in laboratories to accelerate biological discovery and diagnosis of disease.

For use in life science research laboratories, Beckman provides, among other products, centrifuges, ultracentrifuges, liquid scintillation and gamma counters, high-performance liquid chromatography and capillary zone electrophoresis systems, spectrophotometers, pH meters, and associated software programs.

For the clinical diagnostic laboratory, leading Beckman products include clinical and special chemistry systems, diagnostic kits, reagents, and quality controls.

In hospital emergency rooms, Beckman in-

and manufacturing presence around the globe. Its products are currently in use in nearly every biological laboratory throughout the world, and its instruments are even at work on the moon and Mars.

Beckman Instruments has approximately 1,000 employees at three facilities in the Bay Area: in Palo Alto, San Jose, and San Ramon. The company's Bay Area facilities focus on instrumentation, accessories, and supplies for the life science and diagnostic laboratories. Such bioanalytical products help in studying living systems and the mechanics of disease, and are applied to virtually every research discipline, from genetics to immunology to virology.

Beckman developments for the life science laboratory are both legion and legendary. A Beckman ultracentrifuge aided Salk researchers in isolating the virus that led to a vaccine for polio. Other Beckman instruments used in cell fractionation and DNA research have triggered major breakthroughs in bioresearch.

Yet Beckman products make their greatest contributions in workaday lab functions like sample preparation, separation, detection and measurement, and data handling. These analytical instruments are the basic tools used by Nobel laureates as well as quality control chemists around the world.

From its Palo Alto facility, Beckman introduced the first commercial ultracentrifuge in 1949. Since then, the company has been at the forefront of ultracentrifugation technology with innovative systems used to collect cells and other particles from their natural media; separate one cell type from another; and isolate viruses, subcellular fractions, and macromolecules such as DNA, RNA, proteins, and lipoproteins.

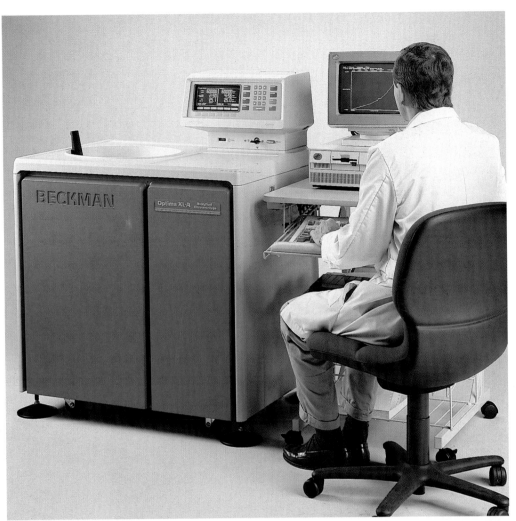

In fact, virtually every major breakthrough in the biological sciences has required an ultracentrifuge during at least one stage of the research process.

Beckman has also been an innovator in the area of liquid chromatography. The company introduced the first all-digital and PC-integrated high-performance liquid chromatography system. Called System Gold, this "personal chromatography" teams advanced liquid chromatography hardware with a powerful personal computer and advanced software.

In addition to maintaining offices throughout the United States, Beckman also operates subsidiaries in most industrialized nations of the world. All are staffed by trained Beckman representatives, including local field personnel, engineers, and applications specialists who keep customers' instrumentation in optimum condition, as well as providing hardware, software, and computer assistance.

Beckman Instruments, Inc., has long maintained a close working relationship with the global scientific community it serves. This close relationship has given the company important insight into the needs of its customers, as well as a tremendous opportunity for innovation.

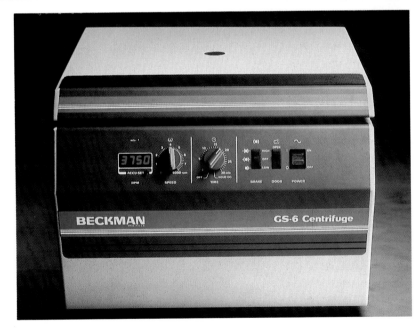

The world for which Dr. Beckman developed his first pH meter has changed dramatically. As the world continues to change, Beckman Instruments will remain committed to fulfilling the needs of its customers and the increasing demands of health care throughout the world.

Oki Semiconductor

Above: Oki Semiconductor has an extensive array of state-of-the-art and next-generation technologies: process, product, packaging, board, and interconnect. This broad offering makes it easy for customers to work with one semiconductor supplier, at whatever level of system solution they require.

Top right: To meet the demands of a growing automotive market, Oki has created innovative solutions including keyless entry transmitters, reliable controllers, and display driver systems.

Oki Semiconductor is one of Silicon Valley's most highly respected and innovative semiconductor companies. Headquartered in Sunnyvale, Oki Semiconductor manufactures memory integrated circuits (ICs) and a diverse line of board-level products for use in computers, telecommunications systems, and automotive and consumer applications.

In addition to its "customer-specific" ICs, including CMOS gate arrays and standard cells, the company is a leader in CMOS microprocessor, memory, microcontroller, and speech-synthesis semiconductor devices.

Oki Semiconductor has the advantage of being a distinctly American company with American creativity, management, and direction, while at the same time being part of a multinational corporation of great size and scope. As one of the three U.S. subsidiaries of Japan's venerable Oki Electric Industries, Ltd., Oki Semiconductor has access to worldwide resources.

A world leader in electronic devices, telecommunications, and information processing, Oki Electric was founded more than 100 years ago. Before the turn of the century Oki Electric built the first telephones outside the United States. More recently the firm was one of the original codevelopers of the cellular telephone, the first to

develop robots for semiconductor manufacturing, and one of the first to produce one-megabit dynamic random access memory parts (DRAMs). The original landless printed circuit board was also developed using Oki Electric expertise.

During its long history of bringing technology to its customers Oki has developed expertise in many different technologies. Today the company has a depth of experience that is difficult to match.

Oki's approach to the semiconductor business is hardly traditional. More than just a component supplier, Oki goes beyond the order-and-delivery relationships systems customers and their semiconductor vendors have traditionally shared. Oki provides support at any level its customers require, from the first stages of systems development to the final steps of deciding the arrangement of chips on circuit boards, from a single component to complete system development.

This system technology approach gives Oki a broader view of its customers' objectives and allows the company to serve as part of each customer's design team to solve overall system problems, adding value at every step in the process.

Oki is the only company in the world that offers standard IC, ASIC (application-specific integrated circuit), packaging, and board-level capabilities, all from the same source. Guided by its systems approach, Oki expertise enables it to apply the best technology at the right level to create the most effective solution.

Oki's Design Centers, one on each coast, are the firm's vital links to its ASIC customers. These centers are private, secure areas where individual customers can work 24 hours a day, either with Oki engineers or independently. Design Center services range from consultation and support for in-house designs to full turnkey development of custom systems from customer specifications.

To ensure that its design resources are readily available, Oki established a computer-aided network that allows data to be transmitted to Oki from any place in the world.

Both of Oki's Design Centers are fully equipped

with industry-leading workstations, mainframes, simulation and layout software, and design cell libraries. And they are expanding rapidly.

In addition, Oki is increasing its focus on application-specific standard products (ASSPs). The company is codeveloping these ASSPs with specific customers for their immediate needs and, with the customer's approval, providing these solutions to other manufacturers.

Sophisticated IC technology is the foundation of all Oki Semiconductor products. The company offers both static and dynamic RAMs in a wide variety of densities and is currently involved in

16-megabit DRAM development. Oki provides a wide selection of both general-purpose and algorithm-specific DSPs as well as floating point products. Oki products include 4-bit, 8-bit, and 16-bit microcontrollers, microprocessors, and their peripherals.

Using advanced CMOS technology, Oki is increasing memory densities while reducing power requirements. Oki recently developed a new submicron silicon-gate CMOS process that provides ultra-high integration and high speeds while using significantly less power.

The company is also pursuing submicron geometries in its BiCMOS technology, which provides the advantages of bipolar and CMOS without the weakness of either. An early innovator in GaAs integration, Oki is at the forefront of GaAs technology, one of the company's highest priorities.

Oki is currently developing new products in the field of voice synthesis and recognition, including voice analysis/synthesis ICs and compact speaker

drivers. The company also offers optical data capabilities and opto-electrical components.

The company's expertise at the IC level has enabled it to develop superior board-level systems and subsystems. Oki provides system-level solutions by combining sophisticated packaging technologies with semiconductor and board-level integration.

Oki also offers broad manufacturing capabilities for all product levels, from ICs to entire systems. Oki's modern facilities incorporate advanced robotics, ultraclean environments, and stringent quality-assurance measures. The company's manufacturing sophistication enables it to pass on the economies of automation to its customers.

The company's intensive research and development program guarantees that its technologies will continue to be state of the art. Committed to play a major role in all aspects of electronics, Oki Semiconductor is vigorously pursuing the technologies vital to the future of the electronics industry.

Left: Developing cost-effective components that provide the greatest density, speed, and performance continues to be Oki's priority.

Below: As one of the top application-specific integrated circuit (ASIC) suppliers worldwide, Oki Semiconductor provides every level of custom capability, from full custom design to semicustom gate arrays, sea-of-gates, and standard cells.

Western Micro Technology, Inc.

Many of the companies developing leading-edge electronic systems today are emerging firms with small operations—too small to buy the advanced technical products they need in sufficient quantities to effectively purchase directly from product manufacturers. For this reason, electronics distribution has grown into a major industry, playing a vital role in the development and manufacture of modern electronic systems.

Western Micro Technology teams up with product manufacturers from around the world to make its advanced components, systems, and subsystems available to these developing firms.

Marshall G. Cox, chairman and CEO of Western Micro Technology, Inc.

Western Micro Technology is one of the fastest-growing electronics distributors in the United States. As a distributor, Western Micro purchases an inventory of products, then markets those products to first and second tier OEMs. The company also adds value to the products it sells by providing technical application support; by testing, marketing, sorting, and subassembling the parts; and by providing credit.

Western Micro Technology, the first true "high-tech" distributor in the United States, was founded in 1977 by Marshall G. Cox and Bernard T. Marren, friends who met while working at Fairchild Semiconductor during Silicon Valley's formative years.

From Fairchild, both men went on to lead major semiconductor manufacturing companies—Cox as president of Intersil, Inc., Marren as president of AMI.

While traditional distributors had been little more than warehousing facilities and order-takers, Cox and Marren designed their company to be different. They created a distributorship that specialized in handling advanced complex integrated circuits (ICs). And, through a highly trained sales and service staff, they provided genuine technical backup support to the engineering departments of customers' companies—a real innovation for what was until then a "low-tech" industry segment. Because this was a first in the distribution industry, Western Micro literally pioneered the concept of technical value-added services.

Today the company is organized to assume a leading position in technical marketing. A specialty distributor serving the major high-tech growth areas only, it meets the needs of companies competing in the growing global economy by locating in those areas where manufacturing demands this unique focus.

A multi-regional distributor, Western Micro has become one of the largest specialty distributors serving the major markets in the United States. The company has grown to include franchised branch offices serving Northern and Southern California, the Pacific Northwest, New England, Metropolitan New York/New Jersey, Philadelphia, and the Southeast. As of this writing Western Micro has plans for future branch expansions into the Pacific Rim, which is the largest market worldwide, and into Europe.

The firm distributes advanced electronic components and computer systems both domestically and internationally. Its Distribution Group sells advanced components from leading suppliers in the United States, Europe, and Japan. In fact, Western Micro is the only distributor in the United States to have franchise agreements with all of the major suppliers from Japan. Five of Western Micro's suppliers—Fujitsu, Hitachi, Mitsubishi, NEC, and Toshiba—are among the world's top 10 semiconductor suppliers.

As a result, the company is able to offer its customers the leading process and product technologies available today, including microprocessors, complex memories of all types, peripheral devices, advanced products such as programmable logic devices, analog circuits, and much more. For original equipment manufacturers, value-added resellers, and *Fortune* 2,000 accounts, Western Micro offers a variety of computer systems and subsystems, including single- and multi-user systems, plus a range of technical service and support programs.

Western Micro's Turnkey Division offers in-house advanced engineering expertise coupled with sophisticated manufacturing and testing capabilities. The company's highly qualified personnel are specialists who deliver a wide range of engineering services for custom memory and logic modules, cable assembly, and testing services.

For custom memory modules, this division provides comprehensive engineering and manufacturing design, prototype, production, and testing services. All of these services are handled in-house, which means the firm can design, assemble, and test all components and boards under one roof.

Western Micro's cable products, which are assembled in San Diego, California, and Ensenada, Mexico, offer competitive pricing and easy accessibility to high-quality cable assemblies. Among the many cable assemblies offered are automated flat ribbon, card edge, custom harnessing, discrete wire termination, DIP plugs, D-subs, pin and socket, receptacles, RFI coax, rings and spades, shielded round cable, and modular plugs.

The company's test labs provide dynamic and static testing, programming, and burn-in of components and subsystems in Durham, North Carolina. One of the largest and most sophisticated independent testing facilities in the United States, the labs utilize advanced testing and handling equipment together with proprietary software. The facility is fully automated at every process level, and is equipped to handle virtually all package types, including surface mount. Advanced flow and tracking systems allow the company to handle extremely high volumes of products.

The test labs operates 24 hours a day, seven days a week, to provide the fastest turnaround possible.

Western Micro also provides its customers with technical seminars and its own in-house training programs. Technical, educational, and product seminars help the firm update its customers and its employees on the latest component and system advances.

Western Micro became publicly owned in 1983 and continues to be one of the fastest-growing electronics distributors in the United States. In December 1990 *Electronic News*, an industry trade newspaper, ranked Western Micro Technology 19th in sales of U.S. electronics distributors, compared with 45th in 1982.

Western Micro Technology continues to pursue its founding goal: to lead the high-technology component and systems distribution industry by offering the most advanced products and providing service that is second to none.

Western Micro Technology's offices in Saratoga, California.

Qume Corporation

Qume Corporation is a Silicon Valley-based manufacturer of page and daisywheel printers, computer display products, and computer supplies and accessories. Through its Data Technology Division the company also offers disk drive storage controller boards and chip sets. Qume's products are marketed around the world through a variety of dealers, distributors, original equipment manufacturers, and value-added resellers.

Qume was originally founded in 1973 as a manufacturer of daisywheel printers for the computer industry. Company cofounder David S. Lee was one of the early developers of the daisywheel, which was the most common type of computer printer before the advancement of dot matrix, ink-jet, and laser printers.

Lee served as executive vice president of Qume until the company was acquired by ITT Corporation in 1978. He stayed with ITT Qume until 1985, when he left the company to become president and CEO of Data Technology Corporation. ITT Qume was sold to Alcatel N.V., a French telecommunications firm, in 1986. Two years later Data Technology Corporation bought ITT Qume and renamed the merged company Qume Corporation. Today Lee continues to head the company's seasoned management team, which includes most of those who helped engineer Qume's success in the 1970s.

Since the merger of ITT Qume and Data Technology, the new Qume has emerged as a company with broad product lines built on innovative technology. Through its own R&D efforts and strategic partnerships with other high-technology leaders, the company has the re-

sources to continue expanding its product lines to stay at the forefront of new developments in display terminals, printers, and disk drive controllers.

As a division of Qume Corporation, Data Technology markets storage controllers, which are sophisticated electronic devices controlling the flow of data between a microcomputer's central processing unit and peripheral storage devices. It also offers a high-performance product line through the development of proprietary application specific integrated circuits (ASICs) and state-of-the-art software and firmware techniques to enhance input/output system performance.

Other devices developed in-house include a range of SCSI host adapters and software drivers allowing quick integration of SCSI devices—such as hard disk drives, tape drives, removable media drives, and CD-ROM drives—into MS DOS, OS/2, Novell, and UNIX environments, and chipsets (integrated circuits).

Since 1978 Qume has been a leading supplier of video display terminals, setting many standards for reliability and ergonomics including detached keyboards, full tilt and swivel screens, and a 25,000-hour Mean Time Between Failure (MTBF).

Continuing its market leadership position, Qume's newest product line, the QVT Series I, is the first family of display terminals to meet the strict Swedish requirements for low electromagnetic emissions at no additional cost. The QVT Series I terminals are price/performance leaders in the alphanumeric terminal market, reinforcing Qume's commitment to supply technologically

advanced, reliable display products to OEMs and distributors throughout the world.

Qume has long been at the forefront of liquid crystal display technology for printers. The firm's CrystalPrint Publisher, introduced in 1988, was the winner of *MacUser* magazine's prestigious Eddy Award as the "Best New Output Device of 1989." The Publisher combines the liquid crystal technology and a Post-Script compatible page definition language with a 32-bit RISC microprocessor controller designed by Qume specifically for graphics applications.

Along with its CrystalPrint line, Qume continues to manufacture and market a variety of laser and daisywheel printers. The firm is currently developing advanced laser printer technologies and plans to emphasize new products in that area in the future.

Qume also has a highly diversified line of after-market supply products supporting both Qume and "other" OEM printers. The products range from a line of compatible laser toners used in over 215 printers to Qumatic software geared to the small business and home office markets.

Since its founding, Qume Corporation has undergone a dramatic metamorphosis that has transformed it from a one-product company into a diversified, low-cost manufacturer of high-quality computer peripherals. In the course of its transformation, the company has built a geographically diversified manufacturing base, with subsidiaries

in Taiwan and contract manufacturing in Singapore, Japan, and the United States.

The company has also developed solid international marketing relationships. Qume has had a growing presence in Europe ever since 1974, where sales offices in the United Kingdom, France, West Germany, and Sweden have positioned it to benefit from the region's coming economic unification.

Likewise, the company has established a broad presence in major Asian markets. Through Compac Microelectronics Hong Kong, a distributor of personal computers and peripherals which the company purchased in 1987, it has also developed a profitable wholesale distribution business in the Pacific Rim—helping to open new sales channels for Qume products as well.

As of this writing nearly half of the company's revenues come from international sales.

Although the majority of Qume's manufacturing operations are in Asia, the company's research and development center is part of its corporate

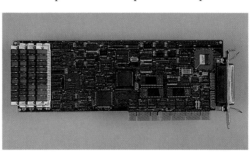

headquarters in Milpitas. This arrangement allows the company to capitalize on both the lower costs of overseas production and the concentration of engineering talent in Silicon Valley. Through its R&D programs Qume introduces new products in a steady stream that continues to broaden the meaning of the Qume name.

Of course in Silicon Valley the name "Qume" is inextricably linked with the company's founder. Lee has received several awards for his contributions to high technology, as well as to the local communities in which he operates his businesses. In 1987 he received the Mid-America Chinese Science & Technology Association Outstanding Achievement Award. Other awards include the Asian American High Technology Convention Award (1985), the Chinese Institute of Engineers—U.S.A. Achievement Award (1983), and the Harvard Business School Association of Northern California's Business Entrepreneur Award (1979). In 1989 and 1990 Qume Corporation's name was added to the *San Francisco Chronicle*'s Top 100 Corporations list.

Crystal Print Publisher II.

EISA SCSI 3290 controller board.

Crystal Print Express.

Sanmina Corporation

When Sanmina Corporation first began manufacturing circuit boards in its original, 5,000-square-foot Palo Alto facility, the biggest fear of the company's founders was that a customer would come out to see the plant.

"We looked so much smaller than the competition," confesses Sanmina co-founder and current chief executive officer Jure Sola, "that we were a little bit embarrassed. But we never failed to deliver what the customer wanted—when the customer wanted it."

Today, with its annual sales approaching $100 million, Sanmina operates seven production facilities totaling more than 200,000 square feet. And its commitment to delivering the highest-quality products to its customers—when they need them—is stronger than ever.

Sanmina was formed in 1980 by Milan Mandaric following the sale of his Lika Corporation, a firm he founded in the early 1970s. The company name is a combination of the names of Mandaric's two daughters, Aleksandra and Yasmina.

Sanmina has established itself as one of the country's leading independent manufacturers of custom-designed printed circuit boards and backpanel assemblies. Printed circuit boards (PCBs) are patterns of electrical circuitry etched from copper and laminated to boards made of insulating material, such as fiberglass epoxy. PCBs are the basic platforms used to interconnect the microprocessors, capacitors, resistor networks, and other electronic components essential to the functioning of electronic products.

Backpanels (also called backplanes) are larger PCBs that house and connect several boards into systems and subsystems.

Sanmina has also developed sophisticated multi-layer products and surface-mount technology to meet increasing demand for PCBs and backpanels with more complex and densely compressed circuitry. Multi-layering, which involves the placing of multiple layers of electrical circuitry on a single PCB or backpanel, expands the number of circuits and components that can be contained on an interconnect product and increases the operating speed of the system.

Sanmina has the capability to efficiently produce commercial quantities of PCBs with 20 or more layers of circuits with track widths of six mils or smaller (approximately half the width of a human hair).

Sanmina provides these interconnect products to leading original equipment manufacturers in the telecommunications, instrumentation, computer systems, and data communications industries throughout the United States and Canada, with some sales in Europe.

Sanmina takes a "solutions approach" to customer service, emphasizing involvement at the early stages of new product development by providing complete PCB and backpanel engineering services. Once engineering of an interconnect product is completed, Sanmina manufactures prototype and preproduction versions of that product on a quick-turnaround basis, allowing the customer to test the product before it goes to the assembly line.

Sanmina's solutions approach has established strong, long-term customer relationships, some of which span the entire life of the company. As of this writing more than 60 percent of the firm's business is repeat business.

This is also one of the reasons Sanmina has earned the designation "certified supplier" to many of its customers. This designation allows

Sanmina Corporation: Providing complete interconnect products to the electronic industry.

Backpanel assembly and testing.

for an exceptional "dock to stock" relationship, where the products Sanmina manufactures bypass incoming inspection and go directly onto its customers' assembly lines.

Sanmina manufactures its products in seven specialized plants, each with its own production overlaps, which enable the company to allocate production based on product type and available capacity at one or more plants. This extremely flexible approach makes Sanmina unique among its competitors.

Each of Sanmina's facilities has its own special expertise. Rather than producing multiple product lines in a single facility or dedicating plants to limited steps in the manufacturing process, Sanmina manufactures each of its products from start to finish in a single, decentralized facility.

Specialized facilities also enable each plant's staff members to enhance their expertise in particular product types, concentrate their attention on fewer priorities, and improve quality control. Also, as customer demand or technology trends change, a particular facility may be redirected without disruption of Sanmina's entire manufacturing capacity.

Sanmina operates two plants in San Jose, totaling 57,000 square feet. The company also operates plants in Santa Clara, Fremont, Milpitas, and Redmond, Washington. The corporate headquarters is located in San Jose.

But, as Sola puts it: "You can't be successful in a business like this just because you've got a lot of fancy buildings and equipment. You've got to have the people, people who are totally committed to the customer and who work together as a team."

More than any other factor, the success of Sanmina is the direct result of the efforts and the high level of commitment of its team of highly qualified people.

"Our people have done things that others said could not be done," says Sola. "For example, before we delivered an assembled backpanel to a customer in two weeks, such a thing was unheard of; it usually took 14 weeks. Today the lead times have come down nationwide because of what our people have achieved. Next to our customers, they are our most valuable resource."

Because of its people and their commitment to its customers, Sanmina has experienced over 25 percent growth annually since its founding. The company currently ranks among the top five independent circuit board manufacturers in the United States and expects annual growth of at least 15 percent during the coming years.

Sanmina Corporation's commitment to utilizing the latest developments in technology, combined with its ability to listen and respond to the needs of the high-technology electronics industry, assures its continued success and the continued success of its most valuable resources: its people and its customers.

Printed circuit board manufacturing.

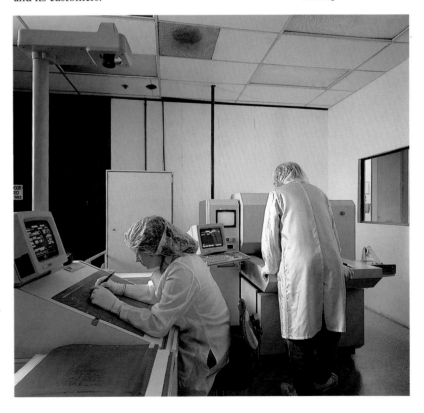

LifeScan Inc.

LifeScan's newest product, One Touch® II, was launched in January 1991.

A customer service representative takes a call from a customer on LifeScan's toll-free phone line.

In the latter part of 1987, LifeScan Inc.—the Santa Clara County-based maker of home blood-glucose monitoring products for people with diabetes—introduced the One Touch® System. On the first day the new home monitoring kit was offered for sale, it generated as many orders as the company's other products typically got in four months. This overwhelming response indicated the success of One Touch and sent LifeScan into double-digit growth.

The One Touch system grew out of the company's commitment to develop products that are easier for the patient to use.

With the introduction of One Touch, LifeScan became the first company to market what are called "second generation" products. The new system requires no timing and no blood removal. With no timing, wiping, or blotting, the chance of patient error is greatly reduced.

In addition, the system has the added benefits of a 45-second test time and automatic storage of 250 test results, which can be recalled from the device's memory. It is the first home diagnostic system to provide "conversational" messages in plain English to guide the patient through the test.

LifeScan has years of leadership experience in blood glucose monitoring innovation. Founded in 1981 to participate in the emerging market for home blood glucose monitoring, the company is based in Milpitas, where it manufactures its products.

LifeScan agreed to be acquired by Johnson & Johnson in late 1986. Johnson & Johnson has a long history of treating customers well. In fact, Johnson & Johnson has a one-page credo which emphasizes its responsibilities to customers first, then employees, the community, and finally stockholders. The acquisition increased LifeScan's resources while leaving its value system—including its devotion to high standards of service to the customer—undiluted.

LifeScan's customer service department has a deserved reputation for outstanding performance. The company's customer service people make autonomous decisions to meet the needs of the customers. At LifeScan they take customer service very seriously and it sets them apart as a leader in their industry.

The company pioneered the use of a toll-free number in its industry. All of its products list the 800 number and customers are encouraged to call with questions about LifeScan products. And when they do call, customers receive courteous and professional responses. LifeScan is proud of its professional staffing in customer service of people with health service backgrounds, such as nurses and dietitians. And everyone at the company is genuinely service oriented.

In order to ensure that its customers can receive the benefit of daily monitoring, LifeScan

maintains a warranty policy with replacement meters shipped to the customer within 24 hours if that customer is experiencing a problem.

When discussing customer service and, in fact, any aspect of LifeScan's business, it is important to have an understanding of the people for whom the company's products are designed: the person with diabetes.

Currently, more than 12 million people in the United States have diabetes mellitus. This includes both Type I and Type II. Approximately 2 million of the patients who are diagnosed use insulin or oral agents. About 58 percent of those using insulin are monitoring blood glucose, while approximately 27 percent of those using oral medications are monitoring blood glucose.

As a result, home blood glucose monitoring has become the largest home health care test in North America. The market is growing as more and more people with diabetes begin to turn to home testing systems.

LifeScan is a company which balances its bottom-line goals with customer-oriented ones. The company's sales strategy focuses on educating health care professionals, such as physicians, pharmacists, and diabetes educators, on the benefits of home testing.

The benefits of home monitoring systems are significant. Evidence indicates that home blood glucose monitoring and the resulting better control of blood glucose levels reduces the long-term complications that are associated with diabetes.

In meeting the needs of people with diabetes, LifeScan approaches its business with its five core values firmly in mind. As with the Johnson & Johnson credo, customers come first, followed by quality, technology, people, and profits.

LifeScan is firmly established as a leader in the large and growing market for blood glucose monitoring systems. Though the company will grow and add other new products in the future, blood glucose monitoring will remain the foundation of any business that LifeScan builds.

Above: This ad for One Touch reflects LifeScan's commitment to its customers— people with diabetes.

Top: An artist's rendering of LifeScan's newest building, which was completed in the summer of 1991.

Integrated Device Technology, Inc.

Integrated Device Technology, Inc. (IDT), was founded in 1980 with a commitment to an innovative computer chip-manufacturing process and a determination to grow into a world-class company. Today IDT, a $200-million operation, is a world leader in the production of the most advanced and highest-performance semiconductor products in the electronics industry.

IDT uses complementary metal-oxide semiconductor (CMOS) technology to design and manufacture complex proprietary and industry-standard integrated circuits (ICs). The company's products are used primarily by manufacturers of high-performance electronic systems in the military, electronic data processing, instrumentation, and telecommunications markets.

By continually refining its own enhanced version of the CMOS process—called CEMOS™—IDT has developed components with four times the speed and 16 times the density of those manufactured using the original process. The company's BiCEMOS process combines the ultra-high speeds of bipolar devices with the lower power and cost of CMOS, allowing for the production of even faster components.

IDT's ability to anticipate and often exceed its customers' technological expectations has allowed it to expand its product offerings to more than 450 devices supplied by eight product groups. The firm's product lines include static random access memory (SRAM) products, specialty memory products (SMP), first-in/first-out (FIFO) products, emitter-coupled logic (ECL) interface products, memory subsystems, FCT logic products, reduced instruction set computing (RISC) microprocessor products, and, most recently, RISC subsystems.

A recognized performance leader, IDT has pioneered many new device functions that have become industry standards. For example, IDT was the first manufacturer to offer 16K SRAMs

with access times less than 100ns. And the company's new CacheRAMs™ open an entirely new market for memories optimized with on-chip logic to fulfill the cache memory requirements of today's fastest microprocessors.

The country's leading supplier of high-speed, low-power SRAMs, IDT offers products with 16K, 64K, and 256K densities in x1, x4, x8, and

x16 configurations. SRAM is IDT's original product line, and accounts for more than 35 percent of the company's sales.

The emergence of a new high-performance microprocessor architecture, commonly known as RISC, has provided IDT with a unique opportunity to establish itself as a leader in the mainstream microprocessor market. RISC-based processors streamline the sequence of simplified instructions stored in high-speed semiconductor memory, allowing the computer to process information much more efficiently than systems using complex instruction set computing (CISC) microprocessors.

IDT's 32-bit R3000 RISC microprocessor allows designers to maximize performance in popular UNIX-based systems. It also improves cost-effectiveness in high-end embedded control applications, and enhances throughput of a wide variety of real-time business and scientific computer systems. IDT is currently shipping 12MHz, 16MHz, 25MHz, 33MHz, and 40MHz products that have up to 28 VAX MIPS capabilities.

To further exploit this new architecture, the firm recently formed its latest autonomous product line, the RISC SubSystems Division. This division provides customers with RISC CPU module products and complete software development solutions to expedite their end-systems to market. The formation of this division makes IDT the only MIPS Computer Systems RISC partner to provide customers with exclusive software/hardware implementation solutions based on the R3000 32-bit microprocessor.

IDT has introduced the industry-standard den-

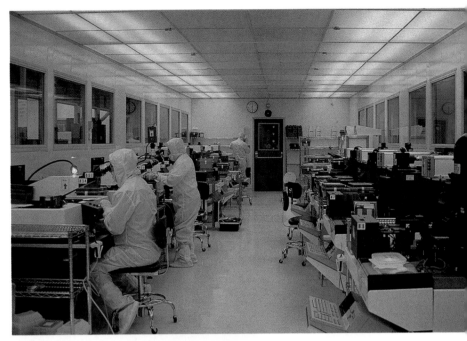

sities and functions in dual-port memories for several years running and is recognized today as the industry leader in this area. The company's recently introduced FourPort™ memory devices allow designers to solve the most complex bus bandwidth and processor connectivity problems in shared memory designs. The FourPort offers more than 10 times the bandwidth performance (160 megabytes) of older communications techniques.

A leader in FIFO memory, IDT offers the industry's largest selection with more than 19 products. For the past several years IDT has pioneered all industry-standard FIFO density, speed, and function improvements.

IDT's CMOS logic family, known as FCT Logic, achieves 50 to 100 percent increases in performance over TTL logic at one-third to one-fifth the power consumption. The latest speed grade, called FCT-C, is the only 4ns TTL logic available and was developed to optimize systems using 25MHz and 33MHz microprocessors.

IDT's logic product line also includes proprietary and speed-leading products in the areas of error detection and correction, digital signal processing, and data conversion. IDT offers the industry's fastest family of fixed-point multipliers and multipliers-accumulators.

The ultimate level of the company's focus on functional integration, IDT's subsystems modules incorporate a variety of components onto a single substrate to create entirely new integrated building blocks. These modules allow customers to achieve levels of integration currently unavailable in monolithic devices.

IDT's ECL I/O SRAMs are the first 64K memories to guarantee 8ns t_{AA} and, therefore, break the 10ns speed barrier.

The company strives to blend the highly focused, energy-intensive entrepreneurial spirit that has long characterized successful high-tech Silicon Valley companies with the larger business perspective of corporate management, which maintains the company's support structures. Thus, the products from each of IDT's eight product lines are designed and marketed by autonomous divisions, which draw on corporate CEMOS process technology and manufacturing capabilities while developing individual market share and profit objectives. Each division has the freedom to develop strategies that best satisfy its particular market needs.

Successful innovation is the foundation of IDT's consistent growth. The corporation, which went public in 1984, has shown a profit every quarter since its founding until the third calendar quarter of 1991, giving it the longest continuous

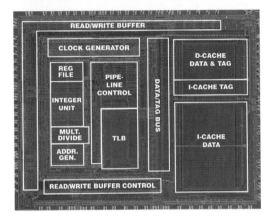

record of profitability of any semiconductor company in the world.

Integrated Device Technology's operations are housed in six facilities (totaling more than 500,000 square feet) in California and Malaysia. The executive headquarters, administrative services, and four of its eight product groups are located on the corporate campus in Santa Clara. The headquarters and manufacturing facilities for the FIFO and ECL product lines are located in San Jose, as are the corporate research and development activities. A test and assembly plant is located in Penang, Malaysia.

The company's newest technology development and manufacturing center is located in San Jose. This state-of-the-art, six-inch, sub-half-micron, Class 1 wafer-fabrication facility employs 800 people. IDT employs more than 2,000 people worldwide.

IDT maintains 20 sales offices in the United States, Europe, Asia, and Japan, with 16 offices in the United States. International markets are served through IDT sales offices in London, Paris, Munich, Taiwan, and Tokyo.

Above: In its wafer fabrication, IDT uses a process called photolithography, in which the microcircuit of the chip is laid out on the silicon surface photographically. In the "yellow room," the development stage of the photographic process is carried out before the wafer goes on to the next step in the manufacturing process.

Left: Die-plot showing the highly integrated functions of IDT's proprietary MIPS RISC R3000-based embedded controller, the R3051.

Mitsubishi Electronics America, Inc.
Electronic Device Group

MITSUBISHI ELECTRONICS IN TECHNOLOGY

From palm-size computers to massive mainframes, from cellular telephones to fiber optic telephone switching systems, accelerated achievements in electronic component technology continue to result in ever smaller, higher performance products.

Whether industrial or consumer, at the heart of today's electronic products are integrated circuits. Commonly referred to as "ICs" or "semiconductors," this is a technology where Mitsubishi Electric continues to support its customers and original equipment manufacturers on a global basis.

Mitsubishi Electric's U.S. subsidiary, Mitsubishi

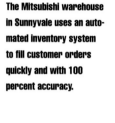

The Mitsubishi warehouse in Sunnyvale uses an automated inventory system to fill customer orders quickly and with 100 percent accuracy.

Headquartered in Sunnyvale, California, the Electronic Device Group of Mitsubishi Electronics America, Inc., employs more than 175 people locally.

Electronics America, Inc., is a leading supplier of electronic products in North America. One of the company's seven divisions is the Electronic Device Group, headquartered in the heart of Silicon Valley in Sunnyvale, California.

As an integral part of one of the world's top 10 semiconductor suppliers, the Electronic Device Group markets and sells a broad line of semiconductors and related electronic components, including:

- memory ICs and memory cards
- microcontrollers
- application-specific ICs (ASICs)
- application-specific standard products (ASSPs)
- optoelectronic devices
- microwave GaAs field effect transistors
- rf power semiconductors
- digital and analog standard ICs
- DC axial cooling fans
- flat panel displays

The group also provides applications engineering support and conducts software research and development from its Sunnyvale headquarters.

Today's high performance, high density, and often compact computer, industrial, and communications products are the result of rapid advances in electronic component and computer technology.

Mitsubishi's Electronic Device Group has played a significant role in this area with the introduction of submicron technology and ultrahigh-

density chip packaging. The company's leadership in packaging expands customers' options to create novel equipment at lower overall systems costs.

For example, the company pioneered the thin small-outline package (TSOP), allowing systems designers to dramatically save on the amount of printed circuit board space taken up by memory chips. This packaging technology has made possible such products as extremely small, memory-intensive laptop and palmtop PCs, indispensable tools in today's fast-paced business environment.

Mitsubishi R&D efforts continue to focus on the technologies that will drive the future, like ultra-thin IC packaging, called "paper-thin packaging" (PTP), as well as extremely high density, 64 megabit dynamic random access memory devices (DRAMs).

The Electronic Device Group of Mitsubishi Electronics America, Inc., markets and sells semiconductor components through a network of regional sales offices in major business centers in North America, and through regional sales representatives and distributors.

The group also participates actively in the setting of electronics industry standards through participation in a number of industry and trade associations, including the Joint Electronic Device Engineering Council (JEDEC) on a national level, and the Personal Computer Memory Card International Association (PCMCIA) and Japanese Electronic Industries Development Association (JEIDA) on an international level.

MITSUBISHI ELECTRONICS IN THE COMMUNITY

Mitsubishi Electronics America, Inc., Electronic Device Group is committed to the semiconductor technologies that will propel its customers to suc-

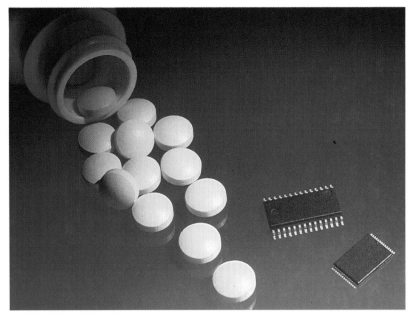

cess in the future. The company is also committed to its employees and their communities.

A long-term member of the local Silicon Valley community, the Electronic Device Group has been in operation in Sunnyvale for more than 10 years. The division employs more than 225 people in North America and is an integral part of the $1.8-billion Mitsubishi Electronics America, Inc., group companies. Collectively, these companies employ more than 4,000 Americans across the United States and Canada.

Mitsubishi Electronics America, Inc., along with the Mitsubishi Electric America Foundation, fosters a philosophy of local support for the communities in which they conduct business. For example, in 1991 the two provided joint donations and became a corporate sponsor of the local Palo Alto-based Children's Health Council Summer Symphony. This fund-raiser is held annually in July at Stanford University's Frost Amphitheatre. Proceeds from the event benefit the programs and services of the Children's Health Council.

TECHNOLOGY PLUS COMMUNITY EQUALS SUCCESS

From spiral escalators to mammoth stadium display systems, from high-output lasers to engineering workstations, few electronics companies have applied their technologies more imaginatively to more products than Mitsubishi Electric Corporation. Mitsubishi Electric's U.S. subsidiary, Mitsubishi Electronics America, Inc., is headquartered in Cypress, California, and is one of the leading suppliers of communications, industrial, and consumer electronics products to the North American marketplace.

As one of the seven Mitsubishi Electronics America, Inc., companies, the Electronic Device Group maintains a commitment to the technologies, innovations, and service that help ensure the local success of its community and the global success of its customers.

Mitsubishi originated the technology for Thin Small-Outline Packaging for integrated circuits in products ranging from laptop computers to engineering workstations.

As a corporate sponsor of the Summer Symphony, Mitsubishi helps the Children's Health Council of Palo Alto obtain the funding to provide diagnosis, treatment, and special education services to local children and their families.

New United Motor Manufacturing, Inc.

In 1989 Elizabeth Dole, then U.S. Secretary of Labor, toured the New United Motor Manufacturing, Inc., (NUMMI) plant in Fremont, stopping for lunch with a group of employees, and observing workers on the factory's second shift. Later, attending a NUMMI Leaders' annual meeting, Dole said, "By moving beyond the adversarial tradition of management versus labor, NUMMI has positioned itself as a model organization."

Formed in February 1984 as an independent California corporation, NUMMI is a joint venture between two of the largest and most successful corporations in the world: General Motors Corporation and Toyota Motor Corporation.

But NUMMI is much more than a search for mutual financial opportunity. NUMMI was conceived as an experiment to see if the Toyota production system, with its emphasis on quality in the process, continuous improvement, and cooperative labor-management relations, could thrive in this country.

To conduct this joint venture, GM and Toyota chose GM's troubled Fremont operation. The Fremont plant, which had a history of labor-management strife and quality and productivity problems, had ceased operations in 1982. The plant required approximately $450 million in equipment upgrades and renovation to prepare it for production.

In 1984, following a historic letter of agreement with the UAW, NUMMI hired the first 26 of an anticipated 1,000 start-up workers. In the letter, NUMMI recognized the union as the official bargaining agent, agreed to pay U.S. auto industry wage and benefit scales, and to rehire from among the laid-off GM Fremont workers. For its part, the UAW stated its readiness to adopt a new spirit of cooperation with management "minimizing the traditional adversarial roles and emphasizing trust and good faith . . ."

In December 1984 NUMMI began production of its Nova subcompact at the newly refurbished assembly plant in Fremont. Today NUMMI's Fremont plant, which sits on 100 acres and has more than 3.7 million square feet of covered space, has the capacity to produce some 220,000 passenger cars per year. Roughly 50 percent of the cars produced there today are General Motors vehicles, with approximately 50 percent produced for Toyota. NUMMI also launched production of Toyota pickup trucks in 1991 and builds about 100,000 units annually.

Though the company has utilized many Japanese management and labor relations techniques, it has not attempted to replicate the Toyota culture at NUMMI. Instead, it has adapted to and complemented American culture to permit the system to function.

Working together in teams of six to eight, NUMMI employees or team members have the direct responsibility for kaizen—the "never-ending quest for perfection." Under the kaizen philosophy, most recommendations for process or production improvements at NUMMI come from production team workers.

Applying jidoka, the quality principle, NUMMI's assembly line is equipped throughout with stop mechanisms, and it is the responsibility of every assembly worker to stop the line rather than pass on defective parts or vehicles.

NUMMI currently employs some 3,500 people, and the company's annual payroll and domestic purchases exceed one billion dollars.

New United Motor Manufacturing, Inc., is an experiment, closely watched by other automobile companies, unions, academia, and anyone concerned with American heavy manufacturing capability. In just a few short years the workers and managers at NUMMI have shown that they can build cars at quality and productivity levels that rival the Japanese. They have shown that cooperation between labor and management can work and that American manufacturers can survive in the global economy.

One of five press lines in New United Motor's stamping plant. This plant produces all the major body panels for NUMMI's cars.

New United Motor Manufacturing, Inc.'s Fremont facility.

Photo by Renee Lynn

12

Marketplace

Silicon Valley's retail establishments, service industries, and products are enjoyed by residents and visitors alike.

Photo by Joseph Sohm/Chromosohm

Pacific Maintenance Company

Pacifico Chioini founded Pacific Maintenance Company in 1931.

Pacific Maintenance Company has been providing custodial services to clients throughout the Santa Clara Valley since 1931. The company specializes in custodial maintenance of professional high-rise complexes and the highly technical environments found in Silicon Valley. Its management and supervisory team have more than 175 years combined experience in all phases of the building maintenance industry.

Pacific Maintenance cleans more than 14 million square feet of floor space each night, providing a broad base of general maintenance programs for a wide range of customers. The company's customer list includes IBM, AMD, Apple Computer, Kodak, Genentech, and National Semiconductor. The company's services include general janitorial work, grounds keeping, laundry packaging, and asphalt and concrete patchwork.

But Pacific Maintenance also provides for the highly specialized custodial needs of the medical, pharmaceutical, and biotechnology industries—as well as space and satellite technology, electronics and semiconductor industries, and computer and peripherals manufacturers.

Pacific Maintenance has been servicing clean rooms for more than 25 years and is today one of the foremost specialists in clean room maintenance. Over the years the company has worked closely with plant cleanliness departments throughout Silicon Valley. Through its constant experimentation with materials, equipment, and techniques, Pacific Maintenance has markedly improved the effectiveness of its own clean room servicing, as well as the industry as a whole. And it has been instrumental in developing definitive,

repeatable, and predictable procedures for bringing any class clean room to certification level and maintaining that level on a day-to-day basis.

The company is a member of the Bay Area's Contamination Control Association and is frequently called upon as a consultant for difficult or unique maintenance problems.

Pacific Maintenance employs nearly 90 full-time, Class 100, Class 10, and sub-micron clean-room janitors. Its clean room personnel are highly skilled in sophisticated cleaning procedures, as well as segregating, indentifying, and combating common and sporadic sources of contamination.

The company employs some 625 janitors, all of whom are required to participate in the hazard communications training program. This training gives them the latest safety information on the many chemicals in use in their industry. The course covers such topics as chemical storage, chemical handling, trade name and chemical mixtures, and chemical characteristics and precautions.

The course also covers basic first aid procedures, access to additional safety and health information, and the nearest emergency phone numbers and locations. Participants must pass a test upon completion of the course to receive certification.

Pacific Maintenance has one of the best records of employee longevity in the valley. Numerous employees have been with the firm for more than 20 years, and most of the janitorial staff has been with the company for at least five years.

Pacific Maintenance Company is a member of the Santa Clara Building Maintenance Contractors Association, and its workers enjoy progressive rate bonuses and benefits.

Pacific Maintenance Company's corporate headquarters, located at 2294 Walsh Avenue in Santa Clara.

Lindsay's Business Supplies and Furniture, Inc.

Lindsay's Business Supplies and Furniture, Inc., is the leading full-service office supplies and furniture dealer in Santa Clara County. The company was founded in 1925 as a bookstore in downtown San Jose by Curtis Lindsay. Lindsay began his enterprise with only four employees, stocking his store with only a few office supply items.

In the mid–1940s the founder's son, Don Lindsay, joined the firm. At about that same time, Elmo Ferrari went to work for Lindsay's, delivering packages by bicycle to customers in downtown San Jose. By 1975 Ferrari had become half–owner of the business with the late founder's son. After Don Lindsay's death in 1983, the company's remaining shares were purchased by Ferrari's sons, Mark and David, and his daughter, Julie. Elmo Ferrari died in 1985 and the management of the company passed to his wife and children.

(From left) David Ferrari, Julie Jarvis, Marie Ferrari, and Mark Ferrari.

Today, with 270 employees and sales exceeding $60 million, Lindsay's is the largest locally owned office products dealer in California. The company distributes its products from offices and warehouses totaling more than 200,000 square feet. Headquartered at its four–building complex at Zanker Road in San Jose, the company has stores in San Jose, Santa Clara, Pleasanton, and Sunnyvale, with sales offices in Pleasanton, San Jose, and San Francisco. The company also maintains a fleet of 40 vehicles for deliveries throughout the Bay Area.

Lindsay's has developed a very loyal customer base and maintains more than 5,000 active accounts in the Bay Area. Its local customers range from large concerns such as Pacific Bell, Tandem Computer, and Sun Microsystems, to small, single–owner operations.

Lindsay's Northern California market ranges from Sacramento to Monterey, but the company also serves customers nationwide. In fact, the company's growing furniture business is both national and international.

Lindsay's contract furniture division was formed in 1983. The division serves the company's customers with a highly trained sales force, design staff, project management group, warehouse and delivery staff, installation crew, and service technicians. And the company's custom printing division provides business forms, letterhead, data sheets, multicolor brochures, and other printing services.

Lindsay's is owned and headed by Marie Ferrari, the current chairman of the board. Her children, Mark and David Ferrari and Julie Jarvis, serve as company president, executive vice president, and executive vice president of human resources, respectively.

Lindsay's is consistently ranked by the *San Jose Business Journal* as the leading office–products dealer in Santa Clara County, as well as one of the area's largest 100 privately held companies. The firm has also been listed among *Facilities* magazine's top 100 U.S. office–furniture dealers.

But more important to the company is Lindsay's standing among its customers. From Sun Microsystems' Supplier Performance Award to Pacific Bell's Quality Partner Award, the company is regularly recognized by its customers for excellence.

The Ferrari family believes in giving something back to the community in which they have prospered. Though they have been involved in many community activities and programs over the years, the Crippled Children's Society of Santa Clara County has been a primary focus of these efforts. David Ferrari serves on the society's board of directors, and the company holds an annual golf and tennis tournament that has raised substantial funds for the organization.

Santa Clara Marriott

The Santa Clara Marriott first opened its doors in 1976 in conjunction with the opening of the nearby Great America Theme Park, then owned by the Marriott Corporation. The hotel was built on 22 acres, surrounded by what were essentially open, undeveloped fields, and it featured 304 rooms.

But a lot has changed since then. The empty fields are gone now, replaced by the Santa Clara Convention Center, Techmart, and the headquarters and facilities of many high-tech companies. And the hotel itself has grown. First in 1979, and then again in 1982, several hundred additional guest rooms were added. Today the Santa Clara Marriott features 754 guest rooms and 23,000 square feet of meeting space, making it the largest hotel between Los Angeles and San Francisco and the 14th-largest in the Marriott chain.

Located just off Highway 101, situated in the heart of Silicon Valley, the Santa Clara Marriott is just 10 minutes from the San Jose International Airport and 30 minutes from the San Francisco International Airport. This central Bay Area location has helped the hotel (Marriott's first in Northern California) to become a frequently chosen venue for conventions and trade shows, as well as both large and small business meetings.

And the hotel is a popular meeting place for nonbusiness groups as well. In addition to corporate gatherings, it is regularly used by state associations and social organizations.

One reason the Santa Clara Marriott is such an attractive group meeting site is the arrangement of its meeting space. The hotel's three large ballrooms are all located on one floor—an important feature that, for example, keeps attendees of meetings with breakout sessions from wandering up and down corridors on different floors—and each ballroom can be subdivided to fit the needs of the individual group. And since the hotel was built on 22 acres, there is an abundance of available parking.

But, though both corporate groups and nonbusiness associations represent a significant portion of the Santa Clara Marriott's business, individual business travelers stopping overnight in Silicon Valley constitute the largest segment of the hotel's customer base.

And because of its proximity to Great America Theme Park, San Jose Mission, and Bay Meadows Race Track—not to mention 10 months of great weather—the hotel is also known as an ideal spot for vacations and weekend getaways.

The Santa Clara Marriott features two restaurants: a garden court, family restaurant for casual dining for the whole family, and Alexander's, one

The Santa Clara Marriott is a popular choice for meetings and conventions, vacations and weekend getaways, and fine dining and catering.

of the South Bay's finest specialty restaurants, with gourmet cuisine, elegant decor, and tableside service.

The reputation of the Santa Clara Marriott's quality restaurants is well-established in the Bay Area—one reason the hotel's off-site catering services are used.

Other hotel facilities include an indoor/outdoor pool, a hydrotherapy pool, four lighted tennis courts for day and night play, and an exercise room. Golf and racquetball are available nearby.

The Marriott Corporation itself was founded in 1927 when J. Willard and Alice Marriott opened their first small root beer stand in Washington, D.C. Today Marriott Corporation is one of the world's leading food-service and hospitality companies, with operations and franchises in 50

states and 26 countries. It has some 200,000 employees, serves roughly 5 million meals per day, and develops more than one billion dollars in real estate each year. The company's principal businesses include lodging, catering, and contract food services and restaurants.

Marriott's lodging operation was also begun in the nation's capitol. In 1957, 30 years after the founders opened their first restaurant, the first Marriott hotel was opened. The firm now operates more than 500 hotels with some 118,000 rooms. Its diversified range of lodging products includes Marriott Hotels and Resorts, Marriott Suites, Courtyard by Marriott, Residence Inn by Marriott, and Fairfield Inn.

Marriott Hotels and Resorts is the largest operator of hotel rooms in the United States, with more than 200 full-service hotels in 38 states and 13 countries. But along with its full-service, traditional hotels, Marriott has also developed a range of other lodging products. Marriott Suites, for example, is an all-suite hotel designed to appeal to the business traveler who wants an upscale, residential atmosphere and to families needing two rooms for the price of one. In 1983 Marriott launched Courtyard by Marriott, the company's rapidly growing chain of moderately priced hotels. The Residence Inn by Marriott, acquired in 1987, is the firm's extended-stay product. And the Fairfield Inns (nearly 500 now operating around the United States) are Marriott's economy lodging facilities.

Marriott is North America's leading supplier of contract food-service management. It serves more than 2,000 clients, producing meals for a variety of businesses and industries, health care facilities, and educational institutions.

The company's other contract services include facilities management and airport operations. And the firm operates nine life-care retirement communities, which provide living quarters and health services for its residents. The company plans to open 309 assisted-living communities sometime during the 1990s.

At the core of the success of the Santa Clara Marriott is the set of simple business principles first expressed by the company's founder, the late J. Willard Marriott, and consistently applied throughout the corporation since its founding. "Take good care of your employees," Marriott said, "and they will take good care of your customers. Provide the customer with good service and a quality product at a fair price. Stay in close touch with your business. Always strive for success and never be satisfied."

Santa Clara Doubletree Hotel

Built to serve Silicon Valley's growing need for a premier executive convention and meeting place, the Santa Clara Doubletree Hotel opened its doors on November 3, 1986. The 500-room luxury hotel is located in Santa Clara, between Techmart and the Santa Clara Convention Center, and next to the Great America Theme Park. This location is easily reached by freeway, and both the San Francisco International and the San Jose International airports are accessible.

The Doubletree stands at the heart of a complex that includes the Santa Clara Convention Center, Techmart, and a full spectrum of recreational opportunities. The hotel's designers, architects Ron Aarons and Giorgio Dazzan,

produced a structure heavily influenced by postmodernism that combines natural textures and contemporary, high-tech surfaces.

The interior of the Doubletree was recently remodeled, and the space captures the spirit of Silicon Valley. The hotel's restaurants and bars are warm and friendly without sacrificing efficiency.

The hotel is directly attached to the 250,000-square-foot Convention Center, and they flow together at both the ground-floor lobby level and the second-floor meeting level.

The Convention Center is an extraordinary facility planned to provide an exciting yet functional accommodation for multiple events. It includes 100,000 square feet of exhibition space, a 25,000-square-foot ballroom, and 12,000 feet of meeting rooms and pre-function areas—plus a sophisticated 600-seat media forum complete with teleconferencing capabilities.

The Doubletree itself has 25,000 square feet of meeting space, which, when combined with the Convention Center's large exhibition space, makes the hotel sufficiently flexible to serve any type of gathering. For example, the 6,000-square-foot Doubletree Ballroom divides into five soundproof meeting rooms, including generous pre-function areas on two sides. And the Grand Ballroom contains 12,000 square feet that divide into four sections.

In addition, three conference rooms, two director's rooms, and a boardroom complete with reception area are all located on the second floor and are luxuriously appointed. And the hotel has

a 60-seat, acoustically perfect learning theater equipped for the latest in audiovisual presentations. State-of-the-art audiovisual equipment is available for meetings upon request, and banquet services are also available.

On the other side of the Doubletree, Techmart provides a five-floor, 300,000-square-foot marketing center for high–technology products such as computers, peripherals, telecommunications equipment, office systems, and software. More than 100 exhibitors from around the world are able to combine marketing and product education in a centrally located showroom in the heart of Silicon Valley.

Each of the Doubletree's 500 guest rooms is spacious, with one king-size bed or two over-size doubles, upholstered chairs, reading lamps, and plenty of room to work. In addition, the hotel has a number of suites, including a presidential suite, two hospitality suites, two VIP suites, five conference suites, and 10 executive parlor suites. Each suite also contains a conference table and chairs, suitable for in-room meetings.

Because of Santa Clara County's mild climate, the Doubletree is able to offer year-round outdoor recreation. The hotel has a heated outdoor swimming pool and whirlpool, and the Santa Clara Golf & Tennis Club maintains an 18-hole tournament golf course adjacent to the hotel. The course, designed by architect Robert Muir Graves, includes a driving range. The club also has eight lighted tennis courts and a clubhouse, which features a restaurant, snack bar, cocktail bar, and golf and tennis pro shops.

The Doubletree has a health club on the third floor of the hotel that includes exercise equipment, a steam room, a sauna, and an express elevator to the pool and spa.

Sticks Restaurant is one of the Doubletree's two eating establishments. Sticks' menu features California-Chinese cuisine. The Caffe Milano features a large, open display kitchen, including a centerpiece brick oven and red, white, and green Italian decor. And the Doubletree's lobby bar is located in the atrium lobby.

The health club at the Doubletree is well appointed with exercise equipment, a steam room, and a sauna.

The Doubletree's 60-seat, acoustically perfect learning theater is equipped for the latest in audiovisual presentations.

The Doubletree stands at the heart of a complex that includes both the Santa Clara Convention Center and Techmart.

The Beverly Heritage Hotel

During the early 1980s business travelers who came to Silicon Valley hoping to find full service hotel accommodations instead often found themselves forced into motels—or even out of the area altogether—because of a lack of rooms.

The Beverly Heritage Hotel was built to fill this gap in hotel services, and continues to meet the special needs of the business traveler today.

The Beverly Heritage opened in February 1984 in the city of Milpitas. Centrally located in the heart of Silicon Valley, the hotel borders the business–rich cities of Santa Clara and San Jose. The San Jose International Airport is just four miles away, and the San Francisco and Oakland International airports are within a short driving distance.

The hotel was built on five acres of what was formerly a dairy farm in what is now the Oak Creek Business Park. In addition to the hotel, the business park comprises 27 computer and electronics firms and two additional hotels.

The area's first full–service hotel, the Beverly Heritage combines the essentials of elegance, service, and corporate economy. Each of the hotel's 200 oversized guest rooms and suites (one–third of the rooms are suites) offers well–lit, oversized desk areas, sitting area, telephones in both bedrooms and baths, plus use of the in–house Computerized Communications Work Center which includes an IBM PC XT and facsimile equipment.

The hotel also offers outstanding meeting and banquet rooms that can accommodate up to 150 people. And though the Beverly Heritage is available for local gatherings, its seven small meeting

rooms were designed primarily with the needs of its guests in mind.

An uncompromising commitment to service is a way of life at the Beverly Heritage, and its high standards are reflected in a variety of personal touches and services, including the hotel's chauffeured airport limousine service; complimentary use of VCRs and videos; cable television, including The Movie Channel, ESPN, and CNN; a choice of morning papers, delivered directly to the rooms; a swimming pool and a whirlpool; jogging trails; bicycles; private Health Club privileges; and continental breakfast served in the hotel lobby.

Illustrative of the Beverly Heritage's commitment to service is the hotel's "Yours For The Asking" program. Like many hotels, the Beverly Heritage keeps a variety of toiletries on hand for guests who have forgotten something like a toothbrush or shaving cream. But unlike other

LOBBY CONCEPT SKETCH   BEVERLY HERITAGE HOTEL

An artist's rendering of the lobby as it will appear when renovation efforts are completed. The hotel's quiet, continental lobby salon will feature a lavish beverage service of international coffees and teas.

The Beverly Heritage Hotel provides luxury with a light California flair.

hotels, the Beverly Heritage also includes personal items such as swimming trunks, neckties, cufflinks, jewelry (both male and female), belts, socks—even suit coats—as part of this complimentary service. And if there's something a guest has forgotten that's not currently available in the Yours For The Asking program, a member of the hotel's staff will go out and get it.

The Beverly Heritage is also proud of its four-diamond (AAA rating) dining establishment, Brandon's Restaurant and Lounge. In a recent *San Jose Mercury News* survey of the restaurants in the Bay Area, Brandon's was named one of the region's top 10 hotel restaurants. Brandon's has also been recognized for excellence by *Epicurean* magazine.

Designed with rich oak, beveled glass, and

classic furnishings, Brandon's is a Silicon Valley landmark. Brandon's is known for its innovative cuisine, which uses traditional methods of cooking in untraditional ways.

Brandon's features aged midwestern beef, an outstanding daily selection of fresh seafood, and a variety of fresh pastas as well as other specialties.

Brandon's Deli, its latest innovation, was created with the businessperson in mind. Modeled after traditional, New York–style delicatessens, the Deli uses the finest kosher meats, breads, and pickles to produce authentic deli sandwiches, salads, and pizza.

Though known primarily as a businessperson's hotel, the Beverly Heritage is also proud to have been chosen by the famous Mirassou Winery from among the many hotels in the area for its popular "Grape Escape" hotel diner package. The Mirassou Winery, the oldest winery in the United States, offers tour packages during the warm summer months.

Unlike the major chains, the Beverly Heritage relies heavily on return business, and that is the key to its success. That the hotel continues to attract so many return visitors is testimony to its service. Most of the hotel's customers come to Silicon Valley from the East Coast, the Northwest, and Southern California. But as part of UTELL, an international reservations network, the hotel also serves an increasing number of business travelers from Europe and Japan.

The Beverly Heritage is conveniently located 10 minutes away from many Bay Area leisure attractions, including the Great America Theme Park in Santa Clara; the Rosecrucian Egyptian Museum and the Winchester Mystery House in San Jose; and 13 California wineries.

In addition, the hotel is equidistant (50 miles) from the major West Coast destinations of San Francisco and Monterey.

The nearby convention centers of Santa Clara (with 250,000 square feet of meeting and exhibit space) and San Jose (with 400,000 square feet of meeting and exhibit space), also attract many domestic and international associations and organizations to the area.

The Beverly Heritage Hotel is an active participant in local community activities and holds memberships in the San Jose, Milpitas, and Santa Clara chambers of commerce; the San Jose and Santa Clara convention and visitors bureaus; and the South Bay Lodging Association. The hotel also holds memberships in Meeting Planner International and the California Hotel and Motel Association.

Above: Brandon's Restaurant and Lounge is a Silicon Valley landmark that offers an outstanding daily selection of fresh seafood as well as a variety of fresh pastas and other specialties.

Left: The hotel maintains a high standard of excellence in all areas of service.

Wolf Computer

Don Wolf, president of Wolf Computer, the largest independently owned computer retailer in Santa Clara County.

During their first six months of operation, the founders of Wolf Computer opened a bottle of champagne to celebrate every single sale.

"Of course, we were so small back then we never had any trouble with inebriation," explains company cofounder and current president Don Wolf. "If we were still doing that today, we'd be in big trouble."

With annual sales exceeding $27 million, Wolf Computer is Silicon Valley's largest independently owned computer retailer. The store was recently ranked by the *San Jose Business Journal* as the second–largest among all computer retailers in Santa Clara County—including the national chains.

Don Wolf and his wife, Anita, opened their Los Gatos–based operation in 1981. A longtime computer industry veteran, Don Wolf started designing computers at Bell Telephone Laboratories in New Jersey in 1953. Anita Wolf, a former nurse, serves as chairman of the board.

Wolf Computer is headquartered at its North Santa Cruz Avenue location in the heart of downtown Los Gatos. Though the company has no plans to add additional outlets, the operation expanded in 1991, doubling its retail space. It's also one of the few retail operations in Los Gatos with its own parking lot.

The store offers a wide selection of computer systems to an expanding customer base. Hewlett–Packard, Apple Computer, and Digital comprise the company's primary product lines, with systems for general productivity, computer–aided design, desktop publishing, accounting, and multiuser solutions. The firm also offers systems from Everex, CalComp, Samsung, and hundreds of others.

Wolf Computer serves three different markets, including *Fortune* 1,000 companies, educators and schools, and small businesses and individuals. Wolf is the Hewlett–Packard supplier for all of the

schools in the University of California system, as well as the University of Kansas, and the University of Texas.

The company also installs and services the products it sells. And, to serve the specialized needs of its customers, Wolf Computer maintains a specialized sales force for each of these markets.

"We really owe our success to our people," says Don Wolf. "We focus not on finding the cheaper system, but a better solution; on finding what the customer needs. If a package doesn't fit, we change it. To do that, you need salespeople who are very technically knowledgeable. I'm convinced we have the best and most knowledgeable sales force in the business."

The firm also offers training for all its customers, at all levels of skill, from novice to expert. The Wolf Computer Training Center (located next to the showroom) offers daily classes.

In addition, Wolf Computer carries more than 500 software titles, including Santa Cruz Operations' UNIX–based applications, Microsoft, Real World, AutoCAD, Borland, and Lotus.

Don and Anita Wolf are very active in the local community. Don is a graduate engineer, an alumnus of Stanford University, and serves on the boards of both Junior Achievement and the Good Samaritan Foundation. The Wolfs are also active in mission work, both in Africa and Mexico.

Wolf Computer features HP Apollo workstations for computer-aided design and other high-end applications.

13

Building Silicon Valley

Developers, contractors, and real estate professionals all help to shape the Silicon Valley of tomorrow.

Photo by Kerrick James

Baycor Construction, Inc.

There is a saying in the construction business that goes, "It takes as long to get ready for a project as it does to build it." More than a mere truism, this saying underscores the importance of practical, cost effective design and planning in today's construction environment—the kind of service the design/build professionals at Baycor Construction, Inc., have been providing the leading property developers and business owners of Silicon Valley since 1985.

Baycor Construction is a leading Bay Area commercial and industrial general contractor and construction manager. The firm constructs and provides construction services for new construction, renovations or rehabilitations of existing structures, building additions, interior alterations or tenant improvements, and seismic or structural upgrades.

The firm's construction services include design and engineering assistance and consultation during the initial phases of building, as well as site selection and site analysis.

Baycor Construction was founded on August 2, 1985, by a group of highly experienced construction professionals. Carl C. Schmidt is the firm's CEO. Responsible for the general management of the firm, Schmidt is a former general contractor with more than 22 years experience in construction in the Santa Clara Valley.

James G. Walker, the company's president, has more than 28 years of experience in the local commercial and industrial market.

Mark E. Lawson, with more than 30 years of worldwide experience, directs the company's construction management and construction audit services.

And Jim Pap Rocki, vice president, construction, is responsible for field supervision, subcontractor coordination, scheduling, quality control, and safety.

All of the principals of Baycor Construction apply their years of experience in a hands–on approach to project management. Each brings a strong design/build background to their clients' projects.

The design/build construction technique has long been favored by developers, facilities managers, and other professional buyers of construction services. This technique has several significant advantages over the more traditional design/bid/build approach.

Through frequent conferences with the owner, builder, architect, and subcontractors, for example, design/build firms are able to establish high levels of cooperation on most projects. This encourages practical as well as attractive design. It also lays the groundwork for quick and effective communication, and for the relationship of mutual trust and responsibility that is the hallmark of the design/build approach.

Because design/build emphasizes teamwork, it also frequently results in substantial reduction of the time required to deliver a project. Construction documents, since they are largely intended for cooperative use within the team, don't need to be as extensive or as defensive as is required by the more traditional process. And it allows for "fast-track" scheduling, in which construction and design proceed nearly simultaneously.

Design/build has tremendous potential for reducing the overall cost of a project. In addition to the savings associated with shorter delivery time, the process involves the eventual guarantor of the project, the contractor, in the earliest planning stages. "No surprises" are the by-words of this approach.

Design/build projects are also much less sub-

ject to disputes than traditionally bid projects. Since there is a single source of responsibility for both design and construction, disagreements are likely to be resolved within the team framework and not involve the owner—or his pocketbook.

Since its founding, Baycor Construction has also been a leader in seismic safety improvements to commercial and industrial buildings. Of the thousands of square feet of seismic safety improvements completed by Baycor, not one building suffered any structural damage during the 1989 Loma Prieta earthquake.

As a result of that disaster, the firm now maintains a crew which does almost nothing but seismic upgrade. The firm enjoys excellent working relationships with the foremost seismic engineering firms in Northern California and offers complete consulting and construction services for repair of earthquake-damaged structures, as well as the sort of preventive improvement which protected many buildings during the 1989 quake.

Baycor has also contributed significantly to the technology of seismic safety, including development of the new, patented chord tie which protects essential panel-to-panel connection in formerly quake-sensitive concrete tilt-up buildings.

Originally based in Mountain View, Baycor Construction recently relocated to San Jose. The company has been involved in commercial and industrial construction projects from the San Joaquin Valley through the Salinas Valley, Monterey, Gilroy, and as far north as Petaluma.

Since its founding, the firm has completed more than a million square feet of commercial and industrial space throughout the area and enjoys a high percentage of repeat clients. "The surest sign that our system works is that people use it again and again," says vice president Mark E. Lawson.

Some of the company's more notable projects include Charleston Place, a four-building, 235,000-square-foot complex of two-story, steel-frame office buildings constructed in Mountain View's Shoreline area for the Mozart Development Company; Black Mountain Spring Water Co., a design/build, three-story, 12,000-square-foot, steel-frame-and-glass curtain wall office building in San Carlos (the project included two stories of headquarters office for the Black Mountain Spring Water Co. and one story of leased tenant space); Capetronic USA in Santa Clara and Adobe Systems in Mountain View, two high-finish entrance lobbies designed and built to convey a sense of contemporary immediacy and high technology compatible with the image of these very competitive firms; and the Grant Road Center in Mountain View, a project which included renovation of existing tilt-up concrete retail buildings and construction of new masonry block and wood frame specialty retail stores.

"Construction is an ancient activity," says CEO Carl C. Schmidt. "People have been stacking bricks and mortar since before the Pharaohs built the pyramids—it's not really a high-tech business. But it is a detail-oriented and management-intensive business. Today more than ever, successful construction projects rely on experienced people making good decisions."

The systems demonstration room at Sun Microsystems in Mountain View, California.

Toeniskoetter & Breeding Inc.

Headquartered in San Jose, Toeniskoetter & Breeding Inc. (TBI) is acclaimed for its efforts in the fields of both development and construction. One of the best known "small" development companies in Santa Clara and Santa Cruz counties, TBI, Development has completed more than 700,000 square feet of quality research and development, office, and mixed-use facilities since its inception in 1983. Its sister company, TBI, Construction specializes in renovation and tenant im-

provement projects as well as general construction and has been responsible for the completion of more than $100-million worth of construction projects during its eight years of operation.

TBI, CONSTRUCTION

The construction side of the TBI business was launched with a strong focus on specialized, high-end tenant improvement projects. The two founding principals, Charles J. Toeniskoetter and Dan L. Breeding, had become acquainted as associates at the Carl N. Swenson Company, a major force in the area's construction industry for years. Toeniskoetter, an MBA graduate of Stanford University, was directing a corporate division responsible for the firm's negotiated projects. Breeding, an experienced superintendent, quickly established himself as the company's tenant improvement specialist, and a close professional collaboration began when a tenant improvement department was established within Toeniskoetter's own corporate division.

Over the years, a strong friendship also developed between the two experienced professionals . . . as did a mutual realization of the growing need for specialized tenant improvement capabilities in the Santa Clara County region.

When the experienced duo established their own company in 1983, they quickly positioned themselves as experts in the area of tenant improvement construction. The firm's early projects included commissions for a number of prominent law firms and accountancy corpora-

The interior of the Toeniskoetter & Breeding headquarters building.

The Toeniskoetter & Breeding headquarters building at 1960 The Alameda, in San Jose, California.

Left and below: The nationally recognized interior space for Bank of the West, located in San Jose, is a Toeniskoetter & Breeding project.

tions, medical and financial institutions, and broadcasting companies; interiors for a number of corporate headquarters facilities; and its own award-winning offices in the restored Cook Mansion. Renovation and general construction were soon added to TBI's corporate repertoire, evolving as a natural extension of the firm's award-winning efforts in restoring and expanding its own offices in a former residential mansion at 1960 The Alameda.

Through the years, TBI, Construction has established a reputation for excellence and dependability reflected in an expansive portfolio that includes a broad range of outstanding (and award-winning) projects. Particularly noteworthy are the nationally acclaimed interiors for Bank of the West's main service branch in downtown San Jose; the distinctive law offices of Atwood, Knox and Anderson, also in San Jose; and the highly specialized surgery center and "cath labs" for Seton Medical Center in Daly City. Granite Creek Business Center in Scotts Valley; the corporate headquarters facility for the PacMed group of companies in San Jose; and Brokaw Business Center near San Jose International Airport are just a few of the firm's key general contracting commissions.

One of TBI, Construction's most prestigious assignments was recently completed on behalf of the Catholic Diocese of San Jose: the restoration and refurbishment of St. Joseph's Cathedral in downtown San Jose. Executed in joint cooperation with Dinwiddie Construction Company, the complex assignment took more than three years to complete. Located on Market Street between San Fernando and Santa Clara streets, the project marked the transformation of a structurally outdated and deteriorating 110-year-old church into an edifice worthy of its new status as "cathedral." The lengthy renovation process encompassed a scope of specialized activities including the carefully engineered reinforcement of the entire structure; the introduction of a second copper-clad main dome as specified in the original century-old design; the relocation of the 27-ton primary altar to a new site within the reconfigured interiors; and the detailed restoration of numerous cupolas, cornices, finials, and marble floors. The new cathedral, dedicated as such in November 1990, was recently cited for a special award for excellence at the 1991 San Jose Development Briefing. TBI is currently at work on a second commission for the diocese: the conversion of an adjacent four-story structure into the Cathedral Center.

TBI, DEVELOPMENT

Just months after Toeniskoetter & Breeding Inc., Construction was established, the firm introduced a separate but affiliated development entity, Toeniskoetter & Breeding Inc., Development, with the intention of developing quality, high-end projects for their own account. Toeniskoetter

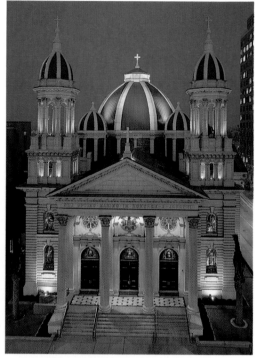

and Breeding brought in Brad Krouskup, an associate from the Swenson Company, to manage the new development operation.

Limiting its development "production" to two or three key projects annually, TBI, Development has emerged as one of the most highly regarded development companies in the area, recognized with numerous awards for professional excellence and known for a consistent roster of quality tenants. Premier locations and distinctive architectural design have also come to be synonymous with TBI, Development projects, and the few company-developed buildings offered for sale have garnered top-of-the market prices. Indeed, two recent sales scored record figures, indicative of their high caliber of design and construction, fine locations, and quality tenants.

One of TBI, Development's most recent projects is Granite Creek Business Center in Scotts Valley. The three-building, 90,000-square-foot complex was the recent recipient of the Extra Mile Award presented by the City of Scotts Valley for "extraordinary attention to quality and concern for the environment" and was also recognized with a prestigious SCOPE award presented by Santa Cruz County. Integrating attractive early California/Spanish-style architecture and a lush natural setting, the complex is home to such high-profile tenants as Borland International, Santa Cruz Operation, and Meridian Data.

Also included in the company's portfolio are

Cochrane Business Ranch in Morgan Hill, Brokaw Business Center in San Jose, and the 133 Mission Hill executive office project in Santa Cruz.

TBI, Development recently celebrated an important and, given today's sluggish market conditions, nearly unheard-of benchmark: full, 100 percent occupancy.

with quality accommodations, outstanding restaurants, and live entertainment on the weekends.

Also included in the partners' acquisitions are a commerce center that encompasses a general store, a sports shop, a bar and lounge, a real estate office, a 7,000-square-foot shipping and receiving center, a gas station, and a minimart that doubles as a mountain bike shop in the summer and a cross-country ski center during the winter months. Also included in the purchase were the area's cross-country skiing operations. Encompassing one of the most extensive cross-country networks in the nation, Bear Valley Cross Country captured a spot on *USA Today*'s "10 Best" list this past winter.

While the Bear Valley holdings are an undeniable labor of love for the team at Toeniskoetter & Breeding Inc., the firm's primary focus remains, as always, the communities of Santa Clara and Santa Cruz counties.

Bear Valley Lodge lies at the heart of Toeniskoetter & Breeding's 215-acre Bear Valley Ranch.

NEW GROUND

In November 1987, TBI broke ground in yet another area with the purchase of a 215-acre property in the Sierra Nevada town of Bear Valley. An appealing year-round destination resort with a popular summer music festival, both Nordic and Alpine skiing, fishing, hiking, and mountain biking, Bear Valley is located 180 miles east of San Jose at an altitude of 7,000 feet and is surrounded by the natural beauty of the Stanislaus National Forest.

Approximately two-and-a-half years after their initial Bear Valley purchase, Toeniskoetter and Breeding joined with their friend, attorney Steve Hallgrimson, to make additional area acquisitions. The concept behind these subsequent purchases was to enhance the overall quality of the area's rich environment with restrained, high-quality development, professional management, and a careful renovation of the existing facilities.

The partners' primary target for renovation was the 53-room Lodge, one of the first Club Med destinations in the United States when it first opened back in the 1960s. Today the newly upgraded and renovated Lodge is once again an important draw for the small mountain community,

Bear Valley Lodge's Cathedral Lounge.

Mariani Development Corporation

It's been nearly 100 years since Paul Mariani, Sr., immigrated to the United States from his native Yugoslavia. Possessing only a third–grade education, but filled with a drive to succeed, he worked hard, acquired land, and—with the help of his children, and eventually his grandchildren—built one of the best-known fruit-growing operations in the then-agricultural Santa Clara Valley.

Today the Santa Clara Valley is better known as Silicon Valley, and high technology has re-

placed agriculture as the region's number one industry. But the name "Mariani" continues to stand for quality, and the Mariani Development Corporation continues to contribute significantly to the health and growth of Santa Clara County.

Mariani Development Corporation is a real estate–oriented investment and development concern. Headquartered in Los Altos, the firm is involved in all aspects of the real estate business, including acquisition, finance, development, leasing, and project management.

Developing exclusively for its own account, the firm has been involved in projects that include commercial, office, industrial, residential, R&D, warehouse, and manufacturing space throughout Silicon Valley. The firm strongly emphasizes research and development projects for local high–tech industries.

The firm's development team is headed by David W. Mariani, longtime Santa Clara County resident and grandson of Paul Mariani, Sr. Of his family's move from farming into real estate development, Mariani says: "There came a point in the evolution of this valley when the value of the land exceeded its agricultural value. That's when we stopped cultivating the soil and started cultivating clients, stopped raising trees and started raising buildings."

Above: Tenants enjoy a prestigious, centrally located corporate environment at Mariani's International Technology Center.

Right: Portofino Villas in Cupertino, a Mariani residential development, offers a high quality of life in a central location.

Mariani's Main Street Financial Center in Los Altos combines a gracious working atmosphere with convenient access to Santa Clara County communities.

The story of the Mariani family is one of the Santa Clara Valley's most prominent success stories. The family settled in the Cupertino area during the early 1900s. Though the area was mostly a grape-growing region in the early part of the century, disease ravaged the plants and farmers switched to prunes.

Paul Mariani, Sr., began growing prunes on his four-acre farm in 1924. As his fruit business prospered he acquired additional land, eventually accumulating thousands of acres.

The next generation of Marianis expanded the family operation into food processing. Paul Mariani, Jr., is credited with marketing the country's first ready-to-eat dried fruit. He also took the family's agricultural business overseas, establishing farms in Australia. And he is noted for establishing the Foreign Trade Zone, a duty-free zone in San Jose.

A well-respected and active member of the local community and a devout Catholic, Mariani was honored by the Pope for his contributions to the church.

When Paul Mariani, Jr., died in 1979, the Mariani family's assets were divided among his children. But the family continues to work closely together in the family partnership. In addition to real estate development, the Mariani Group of Companies maintains interests in agriculture, agribusiness, finance, and banking.

Though Mariani agricultural products eventually became brand-name leaders nationally, by the early 1970s the bountiful orchards the family had accumulated became even more valuable to Silicon Valley's booming electronics industry.

At that time the Mariani family relocated its orchards and turned its direction toward developing its land into major urban communities. With the goal of creating excellent environments for businesses, the Marianis created some of Santa Clara Valley's most prestigious addresses.

Located in San Jose, Mariani Development's International Business Park is a 375-acre research and development/office park. The park's tenants include Becton-Dickinson, Ricoh, IBM, Xerox, Seeq Technology, VLSI Technology, Toys R Us, Castle and Cooke, Inc., and Olympus.

But probably the firm's most famous development is Apple Computer's 100,000-square-foot world headquarters office building in Cupertino.

Other Mariani Development projects include residential developments totaling approximately 1,500 units in various projects in the Bay Area, the Sacramento metropolitan area, and Aspen, Colorado; retail developments in Cupertino; and development, management, and lease-up of more than 1.5 million square feet of research and development, office, and manufacturing space throughout Silicon Valley.

Acme Building Maintenance Company, Inc.

Imagine having to clean a room that's getting the white glove test right afterward. Now imagine cleaning a room in which a skilled technician will be taking an airborne particle reading right afterward—a room already so clean the "dirt" is invisible to the human eye!

Such exacting standards may drive the average janitorial service to hang up its feather dusters, but for Acme Building Maintenance Company, Inc., cleaning high-tech clean rooms is all in a day's work.

Acme Building Maintenance is one of the leading building maintenance companies in Santa Clara County and the largest clean-room maintenance specialist in Silicon Valley.

Independently owned and operated, Acme was founded in 1970 by its current president, San Jose native Henry Sanchez. Some years earlier, Sanchez had joined with a partner to erect a med-

ical office building on the site of a gas station he owned across the street from San Jose Hospital. Sanchez initially served as the leasing manager for the enterprise. As the one responsible for the building's maintenance, he hired the custodial firms that cleaned it. After a few years, Sanchez decided he could do a better job himself than the firms he was hiring. So he sold his interest in the office building and started his own building maintenance company.

In the beginning, Acme Building Maintenance was a one-man operation, selling one-day cleanups. The company later expanded into warehouse and industrial work and eventually began hiring a staff. Soon the company began to land larger contracts, including IBM in San Jose and Stanford University in Palo Alto.

With some 4.5 million square feet of academic space and another 500,000 square feet of student housing, Stanford University was the young building maintenance company's largest contract to date—and a formidable challenge. But Acme met that challenge, and it is testimony to the quality of the company's work that 20 years later Acme is still serving Stanford's building maintenance needs.

Today, under the management of the founder's son, Rick Sanchez, and with more than 600 employees, Acme Building Maintenance is responsible for approximately 24 million square feet of offices, warehouses, and manufacturing space. The company maintains four offices: its company headquarters in Santa Clara (Alviso); a special Palo Alto office on the campus of Stanford University; and two new offices, one in the East Bay and another in Sacramento.

Acme serves a diverse group of clients, large and small, throughout Silicon Valley and the Bay Area. In addition to Stanford University, Acme's client list includes Advanced Micro Devices, Sun Microsystems, Rolm Corporation, Amdahl, San Jose State University, LSI Logic, and Cypress Semiconductor.

Manufacturing facilities account for nearly half of the company's contracts, with colleges and universities constituting about 5 million square feet. The company also cleans about 6 million square feet of administration space (offices) and around 4 million square feet of warehouse and industrial sites.

One reason Acme has been so successful with such a broad spectrum of clients is that the company does more than simply supply janitors. Acme manages each job individually, allocating personnel and resources using computer software and a

data base developed specifically for the building maintenance company. This software enhances Acme's ability to manage large jobs, invoice accurately, and track individual employee performance.

And for its very large contracts (anything more than a 500,000 square feet) Acme installs a permanent, on-site manager who uses the company's customized software and data base to accommodate special requests and clients' changing needs.

Some of the most striking changes in the needs of Acme clients have accompanied the evolution of Silicon Valley and its high-tech environs—the so-called "clean rooms"—where much more is needed than typical janitorial services.

Acme first began marketing its services to Silicon Valley's emerging high-tech companies during the early 1980s. As these companies grew, so did their needs for more sophisticated building maintenance services. And as their needs became more sophisticated, so did Acme's services.

Acme is currently Silicon Valley's largest clean room maintenance specialist. Its staff of trained clean-room custodians has many hours of experience working in a variety of high-tech facilities, including biotechnology and pharmaceutical firms that must conform to rigid FDA requirements.

To train its clean room custodians for this highly specialized work, Acme maintains a training facility at its Alviso offices. This facility provides both videotape and hands-on training in the identification of hazardous chemicals and the use of special types of equipment to filter out dirt invisible to the human eye. All Acme clean-room custodians are carefully supervised on the job by experienced personnel until they are tested and certified for clean-room work.

Clean-room work is particularly challenging because in Silicon Valley these facilities are often in continuous operation. With two and three clean room shifts a day, this often means service around the clock.

As the trend toward miniaturization of high-tech equipment continues, an increasing number of Silicon Valley companies are demanding tighter and tighter controls on their clean-room environments. Some have even constructed submicron clean rooms where the standard of allowable contamination is less than one particle per cubic yard of air.

Acme Building Maintenance Company, Inc., is prepared to meet the increasingly rigid standards of its high-tech clients. Acme has set the standard of performance by which the rest of its industry is measured, and it will continue to maintain that standard for all of its clients.

Above and facing page: Acme Building Maintenance cleans millions of square feet per day, including multi-tenant (high-rise), academic, and manufacturing facilities.

Therma, Inc.

Therma, Inc., has been called the "ultimate family company." With its husband and wife management team, its casual corporate culture, and its company dog (a Yorkshire terrier named Basil) scurrying freely through its hallways and workshops, the company probably deserves that reputation.

But this is hardly a mom-and-pop operation. In fact, Therma is the largest mechanical contactor in Santa Clara County and one of the largest in the Bay Area. The firm consistently wins major contracts throughout Northern California and has even been commissioned by overseas companies in Ireland, Italy, Korea, Singapore, and Taiwan.

Therma's primary customers are industrial users of mechanical contracting services. The company specializes in the design, installation, and servicing of such mechanical systems as air conditioning, process piping, plumbing, refrigeration, special exhaust systems, clean rooms, acid neutralization, energy conservation, and controls.

Founded in 1967, the company's original customers were the young semiconductor and computer manufacturers of Silicon Valley's emerging high technology industries. In fact, Therma has worked on more electronics and semiconductor plants than any other mechanical contractor in the nation. Today the company still installs mechanical systems for the area's leading semiconductor, electronics, biotechnology, and pharmaceutical companies.

Therma also works with the area's largest real estate developers. It is estimated that Therma has installed more than 30 percent of all commercial/industrial air conditioning systems in Santa Clara County.

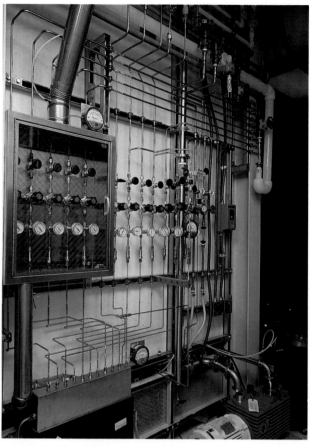

Company president Joe Parisi started the firm in San Jose with his wife, Nicki Parisi. Parisi originally set out to become an electrical engineer, but he switched his studies at San Jose State University after working one summer with a mechanical engineering company. He later worked at Fereday Mechanical as a minor partner, before striking out on his own.

Nicki Parisi is Therma's chief financial officer. Born in Idaho, she grew up in the construction industry. Her grandfather was a local plumbing contractor, and her father owned a mechanical contracting business. She learned about the construction industry as a young girl, going to job sites with her father and later working in his office.

The Parisis have managed their company together since its founding. Joe oversees Therma's sales and manufacturing operations; Nicki manages the firm's finances.

"The reason it has worked so well," says Nicki, "is that we started off small and Joe and I were able to establish our territories—our individual areas of responsibility—early. And as the business has grown, we have each stuck to those responsibilities."

"And besides that," says Joe, "we've always liked working together."

In its early days, Therma catered to the special needs of the valley's emerging high-tech companies, taking on a wide variety of contracting assignments for those firms.

"During our first six months in business," Joe recalls, "we took on all kinds of odd jobs just to make ends meet. We were electrical contractors, sprinkler contractors—anything anybody needed, we jumped in and tried to give it to them."

By working with these young high-tech firms as they evolved, Therma developed special expertise in designing and installing some of the most essential elements of semiconductor manufacturing, such as exotic gas piping, fume exhaust, and acid neutralization systems.

"We even made wet stations (chemical sinks) for those companies for awhile," Joe says. "The industry was very young, and there just weren't enough people making the equipment those new companies needed back then."

At that time Therma also manufactured clean benches and other clean-room accessories, eventually developing a separate company, Modulair, which manufactures clean-room modules. That company was sold in 1985, but still works closely with Therma on many of its contracts.

Therma's first offices were located on Burger Drive in San Jose, and those cramped quarters are legendary among company old-timers (of which there are many). They were so small, one story goes, that, as the company grew and more equipment and personnel were jammed into the space, Joe Parisi's drawing table gradually shrank—courtesy of the company power saw.

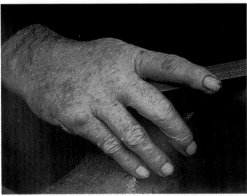

"One day I came back from a sales call," Joe remembers, "and my desk was standing out in the parking lot with a phone on it. That was when I knew it was time to move."

The Parisis soon moved their growing company from its original 4,000-square-foot offices into a much larger 60,000-square-foot facility a few blocks away.

"We decided it would be more fun not to tell the employees about it," says Nicki. "We just moved everything over on Thanksgiving weekend, and when the employees reported for work on Monday, they found a note on the door with maps to the new building."

Today Therma occupies an 87,000-square-foot facility on Ringwood Avenue in San Jose. The facility includes the most modern sheet metal shop in Northern California, where spiral and rectangular duct work is manufactured on automated equipment; a prefabricated piping facility; the most extensive clean-room trailers in the in-

Joe and Nicki Parisi have managed Therma, Inc., since its founding.

dustry for on-site fabrication; and a modern garage for servicing all of the company's 280 vehicles.

Over the years Therma has devised a number of systems and processes that have become high-tech manufacturing standards. Innovations such as the company's first fume scrubbers, acid neutralization systems, and double-contained pipes (for exotic gases) were quickly adopted by early computer manufacturing operations.

The company is also responsible for a number of "firsts." Long involved in energy conservation, Therma was one of the first mechanical contractors to design an air conditioning system for a large building complex that used variable speed motors—an innovation widely employed today that conserves energy and saves money.

More recently, Therma was instrumental in helping the Stanford University Medical School develop an innovative new design for its cadaver dissection tables. The new tables (which Therma is also manufacturing in its sheet metal shop) have individual venting systems that exhaust the formaldehyde fumes that have plagued anatomy students for decades.

"We feel that one of the keys to our success," says Nicki, "has been our unwillingness to limit ourselves and our willingness to recognize a need, wherever we might find it."

Another key to Therma's success is its employees. The company employs some 400 union plumbers, steamfitters, air conditioning mechanics, and sheet-metal workers. And, since Therma designs most of the mechanical systems it installs, the firm also has a 100-member professional staff that includes mechanical engineers, computer-aided design specialists, and systems analysts.

"We have some of the brightest engineers around," says Joe. "We have to design and build clean rooms to increasingly lower tolerances as the electronics industry develops increasingly higher standards. We wouldn't be able to do it without those people."

Therma has always utilized technology to serve its customers, investing more heavily than most mechanical contracting firms in the most modern equipment for its work force. All of Therma's engineers and drafters have access to state-of-the-art computer-aided design systems. And the firm's professional staff is accustomed to interfacing with architects and owners to develop the most practical and cost-effective designs.

"We are very proud of our facilities and equipment," says Joe Parisi, "But we're proudest of our people. We have a coordinated staff of dedicated and loyal employees that has made a major contribution to the growth of this company. It sounds cliche, but they are our most important asset."

Therma has one of the lowest turnover rates in the business. Some of the its employees have actually been with the company since it was

Therma boasts the most modern sheet metal shop in Northern California.

founded. Others have stayed on board until retirement.

"We have a different management strategy," says Joe. "I just don't like that old corporate system of layers of management between me and my employees. I want to have access to them, and I want them to have access to me."

"And we allow people a lot of freedom," says Nicki. "We don't believe in hand holding, and we encourage them to solve their own problems—and they do. They are incredibly creative people. We believe this is a management style that brings out the best in people."

And it's a style to which the company's workers have enthusiastically responded. Therma's employees work long and hard—often giving up their weekends—to make sure the firm's customers are able to keep operating no matter what the circumstances. This dedication was particularly evident in the aftermath of the October 17, 1989, Loma Prieta earthquake. Following that disaster, Therma employees rushed to repair broken pipes and failed systems, working a total of about 5,000 hours of overtime to get Therma's customers back on-line—even though many of them had major quake damage in their own homes that had to wait.

Therma makes a point of taking care of its most important asset, its people. The firm employs a full-time, on-site nurse, who is in charge of the company safety program and a company exercise program. She also administers to minor injuries, and, when a Therma worker is injured on the job seriously enough to require the attention of a physician, she smooths the way to the hospital by calling ahead and making the arrangements.

And, since the company employs staggered shifts to keep its facilities staffed 12 hours a day, Therma also has an in-house restaurant that serves both breakfast and lunch.

Therma also takes care of its customers. The company is unique in that, unlike some successful contractors who seem to eventually outgrow certain clients, Therma continues to accept smaller contracts. In fact, its contracts range from $50 to $15 million.

"We still feel like a little contractor," says Joe. "And I'd like to continue to operate this company like a small company. It's the best way I know to give our customers good service. And you just never know where those small contracts will lead. Our customers, many of whom have become the biggest players in this valley, were just little guys when they started out. But we gave them good service and they stuck with us."

If there is a real key to the success of Therma, it can probably be found in the company's relationship with its customers. The company's early business relationships, developed over nearly a quarter-century, are what have really built the company into what it is today.

The Parisis are actively involved in both their industry and their community. Joe Parisi is the current president of the Santa Clara Valley Contractors Association and a past president of the local Sheet Metal Contractors National Association. He continues to work with others in his industry to improve relations between unions and management.

Nicki Parisi works with the Contractors Legislative Committee, a voice for her industry in the state legislature, and she served on the council of the San Jose Ballet.

Devcon Construction, Inc.

Devcon's partners (from left), Gary Filizetti, Barry L. Ludwig, and Barry C.L. Fernald.

When Devcon Construction was founded in 1976, the idea of teaming an architect and a contractor under one roof—creating the so-called "design/build" contractor—was still a new one to the Santa Clara Valley construction industry—anywhere for that matter. But that combination proved to be a successful one for the company's founders, and today Devcon Construction, Inc., is one of the largest and most consistently successful construction and development firms in the Bay Area.

Devcon Construction is a full-service commercial contractor based in Milpitas, California. Since its founding, Devcon has completed more than 25 million square feet of industrial, research-and-development, and office construction. Devcon's projects include entire industrial parks, multiple office complexes, hotels, mid-rise office buildings, single structure research-and-development facilities, and light industrial buildings. The firm has developed projects in communities throughout California, with a concentration in the greater San Fransisco Bay area.

Among Devcon's more notable local projects are the San Jose Jet Center, a 200,000-square-foot private aviation facility, the San Francisco 49ers Santa Clara headquarters, and the Silicon Valley Capital Club, occupying the entire top floor of the 17-story Fairmont Plaza in San Jose.

Devcon's design/build staff of architects, interior designers, and construction professionals give clients an important edge in the creation of successful building projects. They work as a team throughout a project, coordinating the total development package—controlling time, design, and cost.

But Devcon Construction goes above and beyond the responsibilities of the typical contractor. To ensure that its clients are happy and that the project at hand is built with the highest-quality materials and workmanship, Devcon's construc-

Failure Analysis Associates, Menlo Park, California.

tion professionals are involved from each project's earliest stages.

Devcon is constantly striving to exceed its clients' expectations, as well as its own high standards. To accomplish this, the company's dedicated and experienced professionals do something that is all too rare in business today: they listen to their clients. Clients of Devcon Construction know that they are being heard, that their concerns are being addressed, and that their needs are being met.

And they know that Devcon Construction is with them for the long haul. Just because a particular project has reached completion doesn't mean Devcon's relationship with that project and that client is over. In fact, Devcon treats all its clients as clients for life, and many of the company's ongoing client relationships have existed almost as long as Devcon has been in business.

Since Devcon Construction has grown with many of the high-tech companies of Silicon Valley, it's not surprising that, in addition to its other activities, the firm has developed a specialty in high-technology construction. Devcon builds clean rooms, medical laboratories, radio frequency test rooms, and other ultra-technical and sensitive environments to extremely high standards. As those standards become increasingly more stringent—as the clean rooms become cleaner—Devcon's expertise in this area grows. The more specialized and difficult the project, the more Devcon meets the challenge.

In its early years Devcon was known mainly as a developer of its own projects, with less emphasis on contracting for clients. Today, however, the company's emphasis is largely on providing construction services for corporate clients and developers.

Devcon's own development experience still proves to be invaluable to its clients. The firm is much more in tune with the problems an owner faces than most construction companies. Developing its own projects gives Devcon an opportunity to experiment with new ideas, products,

and materials, providing the firm with knowledge and experience it can then apply to its clients' projects.

Devcon is also in a unique position as a developer to gain experience and to monitor building trends throughout its substantial design and construction work for "owner/user" developer clients. One such trend, due largely to the increase in local land prices, is the construction of R&D buildings with multiple stories, or "vertical construction."

In addition to the trend of vertical construction, there is a movement in the Santa Clara Valley to upgrade the architectural element of industrial structures. Not only does Devcon support this movement toward producing higher-quality industrial buildings, but the firm is also behind the trend toward development of more multifunction buildings, which will allow growth-oriented companies the flexibility to change entire work areas simply and quickly as the need arises.

Devcon Construction has been ranked by the San Jose Business Journal as the largest commercial contractor in Santa Clara County and one of the area's largest privately held companies. The firm is also included among *Engineering News Record* magazine's (a construction–industry trade publication) top 400 construction companies in the United States.

Devcon Construction, Inc., is managed by three principals who maintain a close and constant involvement with the firm's clients. Gary Filizetti is president of the company. A graduate of Santa Clara University, Filizetti oversees all aspects of Devcon's construction activities. Architect Barry C.L. Fernald is the firm's senior vice president. He is a graduate of the University of California at Berkeley and heads Devcon's development and asset management department. Barry L. Ludwig, also an architect, is Devcon's vice president/secretary and a graduate of the University of Oregon. He heads the firm's architectural department.

Fernald and Ludwig are members of the American Institute of Architects, and both have served as directors of that organization's Santa Clara Valley chapter. Devcon Construction is a member of the National Association of Industrial and Office Parks.

Devcon is also a longtime supporter of local cultural organizations and activities, including the San Jose Museum of Art, the Children's Discovery Museum, and the San Jose symphony, civic light opera, and ballet.

In addition, Devcon Construction, Inc., supports a number of community service groups, including the Timpany Center, the Crippled Children's Society, the Christian Youth Organization, and the March of Dimes.

Santa Clara County Department of Social Services, San Jose, California.

SASCO/Valley Electric Company

Above: SASCO has completed the electrical installations on numerous hotels in the Bay Area, including the Doubletree Hotel in Santa Clara.

Right: Rincon Towers in San Francisco, a SASCO/Valley Electric Company project.

Few firms can match SASCO/Valley Electric Company's long history of service to the communities of Santa Clara County. For more than 75 years this full-service electrical contractor has played a key role in the growth and development of the region.

By reputation one of the area's finest firms, SASCO/Valley Electric is one of the oldest electrical contracting firms in California. Founded locally under the name Valley Electric, the company has been operating continuously since 1914. Valley Electric joined the SASCO organization in 1983 and now operates as a division of that corporation.

SASCO Electric Corp. is one of the largest electrical contractors in the United States. *Engineering News Record*, a leading professional trade publication, ranked SASCO Electric Corp. fifth in the nation for 1990. Headquartered in Cerritos, SASCO Electric is a well-known and respected regional contractor, serving clients primarily on the West Coast. The firm also maintains offices in Newbury Park, Newport Beach, Mountain View, and Hayward.

The corporation's operating entities are organized into groups with special expertise in different areas. These include tenant-improvement, industrial,

high-rise, hotel, commercial, service, and special projects. This type of organizational structure has created an entrepreneurial environment which encourages individual achievement within the context of group accomplishment. This effectively combines the advantages of a large company with the drive and intensity of a small company. The operating groups are supported by various corporate departments including engineering, estimating, purchasing, and cost-accounting, ensuring clients the best in service and responsiveness.

SASCO's annual sales exceed $120 million and the company's single-project bonding capacity exceeds $20 million.

SASCO/Valley Electric is headquartered in Mountain View and focuses on commercial light industrial, high-rise, hotel, and multifamily residential projects. Its services range from 24-hour emergency service to multimillion-dollar projects.

The division serves clients throughout the Greater Bay Area, including the counties of Santa Clara, San Mateo, San Francisco, Alameda, Marin, Contra Costa, Santa Cruz, and Monterey. It has also completed major projects in the Sacra-

Left: The Kodak Center is among the projects SASCO/Valley Electric Company has completed in San Jose.

Below: SASCO serves the highly specialized needs of computer companies, such as Apple Computers in Cupertino.

mento area, the San Joaquin Valley, and northern Nevada.

SASCO/Valley's headquarters comprises 45,000 square feet of office and warehouse space on 2.5 acres. Annual sales average approximately $50 million, which would put the division itself among the top electrical contractors in the nation.

SASCO/Valley has completed the electrical installations on numerous major projects in the Bay Area. Completed hotels include the Hyatt Regency in Burlingame, Hotel Sofitel in Redwood City, Doubletree Hotel in Santa Clara, and the Inn at Spanish Bay in Monterey. Major malls include Valley Fair in San Jose and Stanford Shopping Center in Palo Alto. Special projects include the relighting of the Palace of Fine Arts in San Francisco and the renovation of St. Joseph's Cathedral in San Jose.

The division also serves the highly specialized needs of the computer and semiconductor industries. In fact, its client list reads like a "Who's Who" of Silicon Valley's high-tech companies. It includes such major firms as Hewlett-Packard, Apple Computer, IGBM, Sun Microsystems, Intel, NEC, Ask Computers, AMD, and National Semiconductor, among others. Major developer clients include Sobrato Development Cos., Peery-Arrilliaga, and McDandless Development.

SASCO/Valley has installed the electrical systems for two sub-micron clean room facilities for Intel and AMD and is currently completing a third for NEC. These ultraclean environments are an integral part in the production of silicon computer chips.

SASCO has lead the way in the design/build movement which puts a much wider range of contracting services under one roof. Today, with

its professional engineering staff and CAD (computer aided design) capabilities, the company has gone a step further, becoming an "engineer/construct" contractor. This approach provides clients with projects engineered from a value-management perspective.

SASCO/Valley is committed to giving something back to the communities in which it has been so successful. The company actively supports United Way, the YMCA, and Stanford University Children's Hospital, among others. The company is also a member of various local chambers of commerce.

With almost a century of experience, SASCO/Valley Electric has the facilities, personnel, and expertise to provide for its clients' total electrical contracting needs, from design and engineering to installation and maintenance.

In the future, SASCO/Valley Electric Company will continue its commitment to excellence and innovation based on fairness, integrity, trust, and cooperation—principles that have been the key to its success and that serve its customers best.

The Synergism Group of Companies

When Eugene A. Ravizza founded Cupertino Electric in Sunnyvale back in 1954, he had no idea his young electrical contracting company would one day evolve into a group of complementary, but independent, firms. Today each of the electrical construction and consultation firms within the Synergism Group of Companies is a recognized leader in its field.

CUPERTINO ELECTRIC

Cupertino Electric is one of Santa Clara County's oldest full-service, design/build electrical contracting firms. The company was incorporated under its present name in 1958 and has enjoyed steady growth throughout its history. A longtime industry leader, the company has grown into a multimillion-dollar concern with branch operations in San Francisco and Sacramento. A former branch now operates as a separate corporation in Boulder, Colorado. The company continues to take on negotiated work and consistently wins competitively bid contracts throughout the West.

Locally, Cupertino Electric is headquartered at its 15,000-square-foot facility in Sunnyvale, where it employs a staff of 60 in administration, sales, and engineering. The company maintains a field staff of around 310 craftspersons. And the company's 10,000-square-foot support center in South San Jose is staffed by some 11 experienced mechanics and warehouse people.

Cupertino Electric grew up with Silicon Valley, designing and constructing electrical systems for more high-technology companies than any other electrical contractor in the area. A roster of the firm's clients reads like a Who's Who of high tech. Hewlett-Packard, Amdahl, Apple Computer, IBM, Intel, United Technologies Corporation, National Semiconductor, and Lockheed, to name just a few, have all contracted with Cupertino Electric for projects ranging from office complexes to the most sophisticated, high-tech manufacturing facilities.

Though electronics and computer companies continue to comprise one of Cupertino Electric's most important markets, the firm has also designed and built electrical systems for a wide range of clients in other industries. A list of the firm's more notable projects includes, among others, the Fairmont Hotel in downtown San Jose; the Santa Clara Convention Center; and Stanford University's New Children's Hospital, its Beckman Center of Molecular and Genetic Medicine, and its on-campus semiconductor research facility, The Center for Integrated Systems.

Right: An electrician makes the final adjustment to a 480-volt switchboard in a large semiconductor plant wired by Cupertino Electric. Photo by Fred Matthes

Cupertino Electric, Cascade Controls, and Ceitronics provided the turnkey automation, security, CCTv, and fire alarm systems for the San Jose Convention Center.

Recently Cupertino Electric completed statewide installation of Bank of America's Customer Online Information Network. And the company has been involved in several water and waste treatment projects throughout the Santa Clara Valley.

Cupertino Electric was one of the first electrical contractors in the county to utilize computers. In fact, the company has been computerized since the early 1960s. The firm's in-house computerized cost accounting system expedites weekly and monthly job control information; accounts payable; accounts receivable; payroll; financial reporting; and estimating, as well as all state, federal, and union reporting. This system speeds production and assures Cupertino Electric's customers of quality control and the lowest cost.

The company's computer facilities also give its engineers access to state-of-the-art, fully integrated computer-aided design systems. Using local- and wide-area networks, the company employs modern telecommunications technology to communicate electronically to all job sites. This technology allows Cupertino Electric to implement quick changes and engineering modifications which keep the job moving forward.

Electrical contractors of the future are going to continue to need well-trained people—"smart" workers who understand and use modern computer technology. Cupertino Electric recognizes this need and continues to emphasize employee training on its advanced computer systems. The company offers both in-house and off-site programs for its employees, as well as the electrical industry's extensive apprenticeship training for journeyman and foreman electricians.

Cupertino Electric has a history of keeping good employees and maintains one of the lowest turnover rates in its industry. In addition to a rich benefit plan that includes medical, dental, long-term disability and life insurance, the company offers its workers specialized training and a profit-sharing program which has been in place since 1964.

A well-trained staff of dedicated employees is one of the keys to the success of Cupertino Electric. Another is its strong customer base. Many of the company's clients have been doing business continuously with the firm since its founding, and the company's growth has been primarily a function of its customers' needs.

For example, the firm's Colorado company was first established as a branch office in 1978 to better serve a major Santa Clara Valley electronics manufacturer which had needs in that area. That branch office (originally opened in Longmont,

Above: The Center for Molecular and Genetic Medicine at Stanford University's School of Medicine is one of many buildings on the campus that have been wired by Cupertino Electric. Photo by Fred Matthes

Left: An electrician for Cupertino Electric completes the installation of a large emergency generator in a typical Silicon Valley plant. Photo by Fred Matthes

Colorado) is now a separate corporation headquartered in Boulder. It employs some 40 electricians and six office employees.

In 1989 the company acquired Collins Electric of San Francisco to better serve its clients in that city. The 27-year-old company continues to operate under the Collins name as a branch of Cupertino Electric.

Early in 1990 the company established its first branch office in Sacramento (called Cupertino Electric of Sacramento) to serve its customers in that area.

In addition to branching out to serve the San Francisco and Sacramento markets, Cupertino Electric has proven its geographic versatility by the successful completion of projects in Oregon, Arizona, and Nevada. As the firm's customer base

The building automation system for this advanced bipolar semiconductor fabrication facility in Chandler, Arizona, was recently completed by Cascade Controls and Cupertino Electric, Inc. The Rosemount DCS controls the central utility plant, HVAC and hydronic systems, and acid neutralization systems on this site.

continues its steady growth, it is expected that those geographic boundaries will expand even further in the future.

Cupertino Electric is also actively involved in community service and business organizations. The company has a strong commitment to the local community and has long emphasized "giving something back" to the area in which it has prospered. Through the Cupertino Electric Charitable Trust the company makes regular contributions to local charitable organizations.

But the firm gives more than money. For example, after the 1989 Loma Prieta earthquake, Cupertino Electric rewired the damaged Ben Lomond Boy Scout Camp, furnishing materials and electricians for the job. And the company and its employees also contributed $100,000 to the American Red Cross Earthquake fund.

Cupertino Electric continues to operate as an independent member of the Synergism Group of Companies.

An electrician for Cupertino Electric, Inc., works on the 21,000-volt main service panel of a large pharmaceutical plant installation in Santa Clara County. Cupertino Electric was the electrical contractor for this new facility.
Photo by Fred Matthes

CASCADE CONTROLS

Cascade Controls, Inc., is one of the newest members of the Synergism Group of Companies. Formed in 1986, Cascade is an instrumentation and control contractor which provides sales, engineering, software configuration, design, and construction of Distributed Control Systems (DCSs).

DCSs are computerized systems which can be programmed to automatically control or "manage" a wide range of processes and environments—from the temperature, pressure, flow, and level of materials in a refinery to the lighting, heating, and air conditioning in an office building.

Cascade Controls is the exclusive distributor in five Western states for Rosemount, one of the world's leading DCS manufacturers. The Rosemount system is the only industrial grade DCS offered by a major process control and instrumentation company with software specifically developed for the control and optimization of building mechanical and electrical systems.

This highly sophisticated system is most useful in facilities which require tremendously exacting

levels of HVAC control, such as semiconductor "fabs" where component assembly would be impossible without very tight temperature, humidity, and pressure regulation. The system is also applied to the fabs' large, central utility plants, wastewater treatment processes, and is used extensively in toxic gas and chemical monitoring.

In addition to offering process and environmental controls and management, this system creates an on-line data base which gives facilities managers often critical information through operations such as production metering and energy consumption monitoring.

Cascade Controls was the first process control and instrumentation contractor to offer an industrial grade system to the facilities marketplace. Since its founding in 1986 by Raymond Pfeifer, Cascade has grown steadily to become a multimillion-dollar company with a proven track record in its industry. The company has completed design/build facilities automation projects ranging from Class 1 through 1000 semiconductor and bio-genetic fabrication plants, laboratories and research animal facilities, to high-rise office buildings, hospitals, and convention centers.

The company has designed and installed systems for a number of well-known local companies. The firm set up a campus-wide, HVAC (heating, ventilation, and air conditioning) control and monitoring system for more than 75 Stanford University research, classroom, and hospital buildings. It designed and built a system for a Fujitsu Microelectronics chip fabrication facility in Gresham, Oregon, which included utilities, HVAC, acid and HF neutralization, leak detection, toxic gas monitoring and shutdown control, and fire alarm. It provided the DCS system for 115,000 square feet of Class 1000 and Class 100 clean rooms for Lawrence Livermore Laboratories.

Cascade also installed a utilities and HVAC system control, security/life safety monitoring, and fire protection control system in the 400,000-square-foot San Jose Convention Center and parking garage.

Cascade recently completed work on one of its largest projects, Motorola's Advanced Technology Center in Chandler, Arizona. The firm designed and installed control systems for all of that facility's utilities, mechanical, and waste treatment processes.

Cascade Controls, Inc., has proven experience and the professional, financial, insurance, and bonding resources necessary to perform complex, multimillion-dollar controls projects.

SYNERGISM

Synergism, Inc., was established in 1985 as a non-operating holding company which provides the financial support (including banking and bonding needs) to its operating companies. Cupertino Electric founder Gene Ravizza now serves as chairman of the Synergism Group of Companies.

In addition to Cupertino Electric and Cascade Controls, the Synergism Group of Companies includes three other firms: DMA Associates, Ceitronics, and A-D Controls.

DMA Associates was founded in 1962 and was acquired by Cupertino Electric in 1982. DMA provides engineering consulting services for the Synergism Group.

The firm also has expertise in horizontal and vertical power distribution systems (up to and including 20,800 volts), emergency power and energy management systems, sound systems, telephone systems, fire detection, silent and audible alarm systems, security and access systems, and electrical systems for high-tech fabrication.

The firm employs 28 engineers, designers, and draftspersons, and maintains an office in San Jose.

Ceitronics was formed in January 1985 to help the Synergism Group better serve its customers' low voltage and data communications requirements. The firm's principal business is electronic systems contracting, including industrial and commercial application of data and telephone system networks, audio and video systems, fire/life safety and intrusion systems, and electronic transmission systems.

Ceitronics has completed work for many of Silicon Valley's major corporations, including, among others, Hewlett-Packard, IBM, Amdahl, Kaiser Hospital, Bank of America, Lockheed, the Fairmont Hotel, and the City of San Jose.

Synergism's most recent addition is A-D Controls, Inc. Located in Santa Clara, the 21-year-old company is a custom systems integrator for the automation and process control industries.

A-D Controls manufactures control panels which utilize control components such as relays, programmable controllers, single-loop controllers, and other types of panel instrumentation.

The company employs a staff of programmers experienced with a wide range of programmable controllers and SCADA systems. They also develop custom systems as well as configure software packages.

A-D Controls provides complete systems engineering and selection of field instruments for flow, temperature, pressure, level, turbidity, and many other process variables. And the company provides field start-up assistance for all the systems it sells.

Because of the support provided by Synergism, each of these companies is uniquely free to concentrate on its customers' needs. Individually, the firms that make up the Synergism Group of Companies continue to maintain leadership positions in electrical contracting and consulting. As a team, they deliver the best value in the industry.

The Raisch Company

The basic technology of road building has not changed all that much since the days of the Roman Empire. Heavy machinery is now used to move and arrange materials and laser beams now hold grades to pin–point accuracy, but even the most modern road is still made mostly of rock and sweat.

The Raisch Company may not have been building roads as long at the Romans, but for five generations this Santa Clara County–based materials supplier has been keeping Northern Californians on the right track.

The Raisch name has been associated with the Northern California construction industry for well over a century. The company traces its beginnings back to the California gold rush when Gottfried Raisch, the son of a family of German stonemasons, immigrated to San Francisco and started a construction company that built cobblestone streets and installed wooden sewers in the booming city.

The elder Raisch's son, A.J. Raisch, eventually took over the company and followed in his father's footsteps as a road-building contractor, operating the company through the 1930s.

In the mid–1920s A.J. Raisch expanded his operation into the Santa Clara Valley, maintaining offices in both San Francisco and San Jose. Eventually the majority of the firm's business was being performed by its San Jose office.

After earning a master's degree from the Stanford University School of Business and completing a subsequent tour of duty as a U.S. Navy officer, A.J.'s son, A.G. "Bo" Raisch, began working for his father's San Jose organization. In 1966 he became the company's chief executive officer.

Throughout the 1960s the company continued to operate strictly as a road–building firm with supporting

quarry and asphalt concrete plant operations. In 1971 the company entered the ready–mixed concrete business, and the following year it expanded into bridge building, concrete roadway, and channel structures construction.

Today based in San Jose, Raisch is one of the leading construction materials suppliers in Santa Clara County. Bo Raisch's son, Bryan A. Raisch, is the company's current chief executive officer.

The firm operates two asphalt plants, one at the corner of highways 85 and 101 in Mountain View and one outside its Pullman Road offices in San Jose. The firm also operates the Azevido quarry in San Jose, where it manufactures essential aggregate subbases for road construction.

The Raisch Company manufactures and sells nearly 700,000 tons of asphalt and nearly a million tons of aggregate subbase materials each year. A significant portion of the company's products are manufactured from recycled materials. In fact, Raisch is one of the leading road–materials recyclers in Santa Clara County. The firm recycles both concrete and asphalt at its operation in San Jose, and it maintains a recycling operation at the Sunnyvale landfill. Producing approximately 200,000 tons of building materials per year, Raisch's recycling operations help to compensate for the local industry's current shortage of aggregate materials, while preserving the county's landfill sites.

In 1990 the Raisch Company joined with Grade–Way Construction to form Raisch Grade–Way Construction, based in the Stockton/Sacramento area. The new organization is a grading and roadway construction operation, working in both the private and public sectors.

O.C. McDonald Co., Inc.

In 1906 Orin Charles "O.C." McDonald started a one–man plumbing repair business that he operated while raising chickens at his Milpitas ranch. Though O.C. eventually got out of chicken ranching, the mechanical contracting company he founded and passed on to his son, Vic, has grown into a $22–million business and bears the distinction of being one of the oldest continuously operating firms in Santa Clara County.

Still a family–owned and –operated concern, O.C. McDonald Co., Inc., is currently run by O.C.'s grandson, Richard V. McDonald, and his great–grandson, James. V. McDonald.

O.C. McDonald specializes in commercial/industrial plumbing, process piping, heating, air–conditioning, and sheet metal projects. Re-

cently completed projects include the new truck paint facility at NUMMI; piping in the service tunnels below the Stanford University campus; the process and central plant piping at Syntex; the hydronic pumping, waste treatment, and comfort and process heating systems at Lockheed Missiles, Space & Company; and the ice cream piping for Dreyers Ice Cream in Union City. The company also installed the huge outlet conduit that was a vital part of the retrofitting of the Lexington and Stevens Creek dams.

O.C. McDonald has also completed work for El Camino Hospital, Ford Motor Company, General Electric, New United Motor Manufacturing Co., Hewlett–Packard, IBM, Intel, the Los Gatos School District, NASA, New United Motors, O'Connor Hospital, Pacific Gas & Electric, the U.S. Navy and Air Force, the cities of Milpitas, Santa Clara, Sunnyvale, Monterey, and San Jose, and the County of Santa Clara.

Most recently, O.C. McDonald has finished the plumbing and mechanical work on both the

hotel and the condominium complex at the Inn and Links at Spanish Bay near Monterey. The company's largest project to date was the installation of the industrial piping at the San Jose Sewage Treatment Plant.

Unlike most industrial mechanical contractors, O.C. McDonald continues to take on the small jobs—such as home faucet repair—with which it first started. The company operates a full–service retail parts department. And it maintains one of the last union repair service departments in the valley.

O.C. McDonald has moved only twice in its long history. The founder first moved the operation from his chicken ranch to a Santa Clara Street shop in San Jose in 1916. And in 1949 his son moved the company to its current location at 1150 West San Carlos.

In 1943 O.C. McDonald opened a temporary branch office in Fontana to do the mechanical work on Henry Kaiser's new steel plant. During that same period the company built metal lifeboats for the U.S. Navy to help with the war effort.

In 1949 O.C. McDonald installed one of the first air–conditioning systems in the valley for A. Hirsch & Sons in downtown San Jose. And it was the first company in the area to use mobile radios in its service trucks.

From its inception, O.C. McDonald has taken a progressive course to keep pace with growth and development in Santa Clara County. Today O.C. McDonald Co. consistently rates among the top 100 mechanical contractors in the United States.

Left: Performance testing bar and ductwork installed at the NUMMI in Fremont by O.C. McDonald Co.

Below: Equipment installation at Syntax Corp. in Palo Alto by O.C. McDonald Co. illustrates the complexity of modern process piping.

Rudolph and Sletten, Inc.

Visiting Silicon Valley and not encountering a building constructed by Rudolph and Sletten, Inc., is about as likely as coming to California and missing the sunshine. From the Retail Pavilion at the Silicon Valley Financial Center in San Jose to Hewlett–Packard's world corporate headquarters in Palo Alto to Santa Clara's Techmart to the Stanford Shopping Center Mall, Rudolph and Sletten has spent more than 30 years erecting some of the area's best–known and most important structures.

A privately held corporation with more than $350 million in projects under way and more than 600 employees, Rudolph and Sletten is easily one of the largest construction firms in the Bay Area. The company is ranked 42nd in the United States on the General Building Contractors List and was recently ranked 81st in the nation by *Engineering News Record* magazine.

The company was founded in 1960 by Onslow H. Rudolph, Jr., as O.H. Rudolph, Inc. Rudolph (better known to his colleagues as "Rudy") is chairman of the company's board of directors and a fourth–generation builder. During his youth he worked for various construction firms in his hometown of Pittsburgh, Pennsylvania. During World War II he served in the Army Corps of Engineers as company officer of a construction battalion.

After the war, Rudolph worked his way through engineering school at San Jose State University and graduated with a bachelor of science degree in civil engineering. Working with various general contracting firms in Northern California as

a project manager, he gained experience in civil, industrial, and commercial construction.

In 1962 Kenneth G. Sletten joined the firm, and Rudolph and Sletten, Inc., was formed.

Sletten, who is president of the firm, first became involved in construction while attending high school in the Midwest. During summers he worked on contruction jobs in Montana and Wyoming. In 1951 he graduated from the University of Colorado with a bachelor of science degree in civil engineering and was commissioned as a second lieutenant in the U.S. Marine Corps. He later served in engineering and shore party battalions at Camp Pendleton, California, and in Korea.

After the war Sletten went on to attend Stanford University Graduate School of Business, where he earned a master's degree in business administration in 1956. That same year he joined a Northern California general contracting firm, where he worked on large projects in all phases of construction as project engineer, superintendent, and project manager.

The goal of the company's founders was to build a quality–oriented construction organization. Ironically, they never intended to become the area's largest construction firm—only its best. "It doesn't cost any more to build it right the first time," was the company's motto. From the start they hired only the best people, provided them with the best possible training, and maintained the highest standards for every project.

The founders also realized that to maintain these high standards they were going to have to manage their own work. They knew that the early stages of a construction project—the structural excavation and the concrete and form work— were what really controlled the project's schedule and often its overall quality.

Thus, Rudolph and Sletten became a construction manager/general contractor—a contractor who controls a construction project from the ground up. Only in this way could the company deliver its clients the best possible product with the highest quality workmanship, on budget and on time.

Today the firm's work is so well known that 90 percent of its business is negotiated—that is, Rudolph and Sletten is selected by the developer, owner, or architect when the project is first conceived.

The tangible evidence of the quality of Rudolph and Sletten's work can be seen throughout the Santa Clara Valley. Among the firm's landmark buildings are Vallco Fashion Park in Cupertino; Xerox Corporation's research center;

Alza, Hewlett-Packard, and Syntex Corporation headquarters in Palo Alto; the Kodak leasing center and Rolm River Oaks Park in San Jose; Mc-Candless Towers, the Regency Plaza, and the Doubletree Hotel in Santa Clara; and Stanford University's Children's Hospital, Governor's Corner Student Housing, and Peter Coutts Hill Faculty Housing.

South Beach Marina Development, San Francisco.

The firm's list of clients also attests to the quality of its work. Rudolph and Sletten has undertaken construction projects for some of Silicon Valley's most important companies, including ACV Systems, Alza, Amdahl, Apple, ESL, Digital, GTE, Hewlett–Packard, IBM, Kaiser Permanente, Lockheed, Measurex, Raychem, Siliconix, Syntex, Tandem, and Varian.

Rudolph and Sletten's work is also well–known outside the Santa Clara Valley. Probably one of its best–known projects is the Monterey Bay Aquarium. This $40–million project, constructed on Monterey's Cannery Row, is one of the central coast's leading attractions, drawing thousands of visitors every year. For its work on this project, Rudolph and Sletten received an award of national excellence (chosen among 135 entries) from the American Concrete Institute

Arnold and Mabel Beckman Center for Molecular and Genetic Medicine, Stanford.

Governor's Corner Student Housing, Palo Alto.

and has been featured in *Architectural Record*, *Sunset*, *California Builder and Engineer*, and *Concrete International* magazines.

The Skywalker Ranch Technical Building in Marin County, though less well known to the general public, is one of the firm's more interesting projects. The $30–million, two–story movie studio for George Lucas' LucasFilm was designed and built to resemble a turn–of–the–century winery building.

Another conspicuous project, the Metro Center in Foster City, is the location of the firm's new home offices. The Metro Center is a 100–acre, master–planned corporate community that, when completed, will include 1.4 million square feet of office/research and development facilities, housing, shopping, dining, and entertainment complexes, and a five–star hotel. In addition to constructing two of the development's four–story office buildings, Rudolph and Sletten has built the project's centerpiece: the 22–story Metro Tower, which is the tallest building between Los Angeles and San Francisco. The firm currently occupies 30,000 square feet of office space at the site.

Also known for its expertise in the construction of high–technology facilities, Rudolph and Sletten is responsible for the $42–million Center for Molecular and Genetic Medicine at Stanford University, and the Advanced Micro Devices Sub Micron Facility in Sunnyvale, as well as labs and clean rooms throughout Silicon Valley.

Rudolph and Sletten's commitment to its customers doesn't end when a project is completed. In a way, the company's involvement never ends. For example, the day after the Loma Prieta earth-

The Retail Pavilion at Silicon Valley Financial Center, San Jose.

quake shook the Bay Area to its very foundations in 1989, the staff at Rudolph and Sletten put together a list of all the projects the company had completed over the previous 10 years. They narrowed the list down to projects that might have been affected by the quake. And then they visited those sites and offered their immediate assistance.

By making its resources immediately available during this disaster, Rudolph and Sletten helped many clients and former clients stay in business.

Since its founding, Rudolph and Sletten has recognized that its people are its greatest asset. The company understands that, to ensure the firm's growth in the years ahead, it needs educated, flexible, and responsible employees who think for themselves, act independently, exercise judgment, and solve problems.

For this reason the company maintains an aggressive recruiting program. More than a dozen Rudolph and Sletten recruiters comb college campuses around the country every year, searching for capable graduates in civil engineering, construction management, construction engineering, and other related fields. Out of some 300 interviews approximately 50 students are actually flown to the firm's Foster City offices for interviews. Of those, only 10 are offered positions with the firm. Rudolph and Sletten has hired graduates from Arizona, Oregon, Michigan, Texas, Indiana, Iowa, Ohio, and colleges and universities throughout California.

But the firm's recruiting efforts don't stop at college campuses. Rudolph and Sletten also actively recruits from trade programs, searching out the most promising young craftspeople to staff its crews.

Rudolph and Sletten is committed to establishing a work environment in which individuals can grow and where personal achievement is recognized and rewarded. Reflecting this concern for

ucational goals outside the company, offering financial aid for company-approved programs and awarding scholarships for continuing education to children and relatives of employees.

The company is also recognized as one of the most progressive contractors in the area of safety. In fact, "safety" has become an integral part of Rudolph and Sletten's corporate culture. The firm maintains a staff of safety engineers, and every project is assigned a company safety coordinator.

On the first Wednesday of each month the firm takes over a suite at the local Holiday Inn for its monthly "safety breakfast." All company superintendents, project managers, and project engineers are required to attend this meeting, which includes a one-hour presentation from one of the project crews on how they are solving a current safety problem, and/or some interesting construction method they used on their project.

The company's efforts in the area of safety have paid off. In 1982 Rudolph and Sletten was honored by the Associated General Contractors of California with the Safest in the State award, and in 1983 was named as one of the six safest construction firms in the nation by AGC of America, Inc.

Averaging more than $260-million worth of new construction in place during the past five years, Rudolph and Sletten, Inc., looks forward to even greater years ahead.

employee development, the company has provided nationally recognized, formal on-site and off-site training for its people since 1981.

The company's training programs are unique in the construction industry. Even its most qualified employees are required to attend regular, ongoing training. Each class or event is designed to give Rudolph and Sletten employees practical information and skills that can be applied immediately to their work.

Once or twice a month, classes are offered in technical areas, crafts, accounting, estimating, management/leadership skills, and health and wellness. Since the firm promotes from within, these classes give engineers a chance to become project managers, and they give carpenters a chance to become foremen and superintendents.

Certain in-house programs are a company requirement for specific employees—such as first aid/CPR for field personnel, estimating and scheduling for project engineers, and accounting for those responsible for finances. Other programs, such as trades events for craftsmen, and technical management and health programs for superintendents and engineers, are strongly recommended.

Most in-house programs are held at the company's training center. This facility, which seats 35 people comfortably, is equipped with visual aids and has dining and breakout conference rooms adjacent.

Workshops and classes are scheduled to maximize learning and minimize time off work. Most are held in the late afternoon or early evening. Some take place at job sites and involve hands-on experience. Longer programs include meals and refreshments.

The company also offers a wide variety of audio and video self study programs, including built-up roofing; mechanical systems; listening and memory improvement; and reducing secretarial stress.

Rudolph and Sletten supports its employees' ed-

B.T. Mancini Company

The B.T. Mancini Company occupies a unique niche in Silicon Valley's construction industry. As a specialty contractor, the firm provides a variety of exterior and interior building services for the commercial, industrial, and institutional builder.

From raised–access floors to open–web steel joists, from preinsulated wall panels and siding to carpeting and resilient flooring surfaces, the skilled craftsmen and experienced managers of the B.T. Mancini Company have been providing timely and effective service to Silicon Valley builders for some 40 years.

The company has been operated by current president Brooks T. Mancini since 1964, when he purchased the San Jose branch from his father, Brookman Company founder Joseph A. Mancini. Currently headquartered in Santa Clara, the company also maintains offices in Sacramento and Burlingame.

Though the company's primary service area is Northern California and Nevada, B.T. Mancini also performs work in Southern California and a number of western states.

B.T. Mancini's Structural Division furnishes and installs a variety of construction products, including open–web steel joists, floor and roof decking, electrified floor systems, exterior siding, preinsulated wall paneling, curtain wall systems, and exposed metal roofing. This division also erects structural steel for low–rise structures and installs other miscellaneous exterior steel–related products.

The firm's Floor Covering Division furnishes and installs carpeting and resilient flooring surfaces, including sheet vinyls, vinyl composition tiles, welded conductive PVC floors and walls,

rubber–tile floors, as well as factory–finished hardwoods and mini blinds.

The Brookman Company, a division of B.T. Mancini, offers raised access floors, drywall, demountable wall systems, folding doors, and partitions. This division also provides specialty products such as marker boards, tack boards, projection screens, and strut systems, along with assistance in complex installations.

The Brookman Company is the largest Northern California distributor of Tate Access Floors, specializing in fast–track general office and computer facility installations.

Within each of these specialties, B.T. Mancini performs all jobs, from large, complex multimillion–dollar projects, to small, one–of–a–kind assignments, with the same professionalism and dedication to excellence and service. With approximately 200 full–time employees, and covering four craft unions, the company completes between 1,800 and 2,000 jobs per year.

The B.T. Mancini Company's skilled craftsmen and experienced managers have successfully performed thousands of projects, effectively handling every aspect of work within the firm's specialties. Its more notable accomplishments include refacing of the MGM Grand Hotel in Las Vegas; siding of the Trident Submarine base in Washington State; work on the River Park Plaza and the Silicon Valley Financial Center in downtown San Jose; installation of the metal decking for the hotel complex of Harvey's Casino in Lake Tahoe; and the expansion of the Mosconi Center in San Francisco.

With its proven history of timely, on–budget completion, B.T. Mancini Company continues to effectively fill its unique niche in the construction industry of Silicon Valley.

Creegan + D'Angelo

It's almost impossible to travel through Santa Clara County without noticing—if not driving on, shopping at, or doing business in—a project engineered by Creegan + D'Angelo. From the San Jose Convention Center to the Santa Clara County Transit Facility, from the Blossom Hill/Monterey Road Grade Separation to bridges, overpasses, and parking ramps throughout the county, Creegan + D'Angelo has been helping to shape the region for more than 35 years.

Creegan + D'Angelo was founded in 1956 by Elmer D'Angelo and Patrick Creegan. Both founders had been with other firms for a few years before coming together to form Creegan + D'Angelo Consulting Engineers. D'Angelo became president when the company was incorporated in 1973. Creegan left the firm a few years later to pursue other interests.

Larry R. Turl became president of the company in 1988, and Elmer D'Angelo continues to serve as chairman of the board. Creegan + D'Angelo currently employs approximately 140 engineers, land surveyors, technicians, and support personnel. Headquartered in San Jose, the firm maintains regional offices in San Jose, Pleasanton, Fairfield, and Monterey, California.

The firm offers a broad range of engineering services, including civil, structural, water resources, coastal/waterfront, and public works engineering; land surveying and mapping, land-use planning, and feasibility studies.

MOS (Meridian Ocean Systems) is a fully owned subsidiary of Creegan + D'Angelo. MOS is a software-development enterprise specializing in navigation and data management systems for use in sea-floor mapping and submersible vehicle guidance.

Public works is a big part of Creegan & D'Angelo's professional practice. This work includes bridges, interchanges, streets and highways, mass transit, parking facilities, and a host of other projects, large and small.

The firm's skills in land-development engineering have been honed in hundreds of successful projects in the private sector—including commercial, industrial, and residential work.

Creegan + D'Angelo has had extensive experience in new construction and the renovation of existing facilities. Such projects include business and industrial parks, shopping centers, and commercial buildings. The firm has the resources to move a project from initial feasibility studies through construction.

Creegan + D'Angelo also maintains a complete survey division, which utilizes the most advanced surveying equipment available. The firm's survey experience ranges from large-scale cadastral, topographic, and high-order control surveys through the total range of construction surveys.

Water-resources engineering is a growing part of Creegan + D'Angelo's practice. This area broadly includes domestic water supply and distribution, agriculture and landscape irrigation; water reclamation and reuse; collection, treatment, and disposal of municipal and industrial wastes; and flood control and drainage.

The staff at Creegan + D'Angelo utilizes an extensive, firm-wide computer-aided design and drafting (CADD) network for civil engineering design, structural design and analysis, and surveying.

Creegan + D'Angelo is a member in good standing of several professional organizations, including the Society of American Military Engineers, the American Society of Civil Engineers, American Consulting Engineers Council, and the California Council of Civil Engineers and Land Surveyors. The firm has also been recognized for technical excellence in structural engineering.

Bridging San Jose's Monterey Highway and the Southern Pacific Railway, a post-tensioned concrete box girder structure carries six lanes of traffic while spanning distances of up to 266 feet. Creegan + D'Angelo was responsible for the civil and structural engineering design, detour and traffic control, and landscaping for the Guadalupe Corridor Light Rail Transit.

Left: All site engineering for the Santa Clara Convention Center, shown in the center of the photo, was done by Creegan + D'Angelo, as well as the structural engineering for the parking garage. The firm also performed the engineering for widening the Tasman Drive bridge in the lower center of the photo and the design of the pedestrian/golf-cart bridge shown in the center right.

Sobrato Development Companies

John Sobrato, Sr. (seated), and John Sobrato, Jr.

It is impossible to look at the evolution of Silicon Valley and not see the influence of Sobrato Development Companies. From Amdahl's corporate headquarters in Sunnyvale to The Kodak Center in San Jose, from Apple Computer's Cupertino buildings to Santa Clara's Great America Corporate Center and ASK Computer's headquarters in Mountain View, Sobrato Development has left an indelible mark on Santa Clara County.

Sobrato Development is one of the most successful real estate organizations in Silicon Valley. The firm owns nearly 8 million square feet of office, research, and development buildings, and 600 acres of developable land. The property is owned entirely by the Sobrato family without the typical joint venture financial partners.

Sobrato Development specializes in real estate development for high-tech companies. Most of these types of companies require sophisticated interiors such as clean rooms, fabrication and manufacturing areas, and biological and medical laboratories. During its 30-year history, Sobrato Development has developed and built facilities for more than 200 high-technology companies, gaining the expertise along the way to assure that the highly specialized interiors required by these companies are designed and built to correct specification in a cost-effective manner.

Consistently ranked among the top development companies in Santa Clara County, Sobrato Development has long been a leading force in the build-to-suit market. Ever innovative in a highly volatile and competitive business, Sobrato has been responsible for a number of local "firsts." Sobrato was the first developer to build R & D buildings on speculation in Cupertino, the current home of many high-tech companies. It was the first developer to tear down canneries and other heavy industrial plants in Santa Clara County to make room for high-tech R & D facilities. It was the first to build mid-rise office buildings in a suburban context—and it was the first to include parking structures with those projects.

Sobrato was also the first local developer to build a major campus-style complex for a single user. The Amdahl facility, developed and built by Sobrato in partnership with Carl Berg in 1973, was the first campus complex ever built by a developer on the Penin-

sula, and it set a trend that has gained widespread popularity among local electronics firms.

Sobrato has established long-term relationships with many of Silicon Valley's most prominent manufacturers.

Evidence of the firm's contributions to innovative real estate development can be found throughout Silicon Valley in projects for clients such as Apple Computer, Computer Associates, Digital Equipment, Hewlett-Packard, Kodak, Lockheed, LSI Logic, McDonnell Douglas, Motorola, National Semiconductor, Northern Telecom, Synoptics, Western Digital, Xerox, Zycon, and many others.

Since its founding, Sobrato Development has remained a family operation. The tradition began in 1955 when Ann Sobrato developed one of the first "tilt-up" style buildings in Santa Clara County.

"You might say that my mother had a real nose for dirt," says company founder John A. Sobrato, Sr. "She started investing in local real estate when I was still in grammar school. I worked a couple of summers as an apprentice carpenter and eventually followed her into the business."

Sobrato Development built ASK Computer's headquarters in Mountain View in 1986.

At the age of 21, John Sobrato, Sr., founded Midtown Realty in Palo Alto, a firm that specialized in the resale of Eichler homes. At the same time, he teamed up with his mother and began building one building a year for the emerging electronics industry. By the mid–1970s he had sold Midtown Realty to concentrate full time on real estate development.

Like many Silicon Valley businesspeople, John Sobrato, Sr., has had to be as entrepreneurial and willing to take risks as the electronics companies that lease his buildings. Starting in the early 1960s, nearly a decade before the name "Silicon Valley" was even coined, the Sobratos began developing buildings with borrowed money and the hope that a growing business would come along and lease space.

The management staff of Sobrato Development is small, numbering only 16 people. John Sobrato, Jr., handles tenant leasing and runs the company's day–to–day operations, while his father handles creative concepts and approves building designs and property acquisitions.

John Sobrato, Sr., is proud of this lean organization. He says it allows the firm to be more responsive to clients. "We've built our reputation on being responsive," he says. "If someone comes into our office and wants a building, he talks to me or my son. Either John Michael or I are involved all the way through every deal."

Through the efforts of both father and son, Sobrato Development has positioned itself to be even more responsive to major users in the 1990s. The company has employed a strategy of preplanning campus sites so that plans can be drawn and permits can be in place long before a client decides to build. This strategy enabled the firm to deliver a multibuilding campus in six months, instead of the usual two years for Pyramid Technology—an important advantage in an industry as fast–paced as high technology.

In addition to the high–tech and industrial market where the company cut its teeth 20 years ago, Sobrato has recently ventured into an area entirely new to the firm—housing, having built 400 apartments with another 400 under construction.

Diligence, foresight, and timing may be the primary determinants of success for developers, but there's no mistaking the guiding principal behind the success of Sobrato Development Companies. In the words of John Sobrato, Sr.:

"Work for your clients' best interests with a view toward building long–term relationships. Remember, whatever money or service you put into the community will come back and benefit your business tenfold."

The Amdahl corporate headquarters in Sunnyvale is made up of eight buildings built between 1974 and 1978.

One of the largest build-to-suit projects under construction in the nation is the 865,000-square-foot R&D campus for Apple Computer.

Business

Business firms and government offices combine to demonstrate innovative leadership in Silicon Valley.

Photo by Tim Davis

Santa Clara County Historical Heritage Commission

In 1963 a selective inventory was conducted of historic buildings throughout Santa Clara County. The newly formed Santa Clara County Historical Heritage Commission found that 20 of those structures had been demolished just 10 years later. At that rate, the new commission estimated, the rest of the buildings on the list would be gone before the next decade was over.

Ever since that discovery, the 11-member commission has worked tirelessly to stop the destruction of historic structures and preserve the county's historical resources.

In its first year the Santa Clara County Historical Heritage Commission was instrumental in saving a redwood-slab building called Welch-hurst. Located at 16055 Sanborn Road in Sanborn-Skyline Park in Saratoga, this building was originally constructed by Superior Court Judge James R. Welch as a family retreat and hunting lodge. The building's rustic architecture exemplifies the back-tonature movement that flourished at the turn of the century. The use of indigenous building materials in this structure is unique and it is the only one of its kind in the county.

Commissioners obtained approval from the County Board of Supervisors and provided seed money to begin restoration of Welch-hurst. Using its own resources, the American Youth Hostel, Inc., a nonprofit organization, eventually completed the restoration project and permanently maintains the site.

Another example of successful Historical Heritage Commission advocacy is the preservation and reuse of the Woodhills Residence in Cupertino. This historic building was scheduled for demolition until the commission intervened with research, advocacy, and restoration funding.

Unlike its predecessor (the Santa Clara County Historical Landmarks Committee), the Santa Clara County Historical Heritage Commission operates as an independent advisory group to the County Board of Supervisors. The commission investigates, studies, and makes recommendations to the board on such matters as preservation of historic sites, buildings, events, documents, and artifacts; nominations for state points of historical interest; and nominations for inclusion in the National Register of Historic Places.

In addition, the commission is designated to review plans and applications for properties located within three designated Historic Conservation Districts. The commission is also pledged to work with other civic and municipal groups interested in the historical heritage of the county.

Sworn in by the board in July 1973 and funded through the County Parks and Recreation budget, the commission was first asked to compile a heritage resource inventory with listings from unincorporated areas as well as municipalities—something rather unusual at the time.

In addition, a team of architects from Washington, D.C.'s Historic American Building Survey was commissioned to produce a set of scale drawings and photographs of historic buildings in Santa Clara County. During the summers of 1977, 1978, 1979, and 1980, the team compiled historical data and photographs of 30 major historic properties in Santa Clara County. These materials are currently available for display in appropriate locations around the county.

Two editions of the Santa Clara County Heritage Resource Inventory have been compiled and published. The most recent edition is available in all county branch libraries and copies are for sale at the San Jose Historical Museum in Kelley Park.

With the cooperation of San Jose State University, the commission has established a small county records archive at Wahlquist Library on the University campus. Materials in storage include probate records and local business documents.

The commission also gives credit where due with its annual Awards for Excellence in historic resource preservation. Each year the commission selects the best from a list of county-wide nominations of people, projects, and organizations that have achieved excellence in historic resource preservation in the county.

The first of these awards was presented in 1976 to the City of Santa Clara for establishing a local historical heritage commission. Other awards have gone to individuals and organizations throughout the county, including, among others: the *San Jose Mercury News* in 1978, for historical coverage of Santa Clara County; the Los Altos History House in 1978, for the restoration and adaptive reuse of a 1901 residence; the City of Milpitas in 1982, for rehabilitation and site development of the 1828 Higuera Adobe; the City of Gilroy in 1982, for publication of the *Historic Building Study, Volumes I and II*; and the Campbell Civic Improvement Commission in 1985, for adaptive reuse of the historic Campbell Firehouse Number 1 as the Campbell Historical Museum.

In 1990 the commission placed a series of dis-play cases in the lobby of the County Government Center depicting highlights of the county's history. In the same year, four large historical maps were framed and placed at several other locations. Both of these projects have been well received. A current endeavor is the establishment of a county archives committee whose purpose is to protect and preserve the important documents and artifacts of county government and to secure a location where these materials can be stored, curated, and made available to the public.

In 1985 the commission was asked by Windsor Publications, Inc., to sponsor a book on the county's history. This led to the successful publication of *Harvest of Change* by Stephen M. Payne in the summer of 1987 and to the commission's involvement in this book.

The County Board of Supervisors appoints commissioners to four-year terms and they represent all areas of the county. The Santa Clara County Historical Heritage Commission meets monthly in the County Government Center on Hedding Street, and the public is always invited to participate.

Welch-hurst was built in 1913 as a family retreat for James R. Welch, one of Santa Clara County's most prominent Superior Court justices. It is primarily constructed of redwood logs and wooden shingles, which create a rustic, informal appearance and exemplify the back-to-nature movement of the period. The property is currently located in the county's Sanborn-Skyline Park and, since 1979, has been used as an active American Youth Hostel.

The City of San Jose

As the capital of Silicon Valley, San Jose is the center of one of the world's most globally intergrated economies.

In 1971 a popular electronics newsletter first recognized the Santa Clara Valley's singular concentration of high technology companies with the title "Silicon Valley, U.S.A." Today, with most of America's worldwide electronics firms headquarterd in that region, and overseas companies establishing a major presence there, the Silicon Valley may have become the most international marketplace in the world.

The city of San Jose stands at the heart of this international marketplace. With its dynamic urban center, worldwide economic and business linkages, and global cultural ties, it's no wonder *Fortune* magazine refers to San Jose as "the Capital of Silicon Valley."

Formerly a center of agriculture, San Jose was transformed by the technology revolution begun at nearby Stanford University during the 1950s. Today, local firms produce one-fourth of the nation's high-tech exports and comprise the world's highest concentration of entrepreneurial talent.

Nearly half of the 50 largest companies in Silicon Valley have headquarters or divisions in San Jose. The area has more corporate headquarters of *Fortune* 500 companies than Los Angeles and twice as many as San Francisco. And with a growing population of 815,000, San Jose is the West Coast's third-largest city and the 11th-largest city in the nation.

During the 1980s downtown San Jose underwent a dramatic physical renaissance. Under the auspices of the Redevelopment Agency of San Jose, the city worked with the private sector to erect new Class A office and retail buildings, pub-

lic facilities, and luxury hotels; made major transportation improvements; renovated parks; and installed outdoor art, creating an urban core with the kind of amenities—including restaurants, shops, theaters, and museums—found in the major cities of the world. As a result, downtown San Jose has emerged as a vital center of activity for Silicon Valley's business community.

"Downtown Silicon Valley," as San Jose's urban center is called, has also become the transportation hub of Silicon Valley. Its comprehensive network of highways, public transit, and the nearby San Jose International Airport make it the region's most accessible employment center—a real boon to the city's increasingly diverse group of downtown business tenants.

Supporting the surrounding concentration of high-tech firms, San Jose's downtown area has attracted a broad spectrum of tenants for the business community, including banking, consulting, law, public relations, and accounting.

Downtown San Jose also serves the greater metro area with a full array of cultural and entertainment amenities, including the San Jose Convention and Cultural Facilities; the new, 20,000-seat sports and entertainment arena; the San Jose Museum of Art; the Children's Discovery Museum; and The Tech Museum of Innovation, the prototype exhibit for the planned $80-million Technology Center of Silicon Valley.

Complementing its local preeminence, the city of San Jose embodies a globally oriented economy unique among world centers. *World Trade* magazine recently ranked San Jose among the 10

best places to conduct international business in North America. High technology industries and services in particular find a San Jose location paramount to an international presence. Not only do San Jose-based firms produce one-fourth of the nation's high-tech exports, they produce the second-highest per capita exports in the nation (second only to Detroit).

San Jose also attracts foreign investment. In fact, north San Jose has the greatest concentration of Pacific Rim electronics firms in the U.S. And a Silicon Valley presence has become increasingly important to traditional manufacturing industries as they integrate electronic systems into their production processes and/or enter high-tech markets.

San Jose aggressively courts business and maintains a comprehensive economic development program. The city's program—spearheaded by William Claggett, founding director of the city's Office of Economic Development (OED), along with the full commitment of the mayor and the city council—mirrors both the diversity and the entrepreneurial qualities of the San Jose economy.

The city operates one of 10 enterprise zones in California and the only one in the San Francisco Bay Area. All businesses in the zone—which includes the downtown central business district—are eligible for state incentives that include hiring and sales tax credits, a 15-year net operating loss carryover, business expense dedications, and tax-free returns on investments.

Since 1974 the city has sponsored a main foreign trade zone facility under the jurisdiction of the U.S. Department of Commerce. Centrally located, the facility provides easy access to major highways and San Jose International Airport. The zone expedites imported goods through the U.S. Customs process and improves cash flow by postponing duty and excise tax payments.

San Jose also offers its business community a special handling procedure whereby selected economic development projects receive high-level department attention throughout the city's review process. And the city provides access to financial resources for small businesses downtown and in neighborhood business districts throughout the city.

The key to San Jose's successful development of a strong international business climate is the OED's Center for International Trade and Development (CITD). The CITD was created in 1988 by the OED to help local business forge and maintain strategic links with overseas partners, stimulate and direct investment from overseas into the greater San Jose metro area, and help local business understand more about doing business overseas.

Underpinning the successful internationalization of the San Jose economy, the local community reflects many cultural heritages of a truly international population. The largest groups include Japanese, Chinese, Vietnamese, Filipino, and Hispanic communities, which provide San Jose with strong cultural ties to Pacific Rim nations. On a local level, these diverse communities provide residents and businesses with well-established business and cultural networks.

San Jose maintains many of its international cultural ties through sister city relationships and has pioneered the concept of economic partnerships to provide government-to-government linkages with strategic trading partners around the world.

The city of San Jose is a place where economic vitality and a uniquely pleasant way of life go hand-in-hand. The city is committed to ensuring that San Jose long remains an area of strong economic growth, where energetic new companies can prosper and continue to develop products that change the world.

San Jose's The Tech is an extraordinary showcase for the Silicon Valley-born technology that continues to change the world.

Downtown Silicon Valley offers more than centralized business opportunities.

First Franklin Financial Corporation

William D. Dallas, chief executive officer.

When Bill Dallas and his brother, Steve, decided to set up their own mortgage banking firm in Silicon Valley, they chose a location on Franklin Street, just behind the University of Santa Clara, for their first offices. They started their new enterprise with just two employees, and they named the company after the street where they did business.

That was in January 1981. Since then First Franklin Financial Corporation has grown considerably. Today, with 233 employees, seven offices, and nearly $2.5 billion in home mortgages, First Franklin is ranked among the top 10 percent of "Freddie Mac" seller/services and is recognized as GMAC–Residential Funding Corporation's number–one originator of investment–quality products in the United States.

One of the keys to First Franklin's success is its commitment to operate as a full–service mortgage company. "There are a lot of mortgage companies out there," says Bill Dallas, "that only originate loans. There are many that only service loans. And there are many that only fund them. We are one of the few companies that still takes on the whole process."

First Franklin specializes in wholesale loan origination. The firm utilizes interim funds provided by warehouse bankers and other sources to act as a financial intermediary in the origination and purchase of residential mortgage loans, the holding or warehousing and subsequent marketing of such loans to capital market investors, the sale of rights to service the loans, and the ongoing management of a servicing portfolio during the term of loan repayment.

Steven D. Dallas, president.

First Franklin has further expanded its mortgage banking capabilities by creating Residential Home Loan Mortgage Corporation (Ready Mac). Ready Mac is a wholly owned subsidiary of First Franklin, chartered to help home owners obtain CHOICE^SM home loans that don't fit rigid qualification, credit, and other mortgage market guidelines. By pioneering its CHOICE^SM loan (Common Sense Home Loans with Options for Income, Credit, and Equity), the company gives borrowers a way to increase affordable home ownership.

"It is a market that is largely uncharted for mortgage companies," says Dallas. "We're just recognizing a need that is not being filled. And we're fulfilling our charter as a mortgage banker to provide affordable housing for people."

Since its founding, First Franklin has expanded its access to the California mortgage market with additional offices in San Jose, including the firm's corporate headquarters, a regional wholesale office, and Ready Mac's main office. The company serves Southern California, with offices in Westlake Village, Laguna Hills, and San Diego.

"One of the reasons we have grown so quickly," says Dallas, "is that we have always understood that our employees are our most valuable product. We give them what they need to do the job and the authority to do it. And we trust them to evaluate everything in terms of value to the customer."

First Franklin Financial is a member of the Mortgage Bankers Association of America and is an approved seller/servicer for Federal National Mortgage Association (FNMA), Government National Mortgage Association (GNMA), the Federal Home Loan Mortgage Corporation (FHLMC), and several major private–capital market investors.

R.G. Speno, Inc.

Inventing the future mandates a respect for the present and a reverence for the past. In today's litigious society it is necessary to envision the realm of possibilities, which is exactly how the firm of R.G. Speno, Inc., became an instrumental part of the growth of Silicon Valley.

As a commercial insurance brokerage working with the builders, developers, and emerging industries of the valley, Speno witnessed first hand the spectacular changes that have transformed the county from a sleepy agricultural region to the now famous Silicon Valley.

The firm was founded in 1975 by its current director, Ronald G. Speno, who was born and raised in Santa Clara County. Speno built his business—which has been consistently ranked by the *San Jose Business Journal* among the top insurance firms in Santa Clara County—by developing close, long-term relationships with his clients, many of whom he has worked with for more than 20 years. In fact, many of Speno's current clients were also his first clients.

As the Santa Clara Valley has changed, so have the insurance needs of R.G. Speno's clients. Waste management, sophisticated liability needs, and manufacturing contracts all require statistical reviews and assessments of conditions. R.G. Speno assists its clients with these often baffling industry requirements with ongoing reviews and monitoring of programs and requirements.

Speno is a graduate of San Jose State University, an underwriting member of the Council of Lloyds of London, and has been a guest lecturer on property and casualty insurance at both San Jose State University and De Anza College.

The Bond Department was formally created in 1979 when Francis E. Cook joined the organization. At that time there were few independent agencies with an in-house facility capable of rapid bond issuance and response. Cook has brought the Bond Department to its current status of being one of the largest in the area. Since the firm is known for its construction services, the arrival

(Left to right) Frank Cook, Ronald Speno, Mark Speno, and Christopher Lawton.

of the bonding facility allowed for the servicing of all the major contractors involved in the building of Silicon Valley.

Prior to joining the company, Cook was the bond manager for Fireman's Fund Insurance Company in San Jose. Born and educated in the East, he began his career in 1971 in Boston, moving later to Washington, D.C. Cook holds a master's degree in business administration, as well as a C.P.C.U. designation.

Christopher S. Lawton joined the firm in 1984. Lawton, a former branch manager with The Royal Insurance Companies, expanded the firm's reach into new areas with his extensive technical backround and knowledge of coverages. He holds a bachelor's degree in economics from the University of Nevada, as well as a management degree in insurance from the Insurance Institute of America.

Lawton has been responsible for the acquisition of contracts with many of the dynamic insurance carriers represented by R.G. Speno, Inc. This allows the brokerage to service a large variety of industries, offering a diverse program of coverages, while providing competitive premiums. In 1989 Mark A. Speno, the founder's son, joined the firm. Mark Speno graduated from Washington State University with a degree in business administration. Prior to joining the firm, he served as a U.S. naval officer.

State Compensation Insurance Fund

Until 1914, injured workers in the state of California were on their own. No compulsory insurance for on-the-job injuries existed back then, and families were often left destitute when the breadwinner suffered an accident on the job.

But all that was changed that year with the signing into law of the Boynton Act. The act established an insurance system for on-the-job accidents, and at the same time it enabled employers to insure against their liability at the lowest possible cost by creating the State Compensation Insurance Fund.

State Compensation Insurance Fund is California's leading writer of workers' compensation insurance. The fund underwrites more business than its four closest competitors combined, and is the workers' compensation insurance choice of more than 45 percent of California employers.

State Fund is organized as a public enterprise, and is operated on a nonprofit basis. Because it exists as a public enterprise, the fund offers a key advantage to policyholders over other insurers: it is not motivated by profit. Each year State Fund re-

turns a percentage of its premium income to policyholders in the form of dividends, once it has paid out benefits to injured workers and made full provision for adequate reserves, expenses, and taxes.

These dividends are nothing new for State Fund. For more than 75 years it has been keeping workers' compensation costs down for California employers. In 1915 it paid a 15 percent dividend on its first year in business and has paid a dividend every year since.

To assure the easy accessibility of coverage for employers of all sizes, State Fund has located its 21 district offices throughout the state, establishing them in important centers of population and industry, from San Diego to Eureka.

The local State Fund office, located on West Mission Street in San Jose, serves all of Santa Clara County, as well as the nearby counties of Monterey, San Benito, and Santa Cruz. The district employs some 200 people and maintains two legal departments. Plans to relocate the district office to a larger facility south of San Jose on Bernal Road are currently under way.

The State Compensation Insurance Fund district office located in San Jose, California.

Each district office offers every essential workers' compensation service required by the fund's insured and their employees. The fund's sales and safety representatives, attorneys, auditors, claims adjusters, and vocational rehabilitation coordinators live and work in the communities they serve and can respond directly and personally to client needs.

State Fund was established to be fully self-supporting and has always stood firmly on its own two feet. In fact, even its original $100,000 general fund loan for start-up costs granted by the state legislature in 1914 proved unnecessary. California employers responded to State Fund's offer of insurance in such numbers that the loan remained untouched—and was soon returned to the state with interest.

The State Fund contributes substantially to the California economy. Like all insurance carriers, it pays state taxes on policyholder premiums. Since the fund's founding, the State Treasury has received over $223 million in tax dollars from its operations.

And virtually all of State Fund's earnings remain in California. Unlike many private insurers, which have out-of-state headquarters, operations, or stockholders, the fund's earnings are expended as compensation and medical benefits to injured workers, as operational expenses and investments, and as dividend refunds to policyholders.

From the start, State Fund has instituted programs and policies that have served as yardsticks against which its competitors have measured themselves. It has, for example, consistently returned excess premium dollars to policyholders, thus encouraging the spread and continuation of this practice among other insurance carriers.

The fund has also been a powerful force in keeping down the prices of workers' compensation insurance. During 1988, for example, State Fund's singular stand against proposed and unneeded rate increases helped save California employers millions of dollars in premium costs.

Another example is its leadership in group insurance: State Fund pioneered and has always underwritten more group workers' compensation insurance in California than any other insurer. Under these association group insurance programs, statewide safety campaigns help to reduce industry-wide loss experience and related costs.

Just as it works to hold down costs, State Fund also concentrates on producing an exemplary claims product. Toward this end the fund follows an ongoing policy of providing claims staffing levels sufficient to assure manageable adjuster caseloads. In this way it can assure prompt and personal attention to each claim.

As California's population and economy have grown, State Fund has increased the number of its district offices to maintain its high standards of service to its growing number of policyholders.

State Fund has also increased its staff of catastrophic claims consultants. These consultants specialize in helping victims of head trauma, spinal cord injury, multiple amputation, burns, and other very serious injuries. And the fund employs at least one full-time vocational rehabilitation coordinator in each district office.

State Fund has long offered accident prevention services designed to eliminate job hazards, promote safety awareness, and reduce the personal and financial costs of industrial injuries and illness. In fact, State Fund has the largest staff of industrial loss control professionals in California. Services such as safety training, plant and job-site surveys, accident analysis, program development assistance, and industrial hygiene consultation are available to its policyholders.

State Fund also has the largest audiovisual library of safety films and video tapes of any insurance provider in California. More than 1,500 copies of 600 titles are currently available for loan to policyholders.

State Compensation Insurance Fund is dedicated to continuing to fulfill its obligation to assure that all employers are able to insure against their compulsory liability, that they can do so at a minimum cost, and to guarantee prompt, fair, and humane treatment of injured workers and their dependents.

These obligations, designed by the legislature, are timeless and will be just as compelling in the future as they have been in the past.

Under California law it is unlawful for an insurer to promise the future payment of dividends under an unexpired workers' compensation insurance policy or to misrepresent the conditions for dividend payment. Dividends are payable only pursuant to conditions determined by the Board of Directors or other governing board of the Company following policy expiration. It is a misdemeanor for any insurer or officer or agent thereof, or any insurance broker or solicitor, to promise the payment of future workers' compensation dividends. Past dividend performance is no guarantee of an insurer's future dividend performance.

San Jose Convention and Cultural Facilities

During the 1980s, downtown San Jose underwent a dramatic physical renaissance. Working with the private sector, the city erected new office buildings and hotels, renovated parks and transportation, and installed outdoor art, creating an urban core with the kind of amenities found in the major cities of the world.

Today downtown San Jose serves the greater metro area with world-class hotels, gourmet cuisine, cultural arts, and entertainment. At the center of these are the San Jose Convention and Cultural Facilities, which include the Convention Center, the Civic Auditorium Complex, Montgomery Theater, and the Center for the Performing Arts.

The city's newest and largest facility is the McEnery Convention Center, which opened in 1989. Its entry is framed by the largest exterior porcelain tile wall in the world, designed by renowned artist Lin Utzon. Its beautifully patterned terrazzo floors and its vaulted skylight, which runs the length of the 1,100-foot, two-story concourse, make the center nothing short of breathtaking.

Designed and equipped to accommodate users ranging from the international sales force of a *Fortune* 500 company to the local chapter of a regional club, the convention center is truly a state-of-the-art facility. As Northern California's second-largest convention center, it offers more than 425,000 square feet of pre-function, exhibit, and meeting space, food and beverage capabilities to serve banquets for 5,000, and underground parking.

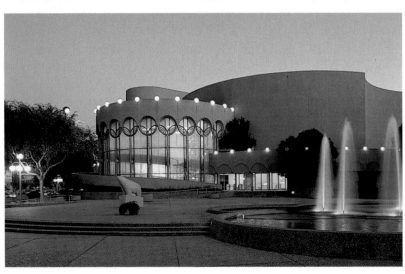

Directly across from the convention center on San Carlos Street is San Jose's Civic Auditorium Complex—perfect for meetings, stage presentations, sporting events, exhibitions, and concerts. The complex features the two-level, 3,060-seat Civic Auditorium with a sound stage, and a combination of fixed seating and open floor space. In addition, the 30,000-square-foot exhibit hall is versatile. By utilizing a moveable, sound-proof wall, users can host two events simultaneously.

Adjacent to the Civic Auditorium Complex is the 537-seat Montgomery Theater, which features full production capabilities and fixed seating. The intimate theater is home to Opera San Jose, San Jose Repertory Theatre, and Children's Musical Theater.

At Almaden Boulevard and San Carlos Street, one block west of the convention center, is San Jose's 2,700-seat Center for the Performing Arts. Built in 1971, it is home to San Jose Symphony, the oldest symphony west of the Mississippi; the internationally toured San Jose Cleveland Ballet, the fifth-largest ballet company in the United States; and the San Jose Civic Light Opera, the largest subscribed musical theater company in the U.S.

Together, the Montgomery Theater and the Center for the Performing Arts offer the greater metro area the finest in theater, musical, and cultural entertainment year-round.

Located within minutes of the Bay Area's major freeways and the San Jose International Airport, downtown San Jose and the San Jose Convention and Cultural Facilities are easily accessed by car or light rail.

THIS FOUNTAIN
IS USING
RECLAIMED WATER

Quality of Life

Medical and educational institutions contribute to the quality of life for Silicon Valley area residents.

Photo by Gerald L. French/The Photo File

O'Connor Hospital

O'Connor Hospital pioneered laser laparoscopy for treatment of gallbladder disease in Northern California.

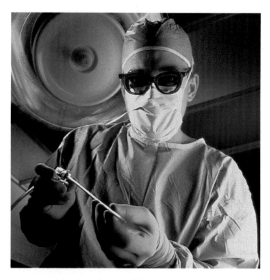

O'Connor Hospital first began serving the communities of the Santa Clara Valley more than 100 years ago. Today, O'Connor continues to be one of the region's leading health care networks, providing accessible, state-of-the-art services with a strong commitment to its community, including the poor.

Located in San Jose, in the heart of Silicon Valley, O'Connor Hospital is a Catholic, non-profit community health care center. The 360-bed, acute-care facility provides comprehensive hospital and health services throughout the Santa Clara Valley to individuals under the care of their private physicians.

The hospital was founded in 1889 through the philanthropic vision of Judge Myles P. O'Connor and the compassionate service of the Daughters of Charity of St. Vincent de Paul, whose health care ministry embodies a special commitment to providing for those in need.

The original O'Connor Sanitarium, which stood at the corner of Race and San Carlos streets in San Jose, was the first private hospital in Santa Clara County and home to one of California's pioneer schools of nursing.

In 1953 the Daughters of Charity constructed a new, modern hospital on Forest Avenue in San Jose, and have since remained at the forefront of medical advancements in the community. For example, in 1969 the hospital installed a prototype linear accelerator, making radiation therapy available for the first time in a local community facility. Soon afterward, O'Connor physicians began performing complex, open-heart surgery. And in 1990 an O'Connor surgical team performed the Santa Clara Valley's first laser laparoscopy operation for the treatment of gallbladder disease.

In 1981 the Daughters of Charity built an entirely new hospital at the Forest Avenue site. O'Connor now holds the distinction of being both the oldest and newest hospital in Santa Clara County.

Today O'Connor Hospital offers comprehensive medical and surgical care, as well as a host of specialty programs.

O'Connor's medical staff of nearly 550 physicians and its hospital staff of more than 1,400 represent expertise in nearly every medical specialty. With a wide range of programs, including business health services, heart care, and cancer care, O'Connor provides specialized service to those with unique needs.

Serving the special needs of cancer patients has long been a high priority at O'Connor. For more than 30 years the hospital has been a leader in providing sophisticated cancer diagnostic and treatment services to the people of the Santa Clara Valley. With the opening of The Cancer Care Center in 1990, O'Connor consolidated all aspects of its cancer care services into a fully integrated, comprehensive, community-based program.

O'Connor's Cancer Care Center blends the hospital's philosophy of healing the whole person with the most advanced medical treatment and state-of-the-art technology in a homelike setting.

O'Connor Hospital has been serving the people of the Santa Clara Valley for more than 100 years.

The hospital's team of highly trained professionals—including a nursing unit dedicated exclusively to cancer care—work together to manage a total care plan for each patient. The most advanced therapies in cancer research are available through a cooperative relationship between O'Connor physicians and researchers at Stanford University and the University of California, San Francisco. For those patients choosing to remain at home, the center offers a variety of home health care options.

To address the special needs of those living and working in Silicon Valley, where stress levels run especially high and many residents are prime candidates for stress-sensitive illnesses such as heart disease, O'Connor has developed a comprehensive array of cardiovascular services. These include prevention, diagnosis, and treatment, as well as special services for the business community.

For example, O'Connor recently expanded its diagnostic services to include electrophysiology and echocardiography analysis, heart catheterizations, and impedance plethysmography. Using this comprehensive testing capability, O'Connor provides cardiovascular evaluations for individuals and business groups through Pro-Fit (located at the area Decathlon Club), allowing physicians to pinpoint problems and recommend treatment.

Sponsoring necessary programs is another of the many ways O'Connor Hospital serves the communities of the Santa Clara Valley. SeniorCircle, for example, is a benefits-coordination program for those over 65 that helps patients coordinate Medicare claims. The Center for Life offers a wide range of obstetric and pediatric services, from pregnancy testing and prenatal care to delivery, postpartum care, and a new pediatrics clinic.

Through its Adopt-A-School Program O'Connor is linked closely with Broadway Continuing High School, providing many students with health care internships, scholarships, and donations for needed school equipment. Because of this program, the hospital was recognized in 1990 for making "the most significant contribution to education in the state of California."

In 1989 O'Connor expanded its service into the underserved South County area with the completion of the Saint Louise Health Center in Morgan Hill. Saint Louise is now a full-service, 60-bed hospital with a 30-physician medical office building, which offers primary and secondary medical services including medicine, surgery, and critical life support. Family-oriented maternal and child health care and 24-hour emergency room services are also available.

O'Connor has also recently expanded its maternal-child health services. The new facilities feature integrated mother-infant care in homelike labor-delivery-recovery suites, and provide childbirth, parenting skills, and basic infant care classes to new parents.

Through its affiliation with Peninsula Industrial Medical Clinic, O'Connor is serving as an example of how health care providers and industry can work together. The clinic provides emergency and follow-up care, such as physical therapy, as well as preplacement physicals and training classes on industry prevention and health maintenance.

O'Connor Hospital is part of the Daughters of Charity National Health System (DCNHS), the largest nonprofit health system in the United States. The DCNHS has 42 major health care facilities with almost 15,000 beds. The DCNHS strengthens O'Connor's business operations by offering opportunities in financial management, group purchasing, utilization of talented resources, sharing of programs, and service development.

Conveniently located near the intersection of interstates 880 and 280 in San Jose, O'Connor Hospital is easily accessible by public transportation. Parking is readily available for patients and visitors. All of the hospital's facilities are fully licensed by the state and are accredited by the Joint Commission on Accreditation of Healthcare Organizations.

Dedicated to healing the sick with the finest physicians and technology available, O'Connor Hospital will continue to be a leading, customer-focused, value-guided, quality health care network of accessible services. And it will continue its century-long commitment to the people and communities of the Santa Clara Valley.

Below: Assisting the elderly is an important component of the Daughters of Charity's mission of service.

Bottom: O'Connor Hospital's mission of service extends to all members of the human family.

TakeCare

California is the birthplace of this nation's oldest health maintenance organization (HMO), group health plans that currently serve nearly 13 percent of the U.S. population's and 46 percent of the Bay Area's health care needs. And one of the oldest and most successful HMO programs in Santa Clara County is provided by TakeCare Health Plan.

"We believe we have four customers, and we try to give them equal weight," says TakeCare president Judd Jessup. "There are the plan members who depend on us for the health and well-being of themselves and their families, the employers who pay for the plans, the physicians who own the clinics, and brokers who consult with employers on their health care needs."

TakeCare Health Plan is a federally qualified, statewide HMO providing health care in 27 California counties. Founded in 1978, the plan provides affordable, comprehensive health care services to subscribers through a network of multispecialty medical groups, individual practice associations, and hospitals.

TakeCare was originally established as a nonprofit organization by Blue Cross of California. It was that organization's first entry into the managed health care market in Northern California.

The firm was converted to a for-profit corporation in 1988.

Today TakeCare is the second-largest HMO in the San Francisco Bay Area. Now publicly traded, the organization operates as a Knox-Keene health care service plan and is regulated by the California Department of Corporations.

TakeCare is a "network" HMO—that is, it does not have physicians and hospitals of its own. Instead, independent medical groups and hospitals contract with TakeCare and agree to provide care to its enrollees. TakeCare has contracts with some of the premier medical groups in the Bay Area, including San Jose Medical Group, Sunnyvale Medical Clinic, Palo Alto Medical Foundation, Redwood Medical Clinic, Camino Real Medical Group, Santa Cruz Medical Clinic, Good Samaritan IPA, Family Medical Clinic of the Peninsula, and Stanford University Clinic. TakeCare also maintains contracts with 176 hospitals statewide.

TakeCare normally contracts with hospitals under a variety of arrangements. Except in life-threatening emergency situations, members are required to receive prior approval from their primary care physician and medical group for hospitalization. TakeCare provides reasonable

Conducting an exercise stress test at Sunnyvale Medical Clinic.

incentives to medical groups for appropriate utilization of hospital services.

In a world of skyrocketing medical expenses, the arrival of HMO-style health care plans is considered by many—brokers, employers, and employees alike—to be a godsend.

TakeCare participating medical groups have no economic incentives to overtreat patients and no pressures from fellow physicians or any third party to undertreat them. TakeCare physicians are paid on a "capitation" basis. This

means that for fixed, monthly payment for each enrolled member, the medical group provides for all covered and necessary ambulatory medical services, including office visits, laboratory services, and X rays. This arrangement encourages timely, appropriate, cost-effective care. This arrangement has also proved attractive to physicians because it frees them from cash-flow concerns.

Also, TakeCare carefully monitors the quality of care its members receive. The firm checks physician performance and undertakes regular member satisfaction surveys—involving both active and disenrolled members. Using annual, network-wide reviews of primary care performance and health outcomes, the firm strives to identify patterns of care. Employing a corporate quality assurance committee and corporate medical director, the firm monitors, reviews, and directs network-wide quality assurance activities.

The firm also utilizes case management review to identify and solve health services delivery problems related to benefits, alternative types of care, provider types, and care setting.

The TakeCare Health Plan is available to employer groups of 15 or more eligible employees. Five basic plans are available to plan members.

The Elite and Classic plans are alike with the exception of a difference in copayment amounts for routine office visits, emergency room visits, and short-term therapy. The Select, Prime, and Value plans feature higher copayment amounts for routine services, resulting in lower monthly premiums for employers.

TakeCare's basic medical plan includes hospitalization, physician services (including routine office visits), short-term therapy, diagnostic X-ray and lab procedures, emergency care, prenatal and maternity benefits, detoxification, and short-term mental health benefits.

The plan also offers supplemental vision, prescription drug, and chemical dependency recovery programs. A supplemental chiropractic benefit was introduced in 1991.

Many of TakeCare's medical groups and contracting hospitals offer extensive health education and health maintenance programs to members. And TakeCare itself has developed a community affairs program that focuses on children's health.

The administration of the TakeCare Health Plan is characterized by its quality service to members, providers, brokers, and employers. Member complaints are typically addressed within five days—and the ratio of those complaints is less than six per 1,000 members.

TakeCare serves about 2,000 employer groups statewide, and the firm has earned a reputation locally for good patient relations and careful attention to medical problem solving in its coverage of some 90,000 plan members throughout the Santa Clara Valley.

TakeCare's local employer groups include Lockheed, IBM, Hewlett-Packard, Amdahl Syntex, United Airlines, SRI International, Stanford University and Stanford University Hospital, and the County of Santa Clara.

Headquartered in Concord, California, TakeCare has regional offices in Orange, San Diego, San Jose, San Francisco, Sacramento, Fresno, and Tracy. The firm employs approximately 185 people.

TakeCare is a member of the California Association of HMOs and is represented on that organization's board of directors.

Assisting TakeCare members in selecting a primary care physician.

Stanford University

Fortune magazine has called Silicon Valley ". . . the densest concentration of innovative industry that exists anywhere in the world." Educators, businesspeople, and government representatives from distant places regularly visit the area, hoping to discover the secret behind this concentration of innovation. What were the key ingredients, they ask, that caused pioneering electronics firms to spring up from one end of Santa Clara County to the other?

Without a doubt, one key ingredient is Stanford University.

Stanford University is one of the world's leading centers for new, high-technology development. Its 660-acre Stanford Research Park, created on university land in 1951, has 55 firms employing some 25,000 people. The two-mile-long Stanford Linear Accelerator Center, also located on university land, is a world center for high-energy physics research. And Stanford has ranked consistently among the top five universities in federally sponsored research.

The university was founded in 1885 by California Senator Leland Stanford and his wife, Jane, in memory of their only child, Leland Jr., who had died of typhoid fever the year before. The university is located immediately adjacent to Palo Alto on 8,200 acres of farmland formerly owned by the Stanfords (hence the nickname, "The Farm.")

Stanford's founders were progressive for their time, establishing a nondenominational residential institution, open to both sexes and affordable to all qualified students regardless of financial means. In fact, there was no tu-

ition at Stanford until 1920, when a charge of $120 per year was instituted.

The university's current student population totals approximately 13,000 undergraduates and graduate students. The 1,567 freshmen entering the university in the fall of 1989 were selected from 14,912 applicants from every state in the union as well as many foreign countries. More than 20 percent of those admitted had 4.0 grade point averages and almost 65 percent were in the top 10 percent of their high school classes.

Stanford's undergraduate student body is among the most diverse of any institution in the nation in terms of ethnicity, economic background, and geographic origin. The 1989-1990 freshman class is well represented by black, Hispanic, Native American, and Asian-American students.

The university's foreign student population comprises citizens from 100 countries. Nearly 70 percent of these are graduate students, about 14 percent are undergraduates, and the remainder are postdoctoral candidates or nonmatriculated students.

Eighty-six percent of freshmen enrolling at Stanford graduate within five years—the national average for all four-year institutions is 55 percent.

Stanford's faculty, which totals 1,325, includes Nobel, Pulitzer, and MacArthur Foundation Prize winners, National Medal of Science winners, and members of the National Academies of Science,

Two Rodin sculptures grace the courtyard in front of the entry to the Inner Quad and Memorial Church.

Engineering, Education, and Arts and Sciences. Between 1974 and this writing, the university faculty has received 122 Guggenheim awards.

In the area of athletics, for the four years preceding this writing, Stanford has won more National Collegiate Athletic Association titles than any other university. The 1989 team champions included both men's and women's tennis, and in 1990 the women's basketball team won the NCAA title. And Stanford had more participants in the 1988 Olympic Games—32 students and six coaches— than any other American college or university.

Stanford's ties to the development of Silicon Valley's electronics industries date as far back as 1909, when the university's first president, David Starr Jordan, encouraged a young graduate student named Cyrus Elwell to start a new business. Jordan went so far as to invest $500 in the firm, which later perfected the vacuum tube as a sound amplifier and a generator of electromagnetic waves, signally the birth of the age of electronics.

The presence of a university with strong academic departments willing to work closely with local companies fueled the growth of the valley's infant electronics industry. But the chief architect of that growth was the late Frederic Emmons Terman, a Stanford professor of electrical engineering who encouraged his students to start companies near campus. Among the students who followed Terman's advice were Bill Hewlett and David Packard. Two others were Dean Watkins and Dick Johnson.

Terman received a big assist from the Stanford physics department in 1937, when Professor William Hansen gave graduate student Russell Varian and his brother, Sigurd, work space and $100 for materials to develop the klystron tube. Their invention became the foundation of radar and microwave communications. It also provided the basic technology for the Stanford Linear Accelerator Center and is now used in cancer treatment.

As university provost after World War II, Terman recognized the potential for combining federal research funds, academic programs, and industrial development. That combination led to the en-

hancement of academic departments at Stanford and to the creation of the Stanford Industrial Park (now called Stanford Research Park).

The first tenant of Research Park was Varian Associates. The park soon attracted the Hewlett-Packard and Watkins-Johnson companies.

Stanford's ties to the local electronics industry were considerably strengthened in 1955, when William Shockley, coinventor of the transistor, located his company, the Shockley Transistor Corporation, in the Industrial Park and joined the university's electrical engineering department as a member of the faculty.

Two years later, in one of the classic spin–offs of its kind, eight Shockley employees left to form Fairchild Semiconductor, where they coinvented the integrated circuit. Several engineers then spun off to form Intel Corporation, where the microprocessor was invented. And the process continued to repeat itself; some 55 electronics firms have since evolved from Fairchild or its offspring.

The park continued to grow, attracting a Lockheed research laboratory that gave rise to the company's Missiles and Space Division in Sunnyvale. Firms specializing in lasers, pharmaceuticals and biochemistry, and other fields followed, among them Syntex, IBM, Beckman Instruments, and Xerox.

Tenants are accepted at the Research Park only if their work ties in with the university's research and instructional programs, thus cementing the ties between Stanford University and Silicon Valley that continues today.

An aerial view of the campus and the Stanford foothills in the west.

Santa Clara University

There is a special synergy between Santa Clara University and the communities that surround its scenic campus.

This has been evident from the university's origins in 1851, when the bishop of Monterey asked two Jesuit priests to create a college in the Santa Clara Valley. California had just become a state, the Gold Rush was booming, and there was a definite need for a strong educational institution in a region experiencing rampant change.

Now, 140 years later, the rush for gold has been transformed into the race to develop high technology. Located in the midst of Silicon Valley, electronic laboratory to the world, Santa Clara has become one of the West Coast's most highly respected centers of rigorous and values-centered learning.

The quality and influence of the university—the state's oldest institution of higher learning—were described in two recent *San Jose Mercury News* surveys. The first cited Santa Clara as one of the 10 most influential institutions in the Santa Clara Valley.

The other story—based on a wide sampling of California's college admissions officers—selected SCU as a "best buy," ranked second among all of the state's private universities for the value it provides in academic quality, campus, and community life. This report echoed the *New York Times* coverage of SCU as the only California independent university in its "Best Buys" guidebook, and the university's perennial *U.S. News & World Report* ranking as one of the most highly regarded comprehensive universities in the West.

What has the university done to earn these accolades? Primarily, it has helped shape the de-

velopment of Santa Clara Valley—and made major contributions to the state and nation—through the leaders it has educated. In every field—law, education, business, politics, social service, and high technology—Santa Clara graduates have taken a leading role.

Although Santa Clara has undergone many changes since 1851, its distinctive tradition of educating leaders for service to humankind has remained constant. This can be described as education for "competence with conscience"—an approach to work and life characterized by critical judgement and an emphasis on making a positive difference in society.

A fascinating blend of tradition and innovation is evident today on Santa Clara's 103-acre campus, which contains some of the oldest buildings in California as well as state-of-the-art computer, engineering, and theater facilities. The beautiful university setting traces its history back to 1777, when Santa Clara de Asis was founded as the eighth of California's 21 missions.

Most of the university's 327 full-time faculty members earned their advanced degrees from the nation's top graduate schools and are distinguished and active scholars in their fields. In the Jesuit tradition, the academic atmosphere emphasizes intellectual rigor, moral and spiritual development, a spirit of inquiry, individualized attention, and concern for educating the whole person.

The university awards degrees through the doctorate level, with 28 undergraduate majors in the College of Arts and Sciences, six in the Leavey School of Business and Administration, and four in the School of Engineering. Professional teaching and counseling credentials are offered through the Division of Counseling Psychology and Education. And the School of Law offers a full range of courses in federal, state, and international law leading to the J.D. degree.

There are many mutual benefits enjoyed and provided by the professional schools in their Silicon Valley location. That such relationships often lead to future employment is indicated by the high proportion (60 percent) of Santa Clara graduates who remain in the area, and the many who staff the executive ranks of such local companies as Hewlett-Packard, IBM, Apple, Amdahl, Syntex, and Lockheed, among others.

Similarly, more than one-third of Santa Clara County Bar Association members graduated from SCU's School of Law, as did half of the county's judges.

At both undergraduate and graduate levels, community relationships are actively fostered. The engineering school's undergrad Co-op Program places students in internships with some 120 local companies.

At the graduate level, the engineering Early Bird Program offers working professionals the opportunity to earn graduate degrees while employed full time. Currently, about 1,500 students representing 250 Silicon Valley companies are enrolled in the program.

The university's MBA program in the Leavey School of Business and Administration is recognized as the area's most distinguished program for working professionals. With a mission of developing leaders who are capable of dealing with rapidly changing environments and who have

broad social and global perspectives, the program enrolls 1,100 students representing some 500 Bay Area companies. The MBA program has nearly 7,000 alumni in management positions throughout Northern California.

Many graduates return regularly for continuing education in the university's Executive Development Center where new frontiers are explored in managing technology, competitive strategy, business ethics, globalization, and understanding diversity.

In another sphere of community service, a program that illustrates the university's commitment is the Santa Clara Community Action Program (SCCAP). Organized and operated by students with faculty support, SCCAP gives participants an opportunity to work in more than 18 local-assistance programs.

Many facilities at Santa Clara are on the cutting edge, from the newly renovated Bannan Engineering complex to Louis B. Mayer Theatre, the site of many student and professional dramatic, dance, and musical productions.

Santa Clara also enjoys a rich athletic tradition and supports a well-balanced program of intercollegiate and intramural sports. Varsity athletic teams—nicknamed the "Broncos"—have enhanced school spirit throughout the university's history. Outstanding recent examples include the 1989 men's soccer team that won the National Collegiate Championship and the women's basketball team winning the 1991 National Women's Invitational Tournament.

Santa Clara's spirit is symbolized by this relatively small university capturing national athletic championships, but the school's larger vision was expressed by its president, Paul Locatelli, S.J., when he wrote in a recent annual report:

"A Santa Clara education means inspiring students and graduates to make a difference in the world . . . We hope our mission of fashioning a better world spreads to corporations, courtrooms, Congress, and beyond. And we believe some of that is happening now as it has throughout the university's 140-year history."

These pages were made possible by a grant from Santa Clara University regent Carole Antonini Rodoni. The university gratefully acknowledges her generosity.

University president, Paul Locatelli, S.J., shown in front of Santa Clara's Mission Church, is a 1961 SCU alumnus and former Business School professor who has been in his present office since 1988. Photo by Charles Barry

Students pass Santa Clara's historic Mission Church at the center of the old campus. The "modern" mission, dedicated in 1928, is an enlarged replica of the original 1777 mission. Photo by Charles Barry

San Jose State University

San Jose State University (SJSU) has been called the "engine that drives Silicon Valley" because so many engineers, managers, designers, and other professionals serving industry in Silicon Valley are graduates of this university. But California's oldest public institution of higher education is not a narrow polytechnic or business school. San Jose State is a regional, comprehensive university that prepares its students for careers in numerous professions, including engineering, business, teaching, nursing, journalism, and design, as well as in the sciences, the arts, and the humanities.

Founded in 1857 to prepare teachers for San Francisco schools, the institution that would one day become San Jose State University first became the California State Normal School. (In the nineteenth century the "normal," or "model," school, patterned on the French *Ecole Normal*, was a leading-edge educational innovation.) Moved to San Jose in 1871, San Jose State developed into a liberal arts college, and, accordingly, in 1935 the name was changed to San Jose State College. Now part of the Califonia State University system, the campus earned university status in 1972 through the number, breadth, and quality of its degree programs and faculty.

Accredited by the Western Association of Schools and Colleges and by many professional accrediting associations, San Jose State University today offers baccalaurate and master's degrees in more than 138 disciplines. These range from such traditional disciplines as music, mathematics, philosophy, and physics to such evolving fields as an interdisciplinary program in Computer-Integrated Manufacturing (CIM).

Present enrollment exceeds 30,000 regularly enrolled students. Another 30,000 students are enrolled through San Jose State University's extended education programs, which reach out into the community with a variety of professional certificate programs.

Excellence in classroom teaching has been the hallmark of San Jose State University since its earliest days. The university's faculty, numbering more than 2,000, are first and foremost teachers. But although good teaching is a requirement for the faculty, they are also expected to be active scholars, contributing to their disciplines through research and other creative activity. San Jose State University operates the Moss Landing Marine Laboratories on Monterey Bay. SJSU faculty are among California's most active participants in joint research with NASA, and the NASA-Ames research facilities are located only a few miles from the campus. The National Science Foundation, the National Institutes of Health, and other federal agencies give consistent support to San Jose State University faculty research.

Many Silicon Valley corporations have established partnerships with San Jose State University. Research by faculty and student teams is often immediately applicable to technical, environmental, or social problems. Applied research experience is an integral part of the education of students in many disciplines at SJSU.

Thus San Jose State University's educational philosophy fits well in Silicon Valley. SJSU graduates are known as "problem solvers," and it is not surprising that they constitute a high proportion

The School of Engineering's new building is one of the premier undergraduate engineering facilities in the country.

of technical and professional staff in many firms. For example, Lockheed recently found that more of its engineers, both locally based and nationally, were graduates of SJSU than of any other university. IBM has reported that only one other university west of the Mississippi has provided that company with more professionals—engineers, computer scientists, MBAs, and accountants—than San Jose State University.

In addition to providing a continuing stream of new graduates with professional and technical skills, San Jose State University is also a resource for working professionals who want to update or upgrade their knowledge and skills. For example, engineers who are moving into management find an MBA program at SJSU that is structured to meet their background and needs. Most professional graduate programs at the university are designed to accommodate students who are fully employed. For this reason graduate courses are usually scheduled during the evening.

San Jose State University takes many engineering and business classes to off-campus sites at local corporate laboratories and meeting rooms, thus assisting area firms in providing opportunities for their technical and professional employees to improve their knowledge and skill levels.

Although it provides extensive off-campus educational opportunities, San Jose State University is also a residential campus. Residence halls on campus provide housing for some 2,000 students. Another 5,000 students live within walking distance of the campus in sororities, fraternities, or other private housing. Although the majority of SJSU students commute from throughout a four-county region, the resident student population makes this a campus that is also a community.

Student activities are provided by more than 150 student clubs and organizations, ranging from the debate team to such club sports as rugby, sailing, and fencing. There are evening events—concerts, lectures, and athletic events—on almost any night of the week. Many of these are open to the community, either free or for a nominal charge.

The San Jose State Spartan athletic teams have a long winning tradition. They compete at Spartan Stadium, located on the south campus grounds approximately one mile from the main campus, in the aquatic center, which has a new, Olympic-size pool, and in the new Event Center. This facility features a 5,000-seat arena, as well as a weight room, handball courts, recreational gyms, and other facilities that are open to all students. The Student Union also provides a multistory facility with cafeterias, a bookstore, art gallery, meeting rooms, and a bowling alley.

Located at the eastern edge of San Jose's resurgent and revitalized downtown, the San Jose State University campus is set in a cosmopolitan urban environment. The San Jose Performing Arts Center, the Convention Center, major hotels, restaurants, and financial institutions are within walking distance of the campus.

The student population at San Jose State University is drawn from the upper one-third of California's high school graduates. Many transfer students enter at the junior year. Most of the student body comes from the surrounding four or five counties and, like the population from which they are drawn, is racially and culturally diverse. Some 40 percent are members of ethnic and racial minorities. Women comprise slightly more than half of the student body. The average age of undergraduates is 25; the average graduate student is 34. Nearly 90 percent are working, and most are working 20 or more hours per week.

San Jose State University provides an affordable, accessible, and excellent educational opportunity for the community that is Silicon Valley. An urban campus located in an ethnically diverse metropolitan center, it is also a residential campus with green "quads" and quiet gardens. A teaching institution, it is also a center for applied research. The dedicated and accomplished faculty contribute their expertise to the community as well as to the campus. They are the unsung heroes of Silicon Valley.

More than 4,500 students, both recent high school graduates and professionals returning mid–career for advanced education, study at SJSU's School of Business.

Tower Hall literally rose from the rubble of the great 1906 quake. It was the centerpiece of a mission–style quadrangle and remains the central element of the campus.

Foothill/De Anza Community College District

Above: Award winning architectural design and landscaping give Foothill College its distinctive look.

Top: Students can always find a beautiful spot on the campus to relax between classes.

Top right: Every season is breathtaking at De Anza College. More than 2,000 evergreen and deciduous trees are scattered over the 112-acre campus.

Right: Several bubbling fountains dot the De Anza College campus and provide meeting places for students.

Located in the heart of Silicon Valley, the Foothill/De Anza Community College District has distinguished itself as a leader among U.S. community colleges. For more than 30 years, Foothill/De Anza has stood for excellence and innovation in faculty, academic programs, and student services.

The district's two colleges—De Anza College in Cupertino and Foothill College in Los Altos Hills—comprise one of the largest community college districts in the country. With a general fund budget in excess of $94 million, it serves approximately 47,000 students each quarter.

Established in 1958, Foothill College is located at the foot of the Santa Cruz mountains on a picturesque 122-acre campus in Los Altos Hills. Some 220 full-time and 350 part-time faculty serve the educational needs of more than 20,000 students per quarter. Classes are conducted days, nights, and weekends on the main campus and at more than 60 sites in the community—including Foothill's Middlefield campus in Palo Alto.

Located on 112 acres in the heart of Cupertino (home of Apple Computer), De Anza College opened its doors in 1967. With an enrollment of more than 27,000 students per quarter, De Anza is one of the largest community college campuses in the nation. In addition to day and evening classes, De Anza offers classes on Saturdays and at 50 locations throughout the community.

Both De Anza and Foothill colleges are fully accredited educational institutions. Academic programs at the two schools lead to associate degrees and parallel freshman and sophomore requirements of the University of California, the California State University system, and private institutions.

And studies have shown that Foothill/De Anza students who transfer to institutions of higher learning do as well at their new schools as those juniors who started as freshmen at the same four-year schools.

An integral part of the educational offering at Foothill and De Anza colleges is a strong, diversified array of career programs employing state-of-the-art equipment and tailored to the local and national job markets. Notable facilities at the two colleges include Foothill's computer center, with one of the most powerful collections of computer systems for teaching in the Bay Area and De Anza's Flint Center for the Performing Arts, a 2,600-seat cultural center.

Foothill and De Anza maintain extensive community service programs, including a vast array of noncredit short courses and public events.

Programs and services are provided not only on each college's main campus, but also throughout the community, at business and industrial sites, recreation and senior adult centers, apartment complexes, churches, and hospitals. As part of their off-campus outreach efforts, the colleges tailor after-hours educational programs, training courses, and counseling specifically to many companies' employee needs.

Foothill College and De Anza College are active members of the League for Innovation in the Community College, a national consortium of leading two-year institutions.

Patrons

The following individuals, companies, and organizations have made a valuable commitment to the quality of this publication. Windsor Publications, the County of Santa Clara Board of Supervisors, and the County of Santa Clara Historical Heritage Commission gratefully acknowledge their participation in *Silicon Valley: Inventing the Future.*

Acme Building Maintenance Company, Inc.
Advanced Cardiovascular Systems
ALZA Corporation
American Airlines
American Electronics Association
Anthem Electronics, Inc.
Aris Helicopters Ltd.
Baycor Construction, Inc.
Beckman Instruments, Inc.
Becton Dickinson Immunocytometry Systems
Berliner, Cohen & Biagini
The Beverly Heritage Hotel
Borland International, Inc.
Brooks, Stednitz & Rhodes Accountancy
	Corporation
BT North America Inc.
California Micro Devices
City of San Jose
Conner Peripherals, Inc.
Creegan + D'Angelo
Devcon Construction, Inc.
Dionex Corporation
Empire Broadcasting, KARA-KLIV
Ernst & Young
EXAR Corporation
Fenwick & West
First Franklin Financial Corporation
Foothill/De Anza Community College
	District
Frank, Rimerman & Co.
Heuristics Search, Inc.
Hoge, Fenton, Jones & Appel, Inc.
Integrated Device Technology, Inc.
Intel Corporation
Ireland, San Filippo & Company
KBAY/KEEN
KPMG Peat Marwick
LifeScan Inc.
Lindsay's Business Supplies and Furniture,
	Inc.
Loral Corporation
LSI Logic Corporation
B.T. Mancini Company
Mariani Development Corporation
O.C. McDonald Co., Inc.

Mitsubishi Electronics America, Inc.,
	Electronic Device Group
MIX 106.5 KEZR
Network Equipment Technologies, Inc.
New United Motor Manufacturing, Inc.
Northern Telecom
Novellus Systems Incorporated
O'Connor Hospital
Oki Semiconductor
Pacific Maintenance Company
Pyramid Technology Corp.
Qume Corporation
The Raisch Company
Romic Chemical Corporation
Ropers, Majeski, Kohn, Bentley, Wagner & Kane
Rudolph and Sletten, Inc.
San Jose Convention and Cultural Facilities
San Jose International Airport
San Jose State University
Sanmina Corporation
Santa Clara County Historical Heritage
	Commission
Santa Clara Doubletree Hotel
Santa Clara Marriott
Santa Clara University
Santa Clara Valley Water District
SASCO/Valley Electric Company
Skjerven, Morrill, MacPherson, Franklin
	& Friel
S-MOS Systems, Inc.
Sobrato Development Companies
R.G. Speno, Inc.
Stanford University
State Compensation Insurance Fund
Sunrise Technologies, Inc.
The Synergism Group of Companies
TakeCare
Tandem Computers Inc.
The Tech Museum of Innovation
Therma, Inc.
Toeniskoetter & Breeding Inc.
Trimble Navigation Ltd.
United Technologies Corporation's Chemical
	Systems Division
Varian Associates, Inc.
Western Micro Technology, Inc.
Westinghouse Electric Corporation, Marine
	Division
Wolf Computer
Xerox Palo Alto Research Center

The stories of these companies and organizations appear in Chapters 9 through 15, beginning on page 265.

Bibliography

BOOKS

Arbuckle, Clyde. *Clyde Arbuckle's History of San Jose*. San Jose: Smith & McKay Printing, 1985.

Burrill, G. Steven/Ernst & Young. *Biotech 90: Into the Next Decade*. New York: MaryAnn Liebert, Inc. Publishers, 1989.

Caddes, Carolyn. *Portraits of Success: Impressions of Silicon Valley Pioneers*. Palo Alto: Tioga Publishing Company, 1986.

Feigenbaum, Ed. *The Rise of the Expert Company*. New York: Vintage Books/Random House, 1988.

Malone, Michael S. *The Big Score*. Garden City, N.Y.: Doubleday, 1985.

Payne, Stephen. *Santa Clara County: Harvest of Change*. Northridge, California: Windsor Publications, 1987.

Rheingold, Howard. *Tools for Thought*. New York: Simon & Schuster, 1985.

Sunshine, Fruit and Flowers. San Jose: San Jose Historical Museum, 1986. (Reprint of the 1896 San Jose Mercury edition.)

Villareal, Jose Antonio. *Pocho*. New York: Doubleday, 1959.

MAGAZINES

California Business
American Electronics Association
SRI International
Chemical Week
Business Week

NEWSPAPERS

New York Times
San Francisco Chronicle
San Jose Mercury News
Peninsula Times Tribune

MISCELLANEOUS

Bay Area Economic Forum. "Market Based Solutions to the Transportation Crisis." May 1990.

Bay Vision 2020 Progress Report. July 1990.

Guadalupe River Park Master Plan. August 1989.

Lowood, Henry. "From Steeples of Excellence to Silicon Valley: A Reappraisal of the Industrial Park and the University-Industry Connection." Palo Alto: Stanford University Libraries, October 1987.

Metropolitan Transportation Commission. Transactions, March 1990 and June 1990.

Metropolitan Transportation Commission. "Transportation Control Measures for State Clean Air Plan." June 1990.

Preservation 2020 Task Force. "Open Space Preservation: A Program for Santa Clara County." April 1987.

Santa Clara County Office of Education. "1989 and Beyond: Challenges and Opportunities for Our Schools." November 1988.

Stanford University. *Stanford: A Centennial Chronology*. March 1987.

Index of Silicon Valley's Enterprises